Blessed are you who take time to listen to difficult speech
For you help us persevere until we are understood.

Blessed are you who walk with us in public spaces
and ignore the stare of strangers,
for we find havens of relaxation in your companionship.

Blessed are you who never bid us to "hurry up,"
and more blessed are you who do not snatch our tasks from our hands
    to do them for us,
for often we need time—rather than help.

Blessed are you who stand beside us
as we enter new and untried ventures,
for the delight we feel when we surprise you outweighs
    all the frustrating failures.

Blessed are you who ask for our help,
for our greatest need is to be needed.

ANONYMOUS

Receiving the Gift of Friendship

PROFOUND DISABILITY,
THEOLOGICAL ANTHROPOLOGY,
AND
ETHICS

Hans S. Reinders

WILLIAM B. EERDMANS PUBLISHING COMPANY
GRAND RAPIDS, MICHIGAN / CAMBRIDGE, U.K.

Published 2008 by

Wm. B. Eerdmans Publishing Co.

2140 Oak Industrial Drive N.E., Grand Rapids, Michigan 49505 /

P.O. Box 163, Cambridge CB3 9PU U.K.

Printed in the United States of America

13 12 11 10 09 08   7 6 5 4 3 2 1

Library of Congress Cataloging-in-Publication Data

Reinders, Hans S.

Receiving the gift of friendship: profound disability,
theological anthropology, and ethics / Hans S. Reinders.

p.   cm.

ISBN 978-0-8028-6232-7 (pbk.: alk. paper)

1. Mental retardation — Religious aspects — Christianity.

2. Friendship — Religious aspects — Christianity.

3. Theological anthropology. 4. Christian ethics.   I. Title.

BV4461.R45   2008

261.8'323 — dc22

2007050291

www.eerdmans.com

Contents

Contents

Part Two
THEOLOGY

Part Three

ETHICS

Contents

Acknowledgments

The project that resulted in this book began in 1994, when I spent a sabbatical year at the University of Notre Dame. After I came back to my alma mater, the Vrije Universiteit in Amsterdam, I had to postpone completing the manuscript. This is not unusual for academics who, after the luxury of undistracted research and writing, return to the responsibilities of teaching and administration. When I returned to the manuscript in later years, there was much in it that I was not satisfied with. In hindsight, the reason was an unclear commitment to theology in a discourse primarily shaped by philosophical questions. It was not until the fall of 2004, when the Center of Theological Inquiry in Princeton, New Jersey, offered me the opportunity to work there, that I was able to get a fresh take on the subject matter of this inquiry. The result was a number of entirely rewritten chapters laying out an unapologetically theological argument. A return to Princeton in the summer of 2006 made it possible for me to complete the manuscript.

I have read parts of earlier drafts of the manuscript at Fuller Theological Seminary, Duke Divinity School, the Center for Ethics and Culture at Notre Dame University, and the Kennedy Institute of Ethics at Georgetown University. I have also read parts of the present book at the Center of Theological Inquiry. I am grateful to all those who participated in the conversations on those occasions. I want to mention, in particular, Wallace Alston, Robert Jenson, Will Storrar, Kathy Morley, and the CTI staff for their support, and I want to express my gratitude for the wonderful time I had in Princeton.

Introduction

The truth of a theory about man is either creative or irrelevant, but never merely descriptive. Any attempt to derive an image from human nature can only result in extracting the image originally injected in it.

Abraham Heschel[1]

1. The Subject

This book makes an unusual claim about unusual people: it says that people with profound intellectual disabilities are people just like other people. At first sight, this claim is not unusual at all. Thousands of proclamations, preambles, declarations, mission statements, reports, and newspaper articles declare that to be true. However, things begin to look different as soon as the question of what distinguishes people from other living creatures arises. Most of the answers to this question will present a version of the commonsense view: this view says that people are different because they have language, they have reason and will and a sense of self, so that they can make up their minds about things and choose what they want, they can pursue plans and ideals, and so on. In other words, the things that human faculties allow people to do or to have are what make people different. Unfortunately, however, peo-

---

1. Abraham J. Heschel, *Who is Man?* (Stanford, CA: Stanford University Press, 1965), p. 8.

1

ple with profound intellectual disabilities cannot do or have these kinds of things. That is, they don't do or have what is said to distinguish human beings from other creatures. Therefore, in light of the commonsense view, to say that the profoundly disabled are just like the rest of us must be a very unusual claim.

There is thus more to this claim than what may appear at first sight, because, if we want to uphold the claim that people with profound intellectual disabilities are people just like other people, then the commonsense view must be false. I know that many readers will want to uphold that claim, which logically commits them to the conclusion that the commonsense view *is* false. But this results in a very unusual claim about usual people: that whatever distinguishes them as human beings, it cannot be the human faculties. If it were the human faculties, people with profound intellectual disabilities could at best be understood as "subnormal," or "subhuman," but not as human beings properly speaking. Since this conclusion would defy the first premise, it follows that what people ordinarily think makes them different qua human beings cannot be true. In that sense, to deny the commonsense view is to make an unusual claim about usual people.

In this book I am committed to making both of these unusual claims. I do believe that human beings with profound intellectual disabilities are people like other people, and I do believe that the best way to understand human beings is not found in the human faculties. It is the burden of this inquiry to make these unusual claims plausible.

When I first began thinking about this problem, my intuitive response — as a Christian theologian — was that the Christian tradition could handle it easily because of the doctrine of the *imago dei*. Since I had never read that God created only some people, not all people, in his image, this doctrine looked promising as a truly universal understanding of human being. The only question that needed to be answered was how the tradition had explained the notion of the divine image. When I started to explore this question, however, it soon became clear to me that the Christian tradition might in fact have been one of the major sources of the commonsense view. The "human being created in the image of God" was taken to mean that human beings are closer to God than any other living creature because of their capacity for reason and will. Discovering that the theological support for this reading was overwhelming across the broad spectrum of Christian denominations was a humbling experience. It made me acutely aware of the odds of this project. Being in denial about what most people believe to be true is not an attractive prospect, either in philosophical ethics or in theology.

Personally, I have great respect for people who live profoundly disabled lives. But can one even say that? Are the people living such lives the proper object of respect? Any contemporary textbook on ethics will explain to its readers that they owe respect to all human beings, because of their capacity for reason and will. These textbooks do not say this because they are contemporary; readers will find the same view in all major Western thinkers, from Kant back to Aquinas to Augustine to Aristotle, to name just a few. One need only substitute "rational soul" for "human being," and one will find the proof for this claim.

The argument that I hope to develop in subsequent chapters will not proceed in the same way of abstract philosophical reasoning that I use here to lay out the problem. The main reason is that this project is not about solving a philosophical problem at all. As a matter of fact, my project is about trying to understand people who live their lives with conditions of profound disability, as well as about trying to understand the people who have committed themselves to sharing their lives with them. Therefore, it is about understanding lives that are way beyond the range of ordinary experience.

The argument will be contextual: it will engage entrenched views and doctrines with regard to thinking about disability. It will be controversial in the sense that I will criticize well-established dogmas held by widely diverse communities of belief, for example, dogmas of the Roman Catholic Church and dogmas of the academic field called "disability studies." My argument will be eclectic in the sense that I will draw heavily on convictions of widely diverse communities of faith. It will also be political in that I will confront the dominant philosophy within the disability-rights movement. I will contest well-established strategies of moral reasoning in the field of bioethics. And my argument will be unapologetically theological because of my conviction that the nature of the question precludes any critical solution that does not involve an account of who God is and what he does. The reason is that the truth about human beings is grounded in God's unconditional acceptance. That is why this book is not about abstract philosophical reasoning; I am not interested in reasons that can "justify" the existence of profoundly disabled human beings. Instead, I am interested in understanding a quite extraordinary kind of commitment.

2. A New Vision

The lives of persons with disabilities in Western society have changed significantly over the last decades: they have gained in the control they have over their own lives; they have gained in opportunities to participate in society; and perhaps most important of all, they have grown in self-awareness. Self-advocacy has turned out to be a very important strategy to bring about these changes. Since the 1970s a new vision is clearly at work that has gradually inspired more and more people to bring about these changes, as one can read in any anthology or reader about the subject, or can hear at any conference addressing disability issues.

The reality of change not only pertains to the lives of people with physical disabilities, but also to the lives of people with intellectual disabilities. Despite the fact that their capacity for self-advocacy is often diminished, there are many other advocates to step in, usually family members and friends. Accordingly, people with disabilities have claimed the right — either for themselves, or others have claimed it on their behalf — to speak for themselves rather than being talked about. They have claimed the right to make their own decisions about their own lives. They have also claimed the right to be treated as citizens with the same rights and opportunities that other citizens enjoy. On the whole, one cannot deny that the change brought about by this new vision has been very significant.

Important as these victories are, however, a lingering sense of disappointment persists. Many persons with disabilities still feel rejected. Despite the positive responses that have greeted them in the sphere of politics and law, similar responses in society at large are much harder to come by. One concept that indicates the truth of this claim will play a significant part in the argument of this book: disabled people are rarely chosen as friends, except by other disabled people. This is especially true of the people about whom I am specifically concerned in this book, people with intellectual disabilities. Friendship is a very rare experience in their lives. People without a disability seldom want to become involved, particularly when it takes a strong commitment to do so. They

4

remain ignorant of what it is to live with a disability, and many apparently want to keep it that way.

It is in reflecting on the lack of friends in the lives of people with intellectual disabilities that one begins to understand the limited nature of the new vision. The new vision has been embodied primarily by the disability-rights movement, particularly in the United States and the United Kingdom. The disability-rights movement has understood the new vision as a charter for political action aimed at equal rights and social justice for disabled people; but there is only so much that rights and justice claims can do. Rights certainly create new opportunities by opening up institutional space, and they are extremely important in that capacity; in creating new opportunities, they affect our lives as citizens. But disabled people, just like other people, are human beings before they are citizens: to live a human life, properly so called, they must not merely be included in our institutions and have access to our public spaces; they must also be included in other people's lives, not only by natural, familial necessity but by choice.

Many people with intellectual disabilities are, for most of their lives, surrounded by family or professional caregivers and support workers. This means that relationships in their lives are either a matter of natural necessity or — as in the case of professionals — of contractual obligation. In the former case, the relationships involve family members who usually carry the burden of responsibility to assist and support the person with the disability because there is nobody else to do so; in the latter case, relationships are based on the fact that the disabled person is a "client" who receives some kind of service from a professional service organization. Both of these kinds of relationships are very important for the disabled person, but neither can establish the one crucial good that disabled people long for: being chosen as a friend. Friendship is of particular value precisely because it is constituted by appreciation. Nobody has to be my friend because of some sort of obligation or role responsibility. No one can be blamed for not being my friend; nor can anyone be questioned about not taking an interest in me. Friendship is special because it is freely chosen. Our friends want us as their friend for our own sake. No other relationships, either professional or kinship, can give what friendship gives.

If one looks at the recent changes in the lives of disabled people from this angle, one can clearly see the nature of the changes that have been the result of political action. By raising issues of equal rights and social justice, advocacy movements have successfully altered the course of public policy. This is particularly true for the United States, where the Americans with Disabilities Act (ADA) has shaped public policy since the early 1990s. Its goal has been to gain access to public spaces and opportunities, both as an end in itself and as a means of gaining control over their lives. To the extent that the disability-rights movement has succeeded, these are very tangible results. But it is important to realize that they have occurred in the domain of citizenship and have left unaffected the domain of personal intimacy. Despite the success they have found in strengthening their status in the public sphere, people with disabilities — particularly intellectual disabilities — experience loneliness and isolation in the sphere of their personal lives.

This kind of observation gives shape to the main aim of this book. Apart from institutional barriers that can be removed by public policy, there are cultural barriers that are entrenched in people's hearts and minds. This is the reason why we need to think beyond rights and justice. In many cases, the lives of persons with disabilities lack the blessing of intimacy: that is, they lack friends, which is the one kind of good that rights and justice claims cannot achieve.

3. Beyond Rights and Justice

Given the above reflections, I will in this study shift the focus of attention from citizenship to friendship. My investigation will go beyond the paradigm of equal citizenship that is found in most of the contemporary literature on disability. As indicated, that literature operates within the political sphere of emancipation, antidiscrimination, and issues of civil rights. It is successful — and considers itself to be successful — to the extent that it contributes to changes in public policy. While I think these efforts are important, and will remain so, I also think we should raise different questions, questions regarding our moral culture. I do not use that term to refer to morality in the narrow sense, as a system of mutual obligations that arise from institutional roles and responsibilities. Rather, I want to use "moral culture" as the domain constituted by the concepts of the good that people pursue in their lives, both individually and collectively.

Questions regarding our moral culture in this wider sense are questions of what it is that makes our lives worth living — "quality of life," in fashionable parlance. Not many people in our society believe that spending time with an intellectually disabled person will contribute to the "quality" of their lives; therefore, it is also true that not many people would know what it is to be a friend of such a person. This is not necessarily their fault. Even though disability is claimed to be "out of the closet," it is still true that many people with intellectual disabilities live in protected environments. It takes an effort to reach out and meet them.

This, then, is the subject matter with which this book is concerned. Our contemporary moral culture disseminates conceptions of a good life that hardly help us to imagine someone with an intellectual disability as a friend. Many traits of our Western culture enable us to see what adequate care and support does for the quality of their lives; but those traits hardly help us imagine what their presence may mean for the quality of our own. Consequently, there is a cultural issue involved here. This is why I believe that we need to change the agenda of ethical thinking about the lives of people with intellectual disabilities.

Because current images of successful and interesting lives in our moral culture do not easily include people with intellectual disabilities, there is a remarkable difference between "insiders" and "outsiders" in this respect. Insiders are people who have learned to share their lives, or part of their lives, with a disabled person. As I have indicated, insider experience is ordinarily limited to either professionals or family members, usually parents. In the personal accounts of parents of disabled children, one is often struck by the fact that they do not value their lives any less than other people do, though they may value their lives for different reasons. For example, parents who value sharing their lives with a disabled child will point out that they live by a different standard of success.[2] Many things that "normal" children learn relatively easily in a short period of time may take months for children with an intellectual disability to master: showing a preference for peanut butter on their

---

2. For these and other observations on how parents regard their lives with a disabled child as a success, see Kathryn I. Scorgie, "From Devastation to Transformation: Managing Life when a Child is Disabled" (Ph.D. diss., University of Alberta, 1996). I have discussed Scorgie's research at length in my *The Future of the Disabled in Liberal Society: An Ethical Analysis* (Notre Dame, IN: University of Notre Dame Press, 2000), pp. 175-92.

sandwich, for example, or picking out the pair of shoes they want to wear today.

With regard to the insider experience of professional caregivers, I have often noticed their complaint that it is virtually impossible to explain to others why working with these children means so much to them. Likewise, I have often heard families lament that other people do not have a clue why living with a disabled kid is just as rewarding as any other life once you have figured out how to do it. This is not to deny that these families experienced, in the beginning, the birth of a disabled child as "devastating"; but they have managed to adjust their conception of themselves as a family in order to include and embrace this child.

All of these observations indicate that different perspectives on "disability" usually reflect different experiences with disabled persons. This at least suggests an experiential gap between the world of insiders and the world of outsiders that is relevant food for thought. It is worthwhile asking how this gap may account for diverging conceptions of the ultimate good of human beings: that is, the difference between insider and outsider perspectives may help to understand diverging conceptions of what it means to live a truly human life.

In this connection, our moral culture in many ways presents families with disabled members with an uphill battle. The culture is replete with images of self-determining bodies and minds, reflecting the deeply rooted cultural belief that the point of our lives is what we are capable of doing. Very often this means that people with intellectual disabilities have no part in them.[3] If the point of our lives is what we are capable of doing, the implication must be that a human life lacking in the capacity for purposive action will be pointless. Many people who are involved in the lives of persons with intellectual disabilities tend to disagree because their insider experience tells them differently. The truth in the stories of their experience must be salvaged, which is one of my aims in this book.

---

3. Don S. Saliers, "Toward a Spirituality of Inclusiveness," in *Human Disability and the Service of God: Reassessing Religious Practice,* ed. Nancy L. Eiesland and Don S. Saliers (Nashville: Abingdon Press, 1998), pp. 19-31.

4. Intelligible Experience

Given the relevance of distinguishing insider and outsider perspectives, there is a point in paying attention to these stories. There are many such stories in which people give an account of their firsthand experience of living life with a disability or sharing their lives with a disabled person.[4] Although I am not a complete stranger to this kind of experience myself, my task in this study is not to contribute to this literature. Instead, my task is to think through the underlying assumptions that need to be understood in order to grasp the truth of what these stories seek to convey.

Let one example be sufficient in this introduction to indicate what I have in mind. It is the story of a profoundly disabled human being.[5] In his book *The Power of the Powerless,* Christopher de Vinck tells the story of his brother Oliver, a profoundly disabled boy. "Oliver could do absolutely nothing except breathe, sleep, and eat. Yet he was responsible for action, love, courage, insight."[6] De Vinck's book grew out of his memories of Oliver, though he did not decide to write those memories down until years after his brother had died. He remembers the experience of a certain mystery about the house — "the house of Oliver," he calls it. It was the mystery of a peacefulness that he attributes to his brother's presence. "I cannot explain Oliver's influence except to say that the

4. Among my own favorites in the Anglo-Saxon literature are Michael Dorris, *The Broken Chord* (New York: Harper, 1989); Christopher de Vinck, *The Power of the Powerless: A Brother's Legacy of Love* (New York: Doubleday, 1990); Kenzaburo Oe, *A Healing Family* (Tokyo: Kodansha International, 1995); Michael Berube, *Life As We Know It: A Father, A Family, and an Exceptional Child* (New York: Vintage Books, 1996). Collections with short stories are: Donald J. Meyer, *Uncommon Fathers: Reflections on Raising a Child with a Disability* (Bethesda: Woodbine House, 1995); Stanley D. Klein and Kim Schive, *You Will Dream New Dreams: Inspiring Personal Stories by Parents of Children with Disabilities* (New York: Kensington, 2001).

5. For reasons I will make explicit later, I take the lives of people with *profound* intellectual disabilities to be the real pièce de résistance for ethical reflection in this area. This is not to suggest that the lives of people with mild intellectual disabilities are less complicated, or that they are less difficult to live. It is only that *if,* as I have suggested, the marginalized existence of people with disabilities has its source in images of the independent self, then positive moral thinking regarding profoundly disabled human beings is obviously the most challenging, as well as most critical, task.

6. De Vinck, *The Power of the Powerless,* p. 31.

powerless in our world *do* hold great power."[7] Oliver could not hold up his head, he could neither crawl, nor walk, nor sing; he never left his bed; he could not hold anything in his hand, nor could he speak. And he never knew what his condition was. Yet his brother remembers how they experienced Oliver: "We were blessed with his presence, a true presence of peace."[8]

Sharing his disabled brother with his family shaped both his life and his view of life, de Vinck confesses. Part of what Oliver's life taught him had to do with purpose. We set our goals and make plans to attain them. But there is a risk in all this activism, de Vinck wants his readers to understand, because it tends to neglect a special kind of attentiveness. We might fail to see "the hidden inside" of things: the extraordinary that can be found in the ordinary, the profound that is hidden in the trivial.

> I have come to believe we are here to tend to the lilies in the field. We do the best we can. If you have a boy or girl like Oliver in your home, you will know what is best for him or her, for your family. . . .
>
> I asked my father, "How did you care for Oliver for thirty-two years?" "It was not thirty-two years," he said. "I just asked myself, 'Can I feed Oliver today?' and the answer was always, 'Yes, I can.'" We lived with Oliver moment by moment.[9]

In his career as a teacher, de Vinck informs us, he often told his students about his brother. He remembers that, on a day when he was describing his brother's lack of response, he was interrupted by one of his students, who raised his hand and said, "I see what you mean, sir; you mean he was a vegetable." "I presume you could call him a vegetable," de Vinck responded to the student, "but we just called him Oliver."[10] De Vinck uses that phrase — "you mean he was a vegetable" — a number of times in his book as an ominous reminder of how experience makes a difference.

However, it is not experience per se that matters, because, to be able to experience Oliver as "the presence of peace," one has to under-

---

7. De Vinck, *The Power of the Powerless,* p. 32.
8. De Vinck, *The Power of the Powerless,* p. 31.
9. De Vinck, *The Power of the Powerless,* p. 31.
10. De Vinck, *The Power of the Powerless,* p. 31.

stand a few things that will make that experience intelligible. What is it that makes some people see human beings like Oliver as a blessing, while others see only "vegetables"? *Experience* cannot be the whole explanation, because it is a fact that not all families with disabled children respond the way de Vinck's family did. The additional explanation has to do with self-perception. Whether or not we are capable of seeing a profoundly disabled boy as a human being depends very much on how we understand our own being as humans. That is what I will argue in this book.

For someone like Christopher de Vinck, the question of whether his brother Oliver has lived a human life is most likely redundant. There is no real difference. Oliver was just Oliver. If there was a question at all, it has been answered by his having lived the life with his family. Living that kind of life has shaped Christopher de Vinck's moral convictions. Thus, the question for us readers of de Vinck's story is: what makes that kind of life intelligible? What kind of perspective can sustain his convictions about Oliver? These are questions about what we take the lives of human beings such as Oliver to represent. Seeing their lives the way de Vinck saw his brother's life depends on a particular set of anthropological and ethical assumptions. The burden of this inquiry is to dig up these assumptions and ask how they can be sustained.

5. The Program

If human beings with profound intellectual disabilities are to be dignified, then the ground of their dignity cannot be found in human agency. That much is clear. Christopher de Vinck answered the question with an indirect reference to agency, as we have seen. Oliver's humanity was never questioned because he could not respond in any meaningful way; rather, it was affirmed because he had the power to move other people. This answer suggests that we have to think about the absence of agency in terms of passivity. Oliver de Vinck's was a life lived in passivity, but, because of what Oliver evoked in other people, his brother did not think any less of it. In view of the cultural celebration of "achievement," this view raises the question of how a life lived in passivity can be a human life, properly so called.

I will take the investigation of this kind of question — and of many others as well — through several stages. The first part of this book sets out to clear the theoretical battlefield in order to prepare for the appropriate setting of the main argument. My overall task is to show how the subjects of intellectual disability, anthropology, and ethics are related. I set the stage in this part of the argument by invoking what I take to be the currently dominant paradigm in ethical thought about humans with disabilities, which is the paradigm found in the disability-rights literature. I am assuming in these opening chapters that many readers will be convinced that the question this book addresses is both interesting and important, but only a few will be convinced that we really need a different anthropology, let alone a theological one, to be able to deal with the ethical questions adequately.

Chapter 1 introduces the question about profound intellectual disability as a question of anthropology: I will show how thinking about human beings such as Oliver de Vinck from the perspective of the disability-rights movement may imply something like an anthropological "minor league." My own "Oliver" in Chapter 1 is a girl named Kelly, whom I have known for a number of years. As the reader will see, Kelly would be the first candidate for an anthropological minor league, if there ever was one. To overturn this conceptual possibility requires that we question the presuppositions that implicitly deny people like Kelly a share in our humanity.

Chapter 2 deals with the first of two versions of a preliminary objection to the present project. It is raised from philosophical quarters that are radically opposed to one another. It says that raising the anthropological question with respect to profound intellectual disability is wrongheaded because the main problem is social and political, not anthropological. This first version represents social constructionism: it suspects that underlying my need for a different anthropology is the paradigm of disability as a natural catastrophe. Because I apparently buy the assumption that intellectually disabled lives somehow contradict human nature, there is a need to change the commonsense view of what that nature *is* in order to include disabled people. Well intended, perhaps, but nonetheless misguided. The real problem is not that we need a concept of human nature that includes persons with intellectual disabilities; the real problem is that our "ableist" culture is informed by views that are oppressive to people with disabilities. They should be regarded as victims of social injustice rather than as products of natural catastrophe. To accept the suggestion that there is a problem with Kelly's humanity is to put the cart before the horse. Disabled people are not the problem; the problem is a society that discriminates against them.

Chapter 3 deals with the second version of the preliminary objection: it says that there is no problem that justifies raising the anthropological question with respect to human beings such as Kelly and Oliver de Vinck. This version comes from Roman Catholic teaching, operating within an Aristotelian framework. It argues that human beings are not identified by a particular set of psychological characteristics but by the fact that they are of human descent. "Man is born from man," as Aristotle puts it. The fact that some human beings lack capabilities characteristic of their species, predominantly reason and will, is not a serious conceptual problem. Following Aristotle, one can argue that every natural kind includes imperfect specimens. Some apples are just more of an apple than other apples, but it does not follow that those other apples are not properly called apples. Something similar can be said of human beings. This view supports the Roman Catholic view of humanity being potentially present in every human being "from the moment of conception." All human beings are included among the image-bearers of God, regardless of their state or condition; so there is no problem with the humanity of profoundly disabled human beings.

Chapter 4 connects the question of anthropology with the question of ethics: the connection is that, in asking how we understand our own humanity, we are in fact asking how we understand the human good and vice versa. This chapter introduces the distinction between the various goods people may pursue in their lives, on the one hand, and the ultimate good of being human, on the other. The distinction allows for the possibility that one can acquire a number of the former goods while still not having a very good life, because one does not participate in the ultimate good. The reverse is also possible. The ultimate good of being human is then identified in terms of "belonging," which is fulfilled by friendship. Even when barred from various goods that people usually think are worth pursuing in their lives, people with profound intellectual disabilities still can be chosen as friends and thus participate in friendship. This chapter shows how this concept of the good brings to light the limits of rights and justice claims.

In Part Two of the book, we will enter the field of Christian theology. Chapters 5 and 6 discuss four different theological accounts of the relationship between Christian faith and disability: a "liberation theology of disability," a "theology of access," a "theology of Christian witness," and a "theology of being human." The aim of my discussion is both to provide an overview of the theological landscape and to show where the arguments and positions each of them presents can be developed further. I will argue that proposals for a liberation theology of disability fail to accommodate questions concerning profoundly disabled human beings because such proposals aim at self-representation as the key to inclusion. The same is true of a theology of access, but for different reasons. The importance of access is in the creation of opportunity for purposive action. This goal defines the good for human beings with profound disabilities in terms of a capacity for agency, which is their weakest spot. The third approach puts us on the right track in thinking about the profoundly disabled as exemplifying the meaning of being God's creatures. Thus understood, they are the rule of what it means to be human rather than the exception. The task of breaking the barriers between "us" and "them" is then redefined as breaking with the illusion of our own strength and accepting our vulnerability and dependency. The remaining question here is why this task should be taken on by particular people, as if it were a special vocation instead of the vocation of every Christian. Finally, the fourth approach exposes the notion that the practice of care and support for disabled people must have a rational ground. In contrast to the other approaches, it argues for the unconditional acceptance of profoundly disabled human beings for no other reason than the love of God. Here the remaining question concerns what this unconditional acceptance means for the participation of the disabled in the ultimate good of being human.

Chapter 7 investigates the doctrine of *imago dei* in order to show that the Christian tradition has struggled with a "double portrait of man": being human as a natural entity and being human as it is before God. The tradition has taught that true human being can only be known in its unique relationship with God, but it has at the same time always maintained that there is human being as it is in itself. In this regard, Chapter 7 argues for a Christian anthropology based on Trinitarian theology. We will see how recent Trinitarian thought has argued for relational being as the main characteristic of the divine life, on which theological anthropology can build. I will try to further the theological debate by arguing that the concept of relational being per se is incapa-

14

ble of doing the work it needs to do. "Relational being" does not necessarily challenge the primacy of the self. I will explore the notion of *ecstatic personhood,* which is grounded in the unconditional love of God. Thus understood, Trinitarian theology provides the resources for showing that true human being is extrinsically grounded in God the Father, the Son, and the Spirit, whose grace allows us to participate in Trinitarian communion. This means that the ultimate good of being human is found in this communion as a movement from God to us. In this way Christian anthropology provides an understanding of our humanity that includes human beings with profound intellectual disabilities. All other alternative approaches will inevitably confront them with criteria they cannot possibly meet.

Part Three of the book returns to ethics in order to explore the practical implications of the theological moves outlined in Part Two. As I have indicated in this Introduction, the key notion I will explore will be friendship. The operation of reversing the order of our theological thinking will continue. It takes its starting point in the notion of friendship as God's friendship with human beings: God's friendship is the gift that precedes Christian friendship and makes it possible.

Chapter 8 will investigate friendship as charity: the theology of Thomas Aquinas will serve as our main source, and we will read it through the lens of Paul Wadell's ethics of friendship. Though Wadell develops a reading of Aquinas within which the virtues appear as the excellences to set us on the road to charity as friendship with God, we learn on closer analysis that the virtues cannot reach this end on their own account, because friendship with God is a gift of the Spirit. Therefore, we have to think about the practical implications of the fact that God's friendship in every instance precedes our friendship with him. The chapter closes with a discussion of Wolfensberger's Christian account of intellectual disability in order to show how the gift of friendship that we receive from God needs to be extended to intellectually disabled persons, "even when not reciprocated."

Chapter 9 returns to the notion of "ecstatic being" and interprets this in terms of being human in relationship that is extrinsically grounded. Here the story of the man born blind (John 9) will guide us to see how the intellectually disabled person can be shown to have a mission when it comes to Christian friendship. Jesus tells his disciples that the man was born blind because God's work can be revealed in him.

The chapter attempts to show how this can be read as a call to trust Jesus' mission, because that is what distinguishes the man who "sees" in recognizing Jesus as the Son of man from the Pharisees and other Jews, who remain in the dark. They rely on their own superiority, and it is Jesus' aim to expose that. The chapter continues with an account of people who have chosen to share their lives with the disabled, the people who live together in the community of L'Arche. Their stories confirm how the people with intellectual disabilities with whom they share their lives become their teachers in trusting God, much in the same way that John's story narrates the mission of the man born blind. We will see how sharing their lives with the intellectually disabled helps people acquire the kind of self-knowledge that is necessary for living their kind of life.

Finally, Chapter 10 seeks to balance the account of Christian friendship in that it considers how our own limitations get in the way of being truthful friends. The chapter explains the difference between Aristotle's concept of friendship and Christian friendship in order to show that Christian friendship is most of all dependent on truthfulness with regard to who we are in relationship with one another. Within these relationships, we must continuously receive the gift of God, but receiving it properly is often the hardest thing to do. Especially in our relationships with people who are utterly dependent, we are tempted to hide ourselves in our own strength. However, God's gift cannot be received in self-possessing strength.

Part One

PROFOUND DISABILITY

Chapter One

One of Us

*It must be clearly affirmed that the disabled person is one of us, a
sharer in the same humanity.*

Pope John Paul II, March 4, 1981

1. Introducing Kelly

Among the factors that have caused the lives of persons with disabilities
to change is the fact that the defect model has been abandoned. A new
vision demands that people be supported in what they can do rather
than being accommodated for their "special needs." This change is significant. Do you see incapacity and neediness? Or do you see possibility
for growth? More and more people have shifted their views to the latter
perspective, and this has opened up more opportunities for people with
disabilities than ever before. The key word is "empowerment." The disabled are more in control of where they live, how they live, and with
whom they live — as well as how they can participate in and contribute
to society. These changes have significantly enhanced the quality of
many lives. But not all persons with a disability have benefited from
these changes, partly because many still live in isolated situations, but
also because the new vision has limitations itself that have not been
sufficiently recognized so far. This is particularly true of people with intellectual disabilities.

There can be no question that the lives of people with intellectual
disabilities are not nearly as good as they could be if their potential and

actual abilities would be more fully appreciated. Much remains to be done; but there is also no question in my mind that improving their lives should not be made dependent on their abilities. It is here that the new vision shows its limitations: it assumes that living a truly human life depends on the quality of agency. Let me explain what I have in mind by introducing Kelly.

Kelly is a young girl I encountered a number of years ago in a group home for people with intellectual disabilities. The director of this home happened to know that I was thinking about a book on people with profound intellectual disabilities. "You should pay Kelly a visit," she said. She told me that Kelly is a *micro-encephalic,* which means that a significant part of the normal human brain is missing in her. When Kelly came to the institution as a baby, there were serious doubts about whether the institution should take her.

The first time I visited the group home where she lives, I found a twelve-year-old redheaded girl who was sitting in a wheelchair, her big brown eyes "staring without seeing," as was my first reaction. I talked a bit to her as a way to make myself feel at ease more than anything else, and I asked the staff a few questions about her. I was invited to stay for the afternoon in order to get an impression of who she was and how she lived. So I stayed. I noticed that the nurses around her had a perfectly natural way of approaching her. For them Kelly was just Kelly, and she could be just as "happy" or "sad" as any other resident in the home. Nonetheless, it appeared that there had been doubts about Kelly's life. This I learned when I interviewed the director of the group home, who told me about their response to Kelly when she was brought to the home as a little baby:

> When Kelly was still a baby, the only thing she seemed capable of doing was to take a deep breath now and then. In her case we did not think of this as something she did, say, as something like "sighing," as if she were lamenting her condition. Instead, we assumed her taking a deep breath was only a respiratory reflex. Until somebody noticed it seemed to depend on who spoke to her. When spoken to by particular voices the changing respiration pattern stopped. Once the voice stopped, she started again. Thank Heavens! At least she could do something, if it was only "sighing." Our Kelly turned out to be human.

Apparently, the recognition of Kelly's humanity was not beyond doubt even among those who cared for her on a daily basis. Kelly is what some people in our moral culture probably would call a "vegetable." Even if one rejects the term and the judgment that it implies, as I think we should, the director's comments answered to some of the most fundamental beliefs of our moral culture. Human being does not count as truly "human" unless it can do something. This belief raised a question mark about Kelly's humanity, and the reason is not difficult to grasp: Kelly never had, and never will have, a sense of herself as a human being. Leaving technical details aside for the moment, standard definitions would rank her as being "profoundly disabled," meaning that for all the important activities that characterize our lives — health, safety, relationships, communication, and so on — she will be entirely dependent on others. Kelly will not reach even a minimal stage of determining what she wants for herself. Words such as "I," "me," or "myself" will never mean anything to her, nor will any other word for that matter. As far as we can tell, Kelly's condition does not allow her any "interior space," by which I refer to the inner life, that part of me where I am with myself. It is concerning this interior space that the language of selfhood becomes intelligible in the first place. If we only realize how crucial this space has been for how human individuality commonly has been valued in the history of Western thought, it does not take long to see why these facts about Kelly's condition may raise questions about her being, questions that could even place her humanity in doubt.[1]

However, the people in the group home where she lived, as I was soon to find out, did not seem troubled by any such questions at all. During that afternoon of my first visit, I noticed a nurse coming in for the late afternoon shift. Entering Kelly's room, she approached her with a spontaneous "you are looking cheerful today." On my subsequent visits to Kelly's group home, I noticed that such descriptions of mental states were quite frequent. One day I came for tea, and as soon as I entered the living room, I was approached by Daniel, a young boy with au-

---

1. Hans S. Reinders, "'The Meaning of Life' in Modern Society," in *Meaningful Care: A Multidisciplinary Approach to the Meaning of Care for People with Mental Retardation,* ed. Joop Stolk, Theo A. Boer, and R. Seldenrijk (Dordrecht: Kluwer Academic Publishers, 2000), pp. 65-84.

tism; he came to me repeating that Kelly looked "very sad," and then he would go over to her wheelchair and stroke her beautiful hair. Others might say occasionally that she appeared to be happy, or that she loved to be bathed. Apparently, Kelly was included in the language that we are accustomed to speaking to and about each other. In any event, she was never approached or spoken to as though she were a "vegetable."

Once I began thinking about these matters, I realized that the use of this kind of language must appear inappropriate when it is seen from the perspective of selfhood that plays such an important role in modern concepts of what we are as human beings. The phrases spoken about her — "looking cheerful," "being sad," "being happy," "loving to be bathed" — all seemed to imply a capacity for having certain mental states, a capacity that is not very likely present in Kelly's case. I then realized a disturbing conclusion that seemed to follow from this perspective: when Kelly lacks the capacity for having mental states such as "being sad," the perspective of selfhood forces us to conclude that the things said about her were in fact said metaphorically. To use the language of mental states to refer to profoundly disabled human beings such as Kelly is to turn that language into metaphor. People speak about Kelly *as if* she were happy, or *as if* she were sad.

I then returned to the notion of doubt regarding her humanity. I realized that the director's relief was wholeheartedly meant to give Kelly's humanity every benefit of the doubt; but people outside her group home may be less inclined to do so. Usually the notion of our humanity is believed to entail more than the ability to produce a sigh every now and then. More disturbing questions arose at this point. At the very least, human agency seems to entail some sense of what one is doing, and having a sense of what one is doing entails the awareness that one's action has a point. Human beings act for a purpose. However, if the capacity for purposive action is what makes us human, where does that leave human beings like Kelly? Should we not say, then, that the language implying that Kelly is a human being must also be spoken metaphorically? People speak about someone like her *as if* she is a human being. Can one speak honestly about Kelly as a human being when one knows for a fact that in her case this predicate is a metaphor?

These thoughts made me very uneasy. Suppose that the people who work with Kelly and her friends would believe something like this. Suppose they believed that they could not speak about her as a human being without deceiving themselves. I vividly remember a scene in which the general director of another institution introduced me to the people of a group home similar to Kelly's. We watched a nurse working with what appeared to be a profoundly disabled young man. They were both laughing: the nurse told us they were playing a game and having great fun with it. When we left that scene, the general director apparently thought that he owed me an explanation. "Of course, that young man has no clue to what's going on, but I greatly admire these nurses. I could not do it." Using the language of playing games with someone with a profound disability, I was to understand, is a form of self-deception for which caregivers are to be admired. They probably could not do their job without the ability to fool themselves, or so this director implied.

Now suppose that the people actually working with Kelly and this young man would indeed believe something like this. What effect would that belief have on their practice of caring? For one thing, they certainly would stop playing games. What could possibly be the point of playing a game with someone who does not have a clue as to what's going on? Of course, I know that you start playing games with your children long before they actually understand what's going on in the game. That is how you enable them to grow into these activities. But with human beings such as Kelly, there is no "growing into" any kind of activity, so why bother? Why bother with a birthday party — or a Christmas dinner? Why have dinners at all? Why not just feed them?

The world within which Kelly is approached as a human being was gradually beginning to evaporate. Examples were multiplying. Can one in good faith say, as I did above, that one is working "with" a profoundly disabled human being like Kelly? Can she really be said to have "friends"? Can she be "happy"? I asked the staff at Kelly's group home some of these questions, to see what they made of all this. In turned out that most of them did indeed believe that a capacity for purposive agency is what gives meaning to human life. They also believed that purposive agency presupposes at least some level of self-awareness. Yet this did not seem to bother them at all when it came to explain how they related to Kelly. For them, Kelly was just someone in need of care, and caregiving was what they did. In doing so, they included Kelly in the language that shapes the meaning of what is going on in her home, which is the practice of caring for people who are dependent on it. They seemed to require no other reason for what they were doing.[2] On the other hand, if the notions of selfhood and of purposive agency are indeed crucial to what it means to live a human life, then the questions I raised are difficult to avoid. What is the point of treating someone as a human being when one's belief about what it means to be human implies that she is not, in fact, a human being?

That was the problem I was stuck with after my visit to Kelly's group home. How could I account for the practice of caring for people like her when some of the most cherished beliefs in our moral culture cannot but cast doubts on their humanity? If I would be pressed to give an account of Kelly's life as a human life, what would I say? If we are inclined — as I was at the time, and still am — to accept Pope John Paul II's claim that Kelly is "one of us," how can we define ourselves in a way that makes this claim intelligible? These reflections suggested to me that there is something seriously amiss when we make selfhood and agency critical to what it means to be human. At least this must be true if we assume that the nurses in her group home are not just fooling themselves when they approach her as a human being.

2. The Hierarchy of Disability

Disability is "out of the closet." People who were invisible have become visible. The general public knows their stories, at least to some extent, and that has put an end to their hidden existence. In the old days it was not uncommon for families to hide disabled children in their homes, or to put them away in institutions out of shame, or because they were worried that their children would be a "burden" on society. These things have changed mostly because of the disability-rights movement, which emerged in the 1970s and 1980s in the United States and then spread to other parts of the globe.[3] It has changed our thinking about

2. See David A. Pailin, *A Gentle Touch: A Theology of Human Being* (London: SPCK, 1992), p. 103. In Ch. 6 I will take up an extended conversation with Pailin's book.

3. On the disability-rights movement, see Joseph P. Shapiro, *No Pity: People with Disabilities Forging a New Civil Rights Movement* (New York: Times Books, 1993); James L. Charlton, *Nothing about Us without Us: Disability, Oppression, and Empowerment* (Berkeley: University of California Press, 1998); Doris Zames Fleischer and Frieda Zames, *The Disability Rights Movement: From Charity to Confrontation* (Philadelphia: Temple University Press, 2001); Richard K. Scotch, *From Good Will to Civil Rights: Transforming Federal Dis-*

disability by insisting on people's right to tell their own story. The general mood regarding disability as a catastrophe usually produced a response of pity and compassion; but the disability-rights movement rejected that response, as well as the assumptions on which it was based. What was traditionally regarded as a matter of charity and benevolence came to be considered a matter of equal rights and social justice. In his well-known history of the disability-rights movement, Joseph P. Shapiro says that the movement testifies to an "ongoing revolution in self-perception" on the part of people with disabilities in which they reject the images of neediness and failure. "There is no pity or tragedy in disability. It is society's myths, fears, and stereotypes that make being disabled difficult."[4]

While I have no doubt that this claim about changing self-perceptions is true, it does reveal at the same time a serious limitation in the ethical framework that is guiding the disability-rights literature. To a very large extent, this literature has little to say about the lives of persons with intellectual disabilities,[5] let alone those, such as Kelly, with profound intellectual disabilities, because the nature of their condition does not enable them to develop a sense of self. Or if it does, their sense of self often has limitations that usually are not true of other human beings. In many cases, developing "selfhood" is the problem rather than the solution for people with intellectual disabilities. But this fact goes entirely unrecognized in the disability-rights literature. I

---

ability Policy (Philadelphia: Temple University Press, 2001); Duane F. Stroman, *The Disabilities Rights Movement: From Deinstitutionalization to Self-Determination* (Lanham, MD: University of America Press, 2003); Jacqueline Vaughn Switzer, *Disabled Rights: American Disability Policy and the Fight for Equality* (Washington, DC: Georgetown University Press, 2003).

4. Shapiro, *No Pity*, pp. 4-5.

5. "Intellectual disabilities" is distinct from "mental disabilities" in that it refers to cognitive impairments rather than conditions of mental illness. The term refers to what, in the United Kingdom, is usually referred to as "learning disabilities." Charlton's otherwise very perceptive book has a remarkable blind spot regarding this distinction. He acknowledges that there is a hierarchy of disability, supported by comments from international disability-rights leaders, who almost without exception say that people with "mental disability" lead the most difficult lives. However, while a number of these witnesses clearly speak of "mental retardation," Charlton interprets them as speaking of mental illness, which means that, even in his hierarchy of disability, the "lowest of the low" are not adequately represented (*Nothing about Us without Us*, pp. 97-99).

am not denying, of course, that in many cases the perception of intellectual disability has resulted in living conditions that are much worse than they would have been had there been positive support. Quite a few people are designated "intellectually disabled" about whom one wonders about their having received the label in the first place. But this is not true of the profoundly disabled human beings to whom the "ongoing revolution in self-perception" fails to apply.

This observation has serious consequences for how the disability-rights movement argues the case for inclusion, because it indicates that the argument itself may well have exclusivist implications. If the important thing to liberate me from social stigma is that I reclaim the authority over my own story, then this is a serious setback for those who cannot possibly know what it is to have a story. Another way of making this point is to say that there apparently exists something like a "hierarchy of disability" that assigns persons with intellectual disabilities in general, and with profound intellectual disabilities in particular, to its lowest ranks.

Recent sociological research confirms the existence of this kind of hierarchy.[6] Those whose intellectual functioning does not allow them to represent themselves are generally perceived as being the "worst off." In addition to pervasive negative attitudes toward people with disabilities in general, there is a hierarchical order of social acceptance of disabilities, within which "mental retardation and mental illness have consistently been identified as the least accepted disabilities in social relationships."[7] This is characteristic of most of those so disabled in that this hierarchical order creates "greater social distance and fewer friendship opportunities." People stay away from persons with intellectual disabilities because they do not consider them to be desirable as friends.

6. For a reflection on this phenomenon from within disability studies, see Anne Louise Chappell, "Still Out in the Cold: People with Learning Difficulties and the Social Model of Disability," in *The Disability Reader: Social Science Perspectives,* ed. Tom Shakespeare (London: Cassell, 1998), pp. 209-20. Chappell's analysis, however, does not move beyond the claim that the theoretical focus on the body in the social model leaves much to be explained for experiences related to impairment of the intellect.

7. Phyllis A. Gordon, Jennifer Chiriboga Tantillo, David Feldman, and Kristin Perrone, "Attitudes Regarding Interpersonal Relationships with Persons with Mental Illness and Mental Retardation," *Journal of Rehabilitation* 70 (2004).

Underlying my argument in this book are two premises. The first is that the hierarchy of disability reflects the hierarchy of moral values in our culture. People move upward on the ladder of cultural attraction because of what they are capable of achieving. The second premise is that this hierarchy of moral values reflects a basic assumption about our human nature, namely, that selfhood and purposive agency are crucial to what makes our lives human in the first place. That is, our culture cherishes the notion that the point of my life is what I make of it; most people with intellectual disabilities are perceived as lacking in the ability to make anything out of their lives. In terms of what our culture regards as interesting, such persons do not make interesting friends. Some of the features that explain their unattractiveness are that their walking and their talking are usually slow, their behavior is often unpredictable and incomprehensible, and their actions are frequently seen as embarrassing. Given this perception, the issue of "friendship" in the lives of people with intellectual disabilities is very much to the point. The realities of their impaired cognitive and intellectual functioning diminish their opportunities for upward social mobility in significant ways. They lose out in our cultural hierarchies. Therefore, they are most likely to stay where they are currently located in these hierarchies. The paradigm of the successful achiever that dominates our careers will make sure that they stay where they are.

The above observations mark the point of departure of my argument in this book. My quarrel with the disability-rights approach is that it does not question this paradigm in any significant way; on the contrary, that approach is entirely dependent on this paradigm. While I do not belittle the importance of equal rights and social justice for any person — with or without a disability — persons with intellectual disabilities need friends more than they need anything else, or so I will argue here. But for my argument to work, I must try to remove notions that tend to make Kelly's humanity questionable. Whatever it means that I am capable of thinking about myself as well as about her while she cannot, it is not crucial to the understanding of what our common humanity entails. That is, notions of our humanity that put selfhood and purposive agency at center stage render the claim that Kelly is "one of us" unintelligible.

3. The Problem and Its Problems

Years have gone by since I first met Kelly. Since then I have only become more convinced of the importance of friendship in the lives of people like her. I also have become more convinced that the issue of friendship is tied to the question of what it means to say that Kelly is "one of us." This is a double-edged question, of course, because I cannot say how I understand Kelly's existence without considering how I understand my own: my conception of my own humanity is at stake within my concept of her humanity, and vice versa. But I have also learned in the meantime that the intellectual interest in this kind of problem is met with suspicion, particularly by parents and family advocates of intellectually disabled children. And rightly so, I should add. Why question the humanity of their children when they already have all the problems they can handle, to be able to support those children and give them a tolerable quality of life? "Intellectual curiosity" is surely not the answer that is going to satisfy the suspicious. Just think of my observations about the people working in Kelly's group home. What was the point of posing my questions to them when they managed perfectly well to treat her as a human being without those questions? Why suggest to these people that what they are doing is unintelligible without an account of what it means for Kelly to be human?[8] So there are problems with raising the question of Kelly's humanity that I need to address before I go on to say anything else.

The first of these problems concerns the issue of what I call "appropriate writing."[9] It is not unusual in the literature on disability to find authors who present their credentials before they start developing their thoughts.[10] Apparently these authors find themselves compelled to ex-

8. See Stanley Hauerwas, "Timeful Friends: Living with the Handicapped," in *Sanctify Them in the Truth: Holiness Exemplified,* ed. Stanley Hauerwas (Nashville: Abingdon, 1998), pp. 143-56. Hauerwas poses the same question: "How do we care for the mentally handicapped in such a manner which would forestall our felt need to provide reasons why we should care for the mentally handicapped, thereby rendering their lives unintelligible?" (p. 144).

9. Hans S. Reinders, "The Virtue of Writing Appropriately. Or: Is Stanley Hauerwas Right in Thinking He Should Not Write Anymore on the Mentally Handicapped?" in *God, Truth and Witness: Engaging Stanley Hauerwas,* ed. L. Gregory Jones, Reinhard Hütter, and C. Rosalee Veloso Ewell (Grand Rapids: Brazos Press, 2005), pp. 53-70.

10. See, for example, Deborah Marks, *Disability: Controversial Debates and Psychological Perspectives* (London: Routledge, 1999), p. xi.

plain why they should be in a legitimate position to say what they want to say. Frequently the author begins by identifying herself or himself as a person with a disability: with very few exceptions, this means a physical, not an intellectual, disability.[11] The need for this identification answers to a moral presupposition of this literature: since persons with disabilities are the subjects of their own experiences, talk of their experiences by other people is patronizing; in fact, taking their own stories from them is showing a lack of respect.[12] Thus, by presenting their credentials as writers in this way, disabled persons can "reclaim their experiences" and "find their own history."[13]

The language of reclaiming indicates a question of intellectual ownership and, at the same time, of intellectual reappropriation.[14] Peo-

---

11. This is true of much of both the theological and the sociological literature on disability: Harold H. Wilke, *Creating the Caring Congregation: Guidelines for Ministering with the Handicapped* (Nashville: Abingdon Press, 1980); Stewart D. Govig, *Strong at the Broken Places: Persons with Disabilities and the Church* (Louisville: Westminster/John Knox Press, 1989); Nancy L. Eiesland, *The Disabled God: Toward a Liberatory Theology of Disability* (Nashville: Abingdon Press, 1994); Deborah Creamer, "Finding God in Our Bodies: Theology from the Perspective of People with Disabilities," *Journal of Religion in Disability & Rehabilitation* 2, no. 1 (1995): 27-42 (Part 1); 2, no. 2 (1995): 67-87 (Part 2); Kathy Black, *A Healing Homiletic: Preaching and Disability* (Nashville: Abingdon Press, 1996). For the field of sociology, see, for example, Mike Oliver, "A Sociology of Disability or a Disablist Sociology?" in *Disability and Society: Emerging Issues and Insights*, ed. Len Barton (London and New York: Longman, 1996), pp. 18-42, 25; Robert F. Drake, "A Critique of the Role of the Traditional Charities," in *Disability and Society*, ed. Len Barton, pp. 145-66; Deborah Marks, *Disability: Controversial Debates and Psychological Perspectives* (London: Routledge, 1999), p. x. In explaining the "emanicipatory approach to the sociological study of disability," Barton lays out some of its key issues. The first is: "What right have I to undertake this work?" (Len Barton, "Sociology and Disability: Some Emerging Issues," in *Disability and Society*, pp. 3-17).

12. According to Jennie Weiss Block, this implies that any attempt to think theologically about disability "must be informed by an understanding of the thinking that shapes the disability rights movement" (*Copious Hosting: A Theology of Access for People with Disabilities* [New York: Continuum, 2002], p. 18).

13. J. Ryan and F. Thomas, *The Politics of Mental Handicap* (Hammondsworth: Penguin Books, 1980), p. 13; Nancy L. Eiesland, *The Disabled God: Toward a Liberatory Theory of Disability* (Nashville: Abingdon, 1994), p. 20.

14. The issue of ownership can also be taken in an economic sense. See Marks, who writes (in *Disability: Controversial Debates*): "It behooves all people working around issues of oppression to acknowledge their own structural location, even if this location is not seen as being immutable, but is rather performed to reflect upon, although not make nec-

ple with disabilities are perfectly capable of representing themselves and should be recognized for their right to do so.[15] Not only should they be in control of their own lives; they should also be in control of what is said about them. What makes living with a disability difficult is not necessarily the impairment itself, but rather the adverse attitudes of prejudice and social stigma. What makes this experience oppressive is the fact that other people wish to explain to you what your life is about — usually in negative terms. In technical language, the disadvantages a disability brings into the material world are reproduced in the symbolic world. Negative images hurt just as much, if not more, than closed doors do. These negative images and the stories that produce them need to be destroyed, so the common argument runs, which is why people with disabilities must be acknowledged as the authors of their own stories. This is the logic behind the claim that they are involved in a struggle for "the power of naming difference."[16] According to this logic, the act of writing about disability issues is a political act of appropriation. Therefore, if raising the issue of Kelly's humanity is appropriate at all, it is definitely not appropriate for just anyone to do so. It takes credentials.

Regarding my own credentials in writing about Kelly and others, it will have to suffice for the moment for me to explain what I intend to do in writing this book. First of all, my raising the question of Kelly's humanity is not a way of introducing the lives of disabled persons as moral quandaries. Moral quandaries are the favorite subject of ethics textbooks: they supposedly teach people correct ways of moral reasoning about "hard cases." My aim in this book is the opposite: my main burden is to eliminate the suggestion that Kelly's humanity presents us with a moral quandary. Regarding my reflections on the metaphorical

---

essarily publicly available, their own personal motives. Failure to reflect on what the member of the privileged group is getting out of the encounter may serve to mystify their own position" (p. xiii). See also M. Oliver, "Changing the Social Relations of Research Production," *Disability, Handicap and Society* 7, no. 2 (1992): 101-15.

15. Charlton, *Nothing about Us without Us*, p. 3; Diane Driedger, *The Last Civil Rights Movement: Disabled People's International* (New York: St. Martin's Press, 1989), p. 28, quoting Ed Roberts: "When you let others speak for you, you lose."

16. Len Barton, "Sociology and Disability: Some Emerging Issues," in *Disability and Society: Emerging Issues and Insights,* ed. Len Barton (London and New York: Longman, 1996), pp. 3-17, 11.

nature of approaching her as a human being, I had to find a different perspective. Since the perspective of individual selfhood was casting her humanity into doubt, it occurred to me that an appropriate move for me to make would be to question that perspective — rather than questioning her humanity. I discarded the notion that the people who approach her as "one of us" are capable of doing so only because they are fooling themselves. In a sense, my aim in this book is very simple: I am trying to understand what makes approaching Kelly as a human being an intelligible act.

In this respect, my inquiry here is radically different from those inquiries in which human beings such as Kelly are introduced to discuss the question of when it is morally permissible to end their lives. It is radically different because I want to explore understanding our humanity in a way that will sustain the effort to include profoundly disabled human beings in our lives, not question whether they should live at all. In other words, this is not the kind of ethical inquiry that is commonly known under the heading of "bioethics"; nor is it about the kinds of issues that hold sway in contemporary bioethics readers.[17] Especially with respect to intellectual disability, the most prominent issues in these textbooks are whether it is morally permissible to abort a human fetus once it is known that the future child will have a severe disability ("selective abortion"), whether there is a moral obligation to prevent disabled lives as much as we can ("prenatal screening for genetic defects"), whether it is morally justifiable to withdraw life-sustaining treatments for disabled newborn infants ("infanticide"). Of course, not all bioethicists come up with the same answers when they discuss these questions. But even though many authors in the field hold that our society has an obligation to provide adequate care for children with disabilities once they are born, there is a current of thought in that field that questions whether they should come to life at all.[18]

The discussion in this book is different. It aims at developing an account of our humanity that eliminates the problem: not by denying dis-

---

17. See, for example, Helga Kuhse and Peter Singer, *Bioethics: An Anthology* (Oxford: Blackwell, 1999).

18. The notorious example is Helga Kuhse and Peter Singer, *Should the Baby Live? The Problem of Handicapped Infants* (Oxford: Oxford University Press, 1985).

ability, of course, but by denying that what constitutes it is *not* crucial to our humanity. The positive question is found in how Kelly's humanity is similar to yours and mine. My hope is that the answer will sustain supportive attitudes toward people with disabilities in general, and toward those with profound intellectual disabilities in particular. The most important thing that this kind of inquiry can do is make people think twice.

However, the aim of my analysis is not only to change readers' minds — if they need changing — but also to advocate participation in the task of sharing our lives with disabled people. Having been a regular guest in Kelly's group home for some time, I know that raising abstract questions about their existence is a futile intellectual enterprise if it is not directed at changing social practices. Thinking about Kelly's life needs embodiment, I have learned. If we are not practically involved, it is very difficult, if not impossible, to understand the practices of care and support for these human beings. I want this book to vindicate the people who have devoted their lives, or parts of their lives, to disabled persons — whether they be families, advocates, or professional caregivers. Given the current role models that dominate our contemporary culture, their practices need this kind of support. This is not only for their sake, I should add, but also for our own: we desperately need countercultural experiences that expose the myth of humans as forever youthful, ideally attractive, aggressively mobile, and physically and mentally strong.[19] This myth is exemplified by, among other things, the current hype about "remakes" and "makeovers" that indicates that the desire to be in possession of our own lives is now extended to our bodies as well. The craving for bodily perfection is but the latest exemplification of that other great myth that holds sway in our culture: that "meaning" is made rather than found. The inevitable implication of this view is that the lives of the Kellys of this world must be pointless. It is no wonder that our culture is interested in the "ethical issue" of ending their lives. In view of these popular beliefs, the question is how to conceive of our lives as truly human so that we will be able to welcome persons with profound disabilities into our midst, as Oliver de Vinck's parents were capable of doing. At the root of the

19. Don S. Saliers, "Toward a Spirituality of Inclusiveness," in *Human Disability and the Service of God: Reassessing Religious Practice* (Nashville: Abingdon, 1998), pp. 19-31.

problem is the fact that our moral culture is replete with images of the good life in which such persons have no part. That fact must also be part of our investigation.

4. No Moral Taxonomy

Apart from the question of credentials, however, there are other problems with raising the problem of Kelly's humanity that we need to consider. One is the problem of appropriate method. The question is not only what to say, but also how to say it. In the bioethical literature, as I have suggested, the common approach to profoundly disabled lives is to regard them as a source of moral quandaries. Their lives are seen as confronting us with "hard cases" of medical decision-making, where medical doctors — together with nurses and families — face issues of "life and death." I will consider this approach briefly in order to show how my investigation is different.

When issues of life and death come up, the question is usually about whether we can distinguish features that make human life worthy of protection. What is it about human life that obligates us to save it? In answering this question, many ethicists have sought to establish a defensible notion of personhood, which they base on the assumption that being a person is somehow critical to the moral obligation not to end human life. If a human being is not recognized as a person, he or she appears to be without moral standing. The assumption underlying this approach is that human life *as such* is regarded as a biological entity that lacks the dignity intrinsic to the human person.

In his recent book *Making Medical Decisions for the Profoundly Mentally Disabled,* Norman Cantor, a professor of law at Rutgers University, follows this same approach to life and death issues concerning human beings like Kelly and Oliver de Vinck. He explains how the question of whether they qualify as persons may be decisive in the withdrawing of life-support systems, particularly with regard "to the interests of surrounding family and caregivers, that is, 'real persons.' "[20] Another question Cantor raises is whether harvesting nonvital tissue can be prohib-

20. Norman L. Cantor, *Making Medical Decisions for the Profoundly Mentally Disabled* (Cambridge, MA: MIT Press, 2005), pp. 14-15.

ited to protect profoundly disabled human beings, for example, when biological material might save the life of a "real" person, or several "real" persons.[21]

With regard to how to resolve such issues, Cantor explains, the common approach is to define the criteria for personhood in terms of psychological and/or social characteristics.[22] Evidently, the most cherished of these characteristics refer to functions of the self, which are located, neurologically speaking, in the neocortex of the brain. It follows, according to some bioethicists, that the interests of human beings whose neocortex is not functioning cannot be said to have the same moral weight as the interests of persons with a functioning neocortex.[23] A well-known argument runs as follows: Without a capacity for self-consciousness, one cannot have a conception of oneself; this necessarily implies that one's life cannot be valuable to oneself.[24] Without self-consciousness, the argument concludes, one's life cannot possibly mean anything *to oneself,* and thus it has no "intrinsic value."

However, Cantor is not satisfied with this argument, because he believes that all human beings should be regarded as persons, even those with profound diabilities. But his support for that belief is surprisingly weak. As a "starter," he mentions that American society recognizes as persons with full moral status all living human beings. Then he shows that the American courts and legislatures have done the same. Next, he suggests that there are social benefits to adopting this position: for example, protecting the profoundly disabled can be viewed as a reminder

21. Cantor, *Making Medical Decisions,* p. 16.

22. Cantor lists about a dozen different philosophical accounts of the criteria for personhood (pp. 17-18).

23. This is the logic exhibited in Kuhse and Singer's book *Should the Baby Live?.* For a few examples of similar positions, see John Arras, "The Severely Demented, Minimally Functioning Patient: An Ethical Analysis," *Journal of American Geriatrics Society* 36 (1988): 938; Allen Buchanan and Dan Brock, *Deciding for Others: The Ethics of Surrogate Decision Making* (Cambridge, UK: Cambridge University Press, 1989); Lainie Friedman Ross, *Children, Families, and Health Care Decision Making* (New York: Clarendon Press, 1998); Peter Singer, *Rethinking Life and Death: The Collapse of Our Traditional Ethics* (New York: St. Martin's Press, 1995). For a critical reappraisal of the concept of personhood in the bioethical literature, see Tom L. Beauchamp, "The Failure of Theories of Personhood," *Kennedy Institute of Ethics Journal* 9, no. 4 (1999): 309-24.

24. John Harris. *The Value of Life: An Introduction to Medical Ethics* (London: Routledge and Kegan Paul, 1985).

of the sanctity of life.[25] But none of his considerations can count as proving anything, of course, because they all make the ascription of personhood dependent on moral and legal convention. One cannot defend personhood for the profoundly disabled by referring to what people believe about them, because, if adherence to certain beliefs justifies the ascription of personhood, then a change in these beliefs may do the opposite.

To close this anticipated gap in his argument, Cantor then provides a theoretical reason for his position. He adduces "conative conduct" — that is, the will to achieve some goal for oneself — as both a necessary and sufficient criterion for personhood.[26] That is to say, profoundly disabled human beings are to be regarded as persons with the full moral status attached to this notion insofar as they are purposive agents. Of course, this implies, as Cantor admits, that there will be profoundly disabled human beings who fail to meet this criterion. To remedy this fault, Cantor relies on the fact that "any profoundly disabled person who does not meet the suggested criterion for moral status (conative conduct) would still receive full legal protection for the practical reasons cited above."[27] Apart from the fact that his argument here is an example of circular reasoning — the "theoretical" reason was intended to sustain actual legal practice, not the other way around — Cantor's argument fails to do anything for all the cases he started with, namely, profoundly disabled human beings who lack consciousness.[28]

As this account of Cantor's argument about personhood indicates, debates in the bioethical literature about who is to count as a human person do not always excel in rigorous logic, even though in actual medical practice much depends on how the question is answered.[29] In general, there seems to be little doubt about this strategy as such. As indicated, most authors proceed by identifying a set of characteristics to

---

25. Cantor, *Making Medical Decisions*, pp. 20-23.

26. Cantor, *Making Medical Decisions*, pp. 25-26.

27. Cantor, *Making Medical Decisions*, p. 26.

28. To succeed in view of these cases, Cantor would have to let go of the capabilities approach, which he fails to do, as his argument implicitly acknowledges.

29. See M. B. Mahowald, "Person," in *Encyclopedia of Bioethics,* rev. ed., Warren T. Reich (New York: Macmillan, 1995); Mahowald observes that many questions about the morality of particular medical procedures are explicitly or implicitly decided on grounds of the ascription of personhood.

determine "personhood," and then continue to test the result against individual cases in order to see whether they can live with the consequences.[30]

In view of this literature, some Christian writers in the field of bioethics have proposed a different account of personhood according to which the human person is conceived of in terms of his or her "relations." My humanity is not dependent on my capacity for self-consciousness, these authors argue, but it is constituted by the web of social relationships of which I am a part. In other words, personhood is not psychologically, but socially, constituted.[31] What often goes unchallenged in presenting this alternative concept, however, is the strategy that produces the rejected outcome. That is, the unchallenged presupposition is that a morally significant account of my humanity is based on a moral taxonomy. In order to be morally considerable — to have "moral status" — I must qualify as a P, which condition is satisfied if I meet criterion S. Only when one accepts this as a valid kind of argument is there a point in arguing that P is more properly conceived of as meeting the criterion of R. That is, arguments of this kind only make sense on the basis of a moral taxonomy.[32]

The methodology in this book for thinking about our humanity does not depend on offering a moral taxonomy: that is, I will not en-

---

30. There is a renowned body of literature on this matter that has become quite suspect in the disability-rights movement (some of the authors are Michael Tooley, John Harris, Helga Kuhse, Mary Anne Warren, and, most prominent of all, Peter Singer). What distinguishes these writers is not the logic of their position, however, but the fact that they are prepared to follow the argument wherever it leads. They can live with outcomes for actual cases that many "traditional" people consider abhorrent. That is, these authors don't reject "counterintuitive" results, because they believe that the intuitions that produce them are obsolete. They find arguments such as Norman Cantor's to be logically confused because these arguments attempt both to respect these intuitions and, at the same time, go beyond them.

31. R. Spaemann, *Personen: versuche über den Unterschied zwischen "etwas" und "jemand"* (Stuttgart: Klett-Cotta, 1996).

32. For a Roman Catholic critique of the liberal position on personhood in the bioethical literature that confirms the method of offering a moral taxonomy, see L. Palazzani, "The Meanings of the Philosophical Concept of Person and their Implications in the Current Debate on the Status of the Human Embryo," in *The Identity and Status of the Human Embryo: Proceedings of the Third Assembly of the Pontifical Academy for Life,* ed. J. de Dios Vial Correa and E. Sgreccia (Città del Vaticano: Librera Editrice Vaticana, 1997), pp. 74-95.

deavor to offer a set of characteristics to convince you that profoundly disabled human beings are also in fact human beings — not only biologically speaking but also ethically speaking. This is because I believe that the procedure is wrongheaded, because taxonomies by definition constitute boundaries and, by the same token, constitute marginal cases. In this book I defend the view that there are no marginal cases of being human. The reason for my claim is theological.

5. A Theological Inquiry

Put positively, my methodology starts from a different assumption. What we are to think about a life like Kelly's I take to be a question of how we understand our own lives. The theoretical task is interpretation rather than classification. That is, rather than classifying what we believe to be the distinguishing characteristics of human beings that make them morally considerable, our task is to interpret humanity — our own as well as that of others — in the light of our existence in this world. In one of his essays on disability, Stanley Hauerwas puts it this way:

> The appropriate moral context for raising the question of the "essentially" human should not be an attempt to determine if some men are or are not human, but rather what we must be if we are to preserve and enhance what humanity we have. In other words, the question of the criteria of the human should not be raised about others but only about ourselves.[33]

According to this principle, the way we regard the lives of other people reflects the way we understand our own, which is no less true of our understanding of the lives of people with a profound intellectual disability.

By way of determining what we must understand about ourselves, what is the underlying assumption guiding my inquiry in this book? It is that there is absolutely nothing important about my being if it were not

---

33. Stanley M. Hauerwas, "The Retarded and Criteria for the Human," in *Truthfulness and Tragedy: Further Investigations into Christian Ethics* (Notre Dame: University of Notre Dame Press, 1977), pp. 156-63.

for the love of God. In the vastness of the universe, both in time and space, my existence is even less than what is contained in the blink of an eye. Only the love of the eternal God can make the difference: it is because of the love of God that our humanity retains its special quality. The traditional theological way of expressing this view has been through the doctrine of *imago dei*. Whatever else it may mean to say that I am created in the divine image, it must surely mean that I am created in God's love, since love is what defines the God in whom Christians believe. This is what makes my existence as a human being incredibly important. For exactly the same reason, it makes the existence of human beings like Kelly incredibly important. Affirming the first claim but denying the second would mean that God loves human beings like me but not human beings like her. I do not see how such a distinction could be defended from a Christian point of view.

In contrast, philosophical accounts of what makes our humanity significant must necessarily rely on some account of our human nature. For example, philosophical naturalism tells us that there is nothing incredibly important about our existence; it is a sheer accident in the history of the universe. All that is valuable to us is only valuable to the extent that it contributes to the satisfaction of what we want. Whatever goods there are, they are such because they are the objects of desire. Good does not exist beyond that. It follows that what we value about our humanity is necessarily grounded in our appetites. In this view there is no meaning that goes beyond satisfaction.

Of course, there are philosophical alternatives to my Christian account other than philosophical naturalism. But I am not sure they do much better. For example, Kantian transcendentalism grounds the significance of our humanity in transcendental reason. But this is far from consoling because transcendental reason can only survive historical criticism on the basis of absolute knowledge, which is not a very plausible notion with regard to human being (*pace* Kantian transcendentalism). What this leaves us with is a kind of historicism, which comes in many varieties in contemporary philosophy. There is no meaning that exceeds the limits of our historical understanding, and this goes for understanding our humanity as well. This position only confirms — albeit in a different way — that whatever we make of our humanity is the result of historically situated cultural constructs. Beyond those there is no meaning.

Nature cannot provide a firm grounding of what it is that makes our humanity special, nor can reason or history. It follows that, if there is anything significant about our existence, it can only be sustained if it is sustained *extrinsically* — that is, from elsewhere, through the love of God. This belief is crucial to my understanding of humanity, whether it be my own humanity or anyone else's. Thus it is also crucial in my understanding of the humanity of human beings such as Kelly and Oliver de Vinck. Only because of who God is, and what he does, can we understand our humanity in a way that sustains their humanity independent of the many and profound disabilities that characterize their lives. That is, their humanity, as well as our own, is grounded adequately only when grounded *unconditionally.* I am convinced that only a theological view can succeed in doing this.[34]

My remarks on how this inquiry will proceed should convey to the reader that it does not in any way set apart human beings with a profound intellectual disability. Nor does it attempt to offer a justification — or give a reason — for their existence, at least not in the sense that their lives are unintelligible unless we can provide a reason for them. It would be difficult to imagine a theological argument implying that, in the eyes of God, Kelly's existence is less intelligible than mine or yours. Something like the reverse is actually true: from the perspective of eternity, my and your existence is hardly different from hers. The issue of "meaning" regarding each of our lives is the same. It is only when we hold on to the perspective of *individual selfhood* that we see them drifting apart; it is only then that we are confronted with the possibility of an anthropological subdivision. Or, to strike a more positive note, it is only because we do not look at their lives as being categorically different from ours that we account for the practices of support in a way that does not set them apart, but includes them in our lives.

To introduce the theological nature of this book in this way may suggest that it aims at a Christian critique of contemporary culture. Though I do not mind criticizing contemporary culture when that is appropriate, I have not written this book for that purpose. The purpose of my analysis here is not to criticize but to empower. Among those who share their lives with a profoundly disabled human being, many would contest the notion that such a person cannot lead a human life, prop-

34. I will return to this claim in Ch. 7.

erly so called. The purpose of this book is to sustain people in exploring the convictions and beliefs that are capable of affirming their judgment in this regard. Second, it would be a mistake to suggest that Christians in this society do not share the dominant view of our moral culture about what it means to be human; as will become evident in the chapters that follow, there is no ground to make this claim. Christian communities are usually not on the frontline when it comes to matters of inclusion. For many people with disabilities, it is still true that it is easier to enter a pub or a cinema than the sanctuary of a church, just to mention one practical problem.[35]

Aside from the many justified complaints about practical matters such as limited access, there are strong historical currents in Christian theology underscoring attitudinal barriers toward people with profound disabilities. There are within the tradition of Christian theology many strands of thinking about our humanity that make interior and self-referential matters central to their conception of being human. In that respect, my aim in this book is not so much intended to be apologetic as it is to be self-critical: it is an attempt to investigate whether the Christian religion can find in itself the resources to develop a view that does not render the existence of profoundly disabled humans inherently problematic.[36]

Finally, it is evidently not true that Christians hold more positive views about profoundly disabled lives than do most other people in our culture, though not many of them would use the word "vegetable." As Kelly has emerged in the first pages of this chapter, I suspect that many readers — Christians and non-Christians alike — would consider her life to be quite atypical of how we usually understand humanity. If so, the reader may well ask why I take her as a test case.

In answer to that question, let me again refer to the hierarchy of disability that exists in the culture. Given the characteristics of Kelly's

35. Deland, "Images of God Through the Lens of Disability," *Journal of Disability, Religion, and Health* 3, no. 2 (1999): 47-79.

36. With regard to finding theological resources to overcome the limitations of theological understanding, my approach is the same as expressed by Nancy Eiesland in her article "Liberation, Inclusion, and Justice: A Faith Response to Persons with Disabilities," in *Impact: Feature Issue on Faith Communities and Persons with Developmental Disabilities*, ed. V. Gaylord, B. Gaventa, S. R. Simon, R. Norman-McNaney, and A. N. Amado, 14 (2002): 2-3.

life, we can safely say that the way our moral culture values our lives, it would render hers as the lowest of the low, dominated as the paradigm is by personal achievement. In view of that valuation, if I were to have as my point of departure the lives of mildly disabled persons, I would fail to bring out the problem in full measure. Many people with a mild intellectual disability are, to a considerable degree, capable of pursuing their own goals in life. That they do not have equal opportunities to do so is nothing less than a shame; and here I agree with the disability-rights movement on the importance of the political struggle. To argue from a perspective of profound intellectual disability, therefore, is not to deny the problems faced by people with other disabilities in this society. Rather, it is to affirm that a concept of being human can be truly universal if and only if it illuminates human existence as such — profoundly disabled persons included. Many people in our moral culture fail to see this, I'm afraid, and that includes many Christians.

6. The Politics of Friendship

In order to clarify the political aspect of the approach I take in this study, however, I must return to my "quarrel" with the disability-rights approach. Admittedly, the disability-rights approach has effectively contributed to the creation of more opportunities for people with disabilities than ever before. Hence it is important to explain why my argument in this book will not follow in its path. The disability-rights approach correctly tackles the social, economic, and political dimensions of exclusion and inequality, which in our society means that the language of rights is the most effective vehicle for launching its claims. However, my support of its claims to equal rights and justice does not necessarily imply that I accept the underlying theoretical framework that produces such claims. At stake here, once again, is the ambivalent nature of rights talk as far as people with intellectual disabilities are concerned.

In order to understand this ambivalence, the reader may wish to be mindful of the sociopolitical history of exclusion. In the wake of Michel Foucault's work, social historians have established that the invention of "liberty" as the inalienable right of citizens in liberal democracies has gone hand in hand with the dehumanization of various groups that the democratic polity believed were out of place. In the nineteenth and early twentieth centuries, the emerging democracies created special places for people who they believed needed to be isolated from the rest of society because they either did not deserve, or could not be entrusted with, the freedoms that healthy and normal citizens enjoyed.[37] Coercive exclusion went hand in hand with the invention of liberal citizenship, as we now know it. The moral justification for the labels of exclusion — "deviancy," "feeble-mindedness," "insanity," and so forth — invariably followed the same pattern: inadequacy or irresponsibility demanded that the rights of the liberal subject be taken from those not living up to its standard.[38] The disability-rights movement has effectively shattered the supposedly "humanitarian" concern that turned those excluded people into targets of "rehabilitation." In doing so, it has successfully repeated the strategy of previous struggles for civil rights, which is why it rightly deserves the name of the "last civil rights movement."[39] Its main strategy has been to acknowledge the subjectivity of humans with disability in telling their own story, using their own language.[40] In this way it has exposed the awkward fit of coerced isolation with fundamental democratic values. It has done so by using liberalism's own weapon of claiming equal rights and social justice for people who have been unjustifiably marginalized.

Thus rights language has once again proved to be the most effective language in our society to open up spaces that remained closed for "displaced" persons, such as persons with disabilities. Nonetheless, it is important to see that rights claims, while necessary, are not sufficient to counteract exclusion simply because of the kinds of spaces they can open.[41] In opening up institutional roles and public spaces they are crucial to our capacity as citizens. But rights cannot open up spaces of

37. Alison Bashford and Carolyn Strange, "Isolation and Exclusion in the Modern World," in *Isolation: Places and Practices of Exclusion,* ed. A. Bashford and C. Strange (London: Routledge, 2003), pp. 1-19.

38. Bashford and Strange, "Isolation and Exclusion," p. 4.

39. See footnote 12 above.

40. Diane Driedger, *The Last Civil Rights Movement: Disabled People's International* (New York: St. Martin's, 1989), p. vii.

41. Hans S. Reinders, "The Good Life for Citizens with Intellectual Disabilities," *Journal of Intellectual Disability Research* 46, Part 1 (Jan. 2002): 1-5.

intimacy, which are the kinds of spaces where humans have their need of belonging fulfilled. Put simply, disability rights are not going to make me your friend.[42]

Given that it perceives inclusion as a political goal, the disability-rights approach derives its strength from what it can do in the public sphere, aiming at how our society shapes its institutions as well as its public spaces. In the context of liberal democracy, however, the public sphere is separate from that other space — called the "private" sphere — where citizens are free to rule over their own lives. By using democracy's weapon of equal rights against its own creations, the disability-rights movement has bought into this division of space into public and private spheres. In doing so it has given away the possibility of addressing the issue of friendship as one of the central goods in our lives. The reason is that, within liberal democracy's division of spheres, friendship is part of our private lives, equal to marriage and family life. Therefore, the disability-rights movement has surrendered the possibility of saying anything about what is for many disabled people one of the fundamental issues, if not *the* fundamental issue: the question of sharing our lives together, not only as citizens but as human beings. If disability rights are not going to make me your friend, neither does reclaiming your own story force me to listen to it. It will only do so when I regard myself, and the purpose of my life, in a light that makes me willing to pay attention to what your life is about. Far from denying the crucial importance of disability rights, and far from belittling the importance of the ownership of one's own story, I do not believe that they will be sufficient to show what it means to say that Kelly is "one of us." And that goes for other people with disabilities as well. "My boy now has all the rights the ADA could possibly assure him of," a mother once said to me about her son with Down syndrome, "but he still has not got a friend."

Given the centers of gravitation in our moral culture, the argument for inclusion has gone toward questioning the ways our society marginalizes particular groups of people. In my view, the processes of marginalization work through the underlying images of who we are.

42. Joseph Shapiro discusses the transition from "pity" to rights; in the course of that discussion he claims that "pity opens hearts" (*No Pity*, p. 23). Lest I be misunderstood, friendship cannot be motivated by pity without becoming corrupt.

The most fundamental question is thus not about how disabled people regard themselves, nor is it about how "we" regard "them." Ultimately, the question is how we — readers and writers of books, if you will — regard ourselves, and our own lives. That question will decide whether or not we are the kind of people who want to share our lives with disabled persons.

No doubt there will be those who read my argument as an argument that "depoliticizes" disability. It would be a failure if it did. Just as there is no ethics that does not rely on a particular anthropology, there is also no ethics that does not have its own politics. What, then, are mine? The politics of my argument that we should go beyond the disability-rights approach is to point out that, if the opening of institutional and public spaces is to become really effective, then we are dependent on moral sources that differ from rights and justice. I do not doubt for a moment that people with intellectual disabilities ought to be treated as equal citizens, but I am equally certain that this concern is not adequately grounded in the moral values of political liberalism. Advocates of disability rights fail to see that the moral values of self-determination and choice they bring to the table in defense of equal citizenship for disabled people are exactly the same values that give other citizens the right not to be interested. Rights create the bonds of citizenship; unfortunately, they do not forge the moral bonds of friendship. Institutional space creates new opportunities that will become effective only because of the support of people. Without people who are disposed to be supportive, opportunities will turn into frustrations. Therefore, the politics of my investigation here is to argue for the inclusion of people with intellectual disabilities in our lives, which is more and greater than including them in our institutions.

7. Terminology

Despite the claim that the crucial issue is how we understand our own humanity, with or without a disability, this book is nonetheless about people with intellectual disabilities, especially profound intellectual disabilities. Of course, not all people with a profound intellectual disability live with conditions as serious as *micro-encephaly.* Difficult as it may be for the "outsider" to imagine, there are huge differences even among people whose developmental stage does not reach beyond the level of a toddler. Who are we talking about when we say "people with profound intellectual disabilities"? To answer this question, I need to say a few things about definition and classification. Before I do, however, I want to offer a preliminary critical remark about semantics.

In this book I will frequently speak first of "people" and "persons," and then often add the prepositional phrase "with disabilities." They are "people first" — before they are anything else.[43] Many writers in the disability-rights movement are careful to use the correct language as a sign of paying respect, and if writing per se is a political act, this makes sense. There is a moral point, then, in following the language that people with disabilities use to refer to themselves. However, there is also something deceptive about the practice of changing the language every few years, as the disability-rights movement has been doing in the last decades. Consider the following passage from a novel, written by the Swedish novelist Majgull Axelsson, about a young woman with a physical disability. The woman is a quadriplegic who stays in a hospital because of her very serious convulsions. She is a bright, intelligent person who absolutely hates to be patronized, which is exactly what some of the nurses do ("Oh, you poor thing . . . "). She remembers that she once attacked a nurse — with her teeth! — because she detested the way this nurse made her subject to "the cause of goodness." She goes on to say:

> It needs to be said. There is no state of being that has worn out so many names as this one; every decade for the last century has spit out some bitter old word and found a new, sweeter one. Thus the cripple became maimed and the maimed soul lame and the lame an invalid, the invalid a handicapped person, the handicapped person disabled, and finally, the disabled became the developmentally challenged.[44]

Old, bitter words are spit out and replaced by new, sweeter ones. It is a ritual that nobody manages to escape. Everybody knows the sequence. "Idiots" became "morons," then "morons" became "feeble-minded,"

43. People First is the name of an organization of self-advocates with intellectual disabilities; visit its website at: www.peoplefirst.org.
44. Majgull Axelsson, *April Witch,* trans. Linda Schenck (New York: Villard, 2002), p. 15.

"feeble-minded" became "mentally retarded," then "mentally retarded" became the "mentally disabled," and finally we have settled on "persons with intellectual disabilities." We do not speak of "feeble-minded" or "mentally retarded" anymore, because it came to be thought, at a certain point in time, that these terms were charged with negative connotations. For that same reason we now prefer not to speak of "the disabled" but of "persons with disabilities." The deception in all this is that we cannot remove the negative connotations of words by changing the language. What induces us to look for new words again and again is not inherent in language but in the attitudes of the people who use the language. Persons with disabilities do not need different words; they need different people. Negative connotations do not reside in words, but in the mind. Negative connotations are attached to words because of how people think about disability; thus, without changing their habits of thinking, people will use new words just as they used the old ones.

Regarding the definition of the term "disability," there are a number of positions to be found in the literature. There are those who believe that it is impossible to offer a universal definition of the term, given its many different uses.[45] To some extent, this is true. The concept of disability falls into the category of what the British philosopher W. B. Gallie has described as "essentially contested concepts."[46] But it does not follow that the term "disability" has no clear meaning. It only follows that definitions of its meaning are dependent on particular semantic communities. Defining the term appears to be a form of verbal legislation, as if it is saying, "If you want to be part of our discourse you need to know that this is how we use the word." Psychologists, for example, will use the definition found in DSM-IV; lawyers in the United States use the definition found in the Americans with Disabilities Act; policy-makers and service-providers throughout the Western world use

45. In the theological literature, this position is found in Weiss Block, *Copious Hosting,* pp. 32-33; see also Pailin, *A Gentle Touch,* pp. 29-30.

46. W. B. Gallie, "Essentially Contested Concepts," in Gallie, *Philosophy and the Historical Understanding* (New York: Schocken, 1968), pp. 157-91. The central idea behind Gallie's notion of "essentially contested concepts" has been explained by John Gray as concepts whose necessary and sufficient conditions of correct application are in dispute. See John Gray, "Political Power, Social Theory, and Essential Contestability," in *The Nature of Political Theory,* ed. David Miller and Larry Siedentop (Oxford: Clarendon Press, 1983), pp. 75-101.

the standard definition of the AAMR (American Association of Mental Retardation). In each case, the definition depends on the goal it is meant to serve. This also explains why the disability-rights movement uses a definition of its own: "A disability is the condition of being stigmatized and marginalized by society."[47]

A position that has gained considerable support in the field is to define "disability" as the effect of a (negative) societal response, and thus distinguish it from "impairment," which is then the physical or mental condition that elicits this response. The principle underlying this distinction is to affirm that there is a condition that causes (some) limitations in bodily functioning — physical or intellectual or mental, or any combination of these three — but to deny that these limitations in themselves justify negative evaluation. Human limitations vary in numerous ways, just as abilities vary in numerous ways. The condition of impairment thus points to human diversity and is, as such, to be considered a neutral fact. The negative evaluation attached to "disability" can then be located in the societal response to this neutral fact. This means that, while the condition of being impaired is a function of a person's body, the person's disability is a function of the way his environment responds to his body. This distinction opens up the possibility of targeting the disability as a "social construct" without targeting the impairing condition.[48]

In this book I don't intend to join forces with any of the semantic communities in the field, and thus I have no stake in elaborating on either definition or classification. What definitions and classifications there are can be abused to reinforce taxonomies that exhibit the logic of exclusion.[49] Having said that, I should add that I find the above distinction between impairments and disabilities helpful, that I don't doubt

47. Quoted from Eiesland, *The Disabled God*, p. 24.

48. The philosopher Susan Wendell succinctly defines a disability as "socially constructed from a biological reality" ("Towards a Feminist Theory of Disability," *Hypathia* 4, no. 2 [1989]: 104-23). See also Creamer, "Finding God in Our Bodies" (p. 35), who claims that disability is a physical condition and a sociopolitical category. She sees "two interrelated factors: the bodily experience of disability and the societal response to these bodies." She argues that "disability can only be fully understood by looking at the interplay between the physical condition and the environment, for each has relevance to theological reflection."

49. This verdict holds across the entire spectrum of moral and political views. In many accounts of the disability-rights movement, there is no place to represent intellectual disability, let alone profound intellectual disability. I return to this claim in Ch. 5.

that negative responses to impairments of any kind are socially constructed, but that I also think that the distinction is not equally powerful with regard to all kinds of disabilities. Here the first condition to come to mind is, of course, the condition of profound intellectual disability. I find it difficult to conceive of a social order in which a cognitive impairment in which a person cannot grasp distinctions between "me" and "you," or between "now" and "then," or "here" and "there" could be effectively regarded as neutral.[50]

My phrase "intellectual disability" is what Americans used to refer to as "mental retardation," but what is now more often known as "developmental disabilities"; this is roughly the same as what the British usually mean when they speak of "learning disabilities." The impairments in question are permanent; they are not a disease or an illness, which distinguishes this term from "mental disabilities" as a reference to psychiatric conditions of mental illness. These impairing conditions may occur at birth or later in life as the permanent effect of an illness or accident. Moreover, these impairments are manifested in limited cognitive functioning, which distinguishes intellectual disability from physical disability. "Intellectual disability" indicates irreversible developmental delay.

The phrase "profoundly disabled" indicates a developmental stage of mental development that has not gone beyond a toddler's stage of development. Whatever else is true of these human beings, it is quite unlikely that one will find them advertised as "being successful" in the way persons with mild intellectual disabilities — the proverbial "happy kid with Down syndrome" — are sometimes advertised in the media. While such kids also have an intellectual disability, and their parents or siblings can inform you about the darker sides of their lives, nobody in their right mind would think of raising a question about their humanity (I do realize that this is an overstatement).[51] Given cultural images of being "successful," or "being happy," things must appear as very different indeed for human beings like Kelly and Oliver de Vinck.

50. I will have more on the subject of social constructionism in the following chapter.

51. For the wonders, the darker moments, as well as the overstatement, read the story told by Martha Beck in *Expecting Adam: A True Story of Birth, Rebirth, and Everyday Magic* (New York: Berkley Books, 1999).

Chapter Two

"Being Human" and "Being Disabled" I

Being cheerful and keeping going is scarcely good enough when one has an illness that will end in an early death. . . . I am not suggesting that all of us with such devastating handicaps probe deeply into the meaning of life, nor that we automatically gain great wisdom or sanctity. But it does seem that our situation tends to make us ask questions that few people ask in the ordinary world.

Paul Hunt[1]

1. A Preliminary Objection

The suggestion that the profound nature of Kelly's intellectual disability renders her humanity questionable will be met with suspicion, as I anticipated in the opening chapter. Disabled people have too often been dehumanized in the history of Western society not to be suspicious about this question. Even though I have explained how the anthropological question is a question about our common humanity, that will hardly be enough to expel the misgivings some readers may have about raising this question in the first place.

Therefore, in this chapter and the next one I will consider a preliminary objection to the present project. In asking how the condition of profound disability affects the nature of being human, I seem to be implying

---

1. Paul Hunt, "A Critical Condition," in *The Disability Reader: Social Science Perspectives*, ed. Tom Shakespeare (London: Cassell, 1998), pp. 8-9.

that this condition affects the core of people's being: in short, being disabled defines being human. The objection I am about to discuss claims that this is a mistake. To question the humanity of profoundly disabled persons is to assume that their being human cannot be accounted for independently from their being disabled, which assumption is false. Human beings like Kelly are not disabled; they *have* a disability.

The issue posed by this objection is how we think "being disabled" is related to "being human." I will consider this objection as it is launched from two different quarters, namely, the sociological literature on disability ("disability studies") and Roman Catholic moral theology (*bien etonné de se trouver ensemble,* as the French put it). From the point of view of disability studies, one would have to say that questioning the humanity of profoundly disabled people is notoriously suspect in that it violates the most important insight in that field, which is that the phrase "being disabled" does not signify a fact about nature, but rather signifies a fact about social environments. Whenever this insight is ignored, the result is usually some notion of "subhumanity"; indeed, ruling out this mistake has been the very point of disability studies. There needs to be a distinction between the person and the condition, which is why we say "persons with disabilities" rather than "disabled persons." Consider James Charlton's way of making this point:

> People with disabilities are conceived, in the first place, as inferior and as the embodiment of bad luck, misfortune, or religious punishment. The disability itself primarily informs the conception most people have about individuals with disabilities. Their humanity is stripped away and the person is obliterated, only to be left with the condition — disability.[2]

The objection is clear: being a human is one thing; being disabled is another. Raising the issue of Kelly's humanity is a mistake because it fails to see that "disability" is a social construct that prescribes rather than describes. That is, the label of "being disabled" prescribes a set of particular (negative) attitudes and beliefs regarding particular people rather than describing a condition inherent to those people. Questioning their humanity is informed by an obsolete metaphysics according

2. James L. Charlton, *Nothing about Us without Us: Disability, Oppression, and Empowerment* (Berkeley: University of California Press, 1998), p. 54.

to which something called "human nature" is defined by a set of particular characteristics that are true of every human. Scholars in the field of disability studies reject this view as "essentialist." My task in this chapter is answering their objection.

In the next chapter I will investigate Roman Catholic moral theology. The same objection to questioning Kelly's humanity is to be expected from that quarter — but for a different reason. The condition of being profoundly disabled cannot raise doubts about the humanity of those who are affected by it because there is no question about their origin. Being of human parentage, in itself, declares that they are human beings. Our humanity is an endowment, not an achievement.[3] Therefore, the fact that profoundly disabled humans cannot claim achievement because of the absence of purposive agency does not affect their humanity in any way. The humanity of human beings is certain from the moment of conception, or so the official position of the Roman Catholic Church teaches, and thus the questioning of any person's humanity is illegitimate.

Let me immediately stake out the response to this objection in general terms and leave the specifics to the exposition of the argument as it develops. When we question the humanity of people with profound intellectual disabilities, this question can have two different meanings: the first regards identification, the second regards qualification. The first is an instantiation of the ontological question: "Is it an x?" In this case, "Is it a human being?" The second is an instantiation of another ontological question: "What is it to be x?" In this case, "What does it mean to be human?" Asking who counts as a human being is different from asking what it means to be human.

Now, if I take the question of Kelly's humanity in the first sense, the answer is not difficult at all, because we can simply follow Aristotle's rule: "Man is born from man."[4] When we ask whether what is said of all human beings applies to the profoundly disabled, we only need to remind ourselves of this one fact. That is all. Note, however, that if we take the question in this first sense, we take it as a question of origin, or *gene*

---

3. I borrow this way of stating the point from a quotation by Ashley Montague in Germaine G. Grisez, *Abortion: The Myths, the Realities, and the Arguments* (New York: Corpus Books, 1970), p. 277.

4. Aristotle, *Physics*, Bk. II, I, 193b8.

sis. People with profound intellectual disabilities are included in the human species because of the fact that they are of human parentage. But when we raise the second question — the question of what it means to be human — we want to know something different. What is the point of being human? This question's intention is very different because, in raising it, we are inquiring into the purpose or goal of our existence. We are raising a question about *telos,* or the end, the purpose, of being human.

With this distinction in mind, we can map the discussion in these two chapters as follows. When scholars in disability studies object to the line of questioning that I have undertaken in this study, we must examine the presuppositions of that objection. Despite their scorn for the metaphysics of "human nature," I will show that there is clearly a concept of human nature involved in their views, a concept that responds to the emancipatory framework that guides their thinking. When disability scholars resist the identification of people with disability as "being disabled," they do so because they take the identification of people as "being disabled" to undercut the ethical and political importance of self-representation. That is, scholars in the field of disability studies are guided by a concept of human nature that understands human *telos* in terms of freedom of the self. But, as I have indicated before, this concept contributes to the source of the exclusion of people with profound intellectual disabilities in the first place.

Something similar is true of Roman Catholic moral theology, but for a very different reason. Roman Catholicism rules out questioning the humanity of people with disabilities because it wishes to include them on absolute grounds. No human being exists that is not from human descent. At the same time, however, writers in this tradition speak a very different language when they speak of being human in terms of its ultimate end. At that point we discern a moral hierarchy that designates human beings as superior to other beings because of humans' capacities for intellect and will. The conclusion from this observation is that, in terms of origin, people like Kelly are human beings all right, but in terms of their final end they cannot be anything other than "defective." There is nothing in their existence that enables them to actively develop the kind of ability that is considered characteristic of being human.

To spell out a detailed response to the objection, I will extensively discuss both versions of it as I have introduced them here. The social constructionist version objects to the approach I have taken because the project buys into the wrong kind of problem: it focuses on being human instead of social context as the source of exclusion. The Roman Catholic version objects to my approach because there is nothing unclear about Kelly's humanity: like any of us, she is born from human parents, which is all one needs to know. The reason for discussing both versions in the same connection, even though they come from opposite quarters, is that the positions that generate them are united on this one point. They both eliminate the task of rethinking human being in terms of this teleology, which is precisely the task this inquiry suggests we need to undertake.

Throughout this discussion I will be referring to persons with profound intellectual disabilities, human beings more or less like Kelly and Oliver de Vinck. No matter how different their lives may otherwise be, they share this one aspect of their being, which is that they both are non-agents: "acting" is not a term with meaningful application in their case. Some readers may hold it against my approach that I have introduced these people as representing the "main character" of this inquiry. Even among persons with profound intellectual disabilities, the lives of these two are quite atypical, they may say. In placing them on center stage, I have construed a "worst-case scenario" that will unnecessarily confront everyone who does not have someone like Kelly or Oliver de Vinck in mind when thinking about our common humanity. In its apparent rejection of ambiguity, my critics may say, the argument smacks of moralism, because it presses an either/or kind of logic that does not leave much room for marginal cases.

My intuitive response to the critique of moralism is to say that I fail to see the mistake. Making a case for the inclusion of disabled human beings does not mean that we leave out those who fail to answer to our most treasured values, such as the value of self-determination — or does it? Thus, when those opposing my project from either social constructionism or Roman Catholicism agree in principle with the aim of inclusion — as they undoubtedly do — why maintain a hierarchy of (human) being that is premised by the faculties of intellect and will? Why not ask how to conceive of our common humanity regardless of any state or condition, not only with regard to our origin but also with regard to our final end? When we pose our question in these terms, we raise a truly universal question, one that relegates no one to an anthropological subdivision.

Of course, this is not to say that there are no significant differences between human beings. Nor is it to deny the impact of the condition of disability. However, the point is to reflect on our humanity in a way that does not lead to the conclusion of disability as defective humanity. I will show that that conclusion is inevitable, for both the social constructionist and the Roman Catholic view, as soon as the question of *telos* is raised. The basis for making this claim is that their normative accounts presuppose a conception of the human person as a *purposive agent*. I would not know how to picture someone like Kelly in such a way that she fits into either of these accounts. To the extent that scholars from either of these fields share this premise, they seldom have much to say that is useful with regard to human beings with profound intellectual disabilities. To overcome this failure, we really need to rethink what it means to be human in a truly universal sense.

2. Social Constructionism

The first version of the objection against raising the issue of humanity is launched from the field of disability studies; the position from which it is to be expected is the social constructionist approach to disability. Social constructionism is a set of theories about the connections between the conceptual schemes that are reflected by our language, the behavior they inform, and the social conditions within which they function.[5] With regard to disability, this means that how we think about "be-

---

5. There are many different approaches united under the banner of "social constructionism." The term refers to a set of views concerning the social nature of how we know the world. As Kenneth Gergen defines the term, *constructionism* represents a range of discourses centered on the social genesis of knowledge (K. J. Gergen, *Realities and Relationships: Soundings in Social Construction* [Cambridge, MA: Harvard University Press, 1994]). In its critical aspect, social constructionism brackets and suspends any pronouncement of the real, according to Gergen: "Constructionism makes no denial concerning explosions, poverty, death, or 'the world out there' more generally. Neither does it make any affirmation. As I have noted, constructionism is ontologically mute. Whatever is simply is. There is no foundational description to be made about an 'out there' as opposed to an 'in here,' about experience or material. Once we attempt to articulate 'what there is,' however, we enter the world of discourse" (p. 72). I owe this quote to Fiona J. Hibberd, *Unfolding Social Constructionism* (New York: Springer, 2005), p. 45. With regard to disability, I will mainly follow Deborah Marks, *Disability: Controversial*

ing disabled" is a reflection of the attitudes and beliefs prevailing in our social world. As it was grounded in this principle, the social constructionist approach to disability resulted in the "social model of disability," which was intended to replace the medical model that had located disability in the individual body as a "defect" and in doing so had created a defective citizenship for people with disabilities due to "natural" limitations, leaving them no recourse to political action.

> The social model challenges the idea of defective citizenship by situating disability in the environment, not in the body. In a society of wheelchair users, stairs would not exist, and the fact that they are everywhere in our society reveals only that most of our architects are nondisabled people who care little about the problem of access. Disability seen from this point of view requires not individual medical treatment but changes in society.[6]

To counteract the notion of natural defects, social constructionists insist that "being disabled" is not a description of a fact about the world; they say that this view is guilty of "essentialism,"[7] which is a philosophical position that reifies social and cultural phenomena by inscribing them into the nature of things as their essential properties.[8] With regard to disability, this means that essentialism construes its meaning

---

Debates and Psychological Perspectives (London: Routledge, 1999). She describes and discusses the social model of disability as developed in the field of disability studies in the United Kingdom. Like most authors in the field, Marks also claims that "the starting point of any critical understanding (i.e., of disability) must be the notion of civil rights and disabled people's resistance to oppression" (p. 2). This means that all "descriptions" of disability function within a discourse of emancipation.

6. Tobin Siebers, "Disability Studies and the Future of Identity Politics," in *Identity Politics Reconsidered,* ed. Linda Martin Alcoff, Michael Hames-Garcia, Saty P. Mohanty, and Paula M. L. Moya (New York: Palgrave Macmillan, 2006), p. 12.

7. Marks, *Disability: Controversial Debates,* p. ix. See also Hibberd, *Unfolding Social Constructionism,* which describes Gergen's view of social constructionism as antagonistic to essentialism because of its commitment to the notion that entities in the world have essential features (p. 17).

8. "Essential" properties here are distinct from "accidental" properties. Whereas the latter can be variable without changing the nature of an entity, the former cannot. The condition of a disability as an essential property (e.g., Down syndrome) determines the being of a person with that condition in the sense that without that condition she would be of a different nature.

as being *intrinsic* to the nature of the person. This is why those committed to the constructionist approach are not interested in asking questions about the natural conditions of individual people. Behind "nature" there is always a social convention.

Furthermore, the constructionist critique of essentialism exposes the latter's tendency to look at unequal opportunities between people as originating from natural conditions. Whenever disabled people's limitations are regarded as the effect of "nature," it appears to be merely *natural* that people with disabilities should have lesser opportunities. This also explains why these people are seen as being necessarily dependent on having their special needs fulfilled by others. Social constructionists expose this strategy of blaming "nature" for social inequality and injustice.

To explain the epistemological claim of the constructionist approach to disability, we may well start with a fundamental question: What is a disability? Of course, there is a popular "commonsense" view: when your body or your mind does not work as it should, you have a disability.[9] Does this mean that having a disability affects you as a human being? The commonsense view has an answer to this question as well: since there is a way of "normal" functioning for human minds and bodies, it follows that, when your body or mind — or both — are functioning "abnormally," then you *are* disabled. Thus, according to the commonsense view, there is nothing wrong with talking about "disabled people" and using the modifier "disabled" to determine the being that they are. When a person's legs do not enable her to walk, or a person's brain does not enable him to speak, then that is what the person *is:* a disabled human being.

Social constructionism contests this "commonsense" view. "Disability is not an entity that a clinical examination can correlate with the numbers on a schedule of impairments," says American historian Paul Longmore.[10] Instead, it is constituted by a complex set of factors, including stigmatized impairments, physical environments, social arrangements, and cultural values. Moreover, Longmore observes, the ex-

---

9. Marks, *Disability: Controversial Debates,* p. ix.

10. Paul K. Longmore, "Why I Burned My Book," in *Why I Burned My Book and Other Essays on Disability,* ed. Paul K. Longmore (Philadelphia: Temple University Press, 2003), p. 238.

perience that comes with the label "being disabled" changes over time; in short, "disability is not a fixed thing."[11] The most important argument for such claims by social constructionists is an epistemological one. It resides in the notion of knowledge as discourse. We do not know things as they are, because we only know things as they are perceived and spoken of. Knowledge reflects the world of the mind, as it is expressed in language; it does not reflect the world as it is.[12] As Kenneth Gergen puts it, there is no fixed relationship between words and the world "because 'whatever is' makes no necessary demands on our language (descriptions, explanations)."[13] What follows is that claims about the nature of disability are not to be taken as referring to the properties of external reality. Instead, the demands of language are to be understood as grounded in particular social practices and institutions. "Disability discourse" is controlled by those practices and institutions that have a stake in defining it. In actual fact, the reality of disability that matters is not "nature" but the practice of labeling people in a way that results in enforcing their marginalization.[14]

Accordingly, as those committed to the social constructionist approach are apt to say, the presence of "disabled people" is inadvertently regarded as inconvenient, annoying, or even threatening.[15] By portraying disabled human beings as "freaks" or "retards," people express anxiety and fear, and at the same time they draw the boundaries around "the others," whom they wish to avoid and exclude.[16] While such boundaries suggest a common feature among people with disabilities, there is no such thing, the social constructionists would say, except for the fact of their marginalized social existence. It is impossible to define

11. Longmore, "Why I Burned My Book," p. 239.

12. See Hibberd, *Unfolding Social Constructionism,* for the link between social constructivism and Kantian philosophy (pp. 169-72).

13. Gergen, *Realities and Relationships,* p. 45; Hibberd, *Unfolding Social Constructionism,* pp. 7-8.

14. Sheila Riddell, "Theorising Special Education Needs in a Changing Political Climate," in *Disability and Society: Emerging Issues and Insights,* ed. Len Barton (London and New York: Longman, 1996), pp. 83-106.

15. T. Shakespeare, "Cultural Representations of Disabled People: Dustbins of Disavowal," *Disability and Society* 3 (1994): 283-301. See also Marks's chapter on cultural images of disability (*Disability: Controversial Debates,* pp. 153-75).

16. M. Oliver, "Social Policy and Disability: Some Theoretical Issues," *Disability, Handicap & Society* 1, no. 2 (1986): 5-18.

"disability" in any coherent way as a universal property, or set of properties, that is *intrinsic to* particular human minds, or bodies, or both. Once we realize the sheer variety among human beings with respect to shape, size, color, or ability, it will be clear that any set of characteristics picked to define "disability" is as valid as any other set. Accounts of disability do not describe an entity — "a disabled human being" — observable from an impartial point of view that is epistemologically secure. Drawing lines and creating boundaries between the "normal" and the "abnormal" must remain arbitrary.

In summary, the constructionist critique of essentialism is grounded in the notion that the social world is not an "object" we can know from an external point of view, because everything we say about it is part of that world, and in some sense changes it. A scientific discourse in sociology is itself part of the social world that it seeks to explain. Social scientific discourse is reflective, we say.[17] The discourse itself is inevitably a part of what it seeks to understand. Therefore, what social scientists say about the social world is necessarily informed by their particular "location" within it: that is, there are no contributions to social scientific discourse other than from "within." These considerations indicate why the constructionist approach to disability rejects the notion that the language of disability refers to particular bodies and minds that can be objectively identified. Disabilities are "made" rather than "found," so to speak.

Given the philosophical claims of social constructionism, this thesis does not hold merely for the nature of disability. If its claims are true, it must hold for everything that we say about ourselves as human beings, including what we say about human nature. There is no objective reality called human nature "out there" that is independent of how we construe its meaning. We have no access to the knowledge of human nature as an objective reality other than through the socially constructed meanings we bring to the attempt to define what that nature is.

17. William Outhwaite, "Naturalisms and Anti-naturalisms," in *Knowing the Social World,* ed. Tim May and Malcolm Williams (Buckingham: Open University Press, 1998), pp. 22-36; see, in the same volume, Tim May, "Reflections and Reflexivity," pp. 157-77; see also U. Beck, A. Giddens, and S. Lash, eds., *Reflexive Modernization* (Cambridge, MA: Polity Press, 1991).

3. The Social Model of Disability

The social constructionist approach to disability became influential in the early 1990s as "the social model of disability."[18] It is not difficult to see why proponents of the social model should oppose the agenda of my inquiry. In questioning the humanity of profoundly disabled human beings, one assumes that the disabling condition affects their being human. This line of questioning is anathema in the field of disability studies as well as in the disability-rights movement. The social model directs our attention to the particularities of society rather than to the particularities of being human. While I am in agreement with the social constructionist approach to the oppression and marginalization that is inherent in social practices and institutions in our society, I nonetheless insist that the question of being human must be addressed rather than dismissed, because social constructionism itself presupposes a particular answer to this question — an answer, moreover, that is in my view part of the problem it seeks to dispel. That is, the constructionist approach reinforces the hierarchy of disability in that it subscribes to an anthropology of political citizenship that excludes intellectually disabled human beings.

Before considering further theoretical developments regarding the social model, let me first point to a practical implication. This is the fact that the logic of this model makes it possible to argue that all human beings are in some sense "disabled." Since most of us have limited opportunities due to social characteristics in some sense, there seems to be no compelling reason to restrict the use of the term "disability" to one limitation rather than another. Obviously, however, people with disabilities themselves may be quite uncomfortable with the notion that all human beings are in some sense "disabled." Consider the following statement by Andrew Solomon, representing the deaf community in the United States:

> It is tempting, in the end, to say that there is no such thing as a disability. Equally, one might admit that almost everything is a disability. There are as many arguments for correcting everything as there are for correcting nothing. Perhaps it would be most accurate to say

18. The publication most commonly referred to in this connection is Mike Oliver, *The Politics of Disablement* (London: Macmillan, 1990).

that "disability" and "culture" are really a matter of degree. Being deaf is a disability and a culture in modern America; so is being gay; so is being female; so even increasingly is being a straight white male. So is being a paraplegic, or having Down syndrome.[19]

While it is obvious that many lives face limitations created by the social world, the implication of this truism cannot be to deny or mitigate the fact that people with disabilities face serious problems that other people do not have to face, limited as they may be in one way or another.[20] This observation suggests that "seriousness" is somehow related to a specific condition, which is a claim the social model of disability would not allow. Take one of Solomon's examples: we may argue, along with him, that being gay in America is a disability, given the social stigma attached to this "condition"; but it is certainly quite different from a condition that does not even allow you to find out whether or not you are gay. Many people with profound disabilities are in this situation — not because they have no sexuality, but because there can be no partner involved in their sexual life.

Obviously, this is only one of many possible examples. It indicates that even if "disability" is socially constructed, it does not follow that the construct does not involve reference to particular natural characteristics — as distinct from social characteristics — of bodily functioning, including both physical and mental aspects. Nor does it follow that some of these aspects do not pose limitations to bodily functioning that are more serious than others. For example, in identifying a person as having a moderate learning disability, we will single out some aspects of her cognitive functioning. Let's say that she is incapable of grasping abstract concepts, such as numbers, and thus is unable to count. Identification in this case presupposes a given set of behavioral characteristics that constitute this person's disability. This set of characteristics will be quite different from the characteristics that identify a person with a profound intellectual disability who is incapable of understanding fundamental deictic words such as "here" and "there," "you" and "me," or "now" and "then." Especially when we look at both persons

19. Andrew Solomon, "Deaf is Beautiful," *New York Times Magazine,* 28 Aug. 1994, 67. I owe this quote to Jennie Weiss Block, *Copious Hosting: A Theology of Access for People with Disability* (New York: Continuum, 2002), p. 35.

20. See Weiss Block, *Copious Hosting,* pp. 34-36.

from the perspective of what they *can* do, we will find huge differences between them that warrant judgments about the seriousness of conditions referred to as "moderate" and "profound."

With regard to both examples, however, it is acceptable that the judgments we make depend on references to certain physical and mental characteristics of the persons involved, without denying that the set of characteristics deemed to be relevant will be "socially constructed." Nor is there a need to deny that how this set is determined will be negotiated between various social, political, and economic interests. Even so, it is clear that such negotiations are about the question of which physical or mental aspects of a person's being will be voted "in" and which will be voted "out." No doubt the mechanisms playing into these negotiations are themselves in turn *also* socially constructed, for example, by means of legal definitions, institutionalized professions, classification manuals, and so on. But none of this changes the fact that their subject matter implies reference to certain physical and mental aspects of being human. To return to the two people I brought up in the introduction, one aspect of the physical and mental being of people like Kelly and Oliver de Vinck that would be referred to in identifying them as "profoundly disabled" is the fact that they don't speak.

In view of these considerations, I am inclined to argue that the theoretical need for a logical gap between "reality" and "perception" is itself a candidate for being explained in social constructionist terms. The social model has proved to be a very effective tool for unmasking the commonsense view of disability as a "natural" condition for which nobody is to be blamed. Apart from locating the blame for the marginalizing of people with disabilities in particular social conditions, however, the social model also prescribes how to overcome these conditions. Tom Shakespeare has said the following:

> In general, it seems that biological determinism has been used to justify social inequality on the basis of natural difference. Social constructionism, in opening up the sphere of free will, choice and the potential for progressive social change, has been associated with positive political developments and liberation strategies. Rhetorically, social constructionism is a very powerful correlative to reactionary arguments. Demonstrate that some experience varies be-

tween cultures, and it becomes very difficult to justify the perpetuation of negative treatment on the basis of nature.[21]

This statement suggests — correctly, I would say — that, as a "correlative" strategy, the social model may have become a mirror image of biological determinism. With regard to this model, I want to consider three subsequent theoretical developments. The first has the notion of "identity" as its key: it argues that the social model of disability is reductionist in its view that disability is nothing but a label to legitimize the marginalizing of a particular group of people in society. In contrast, proponents of "identity politics" argue that disability may be a source of positive identification as well. The second development regards what has been called a "realist version" of the social constructionist approach: it proposes a distinction between "disability" and "impairment" as separating two different kinds of logic in order to be able to acknowledge that disability is also an experience of the body and not merely of social conditions. Finally, there is a poststructuralist account, inspired by Foucault, which rejects "identity politics" as a viable option and eliminates the validity of the distinction between "impairment" and "disability" by arguing that both are socially constructed.

4. "Disability Identity"

Proponents of so-called identity politics, particularly in the American literature, signal the possibility for people with disabilities to have positive identification and engagement based on their own physical or mental characteristics. Obviously, the task of responding to the lived experience of persons with disabilities necessarily includes responding to the experience of their impaired bodies. Shakespeare affirms the same:

> The problem with the strong constructionist account of disability was that it failed adequately to deal with lived experience. Rhetorically, it is a very potent argument for social change: if society creates

21. Shakespeare, "Social Constructionism as a Political Strategy," p. 176.

disability, society can rectify disability. But where people identify on the basis of impairment, then an account of disability which almost totally ignores impairment ultimately fails to reflect personal experience.[22]

Of course, the logic of the social model excludes considering the relevance of physical conditions of impairment. To take them into account as relatively "independent" factors may imply acknowledging the fact that some people may indeed have "special needs" because of their physical condition; it may also imply that some aspects of disability are attributable to natural rather than social conditions. As the feminist philosopher Susan Wendell has argued, "We need to acknowledge that social justice and cultural change can eliminate a great deal of disability while recognizing that there may be much suffering and limitation that they cannot fix."[23] This, in turn, implies that not only social conditions but also physical conditions may be responsible for the fact that people suffer from their disability, none of which the social model of disability has any interest in pursuing, for obvious reasons: to accept this kind of language would be to return to a language that betokens dependency and the lack of control, which for the proponents of the social model has been the main reason to reject it in the first place.

These implications notwithstanding, however, there has been a development in the literature that focuses on "disability" as a source of personal identity. Apparently, this focus has come to differentiate disability studies in Britain from those in the United States: whereas the social and economic dimensions of disability have shaped the object of sociological analysis particularly in Britain, the cultural dimension has been studied more intensely in America in the humanities, particularly in literary studies.[24] Partly in response to the social model, the literary-studies approach to "disability identity" adopts a different strategy. While the constructionist critique rejects the language of "being disabled" for its essentialist implications, we now find people who claim

22. Shakespeare, "Social Constructionism as a Political Strategy," p. 177.

23. Susan Wendell, *The Rejected Body: Feminist Philosophical Reflections on Disability* (London: Routledge, 1996), p. 45.

24. Marks, *Disability: Controversial Debates,* pp. 118-26. See Tom Shakespeare, "Introduction," in *The Disability Reader: Social Science Perspectives,* ed. Tom Shakespeare (London: Cassell, 1998), p. 2, and the literature mentioned there.

that their disability defines, at least in part, who they *are*. For example, Deborah Creamer, an American theologian with a disability, makes that claim in a critique of the question of healing, a particularly sensitive issue for many disabled people who come from religious communities. Most religious traditions, when they speak of disability and disease, have identified "healing" with "cure." Many writers with disabilities reject this notion of healing as cure. Creamer, for example, underscores her rejection of it with the claim that her disability is "an essential part of who I am."[25]

Cyndi Jones, editor of the disability magazine *Mainstream,* and a person who suffered from polio as a child, makes a similar point. She says that, if there were a cure for her disabling condition, she would not take it. Asking her whether she wants to get rid of her disability is like "asking a black person would he change the color of his skin."[26] Jones continues:

> The main thing disabled people need to do is claim their disability, to feel okay about it. Even if you don't like the way society treats you as a disabled person, it's part of your experience, it's part of how you become to be who you are.[27]

We need to sort out several aspects of "being disabled" if we want to understand how these claims to a disability identity relate to the social constructionist position.

One of these aspects is the issue of "ownership" that I referred to in the previous chapter. One could say, for example, that it is perfectly all right for a person with a disability to claim her disability as part of herself without making it all right for me to do so. The American essayist Nancy Meyers, who has multiple sclerosis, refers to her self as a "cripple"; she *is* a cripple, but she adds that she "would never refer to another person as a cripple. It is the word I use to name only myself."[28] Naming oneself "disabled" as part of what one is may be an act

---

25. Deborah Creamer, "Finding God in Our Bodies: Theology from the Perspective of People with Disabilities," *Journal of Religion in Disability & Rehabilitation* 2 (1995): 80.

26. Quoted in Joseph P. Shapiro, *No Pity: People with Disabilities Forging a New Civil Rights Movement* (New York: Times Books, 1993), p. 14.

27. Shapiro, *No Pity,* p. 14.

28. Nancy Mairs, *Plaintext* (Tucson: University of Arizona Press, 1986), p. 11. Marks

of naming that empowers a person. As an act of self-affirmation, it defies the symbolic meaning of one's disability as what should not be. There are many historical examples of this kind of switch, in which a name that is used to defame is turned into a source of self-respect. Whereas the word "disabled" was previously a term others would use to demean people (as were the words "cripple," "moron," "idiot," and so forth), they now have taken ownership of this term to identify themselves positively. In this sense, identifying "being disabled" with "being who I am" clearly does not have the connotation that something is wrong. On the contrary, it can be argued that in this very act one is vindicated as a human being in the full sense of the word.

Furthermore, as Jones's analogy between "being black" and "being disabled" suggests, a distinction is needed between semantics and subjective meaning. Identifying a person as "black" is making a statement that names the color of his skin, and a whole range of negative images may be attached to that meaning, which explains why black people in the United States prefer to refer to themselves as "African-American." But this meaning of "being black" is not necessarily similar at all to what being black means *for that person.* That question is not about semantics but about self-identification. This is why the black consciousness movement in the 1970s came up with the phrase "black is beautiful." Analogously, when Jones asks whether she would want to be cured from her disability, she rejects the idea by claiming that she *is* a disabled person in the sense that "being disabled" is part of what her life means to her. Therefore, what this shift of subjective meaning indicates is that the language of disability identity — "this is who I *am*" — in no way implies a return to essentialism. In affirming that she is disabled, Jones is not making an ontological claim; instead, she identifies herself subjectively as a person with a disability. The language of "disability identity" thus reintroduces "being" into the discussion, but as an act of self-identification it does not necessarily carry ontological content.[29]

---

refers to Mairs's example as a case of "defiant self-naming" (Marks, *Disability: Controversial Debates,* p. 145).

29. If correctly interpreted, statements like the ones we have just seen are misconstrued if they are taken as a return of essentialism. They are an expression of how the person regards his or her own existence. However, note that this cannot be true for people with a profound intellectual disability, who cannot claim their disability as part of who

Considerations such as these have inspired disability scholars in the field of literary studies in their critique of the social model. Because of its tendency to deny or ignore the physical realities that people with disabilities face in their daily lives, these scholars have argued, it leaves conventional representations of human bodies and minds intact. For example, Tobin Siebers has pointed out that the social model implies a successful mastering of one's disability only in terms of being engaged in political activity, which for people whose lack of physical energy does not allow them that kind of activity means a reinforcement of their defectiveness.[30] The principle that "disability" is located in the social order rather than in the body has thus exposed physical difference as an "ideological phantasm," with the result that the disabled bodies as experienced reality have disappeared from view.[31] What people with disabilities are left with is the suggestion that to be free from social marginalization and oppression is a matter of sufficient will power to get involved and get organized. In a sense, one could argue that, following the social model, the emancipation of disabled bodies was effected at least in part by the emancipation from their own bodies. This implies, among other things, that the experience of distress, or pain, is necessarily taken as a *psychic* experience caused by social environments, but never as a *physical* experience of the disabled body itself. Therefore, it appears that the body that occupies the default position in the social model is in fact a body that can rely on its psychological powers because it is not distracted by pain, distress, fatigue; indeed, in this respect it reflects the conventional conception of the able body.

The able or healthy body is, first, a body that the subject cannot feel. The healthy subject is either disinterested in its body or in control of

---

they are. The question then arises whether the legitimacy of talk about "disability identity" is necessarily dependent on self-identification. If being profoundly disabled names what they are, why should the legitimacy of making such a claim be dependent on whether or not they make it themselves? Precisely because they are incapable of acts of self-identification, "being" in their case seems inevitable to carry ontological content.

30. Siebers, "Disability Studies and the Future of Identity Politics," p. 13.

31. David T. Mitchell and Sharon L. Snyder, "Disability Studies and the Double Bind of Representation," in *The Body and Physical Difference: Discourses of Disability,* ed. David T. Mitchell and Sharon L. Snyder (Ann Arbor: The University of Michigan Press, 1997), p. 5.

its feelings and sensations. Second, the health of a body is judged by the ability not only to surmount pain, illness, and disability but also to translate by force of will effects into benefits.[32]

These considerations help us see why "disability identity" could rise as a concern after the influence of the social model of disability had converted many disability scholars to its principles. People may experience their disabilities just as part of who they are and not just a social condition to reject.

One further implication that Siebers spells out is that the social model of disability espouses an ethics of political activism. Following the social model, we are led to assume that people who refer their physical limitations — fatigue and lack of energy, say — to their bodily impairment do not really understand what is happening to them. They seem to be blaming themselves instead of their social conditions, which is to say that they are lacking in political awareness and will power. But, as Siebers points out, this tendency to refer physical states to mental ones is hardly a neutral one. Apart from sending a message of a weakness of will, it also denies the representation of *all* people with disabilities. Consequently, the suggestion that acts of will are essential in overcoming "disability" is indebted to a model of political rationality that presupposes a liberal notion of autonomy, as Siebers explains. It suggests that "emancipation from repression relies on the intellectual and emotional resources of the individual."[33] In this respect, it clearly does not represent people with intellectual disabilities, let alone people with profound intellectual disabilities.

> That one fails to throw off one's physical disability because of mental defect implies a caste system that ranks people with physical disabilities as superior to those with mental ones. The caste system, of course, encourages the vicious treatment of people with mental disabilities in most societies. Its influence is fully apparent in models of political citizenship, the history of civil and human rights, structures of legal practice, the politics of institutionalization, employment history, and the organization of the disability community itself.[34]

32. Siebers, "Disability Studies and the Future of Identity Politics," p. 15.
33. Siebers, "Disability Studies and the Future of Identity Politics," p. 15.
34. Siebers, "Disability Studies and the Future of Identity Politics," p. 16. Although

Apart from the tendency to deny or ignore the physical reality of disability as a lived experience, then, there is in the social model also a tendency, in both theory and practice, to reproduce the hierarchy of disability as explained in the previous chapter. The portrait of the individual embodying its views is that of a self-conscious person who comes together with other like-minded people, equipped with political imagination and the will to bring about social change.

5. The Realist Version of Social Constructionism

Scholars in defense of the social model of disability have taken up criticisms of this nature by responding that they have no problem with the claim that there are physical conditions involved in what our society names as "disability." They only insist that a whole range of normative connotations are attached to this term, which shows that "disability" is not a descriptive term. To clarify this response, they have accepted the distinction between *impairments* and *disabilities* to show how the natural aspect of being impaired is separate from the social meanings ascribed to that condition.

For example, Paul Abberley has rejected what he calls the "bifurcation of impairment as 'personal tragedy' and 'disability' as social response." Abberley is in favor of a view "that does not deny the significance of germs, genes, and trauma, but rather points out that their effects are only ever apparent in a real social and historical context, whose nature is determined by a complex interaction of material and non-material forces."[35] In a more recent article, Abberley pursues this line of thinking by insisting that a theory of disability as oppression must involve a discussion of "the ontological status of impairment," because such a theory must be clear about which aspects of the existing social world it rejects and "delineate the consequences of their posited eradication."[36] While

---

Siebers does not specify the conditions to which the term "mental disabilities" is referring in his usage, what he has to say would apply equally to people with (chronic) mental illness as to people with intellectual disabilities in my terminology.

35. P. Abberley, "The Concept of Oppression and the Development of a Social Theory of Disability," *Disability, Handicap and Society* 2, no. 1 (1987): 12.

36. P. Abberley, "Work, Utopia, and Impairment," in *Disability and Society,* ed. Barton, p. 67.

all scholars remain committed to the focus on "disability" as a social construct, some of them would support consideration of the particular consequences of natural conditions of impairment.[37] However, this does not mean that these authors change their normative position. Deborah Marks writes, for example:

> As such, we need to focus not on disabled people in the abstract, but rather on the way in which labels are produced and reproduced in social interactions within institutional and cultural contexts. Rather than seeing disability as a consequence of natural differences between individual bodies and minds, it can be understood as a result of perceptions rooted in social practices, which mark some differences as being abnormal and pathological.[38]

Statements such as those by Abberley and Marks continue to suggest the separation between two kinds of logic. While the distinction between "impairment" and "disability" allows for the recognition of independent natural conditions, it does not necessarily alter the basic claim of the social model, which is that "disability" names the marginalization and oppression of people stemming from perceptions rooted in social practices, as Marks has it. Nonetheless, there is a strong argument in support of a logical connection between "disability" and "impairment" within the social model itself.[39] When one reads the proponents of the model, impairment is at least tacitly presupposed as a necessary condition of disability. For example, no one argues that people who are discriminated against and excluded because of their skin color are disabled. On the contrary, in the terms of the social model,

37. See also Tom Shakespeare, "Social Constructionism as a Political Strategy," in *The Politics of Constructionism,* ed. Irving Velody and Robin Williams (London: Sage, 1998), pp. 168-81; see also Marks, *Disability: Controversial Debates,* pp. 114-15.

38. Marks, *Disability: Controversial Debates,* p. 79. Marks rejects this view as "dualistic" (p. 119). She criticizes the sociological theory of disability because it fails to see that experiences of impairments are highly variable between individuals and therefore misconstrued with regard to their individual identity when only social responses of exclusion and oppression are studied (pp. 93-94, 124-28).

39. Shelley Tremain, "Foucault, Governmentality, and Critical Disability Theory," in *Foucault and the Government of Disability,* ed. Shelley Tremain (Ann Arbor: The University of Michigan Press, 2005), pp. 9-10. As we shall see, Tremain develops this argument in defense of a Foucauldian approach to disability.

only people who are presumed to *have* an impairment get to count as such.

The distinction between impairments and disabilities is important in that it allows one to acknowledge that being born, for example, with a physical disability is a condition of the impaired body. At the same time, it allows one to say that the marginalization and oppression experienced by people with such bodies does not reflect their bodies per se, but rather the socially constructed meanings attached to it. Thus it appears that both the logical distinction and the logical connection between "impairment" and "disability" allow that the reality of the body informs both our conceptualization of disability and our theorizing about it without being determinative of either.[40] The same view has been expressed by Sharon Snyder and David Mitchell: "The definition of disability must incorporate both the outer and inner reaches of culture and experience as a combination of profoundly social and biological forces."[41] These comments introduce the second theoretical development in the wake of the social model that I will discuss as the "realist" version of the social constructionist approach to disability.[42]

In order for us to understand what the realist position entails, I wish to consider a comment by the Australian philosopher Fiona Hibberd that goes to the heart of the matter. She argues that, contrary to what many social constructionists believe, philosophical realism does not necessarily entail essentialism. Essentialism is the doctrine that an entity has properties, some of which are essential to the kind of thing it is, so that it cannot lose these properties without becoming a different thing. Realism, in Hibberd's view, is the doctrine that entities consist of

40. Paula Moya, *Learning from Experience: Minority Identities, Multicultural Struggles* (Berkeley: University of California Press, 2002), p. 37. I owe this reference to Siebers, "Disability Studies and the Future of Identity Politics," p. 18.

41. Sharon L. Snyder and David T. Mitchell, *Cultural Locations of Disability* (Chicago: The University of Chicago Press, 2006), p. 7.

42. Siebers, "Disability Studies and the Future of Identity Politics," pp. 18-19; see also Marks, *Disability: Controversial Debates,* pp. 17-18. Marks claims that the social model of disability draws on a philosophical realism that says, "some things (such as impairments) exist independently of the way in which they are socially constructed." By contrast, "post-structuralist theory argues that we can only ever grasp 'versions' of the world." Post-structuralist logic entails "that not only disability but also impairment is socially constructed" (p. 17). See footnote 43 below.

properties, but none of these properties are to be taken as essences. In other words, realism does not hold onto the distinction between essential and accidental properties. What the defining properties of an entity are is a factual matter: "It is not a matter of necessity, because to define something in terms of certain properties entails a number of proposals, each of which is open to investigation."[43]

The implication of this is that, while social constructionism is incompatible with essentialism, it need not be incompatible with realism as Hibberd defines it. Evidently, disputes over any proposal for conceptualizing and defining disability will be informed by social contexts and interests; but this does not rule out that they are proposals for how to map a particular phenomenon of the natural world. Such realist proposals indicate that the supposed logical gap between "external reality" and social perception that is sacrosanct in social constructionism is unnecessary to avoid essentialism.[44] As we have already seen, the supposition of this gap is undermined by the fact that the social perceptions of the disability in question are in fact perceptions of physical or mental properties that supposedly don't matter. There is, at this point, always the inevitable question, "the social construction of what?"[45] This is not to deny that our ways of evaluating disability are grounded in social and cultural histories and traditions. Nor can there be any doubt that our understanding of disability is rooted in social practices that as such can be more or less exclusionary and oppressive. But to affirm these claims is not at all to imply that there are no physical or mental realities that are disabling *as such*. It only follows

43. Hibberd, *Unfolding Social Constructionism*, p. 159.

44. Snyder and Mitchell propose a "cultural model of disability" precisely because they think the supposition of this gap leaves important theoretical understandings unexplored. "Some of the key theorists in disability studies have overlooked opportunities to theorize this interactional space between embodiment and social ideology. Strict social model adherents often refer to the biological and cognitive manifestations of difference as 'impairment' in order to situate the phenomenon outside of the concerns of disability studies" (Snyder and Mitchell, *Cultural Locations of Disability*, p. 7). "Rather than lacking a term exclusively referring to 'social disadvantage,' the cultural model has an understanding that impairment is both human variation encountering environmental obstacles and socially mediated difference that lends group identity and phenomenological perspective" (p. 10).

45. Ian Hacking, *The Social Construction of What?* (Cambridge, MA: Harvard University Press, 1999).

that the question about what the realities that define the category are, and why, is a matter of dispute.

Despite the corrections of the realist version on the social model of disability, however, it is put to use within the same practical strategy when it is asked how the realist version enables us to envision social change with regard to the marginalization and oppression of disabled people, we are once again referred to the notion of rational agency as a universal characteristic of being human. The emphasis on disability as a lived experienced of physical reality is justified by the intention to empower people by enabling them to use subjective meaning as a source of positive identity. More generally, the realist version of social constructionism wants to go beyond the binary opposition between a culture's ideology as a closed system and its excluded "others." It is inspired by a vision of moral universalism that is capable of including all human beings. Thus the following view:

> No matter how different cultural Others are, they are never so different that they are — as typical members of their culture — incapable of acting purposefully, of evaluating their actions in light of their ideas and previous experiences, and of being "rational" in a minimal way.[46]

While acknowledging that the realist position is more open than is the social model to differences in how disability can be experienced and how it may inspire political action, we should not overlook the similarities in their basic ethical thrust. The same is true for the view that seeks to target the marginalizing and oppression of disabled people by means of identity politics. For in each case the concept of being human that is ultimately behind the normative claims is inevitably tied to emancipatory ideals of the politics of disengagement that define the modern age. Even as moderate a constructionist view as that proposed by Susan Wendell does not seem to leave them behind. Though she argues that the overly positive celebration of the body in the feminist literature makes living in frail and suffering bodies appear embarrassing, the recognition of the lived experience of these bodies must also

---

46. Satya P. Mohanty, *Literary Theory and the Claims of History: Postmodernism, Objectivity, Multicultural Politics* (Ithaca, NY: Cornell University Press, 1988), p. 198. I owe this quote to Siebers, "Disability Studies and the Future of Identity Politics," p. 19.

be "transcended." Paying too much attention to these aspects of the body will be debilitating, and thus we must learn to free ourselves from these experiences by strategies of "disengagement." Living with a disabled body requires resistance as one cultivates a different sense of one's identity. Hence strategies are needed, according to Wendell, that enable me "to identify myself less with what is occurring in my body."[47]

6. Invention and Discovery

There is a third development in the theoretical reflections following on the rising influence of the social model of disability to be considered. To introduce it, let me draw the reader's attention to an observation from a domain quite different from what we have discussed so far: the widely known response of young parents who face the professional judgment that something is wrong with their newborn baby. Frequently their response is one of denial, at least in the beginning, and they are quite often defiant toward professional judgments per se. For example, they may say that professionals are too preoccupied with their discipline and thus are apt to always find something that is not as it should be. When these parents are informed about a disabling condition in their child, they will often tend to fight this judgment because they believe that the professionals are making it up.

But their resistance usually breaks down when they themselves can no longer ignore what the professionals have discovered in their child. It turns out to be more than just a professional invention. With regard to the social constructionist analysis, we may add that professionals may of course be misguided in their judgment; we may also add that there are obviously cultural particulars entering into the explanation of why and how the facts of the case are recognized, that their professional judgment is shaped by the tradition of their profession and its institutions, and so on. But as I have argued before, none of this does anything to deny that part of what it is to recognize a disability is to know particular facts of physical or mental conditions, including facts about the seriousness of the limitations they impose.

47. Wendell, *The Rejected Body*, p. 175.

This observation allows me to introduce another way of discussing the relationship between social and natural conditions. The key notions are *invention* and *discovery*. The question is whether a particular disability can be discovered independently from particular practical interests rooted in particular social conditions.[48] There are well-known examples of this kind where given conditions are disputed precisely in terms of whether they are inventions inspired by particular social interests or genuinely discovered natural conditions. An example from the mental health field is the dispute about whether schizophrenia is in fact "out there" or whether it is a culturally conditioned model to make sense of otherwise incomprehensible behavior.[49] An example from the field of learning disabilities would be the debate on the ADHD syndrome: that debate is fueled by a suspicion about the interests of drug companies in seeing more diagnoses of children who, according to its critics, are at worst difficult to handle.[50] As we have seen, the realist version of the social model would insist that this dispute is susceptible to rational argument, because whatever the merits of the case on either side of the debate, both positions are defended in terms of the relevant facts as they are identified on either side.[51]

However, the realist view is rejected by the poststructuralist followers of Michel Foucault. Regarding the distinction between invention and discovery, Foucauldians will reject it as utterly misguided. In the domain of truth, according to Foucault, we consider the rules that determine the place of objects within a particular system of knowledge. These objects are not waiting for their discovery by the discipline that is

48. Marks, *Disability: Controversial Debates,* p. 143.

49. See M. Boyle, *Schizophrenia: A Scientific Delusion* (London: Routledge, 1993); see also a discussion on this subject in the *British Medical Journal* 320 (2000): 800 (can be downloaded from http://bmj.bmjjournals.com/cgi/content/full/320/7237/800).

50. See Adam Rafalovich, *Framing ADHD Children: A Critical Examination of the History, Discourse, and Everyday Experience of Attention Deficit/Hyperactivity Disorder* (Lanham, MD: Lexington Books, 2004); see also the *British Medical Journal* (http://bmj.bmjjournals.com/cgi/eletters/-329/7471/907).

51. For a further example, and a very illuminating one in terms of the Foucauldian analysis following below, see Nirmala Erevelles, "Signs of Reason," in *Foucault and the Government of Disability,* ed. Tremain, pp. 51-58. The author interprets the debate on "facilitated communication," a technique enabling people with autism to express their thoughts and experiences in writing, something that experts on the subject deemed impossible.

designed to understand them, as if they were exterior to its discourse and fully formed, only to be correctly described and classified by it. Rather, the reverse is true: discourses form the objects of which they speak.[52] Following Foucault, one would have to declare that disability is an invention created by "policing" institutions and organizations such as professional bodies and the nation state. In Foucault's view, there is only "invention" and no "discovery" at all. Accordingly, we find Shelley Tremain criticizing the social model of disability because of its claim that impairment and disability are conceptually distinct categories between which there is no causal relationship.[53] This claim, Tremain says, mistakenly suggests that the restrictive nature of disability as a social construct is in no way connected to impairment. By contrast, a Foucauldian analysis would show, according to Tremain, how "subjects are produced who 'have' impairments because this identity meets certain requirements of contemporary social and political arrangements."[54] "Impairment" is the invention of a "governmentality," which, according to Foucault's analysis, was created in the eighteenth century in the interest of public hygiene.

The crucial difference that separates a Foulcauldian approach to disability from the social model and its realist critics lies in Foucault's concept of power. Power is not a repressive force that regulates and controls the actions of otherwise independently subsistent entities ("human agents"), but it is the fabrication of entities in discourses that produce information and knowledge of what they "are." Foucauldian "power" creates its own subjects and enables them to act in certain ways, and only in doing so constrains them.[55] Following Foucault's historical genealogy, "impairment" is made knowable when the distinction between the "normal" and the "pathological" marks the beginning

52. Scott Yates, "Truth, Power, and Ethics in Care Services for People with Learning Difficulties," in *Foucault and the Government of Disability,* ed. Tremain, pp. 67-68.

53. Tremain, "Foucault, Governmentality, and Critical Disability Theory," pp. 9-11.

54. Tremain, "Foucault, Governmentality, and Critical Disability Theory," p. 10; see also Bill Hughes, "What Can a Foucauldian Analysis Contribute to Disability Theory?" in *Foucault and the Government of Disability,* p. 82; Barry Allen, "Foucault's Nominalism," in *Foucault and the Government of Disability,* p. 94.

55. Tremain, "Foucault, Governmentality, and Critical Disability Theory," p. 4; Hughes, "What Can a Foucauldian Analysis Contribute to Disability Theory?" p. 81; Allen, "Foucault's Nominalism," pp. 95-96.

of modern biomedicine at the end of the eighteenth century.[56] This distinction "sustains disability as a form of power that both contributes to the formation of an identity and establishes impairment as its necessary and sufficient condition." Consequently, it became possible to "see" impairment and to "say" disability; and, on a Foucauldian analysis, impairments are medical fabrications that constitute disability.[57] Bill Hughes spells out the implications for disabled people:

> To be situated within a discourse of "pathology," is to be delegitimized. Insofar as disabled people have become an object of disciplinary power, they have also become the subject matter of professional groups, whose discourses of expertise have defined and redefined that subject matter. Empirically, this position embodies a reasonable claim, for it explains the oppression of disabled people in terms of the construction of disability as a subject position that disempowering practices have fabricated. The outcome of these practices for disabled people has been the systematic closure of opportunities for agency. By the end of the nineteenth century, confinement, institutionalization, and dependency had become the reality of disabled people's lives. Disabled people became (i.e., were inscribed as) people who could not do things for themselves, who were a burden, a group in need of intensive and intrusive systems of surveillance.[58]

56. Hughes, "What Can a Foucauldian Analysis Contribute to Disability Theory?" p. 82; see also Licia Carlson, "Docile Bodies, Docile Minds," in *Foucault and the Government of Disability*, pp. 133-52.

57. Hughes, "What Can a Foucauldian Analysis Contribute to Disability Theory?" p. 82. Note how this assertion captures the positions we have been considering in a Foucauldian critique, both with regard to "disability identity" and with regard to the distinction between "impairment" and "disability."

58. Hughes, "What Can a Foucauldian Analysis Contribute to Disability Theory?" p. 83. The author does not consider the implication of this view on the history of disability, which is that it only starts in the late eighteenth century. However, several "histories" have been written of intellectual disability that have documented facts about how people with this condition were regarded and treated in the Middle Ages, long before the beginning of modern medicine. See, for example, R. C. Scheerenberger, *A History of Mental Retardation* (Baltimore: Paul H. Brookes, 1983). This observation does not necessarily invalidate the Foucauldian analysis of the discourse of modern medicine and its "invention" of disability; but it does indicate that this discourse is not necessarily the only one that is historically true.

While the Foucauldian analysis clearly has considerable explanatory force, its nominalist tendency reinforces the realist criticism that was aimed at the social model of disability we have discussed above. The point regards the uncompromising rejection of any suggestion that the language of impairment and disability refers to something "out there," a fact about the natural condition of human being that evokes a particular kind of response. There are no such facts because there is no response, and vice versa, because the only thing we respond to is language. Supposedly, the reason for this uncompromising rejection is Foucault's antirealism, which rejects any suggestion of "inherent structure."[59]

Following these ideas, Foucauldian theorists of disability can arrive at remarkable claims — patently false in my view — with regard to impairment and disability as natural realities. They categorically deny the existence of these realities independent from linguistic structures. For example, having noticed in the disability literature the ubiquitous distinction between "impairment" and "disability" as denoting two separate domains, Barry Allen asserts that "nobody is impaired all on her own, through a naturally occurring deficit that her body bears as a biophysical property."[60] Regarding this claim, I invite the reader to consider the following thought experiment. Imagine a blind Robinson Crusoe on his deserted island. For the sake of the argument, imagine also that Robinson has no knowledge of ever having been able to see; hence "blindness" does not mean anything to him. Does he have a visual impairment or not? One thing is immediately clear: Robinson does not know he has an impairment. But does it also follow that he has none? If we could observe him, what would we see? Presumably we would see a man using a stick to get by on his island without stumbling, or maybe he would use his hands, stretching out his arms for the same purpose — the way people do when they are blindfolded. So we would observe that Robinson was blind based on his behavior. The Foucauldian theorist may well ask what this proves, other than that we are in the position to suppose "blindness" because *we* know the concept. At any rate, they would argue, we would have to say that his behavior does not depend on our supposition of blindness. Instead, we should say that his behavior

59. Allen, "Foucault's Nominalism," p. 99.
60. Allen, "Foucault's Nominalism," p. 94.

is an adaptive response to a condition he finds himself in. Following Foucault's concept of power/knowledge as creating certain possibilities for action, the Foucauldian theorist would have to say that the perception of Robinson's behavior is a response, not to a natural condition, but to our ability of "seeing" and "saying" blindness. That is obviously false, for the following reason: it conflates the distinction between knowing and being.[61]

That this is what the Foucauldian theorist would say follows from Allen's own comments on the case at hand. Impairment is not a "naturally occurring deficit" of the body; rather, it is "something added." It is not "something missing," not a "lack" or "absence," but it is an "unasked-for supplement contributed by disciplinary knowledge and power."[62] Evidence for the claim that this view conflates the distinction between knowing and being can be found in Allen's assertion that "it is as impossible for a person *to be 'impaired'* without reference to a statistically constructed 'normal case' as for a person to be a criminal except by reference to law."[63] Clearly, this claim is only true when we read that it is impossible for a person to be *designated* as "impaired" without reference to a statistical norm. The norm does not constitute the condition of being impaired; it only constitutes the label that is attached to that condition within the context of a given social practice.

With regard to "impairment" and "disability" belonging to two separate domains, Allen understands proponents of the social model to be saying that impairment is the bodily reality that is cruelly mistreated by a society that disables people who are impaired. He then says: "What seems more likely, though, is that impairment is itself a product of that cruelty. Impairment is not inscribed in the biological register of nature and merely given in the body. It is an artifact *implanted in the body* by the

---

61. I am aware of the fact that Foucault would not consider this to be a mistake because his nominalism was intended to destroy the notion that there is something like the order of being. Apart from being implausible, the project appears to me as unnecessary to prove the point of Foucauldian power/knowledge as "effective truth," that is, as the capacity of theories, categories, predicates, or labels designating deviation to shape practical reasoning within social practices and institutions. Nothing in the explanation of the marginalization and oppression of disabled people in a society guided by conceptions of "normalcy" seems to depend on Foucauldian nominalism.

62. Allen, "Foucault's Nominalism," p. 94 (italics added).

63. Allen, "Foucault's Nominalism," p. 94.

discipline that measures deviation."[64] Somehow I find that hard to buy. As I have indicated in my observation about parents at the beginning of this discussion, it appears that they tend to believe something like Allen's view, at least when they are first confronted with the professional judgment that something is wrong with their child. They tend to regard this something indeed as "implanted in the body" of their child. But then they have to concede: it does not go away, however energetically they have tried to ignore it. In view of this, I propose we consider the fact that Kelly and Oliver de Vinck don't speak (which is true, of course, for many persons with profound intellectual disability) in light of how Allen concludes his discussion.

> Impairment is real (as real as crimes or money), though not a naturally given abnormality, but rather an artifact of the knowledge that measures the deviation from the norm. Norms and normal cases are like statutory laws and criminals: They exist, they are real, that is, effective, but only because people agree to take them seriously as objects of knowledge. It takes pedagogy to see some difference (which might otherwise be a matter of indifference) as a deficit, deficiency, or abnormal impairment. Impairment has no reality apart from the social mathematics of normalizing judgment.[65]

I contest the plausibility of this claim. In view of my earlier example of human beings who do not understand the difference between "you" and "me," or between "now" and "then," or between "here" and "there," I doubt the possibility of a social order within which this inability would be a matter of indifference. This is not to deny that much of what the Foucauldian analysis has to contribute to disability theory is important; I only deny that its nominalism is part of what makes it important. The truth of the matter seems to be that here, as much as elsewhere in the disability literature, everything comes down to the kind of example one has in mind when making general claims about the nature of impairment and disability. Like most other disability theorists, Foulcauldians apparently have not questioned their generalizations in view of people with profound intellectual disabilities such as Kelly and Oliver de Vinck. I will provide proof to substantiate this claim in the final section of this chapter.

64. Allen, "Foucault's Nominalism," p. 96.
65. Allen, "Foucault's Nominalism," p. 96.

7. Freedom of the Self as Our Final End

It is a great irony of the social constructionist approach to disability that, in spelling out the moral and political implications of the social model, it effectively reproduces a significant part of the social condition of disability. One can find support for this claim in the fact that the social model is about creating space for people with disability for articulating themselves. Whether we consider the earlier stages of its development in critical sociology in the early 1990s,[66] or the subsequent developments of disability identity, with or without realist underpinnings, or the later developments of Foucauldian analysis — in each case the default position is occupied, either implicitly or explicitly, by the disabled person as a purposeful agent competent of self-representation. The social model is thoroughly committed to the project of modern humanism and to the underlying values of this project as exemplified in liberal society. But not only is it committed to these liberal values, it is also committed to the anthropology underlying the concept of citizenship as it is understood in liberal society. In this respect, the social model shows its limitations with regard to people with profound intellectual disabilities. Given the natural realities constituting these lives, it would require quite a stretch of the imagination to picture persons such as Kelly and Oliver de Vinck occupying the default position of the social model. The same holds, of course, for many other people with less severe cognitive limitations.

In this final section I want to provide the evidence for these claims particularly from the work of the Foucauldian theorists of disability. For we have already seen how the political activism espoused by the social model reproduces the hierarchy of disability, but also that it may appear *unlikely* that the Foucauldian analysis would result in the support of a humanist project. Contrary to appearances, however, it clearly does. The poststructuralist analysis of the human subject to which Foucault was committed was intended to show that subjectivity is not a given but is the effect of language. The human subject does not exist

---

66. Diverse as their contributions otherwise may be, this is the common theme of the papers in the volume edited by Len Barton (see above, footnote 14). See, for example, Mike Oliver, "A Sociology of Disability or a Disablist Sociology?" in *Disability and Society*, ed. Len Barton, pp. 18-42; in the same volume, see Susan Peters, "The Politics of Disability Identity," pp. 215-34.

outside the system of signs and signifiers constituted by language, and thus the idea that human subjects can represent themselves by using language as a medium of transparent self-identification must be dismissed as a delusion. Therefore, Foucault rejects the notion of the human individual as a pre-given entity, and replaces it by a notion of the human individual as the result of the exercise of symbolic power. Human subjectivity is not to be mistaken as an originary force but is to be understood as the constituted effect of knowledge regimes.[67]

If this is the case, however, how could a Foucauldian analysis be committed to the humanist project of emancipating people with (intellectual) disability by means of empowering them to self-representation? Here is the answer as found in Erevelles's essay, from which I derived the above account of poststructuralist individuality:

> Thus far, I have supported the poststructuralist critique of the humanist subject. I am, nevertheless, uncomfortable about ending this essay with Foucault's murmur of indifference: What matter who's speaking? It should matter to us who is speaking, because otherwise we would leave unanswered the critical question of agency and its relation to social transformation.[68]

Erevelles suggests that, in light of the Foucauldian critique, the challenge is to rethink agency without producing traditional notions of "essentialized subjectivity." This is particularly significant, she claims, for people who have struggled within the disability-rights movement "to reconstitute for themselves empowering subjectivities."[69]

In a similar vein, Licia Carlson pursues a Foucauldian analysis of the history of "mental retardation" in order to challenge "the self-evident nature of mental retardation *as a particular kind of problem* to be solved."[70] By uncovering the discursive formations that constitute "mental retardation" as an object of knowledge, Carlson hopes to bring to light "subjugated knowledges" that are a critical counterpart of the discourses about retardation "from above." Carlson understands the latter as institutional discourses, philosophical theories, expert knowl-

---

67. Erevelles, "Signs of Reason," pp. 47-48.
68. Erevelles, "Signs of Reason," p. 58.
69. Erevelles, "Signs of Reason," p. 58.
70. Carlson, "Docile Bodies, Docile Minds," p. 134.

edges "produced *about* rather than *by* persons" labeled as "mentally re-tarded."[71] "Subjugated knowledges" I understand to be produced "from below," that is, by disabled people themselves. Carlson's histori-cal analysis shows — along Foucauldian lines — how scientific dis-courses in the nineteenth century created the category of "feeblemind-edness" and produced the "feebleminded" as subjects of education and improvement through a range of oppositions and contested claims and counterclaims regarding "mental retardation" as a classification. This analysis provides Carlson with a theoretical framework that helps "to expose the complex power relationships" that have constituted the "mentally retarded" in the Foulcauldian sense, that is, as "subjects who both act and are acted upon."[72] But in theorizing how their subjectivity is construed, Carlson says that we must take into account "that certain individuals may be unable to participate in this form of philosophical and political discourse."[73] She continues:

> Yet a Foucauldian analysis need not lead to a denial of the lived reali-ties of people who are labeled "mentally retarded," experiences that may be the result of their actual cognitive abilities, and/or the politi-cal, economic, and social consequences of being classified as "men-tally retarded." Rather, the promise of a Foucauldian approach lies in the unmasking of certain power relations that directly affect the ex-tent to which certain voices are silenced, and exposing the dangers of defining and *speaking for* an entire class of individuals. Ultimately, Foucault's work calls upon us to consider how the very existence of mental retardation *as a classification* affects the process of self-definition and conceptions of moral agency for individuals who are thus labeled.[74]

One is curious to know the precise meaning of the "actual cognitive abilities," as distinct from the linguistic fabrications to classify people, that may hinder certain disabled individuals from partaking in the pro-ject; but it appears with regard to "certain individuals" that something — their actual cognitive (dis)ability — seems to escape the structure of

71. Carlson, "Docile Bodies, Docile Minds," p. 135.
72. Carlson, "Docile Bodies, Docile Minds," p. 149.
73. Carlson, "Docile Bodies, Docile Minds," p. 149.
74. Carlson, "Docile Bodies, Docile Minds," pp. 149-50.

Foucauldian power/knowledge. At any rate, the very aim of the project is clear: to establish the moral agency of people with disabilities so that it supports them in the process of self-definition.

Since both these accounts of Foucauldian analysis apparently take recourse to acts of self-representation that Foucault rejected, the question arises how this contradiction can be eliminated. There are two possible solutions, and both are represented in *Foucault and the Government of Disability*. The first solution is to criticize Foucault's work for its inability to articulate the possibility of human agency, which Bill Hughes enunciates in his essay. Though of the opinion that a Foucauldian analysis has great explanatory force with regard to how disabled bodies are produced as disabled subjects, Hughes complains that it has little to offer in terms of practical political action.

> The body is constituted as passive, without agency, the plaything of discourse and text, and a surface ripe for inscription. One might ask: In a disincarnate world such as this would be, how could politics be done? If, as I would argue that Foucault's position with respect to the body suggests, there is no active, creative subject, then politics is reduced to the policing of subjects. Politics is something that is done to people, rather than something that people do. I would argue, furthermore, that such a world would be devoid of responsibility. In short, ethics and politics would be torn asunder.[75]

According to Hughes, Foucault does not acknowledge power as agency, which leads to the conclusion that the politics and objectives of the disability-rights movement must be a futile exercise. That conclusion can only be avoided by introducing some kind of normativity that can "valorize" its aspirations.

This is where the second solution steps in, which offers, according to Hughes, precisely what is needed. Some have suggested that Foucault, in his later work, has addressed the concern about agency in his reflections about ethics. It is the subject matter of his third "historical ontology" — in addition to the ontology of ourselves in relation to truth, and ourselves in relation to power — which regards ourselves in relation to ethics: it is this relationship "through which we constitute

---

75. Hughes, "What Can a Foucauldian Analysis Contribute to Disability Theory?" pp. 85-86.

ourselves as moral agents."[76] Foucault asserts that people are not merely passively positioned by power and subjectification, but "they relate to themselves in active fashion."[77] These relationships of the self with the self, of course, are not to be taken as constituted by the self-affirming subject, but are mediated by cultural models that may inspire the individual to question — indeed, to shape — its own conduct.[78]

From a Foucauldian perspective, the danger here — particularly regarding people with intellectual disabilities — is to supervise their ideals of the self, which betrays the possibility of ethics as the next domain of power/knowledge. To avoid this, we need to empower people so they can resist the power of professionals and institutions to govern their self-images. As Scott Yates reminds us,

> Foucault teaches us that there is a danger in speaking for and above others about their situation, and in formulating programs of resistance *for* them. The problems identified in this chapter are ones that people who live in care accommodation (not academics and social workers) must solve.[79]

Thus the message from Foucauldian theorists on both ethics and disability is clear: it is centered on the relationship of the self with the self as the core of liberating human agency. In this way the Foucauldian project, for all its criticisms of the humanism of the Enlightenment, does not betray its modernist legacy. The domain of ethics certainly does not reinstall the humanist conception of subjectivity, because Foucault's moral agent also finds himself in linguistic structures expressing conceptions of the good life. But in order to avoid circularity, there must be a sense in which the moral agent is not merely acted upon by these cul-

76. Foucault, "On the Genealogy of Ethics: An Overview of Work in Progress," in *The Essential Works of Michel Foucault, 1954-1984,* vol. 1, *Ethics: Subjectivity and Truth,* ed. Paul Rabinow (London: Allen Lane, 1997), p. 262. See Carlson, "Docile Bodies, Docile Minds," p. 148; Yates, "Truth, Power, and Ethics in Care Services for People with Learning Difficulties," p. 67.

77. Yates, "Truth, Power, and Ethics in Care Services for People with Learning Difficulties," 69.

78. Yates, "Truth, Power, and Ethics in Care Services for People with Learning Difficulties," 69.

79. Hughes, "What Can a Foucauldian Analysis Contribute to Disability Theory?" 85-86.

tural ideals. The danger of humanism, as Foucault understood it, is that we impose culturally mediated ideals on "deviating" others. The problem for Foucault's theory, however, is how it can allow moral agents to speak for themselves, when it is "language" that speaks through them. That is, there must be a sense in which the available models enable the moral agent to speak for herself, rather than only to be spoken about, or spoken for, or spoken through. Ultimately, the modernist project, in any of its manifestations, must necessarily presuppose a conception of agency that enables human beings to find themselves.

8. Conclusion

Even though the discussion in this chapter may have suggested otherwise, my critical questions regarding the social constructionist approach to disability are not directed against the social model. Whatever its weaknesses, it remains a powerful tool to bring to light the mechanisms of marginalization and oppression that dominate the lives of far too many disabled people. Instead, my questions are directed against the underlying ethical framework that makes the inclusion of people with disabilities entirely dependent on their capacity for self-representation and self-affirmation. In this regard, social constructionism reinforces rather than criticizes the tradition of thinking about our humanity in terms of our self-reflective capacity. By the same token, it reinforces a conception of human nature in which the nature of our being is constituted by the freedom that asserts itself in our actions. In the context of this book, this is the view that needs to be exposed as part of the problem, and the reason is by now obvious: social constructionism as a philosophical and moral view is very much committed to the modern perspective of individual selfhood that generates all the problems of the hierarchy of disability I discussed in the preceding chapter.

The point of the discussion of social constructionism, then, is this: from the perspective of both the social constructionists and my own theological perspective, the idea that "being disabled" determines the nature of human beings so designated rests on a mistake; but it is important to inquire into the exact nature of this mistake. According to the social constructionist approach, the mistake is that the limitations posed on a person are not the effect of a natural condition but of disabling social environments that can — and thus should — be changed. This analysis is predicated on the view that every human being is destined to determine his or her own existence.

Underlying this moral claim is an anthropological claim about the nature of our being. As human beings, we are free to construe the nature of our own being in the act of self-identification. This freedom is shaped, and thus constrained, by numerous cultural, political, and economic contingencies, but as ontological freedom it is certain. Human beings are the kinds of beings who have their existence as a task, not as a preordained destination. This anthropological claim reinforces the appearance of people with profound intellectual disability as problematic. It characterizes the human being as a being whose primordial relationship of existence is with herself. If we accept that claim, the condition of *not* being related to oneself must negate one's humanity in a fundamental, anthropological sense. If being related to ourselves marks what we fundamentally are qua human being, as distinct from other beings in the world, how could the absence of this characteristic not imply that we are looking at beings that are fundamentally different?

On the basis of these reflections, it seems undeniable that social constructionism repeats the main mistake of its foe, the essentialism of classical metaphysics, on the level of ontology, despite its claim to ontological muteness. This is clear when we look at it from the point of view of human beings with a profound intellectual disability. Neither Kelly nor Oliver de Vinck, nor any other human being with their impairments, is endowed with a capacity to substantiate the freedom of self-identification. The problem with social constructionism is that it leaves intact the anthropology of classical metaphysics that has dominated much of the Western tradition in conceiving the operation of our individual human faculties — the "faculties of the soul" — as the source of our humanity. It is ultimately this conception of our humanity that underscores the perception of people with profound intellectual disabilities as "subnormal." It is not difficult to see why social constructionism, in its constructive aspect, is in effect perpetuating the hierarchy of disability. Within its imagery of empowered people there is nothing to be gained for human beings like Kelly and Oliver de Vinck. In fact, the question of why we should consider them to be human in the first place has become all the more pressing. To uproot the hierarchy of disability, we will need a very different kind of story. My aim in this book is to develop this alternative story from the perspective of Christian belief.

Chapter Three

"Being Human" and "Being Disabled" II

When we are faced with a disabled person we are shown the hidden frontiers of human existence, and we are impelled to approach this mystery with respect and love.

Pope John Paul II, March 4, 1981

1. Roman Catholic Doctrine on Being Human

In this chapter I will consider the second version of the view that raising the anthropological question with regard to profoundly disabled human beings is a mistake. This version is the tradition of Roman Catholic moral theology. As is true for the Christian tradition in general, the Roman Catholic position admits of many different views on many subjects, not the least of which is the question of what it means to be human. It is thus highly problematic to speak of Roman Catholic moral theology in a monolithic sense, given the extensive debate between traditionalists and revisionists in recent times on the central role of natural law.[1] What I will present in this chapter as "the" Roman Catholic view is, in fact, the traditional position that is reflected in the documents and publications of the Roman Catholic Church and the theologians who adhere to that position.

Before I expand on why the Roman Catholic position on being human

---

1. See Paulinus I. Odozor, *Moral Theology in an Age of Renewal: A Study of the Catholic Tradition Since Vatican II* (Notre Dame: University of Notre Dame Press, 2003).

will stir strong reservations about my inquiry, let me summarize what I have presented so far as the thrust of its overall argument. Culturally dominant conceptions of what it means to be human exclude human beings with a profound intellectual disability because such conceptions are predicated on capacities for selfhood and purposive agency. These concepts reflect a longstanding orientation in the tradition of Western thought by which being human is distinguished according to the faculties of reason and will. Since this view apparently does not speak to the humanity of all human beings, there is a need for a fundamental rethinking of this tradition, in particular of its theological origins, because only in this way can we eliminate the theoretical underpinnings of an anthropological subdivision.

This overall argument will be met with critical reservations from Roman Catholic moral theology insofar as it has always defended the humanity of all human beings regardless of their state or condition. As is well known, this defense has been particularly focused in the last decades on ethical issues regarding human life in its prenatal stages. The question that moral theologians have been facing is: When can human life properly be said to be human in the full sense of the term? This question has been crucial in the debate on abortion, but it is also important in a number of other debates in bioethics, for example, in vitro fertilization, embryo experimentation, and, most recently, stem cell research. Each of these issues, from the viewpoint of official Roman Catholic doctrine, turns on the protection of prenatal life. The Magisterium has taken the position that the ontological status of any human being, irrespective of its stage of development, equals that of a human person, and that for all human beings this status obtains from the moment of conception.[2] The defense of this claim has been that human life in its earliest stages — embryonic and fetal — are of the same natural kind as any full-grown human being because they share the same genotype.[3] Any organism that is of human descent is for that

2. In the official doctrine there seems to be no distinction left between a human being and a human person: the two concepts are co-extensive. As Odozor explains, there has been a shift in anthropological thinking in the documents of the Second Vatican Council from a "physicalist" to a "personalist" approach, so that what had been said about "human nature" was from now on said in terms of the "human person," Odozor, *Moral Theology*, p. 286.

3. Joseph F. Rautenberg, "Abortion: Questions of Value and Procedure," in *Moral*

very reason to be regarded as a human being and to be protected as one. Following the "Declaration on Procured Abortion" that was issued in 1974, the position is stated again in *Donum Vitae*:

> From the time the ovum is fertilized, a new human life has begun which is neither that of the father nor of the mother; it is rather the life of a new human being with its own growth. It would never be human if it were not human already.[4]

Being human is biologically determined, then, by the fact that it is born from human persons, male and female. This position reflects Aristotle's rule that "man is born from man." Consequently, if there is an issue about the humanity of some being, all you need to know is whether it is of human descent. Following the classical view — "life from life" — Germaine Grisez argues that it would be more accurate to ask, "How is life transmitted?" than to ask, "When does life begin?" Human life is identified by human parentage.[5]

Consequently, in view of Roman Catholic moral theology, there is no basis for raising the anthropological question with regard to profoundly disabled human beings. My inquiry is thus led astray in raising the issue, despite its (presumably laudable) attempt to oppose any view that makes "being human" dependent on conditions of subjectivity, such as the condition of having a sense of self. It mistakenly assumes that, in order to be able to account for the humanity of *each* human being, we need fundamentally to rethink the humanity of *all* human beings. This step is only compelling when one takes as one's point of departure the current misconceptions of subjectivity as a necessary condition of being human. There is no need to proceed in this way, at least not from the viewpoint of official Roman Catholic doctrine.[6]

Theology: Challenges for the Future, ed. Charles C. Curran (New York: Paulist Press, 1990), pp. 241-63.

4. *Donum Vitae: Instruction on Respect for Human Life in its Origin and on the Dignity of Procreation* (London: Publications of the Holy See, 1987), p. 13.

5. Grisez, *Abortion: The Myths, the Realities, and the Arguments* (New York: Corpus Books, 1970), p. 13. Later in his book Grisez phrases the position in this way: "Life proceeds from life, and human life from human life, in a continuous process. New individuals emerge from existing individuals. Relative to parents, the individuality of the offspring must be admitted to begin at conception" (p. 274).

6. Given my claim that we need to reconsider the tradition of theological anthropol-

2. The Anthropological Ambiguity of Natural Law

However, things are less straightforward than they appear at first sight — even for Roman Catholic doctrine. If we leave the context of the protection of unborn human life behind, it turns out that Roman Catholicism faces precisely the problem that I raised. To explain this, I will borrow a distinction suggested by Eberhard Schockenhoff.

According to Schockenhoff, the term "human nature" suggests that the common nature of human beings is a stable and knowable reality — as far as its ethical and legal relevance is concerned — that cannot be meaningfully called into question.[7] However, as soon as one begins to reflect on the normative content of this term, "living in accordance with one's nature," one encounters a wide variety of possibilities. Historically, "living in accordance with nature" has been understood to refer to *genesis,* or origin, and that view leads to conceptions of a Golden Age to which humankind should return. But at the other end of the spectrum, the term has been understood to refer to *telos,* or end, which leads to concepts that project the ideal of living in accordance with human nature in a future state of utopia.[8]

I propose to borrow the distinction of *genesis* and *telos* to indicate that the Roman Catholic doctrine on being human moves indeed between these opposite poles. On the one hand, there is the view that is

---

ogy in order to solve the problem of humanity, there is another objection to my approach to be expected from Roman Catholic quarters. The view that we need an anthropology grounded in Christian doctrine in order to include profoundly disabled human beings does not take into account the perspective of the natural law tradition (to which Roman Catholicism remains firmly committed in some form). The objection is that, in pursuing a solution to the problem in the field of theology, I am downplaying the insights into human nature accessible to reason itself. I will not deal with this objection in a formal way, that is, as a claim regarding theological epistemology. But I will discuss it on material grounds: the natural law tradition causes a significant problem for Roman Catholic moral theology precisely at this point.

7. Eberhard Schockenhoff, *Natural Law and Human Dignity: Universal Ethics in a Historical World,* trans. B. McNeil (Washington, DC: The Catholic University of America Press, 2003), p. 12. I should make it explicit that I do not mean to present Schockenhoff as representing the Catholic Church's position; I only use his point about the "anthropological ambiguity" of the natural tradition to develop my own question.

8. Schockenhoff, *Natural Law and Human Dignity,* pp. 13-14. The author mentions Seneca as a representative of the first and Rousseau as a representative of the second reading.

stated in many ecclesiastical documents: that a person is given with the genesis of human being because he or she originates from human persons. On the other hand, there is the teleological meaning that is derived from the Aristotelian-Thomist tradition: according to it, "nature" refers to the development and proper use of the powers of intellect and will. That is, human beings attain their true nature only by developing their innate capacities.

The position that defends the concept by which human parentage is both the necessary and sufficient condition of being human has been developed, as I have indicated, in the context of ethical reflection on particular kinds of action, such as procured abortion and embryo experimentation.[9] In this context, moral theology's primary task is to set moral constraints on human action. But ethical reflection is not limited to questions of moral constraint. Even when questions regarding the protection of human beings like Kelly can be effectively answered on the grounds that she is of human descent, this does not answer the question of what it means for Kelly to lead a human life. With regard to ethical questions concerned with human life properly so called, we not only need to identify her origin as a human being; we also need to ask how she participates in our final end as a human being. I will seek to show that the Roman Catholic position does not provide an answer to this second question, other than to say that a human life like Kelly's is defective. That is, the tradition has no positive answer to that question. The reason why profoundly disabled human beings do not lead a human life properly so called from the perspective of our final end is that they do not develop the capacities of reason and will.

In order to substantiate this claim, let us allow the official docu-

---

9. See the analysis by Carol A. Tauer, "The Tradition of Probabilism and the Moral Status of the Early Embryo," in *Abortion and Catholicism: The American Debate,* ed. Patricia B. Jung and Thomas A. Shannon (New York: Crossroad, 1988), pp. 54-84. The logic of the debate is reflected in an exemplary way in Albert S. Moraczewski, "The Human Embryo and Fetus: Ontological, Ethical and Legal Aspects," in *"Humanae Vitae": 20 Anni Dopo, Atti del II Congresso Internazionale di Teologia Morale,* ed. Aurelio Ansaldo (Milano: Edizione Ares, 1989), pp. 339-62. Moraczewski structures the abortion issue by raising the following four questions about the developing human embryo (in this order): "Whether it is an individual human organism," "whether it is a human person," "whether it has the moral status accorded to a born human person," and "whether it has the necessary protection by civil laws" (p. 340).

ments of the Magisterium to speak about the human fetus in terms of human personhood.[10] Claiming that a human person exists from the moment of its conception, the Magisterium retains the focus on the generic meaning of human nature. Consequently, it presents its instruction about the "gift of life" as an instruction on "respect for human life in its *origin.*"[11] The person is what he or she is because he or she is from human persons. The Magisterium finds support for this claim in modern genetic science because, it says, the latter has shown that from the first instance "the programme is fixed as what this living thing will be." Even though science does not decide about theological issues, it does indicate "a personal presence at the moment of this first appearance of a human life," which, given the scientific evidence, is explained by the fact of its genotype. If this is the case, "how could a human individual not be a human person?"[12]

However, adopting the language of personhood raises questions of its own, especially when personhood is examined with respect to the qualities appropriate for human beings in pursuit of their ends.[13] According to Schockenhoff, the understanding of our final end is not in dispute within the tradition. "The Aristotelian-Thomistic tradition," he says, "considers the human person in his physical-intellectual existence and interprets him as a psycho-physical vital unity under the primacy of reason."[14] A human person comes into being by virtue of a rational soul as the substantial "form" of the human individual. This is generally referred to as the "doctrine of hylomorphism." Because the notion of a rational soul is characterized by the powers of reason and will, the doctrine of hylomorphism implies that the human person exists as the union of the rational soul

10. See Brian V. Johnstone, "From Physicalism to Personalism," *Studia Moralia* 30 (1992): 71-96.

11. The subtitle of *Donum Vitae,* see above, footnote 4 (italics added).

12. *Donum Vitae,* p. 13. The debate on moral issues in the sphere of reproduction that continues to generate conflict among Roman Catholic authors turns at least in part on developments in genetic science that have shown that human individuation only occurs after a period of fourteen days. For the various positions in this debate, see the valuable collection of essays in Patricia B. Jung and Thomas A. Shannon, eds., *Abortion and Catholicism: The American Debate* (New York: Crossroad, 1988).

13. Odozor, *Moral Theology in an Age of Renewal,* p. 287.

14. Schockenhoff, *Natural Law and Human Dignity,* p. 14.

with a material body.[15] This doctrine is reflected in the definition of the human person that Boethius formulated in the sixth century and that has been sustained throughout the tradition. According to Boethius, the human person is *naturae rationalis individua substantia* (an individual substance of a rational nature). In view of the lives of profoundly disabled human beings, this definition poses a problem, because the least one can say is that their lives fail to reflect this nature. Therefore, when the Magisterium claims the support of modern science because it has shown that from the first instance "the programme is fixed as what this living thing will be," the conclusion must be that there are beings of human descent — "human persons" in the recent language of the Magisterium — in whom the "fixed" program does not develop at all. This fact by itself implies that these human beings must be different living things. If the program determines what they will be and does not develop accordingly, doesn't it follow that they must be different — not just accidentally but essentially?

In view of the lives of human beings like Kelly, this question cannot but pose a problem for the Roman Catholic position because of its intellectualist conception of our final end. The end of human beings consists in the perfection of their capacities. Aristotle put it this way: "The perfection of its own nature is the end of every object."[16] Foremost among the capacities that determine a human being's "own nature" are the powers of reason and will. This illustrates what I take to be the problem of ambiguity in the Roman Catholic doctrine on being human, a problem that becomes painfully visible precisely concerning human beings with profound intellectual disability. They fit the first conception of the human person, as the Magisterium understands it, the concept of being human according to origin, because they are from human descent. But it is difficult to see how they could fit the second concept, that is, being human according to its *telos,* because they cannot do what human beings do by virtue of their own nature, which is to develop the faculties of reason and will.[17]

15. For a very clear and concise account of this theory, see Joseph F. Donceel, "A Liberal Catholic's View," in *Abortion and Catholicism,* pp. 48-53.

16. Aristotle, *Politics,* p. 1252b.

17. Aristotle did not face the problem of ambivalence between the genesis and telos of being human in this respect, because — as is well known — he did not regard disabled

Returning to the question of how this ambiguity plays out in the domain of ethics, we begin to see what is at stake here. Intervening on behalf of *all* human beings in terms of their personhood from the moment of conception, the Magisterium intends to secure the lives of all those who have a right to life — both the born and the unborn. However, the argument in support of this position does not by itself answer the question about what that right to life is supposed to secure. The answer to that question must be derived from the other position, that is, the one about the end of being human. All human beings are to be protected in order to actualize their potential for becoming what they are meant to be. But, given the nature of that potential as the tradition understands it, how is this argument going to work for profoundly disabled human beings? What is the conception of the ultimate good for human beings, and how do human beings with profound intellectual disabilities participate in it, once the moral injunction against abortion and euthanasia has secured their existence? Securing their existence by force of the argument that all human beings deserve protection for the sole reason that they are of human descent is one thing; explaining how people with profound disabilities participate in the human good is quite another.

3. A Hierarchy of Being

Thus the question is: How are the two concepts of the origin and the telos of being human related? As the text of *Donum Vitae* clearly shows, references to the second concept find their way into the argument that is built on the first. This is clear from what it says, for example, about what is important about the human person. Claiming the support of scientific evidence for the thesis that the human person exists from the

---

children as human beings proper and advised to kill them. His reason for justifying infanticide was that they could not attain happiness. In his *Politics* he observes that "the happiness and well-being which all men manifestly desire, some have the power of attaining, but to others, from some accident or defect of nature, the attainment of them is not granted" (Aristotle, *Politics*, p. 1331b). He then sets out to explore the conditions for fostering happiness that the state should attend to, among which he considers the conditions of healthy procreation to be very important. Anticipating the possibility that the state will not always succeed, Aristotle recommends: "Let there be a law that no deformed child shall live" (p. 1335b).

moment of conception, the document says: "Right from fertilization is begun the adventure of a human life and each of its great capacities requires time to find its place and to be in a position to act."[18] Here we find the two perspectives in one single sentence, which raises the question of how they are related.

The same picture emerges from other documents. In *Veritatis Splendor,* Pope John Paul II places himself squarely within the tradition of Aristotelian-Thomist thought:

> The spiritual and immortal soul is the principle of unity of the human being, whereby it exists as a whole — *corpore et anima unus* — as a person. These definitions not only point out that the body, which has been promised the resurrection, will also share in the glory. They also remind us that reason and will are linked with all the bodily and sense faculties.[19]

Clearly, this statement entails the conception of the human person as defined by the embodied capacity for reason and will. The picture is that of "man as incarnated spirit," indicating the "ontological excess of the human person."[20]

In the encyclical letter *Evangelium Vitae,* John Paul II launched a massive attack on what he called the "culture of death," a phrase that refers in particular to the acceptance of abortion and euthanasia as legitimate medical practice in a number of Western countries. The document finds a "surprising contradiction" in the solemn proclamation of the inviolable rights of the human person that these countries subscribe to, on the one hand, and the denial of these inviolable rights at the moment of birth and the moment of death, on the other hand.[21]

---

18. *Donum Vitae,* p. 13.

19. *Veritatis Splendor: Encyclical Letter* (Washinton, DC: United States Catholic Conference, 1993), p. 76.

20. M. Faggioni, "Life and Forms of Life: The Relationship Between Biology and Anthropology," in *The Culture of Life: Foundations and Dimensions — Proceedings of the Seventh Assembly of the Pontifical Academy for Life,* ed. J. de Dios Vial Correa and E. Sgreccia (Città del Vaticano: Librera Editrice Vaticana, 2002), pp. 67-103. See also Anton C. Pegis, *At the Origins of the Thomistic Notion of Man* (New York: MacMillan, 1963), p. 44: Pegis characterizes the Thomist view of man as "incarnated intelligence."

21. *Evangelium Vitae: Encyclical Letter* (Washington, DC: United States Catholic Conference, 1995), p. 31.

The pope opposes this contradiction by proclaiming the "Gospel of Life," a gospel according to which Christ has come "in order that we will have life, and have it abundantly."[22] In his explanation of what this means, the pope strikes a theological note. Reminding us of the words of the Second Vatican Council, which said that the mystery of human being resides in the mystery of the incarnate God, the pope explains that human beings are not just living organisms like any other form of life. They alone are called to the "fullness of Life," which exceeds their earthly existence because it means a calling to "sharing the very life of God." At the same time, however, this calling includes their earthly existence that is both the initial stage and an integral part of this sharing.[23] The ultimate end of being human, I understand, is the fullness of life, which exists in sharing the life of God. However, the ultimate end does not exist apart from the end of our earthly existence, but includes it.

As it stands, this theological explanation of the "Gospel of Life" does not raise the question I have been asking, because sharing the eternal life of God is primordially a gift that in no way depends on human capacity. It is not that we are called to participate in this life because of what we are capable of *doing*. The papal document makes this point explicit when it declares that human life is a unified process of both our temporal and eschatological existence, which, "unexpectedly and undeservedly, is enlightened by the promise and renewed by the gift of divine life."[24] Approaching the question theologically, this explanation suggests, at least mitigates the problem of undeveloped capacities, since the ultimate end of human life is clearly not dependent on them, but is a gift — an unexpected and undeserved gift. One might even venture to say, as the language of "holy innocents" suggests, that those whose capacities for reason and will have not developed are probably the last to "undeserve" the gift of God since they cannot use these capacities to do evil.

To be instructed further on this subject, let us consider Robert Spaemann's philosophical comment on the anthropology of *Evangelium Vitae:* he intends to show that the pope's theological explanation is not different from the traditional position that is accounted for

22. *Evangelium Vitae*, p. 3, quoting from John 10:10.
23. *Evangelium Vitae*, p. 4.
24. *Evangelium Vitae*, p. 4.

(philosophically) by the insights of natural reason. Spaemann thus accounts for the pope's view in terms of what he calls the "teleological axiom":

> We know fully what something is, only when we know what it is in its final perfection. This is true at least for human beings. We know fully what a human being is, only when we know what he is called to be. This axiom is diametrically opposed to the axiom which dominates our scientific culture and which says: what something is, and therefore also what the human being is, we understand when we know what it is made of and how it came to be.[25]

The calling from which *Evangelium Vitae* takes its point of departure, according to Spaemann, is the one Jesus issued to his followers: "Be perfect as your Father in heaven is perfect." This reverses the angle from which the theological anthropology of the encyclical letter operates. What human beings are is determined by their calling to be followers of Christ — that is, to fulfill the end of their earthly existence — in order to share in the eternal life of God.[26] Presumably, the reason for this move is that Spaemann anticipates the objection that the pope apparently makes his Christian understanding of what it means to be human entirely dependent on revelation, which is something that the Roman Catholic tradition always has rejected.[27] Spaemann says that what the church teaches in this respect is in tune with "age old insights of philosophy."[28]

25. R. Spaemann, "On the anthropology of the Encyclical *Evangelium Vitae*," in *Evangelium Vitae: Five Years of Confrontation with the Society: Proceedings of the Sixth Assembly of the Pontifical Academy for Life, 11-14 Feb. 2000,* ed. Juan de Dios Vial Correa and Elio Sgreccia (Città del Vaticano: Librera Editrice Vaticana, 2001), pp. 437-51. Spaemann is evidently attacking the naturalist approach in science that does not reckon with teleology of any kind; he is not rejecting claims regarding the ontological status of the human embryo that the Vatican has been making in terms of origin.

26. Spaemann, "On the Anthropology of the Encyclical *Evangelium Vitae*," p. 438.

27. Spaemann's concern is confirmed in the text of *Evangelium Vitae,* where it claims that the church "knows that this Gospel of Life, which she has received from her Lord, has a profound and persuasive echo in the heart of every person — believer and non-believer alike — because it marvelously fulfills all the heart's expectations while infinitely surpassing them" (p. 4).

28. Spaemann, "On the Anthropology," p. 439.

However, when the encyclical teaching is then presented in philosophical terms, the teleological axiom is explained in a way that is very different from the theological language used by the document itself. The primary anthropological message of *Evangelium Vitae*, Spaemann argues, is that the life of human persons shows us the very meaning of life, which he explains by saying that in the human person we see the essence of life, because only it is capable of transcending itself and aspiring to be "higher than the other beings living on the earth."[29] As self-transcending beings, human beings crown the hierarchical order of all that is.

With this claim Spaemann invokes all the problems that the Magisterium has been engaged in while disputing with contemporary secular ethicists, who justify abortion and euthanasia in cases where the capacities of reason and will are inoperative. Having argued that human beings are the "summit of creation" because they are capable of ordering nature according to reason, Spaemann concludes:

> To be capable of truth constitutes the dignity of the human person. Only truth liberates man from being trapped in himself, from the inverted centeredness in oneself characteristic of all non-personal living beings. By their actions, human beings are capable to do justice to the things as they are; i.e. they are able to transcend themselves. Self-surrender, self-transcendence, and that is to say: love, is the highest form of life. In this human beings realize themselves as persons.[30]

What happens in this philosophical explanation of the anthropological message of *Evangelium Vitae* is that (1) the ultimate end of human being as the underserved and unexpected gift of being drawn into sharing the life of God is left out of the account; and (2) its place is taken by an account of the "highest form of life" in terms of the perfection of our rational capabilities as humans. Naturally, given the concern that the theological anthropology of the document should not be taken to oppose the insights of natural reason, this replacement is not surprising. What is surprising, however, is the suggestion that the theological perspective does not make a difference.[31]

29. Spaemann, "On the Anthropology," p. 445.
30. Spaemann, "On the Anthropology," p. 445.
31. We will return to this question later in this chapter. The problem it hints at is

Spaemann's argument suggests that *Evangelium Vitae* repeats the same move that we find everywhere, namely, the account of being human in terms of its higher capacities as distinct from the capacities of other beings. The supposition of hierarchical order underlying this suggestion raises the same question here as it does elsewhere: if it is true that the "capacity for truth" constitutes the dignity of the human person, that casts doubt on the dignity of human beings without that capacity. This is the point that contemporary bioethicists have been pressing time after time, and accounts of the Roman Catholic view such as the one presented by Spaemann cannot help but reinforce their point. If the conclusion they draw is to be rejected, this can only be justified by repealing one of the premises of the argument. That is, if it's true that human beings do not lose their dignity even when their capacities for reason and will are undeveloped, then it cannot be true that the perfection of these capacities is the ultimate ground for that dignity.

We may here anticipate someone's objecting that this perspective of the origin of the human being has a much wider scope than its being from human descent, as is apparent in its genotype. "Origin," the objection holds, should be read theologically rather than biologically in that it refers to the fact that God creates the human being in its fullness, just as it finds its ultimate destiny and fulfillment in returning to God. This shows that there is no gap between "origin" and "end."[32] However, it appears to me that this objection makes things worse, because now that it has removed the gap between "origin" and "end," human beings who do not develop their capacities of reason and will are not only excluded from the ultimate end but also from the beginning.[33] Either

---

known in the tradition as the relationship between the "natural" and the "supernatural" end of human being.

32. See Romanus Cessario, *Introduction to Moral Theology* (Washington, DC: The Catholic University of America Press, 2001), pp. 22-31. Cessario writes: "The divine nature abides without potential of any kind; as the Scholastic theologians insist, God is 'pure act.' The Trinity is not a mode of becoming in God, but of being. God is Father, Son, and Holy Spirit. Because God's being is 'to be,' the image of God does not most properly consist in the simple intellectual capacities of the soul by themselves, but these capacities as they dynamically actualize intelligent human life" (p. 28). By this account, profoundly disabled human beings are theologically excluded from being created in God's image.

33. Darlene Weaver brought the objection — as well as the response — to my attention. I will discuss further objections to my claim against the Roman Catholic position below.

way, however, the account of the Roman Catholic position as presented by Spaemann illustrates why there is a question to be answered on behalf of human beings with profound intellectual disabilities.

What we are left with, then, is a question about the relationship between two claims, one regarding the genesis, or origin, of being human, the other regarding its *telos,* or ultimate end. The first is the claim that every human being, regardless of his state or condition, is to be regarded as a person from the moment of conception because he is of human parentage; the second is the claim that the end of being human is the fulfillment of our natural being that consists in the perfection of the capacities of reason and will. The tension between these two claims becomes evident when we look at them from the perspective of human beings lacking in these capacities. It is difficult to avoid the conclusion regarding the second claim, that is, that the lives of these human beings could be anything but "subhuman." My point, of course, is not to suggest that this is what authors committed to the tradition of Roman Catholicism are saying; rather, my point is that the position as described warrants that conclusion.

In the remainder of this chapter I will discuss possible responses to this conclusion. The first response presents us with an Aristotelian account of marginal cases: the fact that this apple is not much of an apple in terms of its qualities — taste, size, shape, color, and so on — does not eliminate the fact that it is nonetheless an apple. Something similar is true of any natural kind, including being human. The second response is the well-known argument according to which human beings do not depend on their characteristic functions, for example, language, rationality, or self-consciousness. Act follows being, not the other way around.

4. Marginal Cases

The attempt to answer my question with an account of marginal cases is built on Aristotle's concept of natural kinds.[34] Even though the lives

---

34. Alfonso Gomez-Lobo, professor of ancient philosophy and metaphysics at Georgetown University, made this suggestion to me during my visit to the Kennedy Center for Ethics. I have not encountered it in the literature so far, so I am entirely responsible for the way it is presented here.

of profoundly disabled people must appear to be marginal cases of what it means to live a human life, it does not follow that their lives are therefore any less human. Differences between human lives are differences in degree rather than kind. In Aristotle's view, natural kinds are classes of beings "that exist by nature," by which he means that "each of them has within itself a principle of motion."[35] Put differently, natural kinds entail beings that produce and reproduce themselves. The fact that human beings bring forth human beings indicates a natural kind in this sense. For the same reason, all living organisms belong to a natural kind.

Now, with regard to natural kinds, Aristotle argues that it is always possible that some instances are central, while others remain only marginal. In order to see how this is possible, we need to look at Aristotle's explanation of how we name being human in various contexts. When we identify being human in various ways, for example, in statements such as "human beings seek to avoid pain," or "this disabled human being has a minimal quality of life," or "human beings who are tall usually have an advantage," we are identifying being human *pros hen,* that is, in reference to "one definite nature."[36] The numerous expressions and claims about human beings that we make are all related to what we take the one nature of the human to be, but they can be so related in various ways. Thus we speak about "human kindness," which indicates affection; about "human sexuality," which indicates capacity; about "human development," which indicates process, and so on. Such examples, of which there are many, show that "there are many different ways in which a thing is said to be, but all refer to one central point."[37] Therefore, as in the Aristotelian concept of being human as a natural kind, it is perfectly possible to speak of "human disease" and even of "human death" as instantiations of the human. The last example — death — is particularly instructive in that Aristotle characterizes the relationship of this expression to human nature as "the one central point," as privation or destruction.[38] To identify a dead body as a human corpse, in this

35. Aristotle, *Physics,* Book II, I, 192b10-13.

36. Here I follow Joseph Owens, *The Doctrine of Being in the Aristotelian Metaphysics: A Study in the Greek Background of Medieval Thought* (Toronto: Pontifical Institute of Mediaeval Studies, 1951), pp. 151-52.

37. Aristotle, *Metaphysics,* p. 1003b5.

38. Aristotle, *Metaphysics,* p. 1003b8.

view, is to express a relationship of destruction to the natural kind of human being. Thus the expression of nonbeing is also part of the underlying unity in the natural being in question.

If we now combine this explanation about the many different ways in which we refer to human beings with what has been said about the teleological concept of human nature that Aristotle developed, then the problem of ambiguity seems to evaporate. The nature of the human being is determined by a formal cause, the rational soul, which assertion has teleological content: human nature has the perfection of our human capacities as end. Of course, there will be degrees of perfection realized in the actual world, so that, from a teleological point of view, we will have a specimen that for a variety of reasons can be further advanced on the road to perfection where others are lagging behind. This difference does nothing to suggest that the latter are not properly regarded as human beings. Therefore, it is quite possible to regard Kelly as a human being properly so called even when it is true that her capacity for reason seems to be absent. There is no ambiguity left.

Let us call this the Aristotelian solution of marginal cases: human beings develop their capacities, some do better than others, some do worse, and some do not develop at all; even so, they still belong to the same natural kind. That is, human beings are defined in terms of their procreation: "Man is born from man." All we need to do is underscore the fact that no being born of human parents can be anything less than a human being. In other words, inferring the claim about origin as a fallback position for the defense of human being as a natural kind can save the teleological axiom. As I suggested in the introduction to this discussion, you don't need to be a perfect apple to be counted as an apple in the first place.

Attractive as this argument may appear at first sight, however, it does not solve anything. The only thing it tells us is that, if you look at it from the question of origin, you will see that the eventual imperfection of a member of a natural kind does not annihilate its being a member of that kind. True, but the problem posed here arises not because of the question of origin but because of the question of *telos*. To stick with the above example, surely the bad apple is an apple from the perspective of origin, but from the perspective of its final end it is not an apple whose being carries any value. It does not count for much. It will be trashed — if someone bothers to pick it up at all.

The moral point of the analogy between bad apples and profoundly disabled human beings is not the garbage can, of course, but the observation that in both cases it is the teleological perspective that revokes the evaluative judgment. We do not have questions about human beings any more than about other living organisms, with respect to their natural kind; but we do have questions about human beings whose lives do not even come close to what many would consider a human life properly so called. As I have argued elsewhere, questions about what to think of disabled lives arise in view of concepts of the human good that make these lives appear as "defective."[39]

In light of this observation, the Roman Catholic position appears to be weakened by the fact that it seeks to answer the ethical issues of our times regarding human life exclusively in terms of its view of the *origin* of being human. But the Aristotelian rule "man is born from man" is never at the heart of what is disputed. Instead, the great divide in the moral landscape of contemporary debate is the question of human *telos*. Accordingly, this is the question that I will explicitly address regarding the lives of profoundly disabled human beings. About this question, the Roman Catholic Church does not seem to have much to say more than that their lives indeed are to be regarded as "defective." This conclusion is inevitable, unless it can be shown that there is no gap between the origin and final end; because what the Catholic Church has to say about the latter is already contained in what it says about the former. As we shall see in the following sections, this is exactly how proponents of the Catholic Church's position defend it.

5. *Agere sequitur esse*

Let us now consider the second response, which turns on the distinction between the human person and his or her functions. Its basic claim is that the human person is not defined by the actual operation of her functions, such as, for example, the capacity for acting on reasons. At stake here is a position that is widely discussed in the bioethical literature. It argues that, because humans are characterized by particular

39. Hans S. Reinders, *The Future of the Disabled in Liberal Society: An Ethical Analysis* (Notre Dame: University of Notre Dame Press, 2000).

functions, the absence of these functions implies that there is no human person properly so called, even when there is a being generated by human parents.

The Roman Catholic objection to this position is that the functions that characterize being human do not exist in themselves, but only as functions of a subject — *subiectum* — that is their ontological condition. To infer the being of a person from acts proper to a person is to presuppose a distinction between a person and personlike acts; but the important point is that the acts of a person follow from the being of the person, not the other way around.[40] That is, the person is the ontological condition of the possibilities of its operations. The latter are the manifestation of the potency of the person, but this manifestation is not to be identified with the person, because the person must exist prior to the manifestation of its potency.

In the context of the debate on the nature and status of the human embryo, Laura Palazzani has defended this argument by invoking Aquinas's version of Aristotle's theory of hylomorphism.[41] Following the Boethian definition of the person, Aquinas argues (according to Palazzani) that the human person is an individual substance of a rational nature whereby the soul is the form of the human body. This "form" or "primary act," as Aristotle puts it,[42] determines the nature of the individual substance. From this *actus primus,* which constitutes the being of the person, we must distinguish its operations as its *actus secundus.*

According to Palazzani, this argument makes it possible to justify the presence in humans of "an ontological principle of unification of the properties and the permanence of functions and acts, present *independent* of their actual exterior manifestation."[43] The failure to un-

40. This distinction is sometimes referred to as the distinction between "person" and "personality," whereby the latter is used in a phenomenological sense, while the former is used in an ontological sense. The person is the *subiectum* of the manifestations that characterize a personality. See, for example, R. Lucas Lucas, "The Anthropological Status of the Human Embryo," in *The Identity and Status of the Human Embryo — Proceedings of the Third Assembly of the Pontifical Academy for Life,* ed. J. de Dios Vial Correa and E. Sgreccia (Città del Vaticano: Librera Editrice Vaticana, 1997), pp. 178-205 (note 52).

41. L. Palazzani, "The Meanings of the Philosophical Concept of Person and their Implications in the Current Debate on the Status of the Human Embryo," in *The Identity and Status of the Human Embryo,* ed. J. de Dios Vial Correa and E. Sgreccia, pp. 93-94.

42. Aristotle, *De Anima,* 412a10-28.

43. L. Palazzani, "The Meanings of the Philosophical Concept of Person," p. 94 [ital-

derstand this, she observes, depends on the failure to distinguish between phenomenology and ontology. "The absence (understood as non-actuation or privation) of properties or functions," Palazzani claims, "does not negate the existence of the ontological referent, which remains such by nature, since ontologically speaking it preexists its own qualities."[44] Raoul Lucas Lucas makes the same argument, as follows:

> It cannot be truly affirmed that there is no person there where manifestations of rationality are lacking. An individual is not a person because he manifests himself as such but on the contrary, he manifests himself as such because he is a person: agere sequitur esse. The fundamental criterion is found in the nature proper to the individual.[45]

Kelly shares the same nature with all other human beings, which means that she is an individual being with a rational soul. The fact that in her case this part of her soul remains inoperative is irrelevant with regard to her being a human person, at least from the perspective of anthropology, because her standing as a human person does not depend on its operations. Act follows being, not the other way around.

There are at least three rejoinders to this argument, however. One is to raise a question about the notion of human acts as "manifestation." The question is: Manifestation of what? When the term means that exterior actions make palpable what is intrinsic to the person — the etymological root of the term "manifestation" — then there is a problem. In the case of profoundly intellectually disabled persons, there appears to be no evidence of an inner source to assume any intellectual capacity on their part. In Kelly's case, I recall that part of her brain is missing, namely, the part where the capacity in question would be located if it existed. If "manifestation" does not necessarily refer to the intrinsic/extrinsic distinction, it may be taken to refer to the distinction between potency and actualization. Thus it might be taken to mean that human being manifests a potency of personhood;

---

ics added]. In the same volume, see L. Melina, "Epistemological Questions with Regard to the Status of the Human Embryo," p. 113.

44. L. Palazzani, "The Meanings of the Philosophical Concept of Person," p. 94.

45. R. Lucas Lucas, "The Anthropological Status of the Human Embryo," p. 198.

even so, the response would have to be that potency as a power to accomplish, or an ability to bring something into effect, also appears to be nonexistent in this case. It is Palazzani's argument that the ontological principle cannot be reduced to its operations. That may be true. But as her formulation of that principle indicates, it does not seem to have any content without reference to an intrinsic potency for these operations. Present in human beings, she says, is "an ontological principle of unification of the properties and the permanence of functions and acts." What is there to be unified without the relevant potency?

Similar reasoning applies to Palazzani's use of Aristotle's distinction between primary and secondary acts. The primary act of being, *actus primus,* in Aristotle's sense means that the soul exists as capacity for the operations proper to it. As Aristotle puts it: "The extent to which a thing has in itself the principle of its generation, determines the measure, if it is not impeded externally, that it will be in potency through itself."[46] But the problem with profound intellectual disability is not the external but the internal impediment, which, following Aristotle's logic, negates the existence of potency "through itself."

My second rejoinder regards the ontological standing of potency as it appears from Palazzani's argument. Her argument runs something like this: the fact that Kelly does not show any sign of human operation is regrettable, no doubt, but this does not affect her status as a human person; whether or not the primary act of being is followed by the secondary act of operation is therefore inconsequential. Whatever else may be the case, Kelly *is* an individual substance of a rational nature as all human beings are, because reason is one of the capacities of the human soul. This is true because the soul is the causal form of her body. However, the question is whether Palazzani's notion of a primary act of being *independent* of a secondary act of operation makes sense at all. If, as Aristotle puts it, "potency is posited in reference to its act," and this means that the act of being constitutes "active potency," then it is hard to avoid the conclusion that without this active potency the act of being remains unfulfilled. If the primary act of being human, an act of the soul as causal form, means the constitution of an active potency proper to its being, then the absence of this po-

46. Aristotle, *Metaphysics,* 1049a13-17.

tency seems to negate the primary act of being.[47] Nonetheless, the Roman Catholic position is that human dignity is "ontological dignity," which means that the human person exists independently of his/her operations. But can he/she also exist independently of the potency for these operations?[48]

This rejoinder, however, seems to gloss over a crucial difference between Aristotle and Aquinas at this point. It has been explained as follows: whereas Aristotle taught the compositeness of the human being derived from the body and the soul as two substances in their own right, Aquinas taught the human being as a substantial unity.[49] The difference depends on Aquinas's concept of the soul as both "incorporeal and subsistent."[50] This claim should not be taken in a dualist sense, because Aquinas, in good Aristotelian fashion, teaches that the human soul is the form of the body.[51] Not *only* is it the form of the body, however, because it also has an operation per se apart from the body. Lucas explains: "The human soul is transcendent; that is, open to the infinite, and possesses being in itself."[52] In this way Aquinas safeguards the soul as being created by God and returning to God after the body is deceased. What Lucas infers from this distinction regarding the human soul is that the being of the soul as ontological principle cannot be undermined by an apparent absence of potency, because it also subsists in itself. It follows that my second rejoinder may have a point against Aristotle, but not

47. If my reasoning here is correct, it follows that Aristotle's view that the intellectually disabled are not real human beings is entirely coherent with his metaphysics.

48. See also M. Cozzoli, "The Human Embryo: Ethical and Normative Aspects," in *The Identity and Status of the Human Embryo,* pp. 260-300.

49. In a sense, Aquinas radicalizes Aristotle because of his doctrine of the immortality of the soul. He thus needs to replace the Aristotelian explanation of the unity of body and soul in terms of compositeness. Thomas argues that the soul as spiritual substance determines *both* the form of the body and the substance of the so formed body, which in Aristotelian metaphysics is impossible. As Father Pegis puts it in his book on Aquinas's conception of the human being: Thomas regards the "composition in man as a form of unity, not a kind of addition" (Pegis, *At the Origins,* pp. 43-44). See also G. Lorizio, "I Believe in the Resurrection of the Flesh," in *The Culture of Life: Foundations and Dimensions — Proceedings of the Seventh Assembly of the Pontifical Academy for Life,* ed. Juan de Dios Vial Correa and Elio Sgreccia (Città del Vaticano: Librera Editrice Vaticana, 2002), pp. 35-51.

50. Aquinas, *Summa Theologica,* I, q.75, a.2.

51. Robert Pasnau, *Thomas Aquinas on Human Nature: A Philosophical Study of Summa Theologica Ia, 75-89* (Cambridge, UK: Cambridge University Press, 2002), pp. 45ff.

52. Lucas, "The Anthropological Status of the Human Embryo," p. 189.

against Aquinas. There is the subsistence of the soul, the divine spark in humankind that is irreducible to any natural condition, including the condition of the rational capacity of the soul as active potency.

This observation brings me to my third rejoinder, which is independent of the first and the second. Granting everything expressed in response to my question so far, what in fact does the Roman Catholic position amount to? The human being is what it is by virtue of an ontological principle, not by virtue of any of its potential operations. This being comes into existence at the moment of its conception, infused with a soul by an act of God. This infusion is both the necessary and sufficient condition of its dignity as a human being. Not even the absence of potency can annihilate this dignity. What does this thesis amount to with regard to human beings like Kelly? Well, since we have eliminated all references to the potential actualization of her being — including the rational capacity of the soul as active potency — there is nothing left to identify Kelly's ensouled nature other than her human body. Since we have no way of identifying her as a human person other than by the fact that she was conceived as a human person, it follows that the counterargument boils down to what I have already conceded. Regarding its origin, a human being is necessarily and sufficiently identified by its being from human descent. But this leaves the problem I posed at the beginning of this chapter exactly where it was when we started this discussion. Kelly's life has no significance whatsoever from the perspective of the human *telos* (as defined by the Roman Catholic position) because the human *telos* involves not only the actualization but also the potency of a rational soul.

6. Potentiality and Actualization[53]

So the remaining claim is this: when it is not actualization but the potency of actualizing human capacities that matters, we must face the

53. The literature I have consulted to understand the concept as it appears in the thought of Aristotle and Aquinas uses both the terms "potency" and "potentiality" as translations of the Latin term *potentia;* some use these English terms interchangeably (see, e.g., Leo J. Elders, *The Metaphysics of Being of St. Thomas Aquinas in Historical Perspective* [Leiden: Brill, 1993], pp. 158-69). On the terminology and its translations, see Pasnau, *Thomas Aquinas on Human Nature*, p. 145.

fact that not all human beings seem to have this potency, even when they are of human descent. According to the Catholic tradition, this cannot be true conceptually; that is, to be of human descent is to have the potency of a rational being. Denying this would result in a contradiction in terms: a human being that is not a human being. In my view, however, the contention is empirically true. The lives I have described so far are proofs of this claim.

A further point of clarification of this conflict regards the relationship between potentiality and actualization. We have learned from the above defenses of the Magisterium's position that there is no relationship of dependency between the two. The potentiality of intellect and will is the potentiality of the rational part of the soul: that is, it has ontological standing of its own and is thus independent from being actualized in the body. Since the relation between potentiality and actualization is not one of dependency, the question arises how this relation should then be conceived. The answer, as we will see, is that potentiality is not dependent on actualization, but the two are correlative.[54] Should this relationship of correlativity be entailed in the Roman Catholic position, the second response to my question regarding the origin and final end of being human finally collapses, because there are human bodies that lack even a minimal potency for developing intellect and will.

To account for a correlation between potentiality and actualization in being human, we may return to Aquinas's teaching that the soul is united with the body as its form.

> It is clear that the first thing by which the body lives is the soul. And as life appears through various operations in different degrees of living things, that whereby we primarily perform each of all these vital actions is the soul. For the soul is the primary principle of our nourishment, sensation, and local movement, and likewise of our understanding. Therefore this principle by which we primarily understand, whether it be called the intellect or the intellectual soul, is the form of the body.[55]

Despite its incorporeality and subsistence, the intellectual soul as form works on the potentiality of the human body. In the *Summa Contra*

54. Elders, *The Metaphysics of Being*, p. 162.
55. Aquinas, *Summa Theologica*, I, q.76, a.1.

Handwritten margin note: *Aquinas on conception vs ensoulment*

Gentiles, Aquinas argues that "the human body . . . is temporarily prior to the soul. It is not then actually human, but only potentially."[56] This not only shows that Aquinas clearly identified this "potentiality for the soul" as a potentiality of a biological entity; it also indicates that he regarded it as a developing biological entity, which allowed him to say that the human body in its fetal stage is ensouled after it has developed the appropriate organ. "Since the soul is united to the body as its form, it is united only to a body of which it is appropriately the actuality. But the soul is the actuality of a body with organs."[57] Even though the intellectual soul has its existence from itself, independently from the body, this does not mean that the two are not related. In fact, Aquinas formulates something close to correlativity when he says that, because the intellectual soul has to gather knowledge from individual things by way of the senses, it has to be united by a body suitable to its operation. "A body is not necessary to the intellectual soul by reason of its intellectual operation considered as such, but on account of the sensitive power, which requires an organ of equal temperament."[58] Because the intellectual operation, "considered as such," is immaterial, the soul does not need a body; because it is the operation of a human soul, it requires a suitable body. Not dependency, but correlation.

These observations clearly indicate that Aquinas did not hold the position of the Roman Catholic Church on the origin of human being at the moment of conception because he believed ensoulment to occur somewhere during fetal development.[59] It is certainly a problem for the Catholic Church not to find unequivocal support for its position in the teaching of its greatest theologian, but this does not necessarily make the position untenable. After all, Aquinas may have been mistaken. Unfortunately for its defenders, however, this is not end of the story.

To see why, let me return to the argument for human personhood to begin at the moment of conception that is found in *Donum Vitae.* Sci-

56. Aquinas, *Summa Contra Gentiles,* II, 89. I owe this quote to Pasnau, *Thomas Aquinas on Human Nature,* p. 121.

57. Aquinas, *Summa Contra Gentiles,* II, 89.

58. Aquinas, *Summa Theologica,* I, q.76, a.5.

59. Pasnau, *Thomas Aquinas on Human Nature,* p. 110. Pasnau draws on G. R. Dunstan, "The Moral Status of the Human Embryo: A Tradition Recalled," *Journal of Medical Ethics* 1 (1984): 38-44, and John Connery, *Abortion: The Development of the Roman Catholic Perspective* (Chicago: Loyola University Press, 1977).

entific evidence has proved that the "biological identity" of the human individual is already constituted in the zygote resulting from fertilization. This supports the notion of "a personal presence at the moment of this first appearance of a human life," according to *Donum Vitae,* which leads it to wonder: "How could a human individual not be a human person?"[60]

60. See above, footnote 12. The entire passage reads:

This Congregation is aware of the current debates concerning the beginning of human life, concerning the individuality of the human being and concerning the identity of the human person. The Congregation recalls the teachings found in the Declaration on Procured Abortion: "From the time that the ovum is fertilized, a new life is begun which is neither that of the father nor of the mother: it is rather the life of a new human being with his own growth. It would never be made human if it were not human already. To this perpetual evidence . . . modern genetic science brings valuable confirmation. It has demonstrated that, from the first instant, the program is fixed as to what this living being will be: a man, this individual-man with his characteristic aspects already well determined. Right from fertilization is begun the adventure of human life, and each of its great capacities requires time . . . to find its place and to be in a position to act." This teaching remains valid and is further confirmed, if confirmation were needed, by recent findings of human biological science which recognize that in the zygote resulting from fertilization the biological identity of a new human individual is already constituted.

Certainly no experimental datum can be in itself sufficient to bring us to the recognition of a spiritual soul; nevertheless, the conclusions of science regarding the human embryo provide a valuable indication for discerning by the use of reason a personal presence at the moment of the first appearance of a human life: how could a human individual not be a human person? The Magisterium has not expressly committed itself to an affirmation of a philosophical nature, but it constantly reaffirms the moral condemnation of any kind of procured abortion. This teaching has not been changed and is unchangeable.

Thus the fruit of human generation, from the first moment of its existence, that is to say from the moment the zygote has formed, demands the unconditional respect that is morally due to the human being in his bodily and spiritual totality. The human being is to be respected and treated as a person from the moment of conception; and therefore from that same moment his rights as a person must be recognized, among which in the first place is the inviolable right of every innocent human being to life. This doctrinal reminder provides the fundamental criterion for the solution of the various problems posed by the development of the biomedical sciences in this field: since the embryo must be treated as a person, it must also be defended in its integrity, tended and cared for, to the extent possible, in the same way as any other human being as far as medical assistance is concerned.

If we reconstruct this argument in a more formal way, it says that (1) human beings develop as human persons by virtue of their natural capacities; (2) scientific evidence shows that each human being from the moment of its conception has these natural capacities because it shares the genotype of its parents. It concludes from these premises that (3) each human being must thus be considered as a human person from that moment onwards. While it is generally undisputed that (1) and (2) are true, it is also obvious that (3) is only true on the further premise that the natural capacities are an *active* potency of the soul that is *inherent* to the developing biological entity from its beginning.[61] Without this further premise, it would still be possible to hold — as Aquinas did[62] — that human personhood occurs at a later stage, when the brain has developed into the organ capable of rational activity. *Donum Vitae* assumes this further premise to be true when it says: "From the first instant, the program is fixed as to what this living being will be: a man, this individual-man with his characteristic aspects already well determined."

These observations show not only that there is a difference of opinion between the official position of the Magisterium and Aquinas on this point, but also that both assume the correlation between the intellectual soul as a formal, immaterial principle and a capacity for the functions of the intellect that reside *within* the developing human body. This correlation is also found in other ecclesial documents. For example, *Veritatis Splendor,* having reminded us "that reason and free will are linked with all the bodily and sense faculties,"[63] explains that, guided by reason and virtue, we discover in the human body "the anticipatory signs" of the gift of self. It then states:

---

61. The distinction between *potentia activa* and *potentia passiva* is found in Aquinas (*Quaestiones disputatae de potentia dei,* q. 1). The first is a potency that is capable of bringing about some change; it is actualized "from within." In contrast, the second is a potency of being changed by something else; it is actualized "from without" (Elders, *The Metaphysics of Being of St. Thomas Aquinas,* p. 164).

62. See n. 61 above. Aquinas was following on what he had read in Aristotle: "As the body is prior in order of the generation of the soul, so the irrational is prior to the rational" (Aristotle, *Politics,* 1334b, 20-22).

63. See n. 19 above.

> Since the human person cannot be reduced to a freedom which is self-designing, but entails a particular bodily structure, the primordial requirement of loving and respecting the person as an end and never as a mere means also implies, by its very nature, respect for certain fundamental goods.[64]

Despite the allusion to Kant, one recognizes the Roman Catholic pattern: the human person cannot be reduced to functions constituting the self as the source of its freedom, which implies that there is no relationship of dependency between the two. At the same time, there is a correlation of potentiality and actualization in that the human person presupposes a "particular spiritual and bodily structure," which from the moment of conception develops the "anticipatory signs" of the gift of the self.

To sum up this extensive discussion, Roman Catholic scholars are surely right in their insistence that the potentiality for developing the functions of the human intellect is not to be reduced to their operations. Aristotle entered the debate on the metaphysics of potency with the same view. Even though the existence of a capacity can only be known from its activity, he argued, it does not follow that a capacity only exists when it is used, because prior to the activity there must be a capacity to act.[65] But, despite this ontological differentiation, this capacity to act requires a body that is suitable to its actualization. At any rate, that is what Aquinas believed. In view of his doctrine of the unity of body and soul, he understood potency and act as correlatives, as did Aristotle.[66] More important, on the point of correlation, however, is the fact that the Roman Catholic

---

64. *Veritatis Splendor,* p. 77.

65. Elders, *The Metaphysics of Being of St. Thomas Aquinas,* p. 160. See also Stanley, who in a different context characterizes Thomas's view in the *Summa Contra Gentiles* to be that intrinsic qualities of the natural inclination of being human must be founded on the properties of the nature in which it resides, but it does not follow that these properties (e.g., the operations of reason and will) determine the inclination itself. Being human is not primarily intellectual, but is primarily directed by an inclination to an end. The inclination, or intrinsic tendency, that Aquinas speaks of is found in all intellectual and non-intellectual beings; of its very nature it precedes all knowledge and all volition. See Gerald F. Stanley, "Contemplation as Fulfillment of the Human Person," in *Personalist Ethics and Human Subjectivity,* ed. George McLean (Washington, DC: Council for Research in Value and Philosophy, 1991), appendix.

66. See n. 53 above.

Church does not diverge from its most venerated teacher. Being human is a personal presence residing in its biological potential that enters the process of actualization from the moment of conception.

The final conclusion must be twofold. The Roman Catholic doctrine on being human can indeed be said to regard the question of our final end as answered by the question of our origin, but its claim to a personal presence embodied in the human zygote shows that it understands this presence not to be separated from its biological substratum. This understanding runs counter to the fact that some human beings do not have a potential for the activity of reason and will residing in their bodies.

7. The Theological Option

In view of this conclusion, there is a response from Roman Catholic quarters that could solve the problem; but this would require locating the solution in the domain of theology. What this solution would be like has already been indicated in the theological anthropology of Pope John Paul II. That is, when the question of our humanity is approached from the ultimate end of sharing the life of God, then the absence of potency does not create the difficulty it does when the question is approached from the perspective of Aristotelian metaphysics. For then it can be said that fulfilling the ultimate end of being human is God's gift. This means that human fulfillment is ecstatic, that is, "from elsewhere" — namely, from God the Father, which is the same as saying that the final destiny of being human is not of our own making.

Presumably, this solution will not be acceptable because Roman Catholicism does not allow theological explanation to be pitched against natural reason, at least not in the domain of anthropology and ethics. The tradition holds that the ultimate end of being human is the proper object of reason, not of faith. More precisely, the tradition maintains a distinction between the natural and the supernatural end of being human. While the first is fulfilled in the perfection of the human faculties through the operation of intellect and will, and is thus attainable by natural reason, the second consists in the *beata visio dei* (seeing God face to face), which is fulfilled in the next life by the gift of God's grace.[67]

67. See Wolfhart Pannenberg's criticism of this classical distinction in Roman Cath-

This distinction enables the proponents of the tradition to argue that some human beings may not attain perfection because they lack the natural capacities that are its object, but it does not follow that they cannot participate in the ultimate end of being human. Sharing the life of God is an end that we are drawn into; it consists of a perfection that is not fulfilled by our own doing. Differences in perfection of intellect and will between human beings are insignificant when compared with the infinite difference in this respect between all human beings and God. Being more or less disabled in intellectual and moral capacity is thus irrelevant when it comes to our ultimate end as it is understood by faith.

Assuming that this is a legitimate interpretation of the distinction, what does it show?[68] It shows that the vacuity of the notion of potentiality need not be the end of the story. Even in the rare cases where there is apparently no possibility of actualization, there still would be a way to bridge the gap between the genesis and telos of being human. No human being will be excluded from our final destination because of limited or unfulfilled human capacities.

Despite the ambiguity that I have tried to uncover in the Roman Catholic position, I don't think this interpretation would be acceptable for the reason I have already mentioned: its implication would be to "save" the humanity of some human beings by moving into the domain of theology. Accepting this move would be accepting at least the following two premises: a theological perspective is required for an account of

olic thought (W. Pannenberg, *Anthropology in Theological Perspective,* trans. Matthew J. O'Connell [Philadelphia: Westminster Press, 1985], pp. 499-500). Pannenberg acknowledges that the distinction brings out in its own way the historical character of being human as in movement from the first Adam to the second, but then adds: "It is also burdened with difficulties, since an 'essential nature' understood according to the philosophical concept of *physis* is incapable of supernatural completion. Conversely, a 'nature' that is ordered to supernatural fulfillment no longer corresponds to the concept of nature in classical Greek philosophy."

68. There is reason to doubt this assumption when we take Aquinas's word for it. In explaining charity as the friendship with God, Aquinas says that in our physical existence — or "sensitive and corporeal nature" — there is no communication with God; only in the spiritual life of our minds "there is communication or fellowship between us and both God and the angels" (*Summa Theologica,* II, II, 23, 1). This claim throws doubt on the attempt to save the universality of being human from the perspective of the supernatural end.

our humanity that is truly universal (as I have claimed in the first chapter); and the crucial importance assigned to the human faculties should be reconsidered (as I will argue in later chapters).

In fact, both premises amount to the same principle, which reflects what this inquiry is pursuing. Because in some human beings there are no intrinsic qualities to build on, any anthropology and ethics that proceeds from such qualities cannot be truly universal for that very reason. By the same token, we can infer that any anthropology and ethics that claims to be truly universal in the face of profoundly disabled human beings cannot but proceed from the principle that whatever quality there is to build on must be extrinsic.

Given its venerated principle that anthropology and ethics build on the natural powers of "man," it is doubtful that Roman Catholic moral theology will be allowed any concession in that direction.[69] Thus it seems that we are left with the conclusion I have stated before: in view of the Roman Catholic doctrine of being human, Kelly's life has no significance from the perspective of the human telos. This does not rule out that her humanity can be affirmed from the perspective of its origin — following Aristotle's rule — but it does rule out her participation in any understanding of human life properly so called.

Not surprisingly, given the arguments we have discussed, the final conclusion is disappointingly confirmed in Spaemann's book on human persons.[70] There Spaemann raises the question of whether all human beings are persons, including the profoundly intellectually disabled, and then answers affirmatively by referring to their origin. The argument to sustain this claim follows the steps we have been considering. From the Roman Catholic point of view, there is no distinction between the human being and the human person: all human beings are persons. Facing the objection that human personhood becomes mani-

---

69. I say "doubtful" because there have been attempts in Roman Catholic thought to overcome the distinction between the natural and the supernatural in the traditional sense. The best-known example from the last century is Henri de Lubac, *The Mystery of the Supernatural,* trans. Rosemary Sheed (London: Chapman, 1967). For an attempt in the other direction, attributing to Aquinas the view that both "contemplation" and "vision" are "natural ends of human being," see Stanley, *Contemplation as Fulfillment of the Human Person.*

70. Robert Spaemann, *Personen: Versuche über den Unterschied zwischen "etwas" und "jemand"* (Stuttgart: Klett-Cotta, 1996).

fest in certain kinds of acts, and that it is thus nonsense to claim personhood for beings incapable of these acts, Spaemann answers that the objection fails to understand the most crucial point. Unless human beings are regarded from the very beginning as persons, there is no point in doing so at a later stage, for example, when they show the right "signs" that force us to recognize their right to be included.[71] A human person is not just an instance of a natural species but a member of a family related through birth. Humankind is not constituted by a set of observable properties but by a community of genealogy.[72]

This is ultimately the ground for the Roman Catholic concept of the person. This position is consistently defended, but it also consistently creates the same problem in the domain of anthropology and ethics when it comes to give an account of profoundly disabled human lives. Because it defines the human good in terms of our capacities for reason and will, there is no way in which human beings with a profound intellectual disability can be said to participate in the human good. They are part of a community of genealogy; they cannot be part of a community of teleology.

The implications of this impossibility are serious, not only in a formal sense of incoherence, but also in a moral sense. For it necessarily informs a negative picture of profoundly disabled lives. To give two instructive examples of this, consider first the view stated by R. L. Lucas. Claiming that human dignity resides in our intrinsic being, he says: "For this reason. . . the sick or handicapped human body enjoys the same value, dignity and rights as the healthy body. Illness is an evil, but not an absolute evil, such as to be extirpated at any cost."[73] Given the logic of the argument, this is indeed all that there is left to say. The handicapped human body represents an evil, albeit not an absolute evil. Similarly, Spaemann argues, human beings with profound disabilities are not considered to be "normal"; instead, we consider them to be "sick."[74] Like other human beings, and unlike animals, the profoundly disabled *have* their nature; but in their case "their nature is defect, and

---

71. Spaemann, *Personen,* pp. 254-59.

72. Spaemann, *Personen,* p. 256.

73. R. L. Lucas, "The Anthropological Status of the Human Embryo," p. 190.

74. Spaemann, *Personen,* p. 259: "Der Debile, mit dem wir nie in personale Kommunikation auf Gegenseitigkeit treten können, wird von uns unvermeidlich nicht als 'normal,' sonders als krank betrachtet."

therefore, also their having this nature is defect."[75] I believe that these statements are sufficient to suggest that there is something amiss with the position that produces them.

Therefore, I regard the foregoing discussion sufficient to conclude that Roman Catholic moral theology's objection to my raising the problem of Kelly's humanity — in the sense I have explained — fails. The basic tenet remains that, as a human being, she is an individual substance of a rational nature even though in her case this nature does not qualify the individual substance that she is, not even in terms of its potentiality. Since everything that is important about human life, according to the Roman Catholic view, is necessarily related to the perfection of our natural capacities, the life of the profoundly disabled human being can only be recognized as a manifestation of natural evil. I take this to warrant the claim that the Roman Catholic objection itself implies a view of human nature that is part of what needs to be replaced. At the least, the logic of Aristotelian entelechy seems to imply that, from the point of view of the good, we will have to say that some human beings are more human beings than others. Exactly the same follows from the hierarchical taxonomy that makes the self-transcending subject the summit of all of creation. Of course, I do not mean to imply by these comments that the Roman Catholic Church would in any way take for granted the ethical implications of its doctrine of being human that I have tried to delineate in this chapter. I am afraid that the truth of the matter is that this doctrine has never been probed in the face of human beings such as Kelly and Oliver de Vinck.

Therefore, it is my conviction that Christian theology should rethink any view that has these implications — or that lacks the grounds to deny them. Theology's point of reference is the belief that we are God's children because God is our loving Father. Christians, together with Jews and Muslims, believe that all human beings are created in the divine image. They do not believe that God created only some human beings in his image. To put it succinctly, but not inaccurately: Christians claim that there are no marginal cases of being human in the loving eyes of God the Father.

---

75. Spaemann, *Personen*, p. 259: "Auch sie haben eine Natur. Aber weil ihrer Natur defekt ist, ist auch das Haben der Natur defekt."

8. The Disabled Person as Mystery

There is yet another response from Roman Catholic quarters, however, that does seem to recognize a tension between these two claims, while at the same time refusing to accept any ambiguity about the status of people with disabilities. In an address during the International Year of Disabled Persons in 1981, Pope John Paul II claimed that the disabled person "is a fully human subject whatever the state or condition of his or her disability with the corresponding innate, sacred and inviolable rights."[76] In explaining this statement, the pope reaffirmed the official position of the Magisterium by saying that "a human being possesses a unique dignity and an independent value from the moment of conception and in every stage of development, whatever his or her physical condition." Anticipating the apparent question with regard to particular kinds of disabling conditions, the pope confirmed:

> A disabled person, with the limitations and sufferings that he or she suffers in body and faculties, emphasizes the mystery of the human being with all its dignity and nobility. When we are faced with a disabled person we are shown the hidden frontiers of human existence, and we are impelled to approach this mystery with respect and love.[77]

Profoundly disabled human beings confront us with a "mystery" in that they show us the frontiers of human existence, but this in no way detracts from their dignity and nobility as humans.

What should we make of this response? In many ways the notion of mystery is quite accurate when it comes to the lives of some people with intellectual disabilities, because we can only guess at what they experience. But in the case of Kelly's life, we are less uncertain about this: in her case, "experience" appears to be nonexistent. However, we can safely conjecture that the pope would say exactly the same thing about Kelly. Her life is also a "mystery of the human being," with all its dignity and nobility.

76. John Paul II, "The International Year of Disabled Persons," in *Ministry With Persons With Disabilities*, Vol. II: Resource File, section III. A., Church Documents, ed. Janice Lalonde Benton (Washington, DC: National Catholic Office for Persons with Disabilities, 1987).

77. John Paul II, "The International Year of Disabled Persons."

If this conjecture holds, it implies that the term "mystery" is not intended to signify a lack of understanding on our part. The pope was not suggesting that we need more scientific research to clarify Kelly's humanity. Rather, the language of mystery is intended to signify reverence for human life that is lived under conditions that defy judgment.[78] On this point one cannot fail to notice the "limitations and sufferings" of disabled lives that lead the pope to speak in this way. In other words, in speaking of mystery the pope was not referring to origin but to purpose and meaning. This is the mystery that remains: How can human beings be human when their condition actually defies the development of natural endowments that supposedly make their lives properly human? The pope's address leaves us wondering about the teleological nature of human life in the case of these human beings.

The pertinence of this question also holds for the Aristotelian solutions that we probed. Nobody has any doubts about the human nature of people with profound disabilities in the sense of their originating from human descent. Neither Kelly's nor Oliver de Vinck's humanity is in dispute in that sense. The remaining problem emerges as soon as we regard their lives from the perspective of the human good. Questions about the good entail questions about purpose — the end of being human. As I have indicated, in engaging contemporary bioethics on issues such as abortion and euthanasia, the Magisterium has been primarily concerned with the *protection* of human life, for which it seeks to provide a ground that is intrinsic to being human. This is the crucial point at issue. Note how Mauro Cozzoli puts it:

> There is no handicap, no matter how crippling, that can annul or reduce the value that a human being has in himself. He is not relative to anything or anyone (other than God), so as to derive his own dignity from another or from others. His dignity is consubstantial with his being a human individual.[79]

78. In any case, it is worth noting that the notion of mystery is conspicuously absent in the reflections that came out of the meetings in the Vatican cited earlier in this chapter. The tone and tenor of the encyclical *Evangelium Vitae* is different, however, not in material content but in the language in which it is cast. Referring to the pastoral constitution *Gaudium et Spes* of the Second Vatican Council, the pope relates the mystery of the human being to the mystery of the Incarnation.

79. M. Cozzoli, "The Human Embryo: Ethical and Normative Aspects," p. 281.

This insistence on a principle *intrinsic to our being* as the indisputable ground of our dignity as persons runs into grave problems once it is confronted by the question I am raising in this book. I am tempted to say that, for human beings like Kelly and Oliver de Vinck, everything may depend on what Cozzoli places in parentheses in the above quotation.

We have already seen the negative accounts of disabled lives — "evil," "defect of nature," "limitations and sufferings" — that follow from the Aristotelian-Thomist concept of the human good. The position put forth by the Magisterium leaves no basis whatsoever to account for disabled lives from a teleological point of view other than their failure to qualify as human lives properly so called. I am not arguing against the Magisterium's stance against liberal bioethics that the origin of human life is a sufficient reason for is protection.[80] But we need not only be able to identify a profoundly disabled infant as a human being in the sense of origin; we also need to face the task of saying what the end of that child's life as a human being is — from a Christian perspective. That is why ethical reflection on the lives of persons with profound disabilities must go beyond questions of rights and protections.

This claim (which I will defend in the next chapter) is certainly consistent with the teleological structure of traditional Roman Catholic moral teaching. However, for us to fit people with profound intellectual disabilities into that structure, we need a different story of who and what we are. We certainly know that persons with profound disabilities belong to particular families, having been procreated by their parents. But, as their parents themselves will be the first to admit, beyond this bare fact are many experiences — good and bad — to be accounted for when it comes to the question of how to live together with profoundly disabled persons and share their lives with them. That question is a question about the final end of human being.

---

80. Lest these remarks be misunderstood, let me emphasize that the point is not to suggest that questions about rights and protections are less important than questions about the human good. They are not. In some ways they are necessarily prior, not logically but practically. Human lives obviously need protection first if there is to be any point in arguing for a particular conception of how they may best be lived. It seems to me that the Aristotelian principle that human beings are identified by human parentage answers the question of who counts as a human being unambiguously.

Chapter Four

Profound Disability
and the Quest for the Good

Their families say just keep them in that place
No one out here can bear to see their faces
We don't believe that they're deprived
Besides we have a right to our own lives
Their families say just keep them in that place
The lawyers say they'll help us change things in the court
It's the only way to open up the doors.

From "The Promised Land,"
a song by Karl Williams and Ruthie Beckwith

1. A Different Agenda

In the previous chapter I concluded that the ethical question with regard to human beings with profound intellectual disabilities is not
only a question of origin; it is also a question of end. The question of
the end, or *telos,* of our being human is a question of meaning and purpose. When we use the pronoun "our" in such a question, we commonly intend to make a claim to something that holds for each human
being. However, the accounts of "our" humanity that we have been
considering thus far do not succeed in this respect. This has been
shown to be true of accounts that are as widely divergent as Roman
Catholic moral theology and social constructionism; but it is also true
of the disability-rights movement. In each of these accounts, the end of
being human is dependent on the capacities of reason and will. In the

one case, the end of being human is to develop these capacities in order to attain moral perfection; but the notion of perfection of human capabilities casts a dark shadow over the lives of the profoundly disabled. In both other cases, the end of being human is primarily understood in terms of moral freedom; but here the lack of development excludes profoundly disabled people from the value of self-identification and self-affirmation. Either way, the lives of such people cannot but appear as defective.

The task ahead is to rethink the question of the final end of being human in view of these outcomes. It is a question posed at the intersection of the disciplines of anthropology and ethics, where the question of the meaning and purpose of being human coincides with the question of the human good. There must be a connection between the two. For example, if being human is defined in terms of "sociability" — "to be human is to share one's life with others for the sake of a common good" — then one cannot define the ultimate human good in a way that disregards sociability, for example, in terms of happiness as pleasure. Similarly, if freedom of the individual is the ultimate end of being human, then a human being must be the kind of entity that is characterized by capacities that enable freedom, such as the capacities of reason and will. These examples indicate that what it is to be a human being is connected to what it is to be a *flourishing* human being. That is, from the perspective of our final end, anthropology and ethics are connected in the question of the ultimate good of human being.

In this chapter, therefore, I will explore the question of final end as the question of ethics. What kind of reflection is involved in raising this question, and what does it imply for the subject matter of this book? What does a concept of the good for being human entail? How is it possible that all human beings participate in the human good, regardless of their state or condition, and what does this imply for the nature of our conception of the good? These questions will set the stage for the construction of the main argument in Parts II and III.

In general, it is fair to say that the ethical literature that addresses disability is mostly concerned with the discussion of practical moral "issues," especially as they arise in the context of daily practices of care and support. Very often this literature uses models of ethical analysis that have been developed in the context of medical ethics and bioethics and take the form of resolving hard cases and dilemmas by laying out moral rules and principles. The resulting analysis commonly produces "ethical guidelines" that are to be applied in the decision-making process within the practices of care and support. Working with the proposed rules and principles should enable us to draw distinctions between the morally right, the morally wrong, and the morally permissible. The ethicist's task is to assist in identifying moral boundaries and to set limits on what people may or may not be morally justified in doing. By contrast, the ethical question I am raising in this chapter is about the ethical evaluation of human life as a whole, rather than that of incidental actions in particular contexts. It focuses on the question of whether there is an end in living a human life: in other words, it prioritizes the quest for the good instead of the quest for right action.

In making this distinction I am not denying that the evaluation of incidental actions may also be framed in terms of the good these actions are intended to bring about. But with regard to our actions, the good is necessarily fractured; that is, a human action may or may not result in *a* good, but that good is necessarily a partial good, often to be evaluated in the light of other possible goods. As the literature on ethical decision-making abundantly shows, "moral issues" are frequently understood as questions about justifiable tradeoffs between conflicting goods. The determination of right action seems to presuppose a plurality of goods that are potentially in conflict, and the task of ethical reflection is seen as the task of resolving such conflicts. Again, the evaluation of human life as a whole, by contrast, presupposes a focus on *the* good. It considers the plurality of goods in view of whether there is an understanding of being human that transcends it. In other words, it presupposes the question of whether there is an *ultimate good* of being human.

I will thus take up this question in the context of a teleological conception of ethics. Within such a conception, what is seen as the distinctive feature of our common humanity informs the meaning and purpose of human existence, not only our own but anybody's — regardless of their state or condition. The main objective is to conceive of the ultimate human good in such a way that the result does not regard the lives of human beings with profound disabilities either as "defective" or as only marginally participating in the good.

There are two reasons for redefining the task of ethical analysis in this sense. Given the fact that many people with profound intellectual disabilities will never be capable of conducting their own lives, the moral principles and values most central to ethical reflection in liberal society are of little help. I am not denying that we should do everything to support people in developing whatever potential they have. Even so, there is no escape from the teleological question. We cannot be content with raising moral questions about what we are allowed or are not allowed to do, because in taking responsibility for the profoundly disabled we cannot avoid raising the question of what kind of life we think is worth pursuing.

The second reason is closely related to the first. In our moral culture, ethical reflection on vulnerable and marginalized people is predominantly shaped by the political values of equality and justice. As I have shown, we see this predominance clearly in the disability-rights movement and in the social constructionist approach to disability, and we will find much of the same in the literature on disability theology. Ethical reflection of this kind aims to protect and promote well-being, as well as freedom and opportunity. In our society the dominant currency to warrant the moral claims to these goods on behalf of marginalized people is the language of rights. However, rights claims can only do as much for vulnerable people as can be enforced on others. The recognition of rights includes people in the community of citizenship, but it does not, per se, include them in the community of the good life. Therefore, rights claims cannot address an essential part of our responsibility in support of people with intellectual disabilities. As is abundantly clear from their current lives, it is quite possible to treat them within the limits of their moral rights without engaging their social and cultural isolation. Claiming equal rights and social justice for disabled people is a way of trying to improve their share of the various goods that our society distributes among its members. Although that is in itself a commendable goal that we must continue to pursue, it does not address the most fundamental question, which is a question of belonging. And the key to that question is to ask why so many people with disabilities do not have friends.

2. The Good of Being Human

What does the notion of an ultimate good of being human entail? If we were to ask people whether they consider themselves to have a good life — and if so, why — they would most likely mention a variety of good things that, when taken together, add up to their own view of a good life. Nevertheless, the sum of any number of goods — family and friends, health, an interesting job, a steady income, a nice place to live, and so forth — may not amount to a life that answers to a conception of the ultimate good. Quite a few people in our Western society seem to have acquired most of the goods on the above list and still have the feeling that there is something missing, the fulfillment of some "higher" purpose in life. On the other hand, many people are perfectly happy with the same set of goods simply because they don't believe life has any higher purpose.

In other words, the notion of the good life can have at least two different meanings. One refers to the enjoyment of the collection of various goods that is acquired during one's lifetime; the other refers to a conception of the ultimate good as the end of living a human life, which transcends the meaning of these various goods, and from which the importance of these goods can be evaluated. To explore this distinction a bit further, let us consider a reflection on the nature of the good by Paul Hunt, an early disability activist in Britain with a severely disabling and progressive illness.[1] One of the challenges that people with disabilities pose to others in their society, according to Hunt, is the fact that they are unfortunate. They do not enjoy many of the goods that people in this society are accustomed to, for example, the opportunity to marry and have children, to earn money, the freedom to move around in a house of their own, and so on. Thus the disabled are underprivileged, says Hunt; but the question is how this affects the evaluation of their lives.[2]

> If the worth of human beings depends on a high social status, on the possession of wealth, on a position as parent, husband, or wife — if such things are *all-important* — then those of us who have lost or never had them are indeed unfortunate. Our lives must be tragically

1. Paul Hunt, "A Critical Condition," in *The Disability Reader: Social Science Perspectives*, ed. Tom Shakespeare (London: Cassell, 1998), pp. 7-19.
2. Hunt, "A Critical Condition," p. 9.

upset and marred forever; we must be only half alive, only half human.[3]

Hunt does not doubt that most people act as if these goods are all-important to a fully human existence; but he brings in another point of view about these goods.

> In my experience even the most severely disabled people retain an ineradicable conviction that they are still fully human in all that is ultimately necessary. Obviously each person can deny this, and act accordingly. Yet even when he is most depressed, even when he says he would be better off dead, the underlying sense of his own worth remains.[4]

Clearly, Hunt is talking about people whose disability has not (yet) affected their capacity to reason; but this does not undermine the logic of his point. Life can be fully human "in all that is ultimately necessary" even though it is deprived of the goods that most people usually regard as all-important. Hunt does not tell us what the ultimate meaning of a fully human life is, but this does not undermine the logic of his point either. His point is that whatever is ultimately necessary for a fully human life must be a good of a different nature. It does not have to be a good that sums up or contains all the other possible goods. The good of a fully human life, whatever it is, is not necessarily equal to the sum total of all the various goods that can be realized in a unified human life — nor is it of the same kind.

The reason that it is not the same kind of good, says Hunt, is that it can be obtained even though one's score on these other goods may be very poor. If it were of the same kind, Hunt implies, the most likely outcome of our quest for the good of being human would be something like the average life of many middle-class people in Western society. Their lives usually consist of accumulating a wide array of social, economic, and cultural goods — a well-paying job, a nice house, free-time activity — that, combined with the personal goods of marriage and family, pretty much sum up what they seek to achieve in their lives. Thus conceived, the accumulation of a variety of goods taken together consti-

3. Hunt, "A Critical Condition," p. 9.
4. Hunt, "A Critical Condition," p. 9.

tutes the good life. However, Hunt suggests that a fully human life is not necessarily made up of such an accumulation. If it were, people with disabilities could never have a fully human life, because their impairment would always bar them in some measure from attaining some of its goods. This would be true for most of the people in impoverished countries as well. To maintain that all the "goods" we Westerners ordinary accumulate in our lives are *all-important* would be to imply that the lives of such people are unfortunate, indeed, *nothing but* unfortunate. More important, it would also imply that, because of what they lack, their lives have to be qualified as only "half human."

It is important to emphasize that Hunt's argument does not imply that the list of accumulated goods is trivial. His denying that such goods are all-important in no way implies that they are unimportant. Nor does the argument imply that we should disregard the goods that result in the pleasure of the body. Particularly for people with intellectual disabilities, food and drink items such as coffee, candy, snacks, fries, and so on — all such goods are very important, even to the point where they need to be restrained in their consumption in order to maintain good health. For people with profound intellectual disabilities, the importance of bodily sensations — color, texture, and sound — has been recognized and supported in recent times with the creation of environments where these sensations can be experienced. Generally, disregarding the goods of the body would be disregarding the body as such, which would imply some kind of anthropological dualism. We need to avoid that. But it is not therefore necessary to accept a view that makes the human good coextensive with the accumulation of what can only be conditional goods.[5]

What follows from this argument is that the ultimate good of being

---

5. Hunt's argument is reminiscent of the structure of Augustine's argument in *De Civitate Dei,* Bk. XIX, where he argues why the wide variety of good things that people value cannot be equivalent to the ultimate good. Not only do philosophers not agree on a list of necessary goods — e.g., Augustine discusses a work of the philosopher Varro, who records a list with 288 possible goods he found in the works of his colleagues — the nature of these goods is such that they can be lost, can be changed into their opposite, and, therefore, cannot be relied on. Augustine's argument aims at a conception that locates the ultimate good in the heavenly city, that is, in the life hereafter, but this does not alter the logical point: that the ultimate good is different in kind from the variety of goods people usually seek in their lives. I will return to Augustine's argument later in this chapter.

human is not necessarily equivalent to the optimal accumulation of the kinds of goods most people in our culture consider constitutive of the good life. Hunt's notion of the "ultimately necessary," whatever it is, has the nature of a "hyper good," to borrow Charles Taylor's term, such that one may lack a large portion of the accumulated goods and still consider oneself to have a good life because of it.[6] Alternatively, one may have an above-average share of the accumulated goods and still have the sense that something is lacking. "Hyper goods" relate to the question of what kind of life we think is worth pursuing. This question cannot be answered simply by pursuing the kind of life that other people in our society consider good, because, as Hunt's argument shows, to do so would make some people's lives inevitably appear unfortunate, even tragic. If the human good is "really" good, it must be good with respect to each of our lives. Therefore, we cannot be content with a concept that some of our lives are not fully human lives because of the goods that cannot be realized within them. Redefining what is ultimately good for human beings — "what is ultimately necessary," in Hunt's terms — is required in order to avoid the implication of an anthropological subdivision with regard to the good life. There is no other way of defeating the claim that living with a profound disability is a life not worth living than arguing for a conception of the good that shows this judgment to rest on a mistake.

I take the point of Hunt's reasoning to be philosophical, not sociological. He is not making a claim about whether or not most people in our culture actually support this view. Presumably, even in affluent Western society, many will accept that the human good is not coextensive with affluence. If they do, they presuppose another kind of good, conceptually at least, that lies beyond the variety of goods that they are accumulating, which is the kind of good that is "ultimately necessary." At any rate, this is the view we find in many accounts of people who are living a disabled life, or are sharing their lives with disabled children or siblings. Whatever unfortunate aspects there may be in such lives, they do not cancel the possibility that those lives, nonetheless, can be very good.

---

6. Charles Taylor, *Sources of the Self: The Making of Modern Identity* (Cambridge, UK: Cambridge University Press, 1989), p. 56. In borrowing Taylor's term, I am not implying that I share his realist conception.

As just one example that befits Hunt's argument, consider a young mother of a child with a disability: even without the prospect of a stable condition for her child, and though she has a lot to worry about, she may tell us that having this child makes every day of her life a joy.[7] Nonetheless, many of us may consider her life very unattractive, given all the things she has to worry about. Presumably, this is the kind of example that Hunt has in mind when he suggests that people with disabilities tend to ask questions about meaning and purpose that do not seem to bother other people.[8] The question of what is ultimately necessary for a fully human life is such a question.

In this book I will pursue this question in terms of belonging.[9] Despite the claims to various kinds of goods that disabled people are entitled to, just as other members of their society are, the ultimate good is about belonging — or so I will argue. Belonging is of itself necessarily other-dependent: wherever you belong, you only belong there because significant others in your life will confirm that you do. In our moral culture, "belonging" is for many people primarily mediated by family, and that is true for many people with disabilities as well. Whatever the importance of one's family, however, being part of it does not exhaust "belonging." This is because family ties depend on natural necessity. We are born into families; more precisely, we are born into *this* family, whether we like it or not. But those who are significant others in our lives are not limited to family members. A full sense of belonging is created by a different relationship, one in which others affirm our sense of belonging, but not because of natural necessity. Not only have I not been able to choose my family; neither has my family been able to choose me. A full sense of belonging does not depend on choice but on being chosen. Therefore, it is more properly found in relationships with friends than within the family. This does not, of course, exclude the

---

7. This statement was made by Brianne Jourdin-Bromley, the mother of Kenadie, a three-year-old girl with primordial dwarfism: the girl is about 26 inches tall. Brianne admits that when Kenadie was born, and her condition turned out to be critical, their life fell apart — "not just a part of you, but all of it." She adds: "Your plan is gone." Hers is an example that could be multiplied by many other parents of disabled children who have learned to take life as it comes and enjoy it one day at a time.

8. Hunt, "A Critical Condition," p. 8.

9. See Jean Vanier, *Community and Growth,* rev. ed. (New York: Paulist Press, 1989), pp. 13-18; *Becoming Human* (London: Darton, Longman & Todd, 1989), pp. 35-68.

possibility for family ties to be similar to bonds of friendship. We usually don't think that we would rather have different parents, or different children, because we really love those we have and would not exchange them for any others. Nonetheless, even though family ties commonly establish loving relationships, they certainly do not guarantee them. Unfortunately, this is often seen in the lives of people with disabilities, especially people with profound disabilities, who are frequently abandoned, which creates great wounds in their lives, as profoundly disabled as they may be. Like any other human beings, people with disabilities need to be chosen as friends.

Establishing the case for friendship as the ultimate good of being human will require a kind of reflection that is very different from thinking about right actions with regard to hard cases and moral dilemmas. In this chapter I will take only a first step in that direction. As I develop the argument, I will add further elements to my critique of the disability-rights approach. The focus on disability rights fails to envision the moral domain constituted by friendship. I will argue that a truly universal concept of a fully human life can only be established when we take friendship to be at its core. This argument can only work if it does not make friendship dependent on human agency, but that is a claim to be postponed to Part III. Even though the intellectual and moral faculties of most people with intellectual disabilities are under-developed, this does not preclude them from the possibility of being chosen as friends. Friendship is a possibility that may be realized for any human being, regardless of her or his condition. We will realize what is ultimately necessary for these people when we know how to be their friends.

3. "Disability Culture"

Let me continue my engaging of the disability-rights approach by pointing out a development that seems to express a concern similar to what I have been suggesting above. Within the disability literature, there is an emerging interest in the issue that is introduced under the heading of "disability culture."[10] Identifying "disability pride" and "diversity," this

10. On the notion of a "disability culture," see Steven E. Brown, *A Celebration of Di-*

notion of culture signals a shift from matters of access and participation (rights and justice) to cultural representations and self-portrayals of people with disabilities in terms of their "alternative values."[11] While the first has been a struggle for redefining the moral boundaries within society, the development of a disability culture is aiming at establishing much more than this. The aim is to promote pride in disability as a positive identity that can be seen in the cultural activities created by people with disabilities themselves.[12]

Thus there is an emerging interest in moving beyond the paradigm of rights by paying attention to "value." One way to describe the development of disability culture would be to say that the politics of equal access has been expanded into a politics of identity.[13] This may suggest that the limitation of the disability-rights approach that is the subject of my criticism has already been taken on within that approach itself. But, as we shall see, this interest is expressed in ways that continue to presuppose the anthropology of liberal citizenship I have described in

---

versity: An Annotated Bibliography about Disability Culture, 2nd ed. (Las Cruces, NM: Institute for Disability Culture, 2002). James L. Charlton, *Nothing about Us without Us: Disability, Oppression, and Empowerment* (Berkeley: University of California Press, 1998) discusses what he calls the "moral meaning of disability" as an argument about the good life in terms of disability culture; see also Nancy L. Eiesland, "Barriers and Bridges: Relating the Disability Rights Movement and Religious Organizations," in *Human Disability and the Service of God: Reassessing Religious Practice,* ed. Nancy L. Eiesland and Don E. Saliers (Nashville: Abingdon Press, 1998), pp. 200-229.

11. Paul K. Longmore, "The Second Phase: From Disability Rights to Disability Culture," *Disability Rag and Resource* 15 (Sept./Oct. 1995): 6-7. See also Longmore, *Why I Burned My Book and Other Essays on Disability* (Philadelphia: Temple University Press, 2003), Ch. 11. The most celebrated case for disability culture has been the experience of deaf people on Martha's Vineyard: see Nora Ellen Groce, *Everyone Here Spoke Sign Language: Hereditary Deafness on Martha's Vineyard* (Cambridge, UK: Cambridge University Press, 1985).

12. See the mission statement of the Institute for Disability Culture: "Our mission since 1994 has been to promote pride in the history, activities, and cultural identity of individuals with disabilities throughout the world" (www.dimenet.com/disculture).

13. See Longmore, "The Second Phase," p. 224, where he speaks of two complementary aspects of the disability movement. Longmore's essay is somewhat disappointing in what it has to say about disability culture. Two-thirds of his essay is about the "first phase" and thus not about culture at all. Most of what he has to say about the latter is about disability studies. Since he defines that as being in service to the disability-rights movement, it does not tell us much either.

Chapter One. Not only does the notion of a disability culture rely on the crucial importance of self-representation by people with disabilities; it also emphasizes the political nature of this development. Here is how the notion of a disability culture is expressed on a website called, quite appropriately, *Disability Cool:*

> Disability culture is: pride in being who we are and translating our pride into changing the way media portrays us. It's reveling in sharing common experiences and enjoying the company of one another. It's recognizing the role we have as legitimate members of society and the value of our lives. It's being proud of our history and not feeling isolated. It's buying products developed and sold by other people with disabilities with our symbols on them. Disability culture has its greatest influence when people with disabilities write their own books, do their own research, paint, draw, film, and express themselves through the use of language and image.[14]

"Enjoying the company of one another" surely addresses the concern I have expressed earlier in this chapter, just as the entire quotation suggests that the disability movement itself is experienced as a space of belonging. Consequently, there is everything to be said for disability culture because it pays attention to those matters that rights do not address. It is equally clear, however, that the very aim of the disability culture puts it under the same rubric as some of its predecessors, for example, "women's culture" and "gay culture." Constitutive of these cultures is the value of self-identification and self-affirmation, which are the main characteristics of the politics of identity. To the extent that this is the case, disability culture inevitably reflects the same limitations of the disability-rights approach's theoretical framework that I observed in Chapter 1.

It is accurate to say, then, that should disability culture identify a limitation in the main strategies of the previous era, it does so mainly by redefining the nature of political action.[15] It does not identify the

---

14. I owe this reference to Eiesland, "Barriers and Bridges: Relating the Disability Rights Movement and Religious Organizations," p. 212.

15. The shift reflects the same development that we have found in the more recent literature about the social constructionist approach to disability, which introduces the "politics of identity" to acknowledge the embodied experience of people with disabilities. See Ch. 2 of this book.

limitation that is reflected in the notion of a hierarchy of disability. Again, this in no way denies that people with disabilities deserve full support in destroying negative images of disability that our "able-bodied" culture produces. It is to deny, however, that "disability culture" as it is presented is sufficiently inclusive for people with profound intellectual disabilities Whenever the lives of disabled people are portrayed, one rarely finds a positive account that includes people with profound disabilities.[16] It is thus crucially important to go beyond a philosophy that presupposes a conception of the human good exclusively built on the capability of self-expression and self-affirmation. Without acknowledging this limitation, the disability-rights approach will leave unchallenged the barriers that produce images of the lives of people with intellectual disabilities as more or less "defective."

As it stands, the philosophy informing disability culture can be summed up in the principle that a good life for me is one that I myself can proudly affirm as my own. It is important to be clear about what this principle entails for people with an impaired sense of self. Not only does it presuppose that having a good life requires a particular psychological condition, but also that having a good life is dependent on what I can choose to do with my life. Conceptions of the good that make it dependent on "choice" presuppose that your life will be better to the extent that you are able to realize the set of conditions you would have chosen had there been a choice. It is often said that in liberal society the good life is lived "from the inside," which means that good lives are "first-personal." This not only shows that liberal conceptions of the good have subjectivity as a necessary condition; it also shows that these conceptions assume that the good life is constituted by a particular kind of first-personal *act*. Decisive is the fact that I can positively identify my life as my own because it is what I want it to be: "pride in who I am" and "reveling in sharing common experience," as the above account of the disability culture puts it. In other words, such a conception of the good is decidedly activist: it sends the message that the good life is of our own making, which is, of course, the message of modern culture per se — the same culture that "produces" disability.

By way of contrast, let's consider a different conception, which does not so much eliminate the role of subjectivity as construct it differently.

16. See the references in n. 6 on p. 26, above.

Subjectivity appears in this conception not primarily as act, but as response. Its modus operandi is not that of a project but of an encounter. As an example, consider the following reflection by Mrs. de Vinck, mother of Christopher de Vinck and his profoundly disabled brother, Oliver.

> For many, many years, I was confined to the house, alone and without the support of relatives or friends. My husband was at work all day and I was with Oliver and the other five children. This enforced seclusion was difficult for me; I had a restless, seeking spirit. Through Oliver I was held still. I was forced to embrace a silence and solitude where I could "prepare the way of the Lord." Sorrow opened my heart, and I "died." I underwent this "death" unaware that it was a trial by fire from which I would rise renewed — more powerfully, more consciously alive.[17]

Had Mrs. de Vinck pursued the life she wanted for herself, she probably would not have chosen the life that eventually became hers. As a matter of fact, the woman whose "restless, seeking spirit" longed for a different life had to "die" in order for a new self to emerge. If she had conceived of the good life in terms of self-expression and self-affirmation, Mrs. de Vinck probably would not have allowed this to happen; she would have resisted, or at least resented, her "fate." As we know, emancipatory feminism has rejected this kind of self-sacrifice precisely because, as Mrs. de Vinck testifies, it is a response to a role that is not voluntarily assumed. Somehow, though, the account she gives of her life transcends the absence of choice. She learned to see her life with Oliver as a gift; she inferred that acceptance creates unexpected rewards of its own.[18]

Of course, people who believe in "choice" may also recognize that their lives are gifts. If they do, however, they tend to understand this in terms of life's contingencies. "Choice" is central to one's moral views if one believes that the meaning of whatever is happening in one's life is to shape the possible and the impossible. That is, life's conditions are

17. Christopher de Vinck, *The Power of the Powerless: A Brother's Legacy of Love* (New York: Doubleday, 1990), p. 94.
18. Elsewhere I have discussed this kind of experience in terms of a transformation of the self; see Reinders, *The Future of the Disabled in Liberal Society*, pp. 175-92.

given as the conditions of choice; they have no meaning attached to them other than that. Mrs. de Vinck's account is different precisely in this respect: there was meaning to be found in certain things even when she would never have chosen them to be part of her life. The important distinction here is the distinction between the *gift* of life and the *givenness* of life. When "choice" dominates one's moral view, life appears as *datum,* but not necessarily as *donum. Datum* refers to "gift" as contingency: there is givenness, but there is no giver. In contrast, *donum* refers to givenness that implies purpose. The gift of life implies a giver who may have had a purpose in mind by "sending" whatever it is that happens to you. This is clearly how Mrs. de Vinck came to envision her life when she learned to see her caring for Oliver as a way of preparing to receive the gift.

It can be argued, of course, that Mrs. de Vinck's account of her own life can also be read as being about self-expression and self-affirmation. If so read, there is nonetheless an important difference: what she expresses and affirms is not a life that has the choosing self as its object. The choosing self is precisely what in her view had to die in order for the new self to rise from its ashes like a phoenix. For people whose moral views are dominated by "choice," life may also be a gift, but only in the sense that it provides them with a given set of opportunities to choose from. In the moral universe of such people, the choosing self is very much present at center stage. This explains why "choice" in itself is without boundaries, because it presupposes that the good life for human beings is coextensive with a chosen life. What follows is that "goodness" and "meaning" is conferred on people's lives by virtue of their own authorization. As we have already seen in Chapter 1, this is usually expressed by the claim that people need to be respected as "the authors" of their own lives, which supposedly is true for people with intellectual disabilities as well. In order to have a life that is properly called "good," they must be in control of how they choose to live their lives. The good life results from their own project if it is to be a good life *for them.*

It will be clear that this conception of the good life excludes all those incapable of purposive agency. It excludes those human beings who, because of their impairment, cannot affirm their own being. Given the account of a "disability culture" I have traced above, it follows that its emphasis on self-expression and self-affirmation as the essence of that culture reinforces once again the hierarchy of disability I discussed in the first chapter. Consequently, if there is to be an inclusive account of the good life for human beings, it cannot depend in any way on the centrality of the choosing self. In this respect, the lives of people with profound intellectual disabilities pose a serious challenge to our ethical thinking. Moral views that place the choosing self on center stage inevitably will cast serious doubts on whether their lives can be good and meaningful at all. Therefore, an important task of this book is to criticize conceptions of the human good that generate these doubts, and to scrutinize the premises on which they rest.

4. The Ethics of Access

If one goes through the disability-rights literature to understand the kinds of goods that equal rights and social justice are supposed to secure, one cannot fail to notice the ubiquity of *spatial metaphors* that are universally expressed in these claims. As this literature makes abundantly clear, people with disabilities insist that barriers that exclude them from full participation be removed, which indicates that their claims are about space and equal access to space. They seek the elimination of barriers and boundaries when it comes to buildings, services, jobs, schools, recreation parks, clubs, and housing. They also seek the elimination of barriers and boundaries in the symbolic world, the kind that exist, for example, in discriminatory language. Consequently, metaphors of space abound in claims about "opening up" and "widening" and "broadening" our horizons to welcome difference and diversity in our communities. Equal rights and social justice demand that public spaces in all of these locations no longer be exclusively occupied by "temporarily able-bodied" people, and that they be opened up to people with disabilities so that exclusion stops and inclusion can begin.

However, the various goods to be secured by these claims are goods that are sought because they create opportunities for human action; and the logic driving such demands is that, in order to live a fully human life, people must be enabled to do things. Disability-rights claims are thus claims to moral space for *action:* it is when people have access to housing, jobs, and education that they can begin to find their own way of living their lives. The same goes for the other kinds of goods, such as the material goods of physical accessibility to public spaces, or the psychological goods of respect and self-esteem. People with disabilities seek all these goods because they enable them to be in control of their own lives, as well as of the stories told about their lives. In this view, the aim of claims to equal rights and social justice is to establish the conditions of individual freedom. It is when people have opportunities that they can explore for themselves how to live their lives.

This is the logic that much of Western moral culture presupposes in its views of what it means to be human. It also underscores the disability-rights literature. It explains the ubiquity of its spatial metaphors and shows that the need for legitimate space for action is grounded in the capacity for human agency that enables us to explore life's opportunities as they present themselves to us. It is because of these opportunities that we can choose who we want to be rather than having our lives determined by powers beyond our control. At its most fundamental level, the disability-rights literature confirms the anthropological claim to human freedom as an *intrinsic* quality. Therefore it favors independence and self-determination. We can see the close connection between the anthropology of liberal citizenship and the ideal of human freedom as the ideal of the choosing self. It explains why self-representation and self-affirmation are regarded as important, particularly for people with disabilities. These are crucial values because they change the "cannot do" usually attached to the perception of disability into the "can do" usually attached to the affirmation of citizenship.

However, in its celebration of individual human freedom as a "hyper good," the disability-rights literature fails to address the needs of human beings for whom purposive agency exists only at the fringes of their lives, or does not exist at all. Even when we take into account, as we should, that the capacity for agency comes in degrees, the fact remains that some human beings are very far from knowing what it is to choose for themselves what they want. And to the extent that choosing for oneself what one wants depends on the capacity for self-identification and self-affirmation, the logic underlying human freedom as a "hyper good" has marginalizing effects. Not only does it pose human agency in control of itself on center stage; it also implies that some human beings

139

belong at best only at the fringes of its conception of the human. The spatial metaphors supporting access to public spaces for action will inadvertently produce spatialization at the margins for people with profound disabilities.

Therefore, the disability-rights approach to inclusion endorses a view of being human that turns the inclusion of these people into an uphill battle. More than anything else, the disability-rights movement has hammered home the claim that the notion of "disability" is a disabling notion per se; by implication, the proper way to think about people with disabilities is to focus on what they can do rather than on what they can't do. However, in pushing action as the rationale for its claims to equal rights and social justice, the disability-rights movement has made life for the "temporarily able-bodied" much easier than it should have been; for it has left intact their most cherished treasure, namely, their self-image as "doers" and "achievers." In fact, it has done nothing but reinforce that self-image.

How very convenient for me, and for the likes of me — readers and writers of texts, shall we say — that people with disabilities only demand a relationship between equals. A relationship of equality is usually understood in terms of reciprocity. Nowhere am I asked to change in any way; I am only asked to allow people with disabilities to have the opportunities to act that I have. That is, I am only asked to imagine myself in their position and then to consider how I would feel being excluded as they have been. Actually, disability-rights advocates frequently appeal to my enlightened self-interest in helping me to consider the possibility that one day I myself may be dependent on the recognition of these rights. This is how Joseph Shapiro makes the point:

> The disability movement, however, is a reminder that all Americans have a mutual investment in protecting civil rights. As people with disabilities point out, anyone can join the nation's population of 49 million persons with disabilities at any time.[19]

19. Joseph P. Shapiro, "What the ADA Teaches Us about the Value of Civil Rights," *The Journal of Religion in Disability & Rehabilitation* 2, no. 4 (1996): 43-47; see also Diane Driedger, *The Last Civil Rights Movement: Disabled People's International* (New York: St. Martin's Press, 1989), p. 2.

This appeal to enlightened self-interest is not at all uncommon for a defense of equal-rights claims in contemporary moral philosophy.[20] What is asked of the "temporarily able-bodied" in this philosophy is precisely to consider the temporary nature of their able bodies, which, if they do, will make them see their own interest in considering the reversibility of places in the moral fabric of society.

What strikes me as quite mistaken in the appeal to enlightened self-interest is the suggestion that it has any force of constituting a *moral* obligation. All that this appeal does for me is to demand that I respect disabled human beings because, if I eventually end up in the same position they are in, I would expect the same from others. Whether this rule has any consequence for what I am motivated to do must thus depend entirely on how much weight I will give to the eventuality I am envisioning. This weight may not amount to much, assuming that I am a self-interested person. Suppose I say that, if that bad eventuality should take place, against all odds, I would rather be dead. So I carry a do-not-resuscitate order with me wherever I go. Given that this is my view, how can enlightened self-interest bind me to the interests of disabled persons? As is the case with all appeals to self-interest as a basis for moral obligation, they only work for morally disposed people.

The most important failure of such appeals, however, is that they presuppose that morality takes the form of social constraint. This is what limits rights and justice claims. Nowhere are citizens challenged in their belief that what makes them special as human beings is determined by what they are capable of accomplishing. Nowhere do rights and justice claims leave them questioning their self-affirmation as doers and achievers. The only thing we are asked to do is to make room for people with disabilities, stop calling them names, and grant them the opportunities that we want for ourselves.

This way of looking at the logic of the claims to equal rights and social justice reveals what I consider the most serious weakness of the approach based on it. Like most of modern political philosophy, it defines

20. The most influential of such defenses is found in John Rawls's widely acclaimed work *A Theory of Justice*, which makes our recognition of the rights of other people dependent on the recognition that we may eventually find ourselves in their place. For a discussion of Rawls's theory from the perspective of people with intellectual disabilities, see Reinders, *The Future of the Disabled*, Ch. 8. For further references to similar arguments based on enlightened self-interest, see p. 178, n. 21, below.

a negative relationship. The disability-rights literature argues, explicitly as well as implicitly, that if I want to avoid ending up in the position of a disabled person, I'd better acknowledge the claims to equal rights and social justice. Beyond that, I am entirely secure in the freedom of minding my own business, whatever I take that business to be.

I consider this to be its most serious weakness because human beings with intellectual disabilities, and particularly those with profound intellectual disabilities, are not going to thrive on negatively defined moral relationships. In endorsing the logic of enlightened self-interest, the disability rights literature has left me off the hook with regard to the most critical issue. In my listening to persons with intellectual disabilities, it has struck me that they long to share their lives with others, but not necessarily in the sense of being admitted, or allowed to be present, as a matter of their right. They do not seek to be tolerated because of claims to equality and justice; they long to share the lives of people like me because they want to be chosen by people like me. In other words, they want to belong, not on grounds of moral equality, but on the grounds of my predilection. This longing confronts us with a question that rights and justice claims cannot possibly address. If I am to choose a disabled person, there must be a desire on my part, a predilection, on the grounds of which her presence is desirable.

What ultimately prevents people with intellectual disabilities from full participation in our society is the fact that they are generally not seen as people we want to be present in our lives. We don't need them.[21] Not being wanted by significant others, as every psychologist can tell, is the cause of serious personality disorders in many people. In the lives of intellectually disabled persons, the role of valued significant others falls mainly to their relatives and to their professional caregivers. Apart from those relationships, their lives usually do not include many significant others, which means that the most important social role in human life is rarely open to them. They are rarely chosen as friends.

The failure in the disability-rights literature to address this point is

21. Here again the danger of considering their presence as valuable *for us* reappears. This danger is apparent in arguments claiming that people with disabilities have positive things to contribute when they are enabled to participate in our clubs, our schools, our workplaces, our churches, and so on. However well intended they are, such claims are wrongheaded because they claim the presence of persons with disabilities on grounds of instrumental value. I will return to this point below.

seen in the fact that, among the many authors in the field who promote "community care," there are only a few that insist on finding friends in the community as a necessary condition for the success of this policy.[22] Life in our local communities may not be all that salutary for disabled people if they do not have friends. However, it should not be surprising that the importance of friendship is rarely taken into account. Rights and justice claims have the capacity to open up public spaces, but they do not suggest what to do with them.[23] No doubt people with disabilities should be allowed access to institutions and organizations, which is what rights and justice claims on their behalf can secure. However, these claims do not command moral attitudes other than those necessary to pay respect to their rights. That is, they do not command attitudes of fellowship and friendship.

Experiencing fellowship and friendship is important for people with disabilities not only because of their mental health, but also because to be friends with others, I will argue, is what we are meant to be. To establish a convincing argument for the recognition of equal rights and social justice, an appeal to my enlightened self-interest may be successful, depending on whether I am sufficiently aware of my own vulnerability as a merely "temporarily able-bodied" person. A convincing argument for friendship, however, requires something entirely different. I need to change as a person. Particularly, I need to change with respect to how I regard my own humanity. This is why I said in Chapter 1 that "self-image" is an important key in ethical reflection on the lives of people with disabilities. When I am convinced that the value of my life depends on what I make of it, the unaccomplished lives of people with disabilities must appear as defective to me, which is hardly a basis for being attracted to friendship with them. Thus the crucial question is what concept of the human good makes me consider the possibility of being such a friend, and how I get to the point of trying. My objection to the ethical framework underlying the disability-rights literature is that it cannot even begin to address such a question.

22. A. Novak Amado, ed., *Friendships and Community Connections Between People With and Without Developmental Disabilities* (Baltimore: Paul H. Brookes Publishing Co., 1993). A pioneer in this area is Robert Perske; see Perske, *Circles of Friends: People With Disabilities and Their Friends Enrich the Lives of One Another* (Nashville: Abingdon Press, 1988).

23. On this point, see also Hans S. Reinders, "The Good Life for Citizens with Intellectual Disabilities," *Journal of Intellectual Disability Research* 46, part 1 (Jan. 2002): 1-5.

5. Distinct Motivations

To sustain this objection, let me return to the spatial metaphors in the disability literature. The spaces to which access is demanded as a matter of equal rights and social justice, I have argued, allow for the pursuit of various kinds of goods. They may be physical locations, such as buildings, that are accessible once the barriers for entering them are cleared. Alternatively, they may be social "locations," such as roles and positions, or programs for which people with disabilities were not hitherto eligible, such as becoming a homeowner or the minister of a church. Alternatively, they may also be symbolic "locations" that are occupied by images and stereotypes grounded in "ableist" languages and concepts, which create cultural barriers to disabled persons expressing themselves. Following the disability-rights literature, the main task in deconstructing and reconstructing these locations is to make sure they are opened up for persons with disabilities. Let us think about what might be required in each of these cases to make this happen.

For example, if buildings need to be made accessible, we must change the regulations for appropriate building and specify regulations for accommodating existing buildings. In the case of positions and opportunities, the rules that need adjustment are procedural: if people with disabilities need to have access to a certain kind of job, or a particular kind of benefit, the criteria for eligibility that previously ruled them out must be changed. Furthermore, the proper authorities must implement mechanisms of control and redress in case the new procedures are ineffective to remove existing barriers. Something similar is true for opening up symbolic spaces. As an example, consider the issue of how to name persons with disabilities. In previous times, the power of naming was within the domain of medicine; that was later transferred to the domain of psychology. Reclaiming the power of naming, however, disability-rights advocates adopted the rule that how disabled people are named and identified should be decided by the people with disabilities themselves. Consequently, as each of these examples indicates, what is crucially needed is a change of the rules that control access to these spaces — physical, psychological, and spiritual.

However, breaking down existing barriers is not only a matter of changing the rules that uphold them; the new rules that replace them must also be followed. Here the question is: What makes people follow these new rules? When we think of it, we will see that there can be a variety of reasons for doing so. For example, as a scholar who is in conversation with the field of disability studies, I may be keen on using "correct" language simply to avoid the risk of being ignored if I don't. Public institutions may create accessible buildings because there will be expensive lawsuits followed by considerable fines if they don't. Organizations depending on public support may want to include people with disabilities in their membership for reasons of projecting a positive image. In many cases, as politicians and lawmakers know very well, people follow new rules not because they are convinced that they are right but because they fear the sanctions that will otherwise be imposed. With regard to such cases, moral philosophers speak of actions that stem from "external motivations." It is not the rule itself, but other people's response to my failure to comply with it, that motivates me to follow that rule. People may comply with the rules for reasons of self-interest: they do not want to pay the price for failing to do so. If this is the case, they lack a moral motivation on "internal grounds." The reason for changing their behavior is not their support for the objectives of the rule. By changing their behavior they only mean to create an appearance; the change does not spring from sincere commitment.

In the example of my using politically correct language, my motivation has nothing to do with paying my respect to disabled people, but only with my interest in not being ignored by fellow scholars in disability studies. Perhaps I will not be invited to give presentations at conferences, or I will not be allowed to publish in certain journals if I don't use politically correct language. Similarly, an executive who is responsible for making his building accessible to wheelchair users may feel the need to comply with the new regulations; but because he is not sincerely motivated, he may dispense with it at minimal cost, making wheelchair users feel as though they are sneaking in the back door. The dean responsible for admitting students with a disability to her school may follow the correct procedures and yet obstruct the objective of those procedures by refusing to offer facilities for extra needs, such as flexibility in class hours or resources for extracurricular support. The leadership of the congregation can decide to start a program for celebrating disabled church members to make them feel at home in their church, but they may fail to assist in dealing with transportation problems. Many similar examples can be drawn from the disability-rights literature.

What each of these examples shows is that breaking down the barriers of exclusion can be done in ways that are barely supported by appropriate motivations. Complying with regulations in a normal way, paying lip service to their objectives, saying one thing but doing another, hypocritical affirmation stemming from self-interested motives — all these behaviors take place and have many faces. And in each of these behaviors we find the operation of "external" rather than "internal" motivation. As we shall see, this aspect of motivation highlights an important point about claims to equal rights and social justice. By their very nature, these claims presuppose the absence of internal motivation on the part of those whose behavior needs changing. That's why we have the language of rights and justice in the first place; and they have been named, quite appropriately, "the colder part of morality."[24]

We have and use these regulations because we need devices that will coerce people to do what they are otherwise not inclined to do. For example, nobody would have any need to claim the right of disabled students to enter an educational program if the school offering the program had its doors wide open and welcomed them in person on its doorsteps. If people's hearts and minds were already open to include persons with disabilities in their congregation, rights and justice claims to that effect would be pointless. Because people may not be internally motivated by the goods the new rules of access seek to secure, we use claims to equal rights and justice to make them comply, irrespective of their own particular motivation. Thus we find descriptions of how these rules come to be enforced by law in terms of "from good will to civil rights."[25]

If people were internally motivated to support the objectives of inclusion, the very language of rights and justice would be redundant. But because we are not in that situation, we do need rights and justice claims, though they can only remedy a limited range of social evils. They undoubtedly represent an important tool for change, but the

24. John R. Lucas, *On Justice* (Cambridge, UK: Blackwell, 1980).
25. Richard K. Scotch, *From Good Will to Civil Rights: Transforming Federal Disability Policy,* 2nd ed. (Philadelphia: Temple University Press, 2001).

change they can effect is predominantly of a legal nature. They cannot force people into changing their attitudes. To quote from Stuart Govig, a theologian with a disability: "The stairs may have been made accessible, but the stares remain."[26] Govig says:

> The stare barrier is another matter. In battling it to gain compassion and human rights we confront more elusive enemies: hidden fears and habits of "keeping one's distance." Persons with disabilities meet people who refuse to look their way at all, a degrading and humiliating experience. Or, they meet indifferent people, or those bent on satisfying their curiosity, an irritating experience.[27]

Whether one takes this to be a serious problem largely depends on whether one believes that, in compliance with rights and justice claims, people will also change their moral attitudes over the long haul. There are different opinions on this question, which is due not only to different perspectives but also to different experiences. Looking at the Unites States after fifteen years with the Americans with Disabilities Act, one gets a mixed message. The results have significantly changed the lives of many people with disabilities in the United States; at the same time, complaints about negative attitudes toward disability continue to be voiced in the literature. This is how the President's Committee on Employment for People with Disabilities assessed the situation in 1999:

> Over the last decade, many changes have taken place in the fabric of life for persons with disabilities. Laws have been passed that are breaking through many of the barriers, which have kept people with disabilities out of the mainstream. However, we cannot legislate against attitudinal barriers; that is the one frontier which each of us must confront. We must all work to remove the negative and stereotypical attitudes from our minds, writings and actions. For too long, people with disabilities have been depicted as caricatures — some

26. Stuart Govig, *Strong at the Broken Places: Persons with Disabilities and the Church* (Louisville: Westminster/John Knox, 1989), p. 11.

27. Govig, *Strong at the Broken* Places, p. 12. My argument here is to point out that "human rights" are questionable as an effective means to change the behavior of people who are in the habit of keeping their distance. The reason is that the nature of rights is to bind us externally, not internally.

evil, some to be pitied and all to be avoided. None of these images reflect people with disabilities who have skills and talents needed by today's employers.[28]

In other words, the law can legislate behavior, but not attitudes. Whether or not one takes this statement to be categorically true, it seems to be clear that the law is not well suited to force people into welcoming and appreciative attitudes regarding their disabled fellow human beings. Many disabled people who have experienced discrimination voice this concern. Consider a passage from a song by the self-advocacy group Speaking for Ourselves, which came out of a meeting celebrating the inauguration of the Americans with Disabilities Act in 1992. It makes clear what these people expected from their non-disabled fellow humans:

> You're gonna see me,
> in some place new.
> You may be angry,
> but won't be a thing you can do.
> You can bolt all your padlocks,
> bar all your doors.
> I'll hire me a lawyer
> and see you in court.

The chorus joyfully adds to the verse: *"Hey, hey, hey, for the ADA."*[29] I take

28. Quoted from the President's Committee on Employment of People with Disabilities Education Kit (1999): www.pcepd.gov/pcepd/pubs/ek99.

29. The title of the song is "Americans With Disabilities Act Song." The complete text of the song runs as follows:

> The curbs are cut, the ramps are down.
> The lifts are in, so gather 'round.
> The clouds are gone and the sky is blue.
> We got our rights in 1992.
> Chorus: Hey Hey Hey for the ADA
>
> Gonna find me a job, gonna ride the bus.
> You kept us down for so long,
> but now there's no stopping us.
> Chorus: Hey Hey Hey for the ADA
>
> Gonna get an education, check into a hotel room.
> And when they start selling tickets,

these lines to underscore in crystal-clear language that organized groups use legislated rights to get from the public and institutions what they otherwise are not inclined to let them have, or do, or enjoy — such as the right to a home of one's own and an education, or the right not to be discriminated against. As the president's committee points out, however, these rights cannot remove the social evil of avoidance, or of stereotyping and caricature. Rights and justice may succeed in the remedying the results of aversive behavior, but they do not remedy the aversive attitudes that produce the behavior. Self-advocates celebrating the ADA would no doubt prefer no angry faces and no stares. They would undoubtedly rather not use the right to go to court; but if you want to force people into a position where they have to comply, this is what you need to do. They will decide to comply with the new rules for reasons of enlightened self-interest: to avoid being sued. Depending on political circumstances, they may even think it expedient to feign support for these rules.

The distinction between external and internal motivation illuminates the limitations of rights and justice claims. By their very nature, such claims motivate primarily externally; that's their point. They coerce people into compliance even when they may not consider the objectives of the rights in question to be *good*. This is not to deny that rights claims can motivate both internally and externally; but when they motivate internally they are redundant, because then people already support the good to be secured by these claims. They need no push in the right direction because they are already attracted to it, which is in the nature of the good. In contrast, rights claims push people in a direc-

---

might even take a ride to the moon.
Chorus: Hey Hey Hey for the ADA

We're gonna take our place, play our part.
Lord, we've been praying for this day,
with all our hearts.
Chorus: Hey Hey Hey for the ADA

You're gonna see me, in some place new
You may be angry, but won't be a thing you can do.
You can bolt all your padlocks, bar all your doors.
I'll hire me a lawyer and see you in court.
Chorus: Hey Hey Hey for the ADA

©1992 Karl Williams and Speaking for Ourselves

tion they would otherwise not be inclined to go. Rights push; the good pulls.[30] This is an important distinction in light of what I have said about negatively defined moral relationships. Recognition of equal rights and social justice for people with disabilities constitutes opportunities for action; it does not constitute positive relationships with other people per se. However, people with intellectual disabilities are particularly dependent on these relationships. They deserve to be chosen because of who they are, not because of the law, not even because of a respect for their human rights. They are not merely to be tolerated because of a response to claims to equality and justice. As our fellow human beings, they deserve to belong on grounds of our predilection; they deserve to be chosen as friends.

The foregoing analysis has put us in the position of going one step further with respect to the ultimate good of being human. The ultimate good is not necessarily coextensive with what all people desire, but with what is desirable for all people because of the human beings they are. Therefore, the human good must be what we all can participate in. Friendship is this kind of good. It is constituted by what is most desirable for being human regardless of its state or condition. Thus it motivates internally, that is, for no reason other than itself. Since this is not a matter of moral consensus, the argument must show that friendship is at the heart of our humanity because it reflects what our humanity consists in. That is, friendship is not at the heart of the good life because it is universally desired, but because it is universally desirable, given a particular understanding of what our humanity *is*.

6. Participation in the Good of Being Human

Let me summarize the argument in the foregoing sections. In giving priority to rights and justice that will support people with intellectual disabilities, the disability-rights literature must rely, at best, on respect for people's moral standing as citizens; at worst, they must rely on the enforceability of rights that can induce people to comply for reasons of enlightened self-interest. Neither scenario is in any way sufficient to es-

30. I borrow the terminology from Robert Nozick, *Philosophical Explanations* (Cambridge, MA: Harvard University Press, 1981).

tablish positive relationships. That is, they are in no way sufficient to welcome disabled people into our midst — into our institutions, or into our communities, or into our individual lives. All of these concerns can only be addressed effectively when we shift to the question of how disabled people participate in the human good. In the following chapters I will seek to make this argument work by proposing a conception of the human good that has being chosen as a friend at its core.

As I have indicated earlier in this chapter, such a conception presupposes a distinction between a variety of goods, on the one hand, and an ultimate good — a "hyper good" — on the other. To prepare the ground for the task ahead, I will conclude with one further reflection on this distinction. In one of his rare essays addressing the topic, Wolf Wolfensberger, the American "godfather" of normalization theory, introduces it in the following way:

> From the perspective of the prevailing materialistic worldview, the good life for retarded persons would probably have to be defined entirely in terms of materialistic and emotional welfare. However, I will attempt to delineate the issue from a Christian perspective; within such a perspective, considerations of material and emotional welfare are important issues, but not ultimate ones.[31]

In Wolfensberger's conceptualization, items of materialistic and emotional welfare cover the list of goods that, taken together, may constitute a good life; but they do not cover the "ultimate considerations" that are for him inherent in a Christian perspective. He thus aligns himself with the Augustinian concept according to which there are many possible goods in our earthly existence; but they can only be properly appreciated from the point of view of our destiny, which for Augustine is to be residents of the "city of God," in which we will enjoy God's friendship. Considering the distinctions drawn above, this view makes good sense: items of materialistic and emotional welfare do not presuppose a conception of life's final end per se, but they are nonetheless very important. So the lives of persons with profound disabilities can be evaluated from two per-

---

31. Wolf Wolfensberger, "The Good Life for Mentally Retarded Persons," in *The Theological Voice of Wolf Wolfensberger*, ed. William C. Gaventa and David L. Coulter (Binghamton, NY: Haworth Press, 2001), pp. 103-9 (reprinted in *National Apostolate with Mentally Retarded Persons Quarterly* 15, no. 3 [1984]: 18-20).

spectives on the good life: in one view, their lives are good when they enjoy a list of particular goods; in another, their lives are good, just as all other human lives are good, when they answer to a higher purpose, an ultimate goal, or a final end. The two views are not mutually exclusive, at least not from a Christian perspective, nor are they mutually dependent.

In raising the question of ethics regarding profoundly disabled lives, I will follow Wolfensberger as I reflect on the good of being human in the second sense rather than the first sense. It is worth mentioning that my inquiry in this book distances itself from the way the question of the good life is usually addressed nowadays in the social scientific literature under the rubric "quality of life."[32] In the evaluation of residential services for people with disabilities, service providers use the notion of "quality of life" as a measure to assess the care and support they offer their customers. In the contemporary literature, a widely accepted way of conceptualizing the "quality of life" notion is in terms of a person's performance in various domains of human life, such as, "health," "relationships," "occupation," or "leisure." One can develop a checklist of items for each of these domains: for example, for the domain "relationships," the checklist may ask about whom the person meets, on what occasions, how often, for what purpose, and so on.[33] One can imagine how this procedure results in an overview of a person's performance on the "QoL-scale," which then enables the service provider to determine points of improvement. It is much more difficult, however, to imagine how a person's performance in the various domains could tell you anything about the overall "goodness" of her life. The emerging picture will be a mixed bag: the goods she enjoys need not be limited to Wolfensberger's "material and emotional" goods, because we can add social, spiritual, and any other kind of good we deem important. However, we would still be missing a way to assess whether, and to what extent, the goods she acquires amount to a life that is really good.[34] That is, we would still miss an assessment based on a concept

32. R. L. Schalock, *Quality of Life: Perspectives and Issues* (Washington, DC: American Association on Mental Retardation, 1990); Robert S. Schalock and Miguel Angel Verdugo Alonso, *Handbook on Quality of Life for Human Services Practitioners* (Washington, DC: American Association on Mental Retardation, 2002).

33. See, for example, R. L. Schalock and K. D. Keith, *Quality of Life Questionnaire Manual* (Worthington, OH: IDS Publishing Company, 1993).

34. Social scientists seem to be satisfied with using the instrument of expert panels

ethical naturalism
- natural desires
- no external desire

of the ultimate good — Wolfenberger's "ultimate considerations" — that is *external* to the goods acquired.

Why should this matter? Well, to begin with, for a concept of the ultimate good to be truly universal, it is necessary that it not consist of the sum total of a variety of goods, as I have argued earlier. That is, if it is to be possible for all human beings, regardless of their state or condition, to participate in the good, then a concept of a sum total of goods could not include human beings with profound disabilities. They would lose out because of their very limited capacities to enjoy a wide range of goods that would be included, notably all emotional, social, and spiritual goods. If there is to be a truly universal concept of the human good, it must be a concept within which the good is not dependent on such capacities.

There are, of course, a number of positions that exclude any such concept. First, there is the position of ethical naturalism, which precludes the very idea that there is such a thing as an ultimate good for human beings. Ethical naturalists hold that "good" equals the satisfaction of natural desires: in their view, no standard for "goodness" exists that is external to the good of satisfied desires. This is because there is nothing desirable beyond the satisfaction of what one actually desires. Even the good of meaningful human experience would fall into that category. That is, there is no standard or basis for the evaluation of satisfied desires.

From the perspective of ethical naturalism, therefore, the good necessarily equals the maximization of the satisfaction of desires. Hence, anyone who believes this will be content with a concept of the human good consisting of a plurality of realized goods. In view of the goal of maximizing satisfaction, the only concern would be to ask for a minimal level of satisfaction in the various domains that would represent a threshold value below which a person's score would be unacceptably low.[35] Even though this position may not be widely accepted in a theo-

---

to deal with the apparent problem of the scientific objectivity of such judgments. For a critical discussion, see Chris Hatton, "Whose Quality of Life Is It Anyway? Some Problems With the Emerging Quality of Life Consensus," *Mental Retardation* 36, no. 2 (1998): 104-15.

35. This may be called the "basic needs" approach that distinguishes among several needs that being human seeks to fulfill, and marks those that have priority in a scheme of providing them at least with what they basically need. An important source for this kind

retical sense, in actual practice it is widely accepted — at least implicitly — because the approach of assessing "quality of life" operates on the same assumption. Or, perhaps better, this approach reflects a posture of metaphysical abstinence in that it does not address the question of an ultimate good, presumably because it is serviceable to caregivers who operate in a pluralist society. On this assumption, a transcending concept of what it means to live a truly human life must fail because there is no universally valid way of answering it.

By contrast, those who do believe that this question has a universally valid answer will be worried about the equation of a plurality of acquired goods with the good life. For example, both Kantians and Aristotelians, each in a different way, hold that the ultimate human good cannot exist in a sum total of various goods. Their reason for holding this view is the same: the goods that human beings may enjoy can be used for degrading purposes. Kantians and Aristotelians believe that there is a conception of the ultimate good of being human that every rational person should accept, and that it consists in the proper use of the human faculties. For Kantians, the good ultimately depends on respect for oneself as a free human being endowed with the capacity for reason; for Aristotelians, the good ultimately depends on the perfection of the same. Of course, from the perspective I am offering in this book, both these conceptions are unacceptable because they depend on the operation of faculties that not all human beings possess, not even potentially. Therefore, by definition they result in a category of the subhuman as far as the ultimate good of being human is concerned.

What we have so far, then, are two mutually exclusive and equally unattractive philosophical positions concerning the question of the good life for people with profound intellectual disabilities.[36] "Nature"

---

of approach has been Maslow's theory of the hierarchy of needs. See A. Maslow, *Motivation and Personality* (New York: Harper, 1954); see also G. Norwood, *Maslow's Hierarchy of Needs* (2006): http://www.deepermind.com-/20maslow.htm; and W. Huitt, *Maslow's Hierarchy of Needs: Educational Psychology Interactive* (2004, Valdosta State University): http://chiron.valdosta.edu/whuitt/col/regsys/maslow.html.

36. The Aristotelian view has been discussed in terms of an account of marginal cases that would open the possibility to circumvent the negative consequence of a category of subhumanity (see Ch. 3 above). For a discussion of the Kantian view, see Reinders, *The Future of the Disabled*. With regard to ethical naturalism, the main point of contention

— regardless of whether it is understood in a naturalist, an Aristotelian, or a Kantian sense — does not define "goodness," at least not in the Christian (i.e., Augustinian) understanding of being human that I will defend in my analysis. Within an Augustinian perspective, the final end *(telos)* of being human is properly understood in terms of a relationship with God. How we are to account for this is a question that we will have ample opportunity to discuss in the next chapters. To get started on that discussion, I propose that we first take stock of what theologians have been saying about disability in recent decades.

———————

would be its claim that "being human" is in itself not a morally relevant description. The position taken by Peter Singer would fall into this category, as one can see, for example, in his assessment of the Great Ape Project (Paola Cavalieri and Peter Singer, *The Great Ape Project: Equality Beyond Humanity* [New York: St. Martin's Press, 1994]. The claim that "being human" is as such a morally relevant description relies, according to Singer, on "speciesism." A discussion of this notion falls outside the scope of my argument. One way of suggesting how the argument against Singer's position on speciesism might go would be to say that it would not be important to him that a chimp could not be his son. Similarly, if Singer was to have a profoundly disabled son, it couldn't matter to him what it would be to say that his child was a human being. That is, given his ethical naturalism, the question of natural kinship could not matter to him other than on utilitarian grounds, which simply seems odd. With regard to the underpinnings of the Great Ape Project, see also Nora Ellen Groce and Jonathan Marks, "The Great Ape Project and Disability Rights: Ominous Undercurrents of Eugenics in Action," *American Anthropologist* 102, no. 4 (2000): 818-22.

Part Two

THEOLOGY

Chapter Five

Theology and Disability I

*In the face of the retarded we are offered an opportunity to see God,
for like God they offer us an opportunity of recognizing the character of our neediness.*

Stanley Hauerwas

1. Introduction

Today there still is no extensive body of literature on Christian theology
and disability. Given the fact that many people with disabilities continue to exist on the margins of our society, this should not come as a
surprise. Unless one could expect that the life of the church would be
different from that of society in general there is no reason to think that
theologians have greater sensibilities in this respect. On the whole, they
do not.

Most of the material that does exist comes from North America and
the United Kingdom. Furthermore, much of that material is strongly influenced by the disability-rights approach. This is particularly true for
the work that originates in the United States, where many Christian authors explicitly join forces with the disability-rights movement. Their
main objective, it appears, is to change existing practices both in the
church and in theology. These authors tend to believe, though there is
evidence to the contrary, that the leading forces in this struggle are
from outside the Christian community.[1] Their assumption seems to be

1. See Deland, "Breaking Down Barriers So All May Worship," *Journal of Religion in*

main objective

that change must come from outside. Guided by the core values of liberal democracy, the disability-rights literature often presents "theology" and "church" as objects of resistance rather than as agents of change.

When committed to the disability-rights approach, those writing on theology and disability often forget to ask what a distinctively theological voice might contribute in the struggle for inclusion. Nor do they pay much attention to the question of how the philosophy of the disability-rights approach relates to the fundamental beliefs and practices of the Christian tradition. In this book I take that question to be very important. My main objective is to think theologically in a way that does not reproduce the "hierarchy of disability," which is what the disability-rights approach by implication does. We may take the position of profoundly disabled human beings within that hierarchy as a litmus test. As we have seen, the key issue in the disability-rights approach is self-representation. This means that we do not get much from it with regard to those who cannot represent themselves — other than the claim that they need adequate representation by others. No coherent argument regarding profoundly disabled people can be made via a philosophy that has self-representation as a necessary condition of inclusion. That its argument for the inclusion of disabled people is grounded in the anthropology of liberal citizenship, which creates serious theoretical problems concerning people with intellectual disabilities, is something that seems to escape most of those writing in this field.

The task of developing a theological anthropology that does not make the same mistake proves to be a very demanding one indeed. Rethinking our fundamental beliefs regarding being human is a theoretical undertaking driven by an eminently practical concern, but it will take us deep into the tradition of Christian theology before we get to where we want to be. The task of considering *how* concepts of the human and divine are construed raises important issues in theological method. But if we do not consider this, we may fail to see that, in thinking about "disability," we are often only thinking about a select group of people with disabilities. It is important to pay attention to such matters

---

Disability & Rehabilitation 2, no. 1 (1995): 5-20. This article presents steps and documents from various churches and their organizations from the 1970s indicating that church initiatives were developing at the same time the disability-rights movement got into gear.

because of how methodologies work: they organize our ways of seeing reality, which implies that our methodologies are both revealing and concealing. By making some aspects of reality visible, they make other aspects invisible. Thus, if one is uncritical of one's own methodology, one necessarily fails to see the limitations of what it is both capable and incapable of showing.[2]

However, it does not follow that since each of our ways of seeing reality has its limitations, they must therefore be equally valid. Different methodologies are usually, though not necessarily, driven by different moral concerns. In the context of my analysis, many of those writing on theology and disability are driven by concerns about "access."[3] They claim that both the church and theology need to open up institutional, procedural, and symbolic spaces for persons with disabilities. My own concern is different because I do not regard "space" as the crucial issue: the reason is that, in the end, participation does not depend on space but on commitment. In philosophical language, space is a *necessary* but not a *sufficient* condition for inclusion. What enables me to participate in my own social world is not the fact that I am allowed to live my life as I want to (which is what "space" can do for me), but that there are people who are committed to me and want to be part of my life. Ulti-

---

2. See Deborah Creamer, "Finding God in Our Bodies: Theology from the Perspective of People with Disabilities," *Journal of Religion in Disability & Rehabilitation* 2, no. 1 (1995): 34. Creamer argues for a theology of disability from a liberation perspective, "to create clearer and truer pictures of God." However, Creamer observes that it is important to keep reminding ourselves of the fact that disability is a multifaceted phenomenon: it includes not only impaired bodily function but also poverty, race, and gender. Disability and diversity go hand in hand. This leads her to make an epistemological point: the knowledge of God is a puzzle, and "each of us offers a piece of the puzzle" — hence the importance of diversity (p. 33). As long as people with disabilities are excluded, they cannot contribute their piece of the puzzle. "Only after access is gained can concrete and constructive theological reflection be possible" (p. 35). See also Helen Betenbaugh, *A Theology of Disability* (Dallas: Perkins School of Theology, 1992), pp. 3-7.

3. See Jennie Weiss Block, *Copious Hosting: A Theology of Access for People with Disability* (New York: Continuum, 2002): "The first and primary goal of any disability theology is access and inclusion" (p. 99). Other examples are Harold H. Wilke, *Creating the Caring Congregation: Guidelines for Ministering with the Handicapped* (Nashville: Abingdon Press, 1980); H. Oliver Ohsberg, *The Church and Persons with Handicaps* (Scottsdale, PA: Herald Press, 1982); Stewart D. Govig, *Strong at the Broken Places: Persons with Disabilities and the Church* (Louisville: Westminster/John Knox Press, 1989); and Helen Betenbaugh, *A Theology of Disability.*

mately, human participation does not depend on personal freedom but on shared practices of communion, which is why I believe that the issue of participation must ultimately be construed as an issue about friendship rather than citizenship.

Another important difference is that my inquiry in this book is not primarily interested in a theology of disability: I am not looking for my own niche in the theological literature where issues of disability can be properly addressed. Instead, I wish to confront longstanding convictions in the Christian tradition with implications of exclusion that have never been properly questioned. To avoid these implications, the church needs to find ways of thinking about being human that do not support the distinction between people with and without disabilities. I believe that friendship is the key to this attempt. Every human being is worthy of being chosen as a friend simply because that is what God does — choose us to be friends. We need friendship if we are to flourish as human beings. The theological justification for this claim is that friendship with our fellow creatures is our vocation. This is what we are created for. With respect to the philosophy of disability rights, this means that the prime source of participation and inclusion is not political but ethical. That is, rights to access for people with disabilities will only enable them to flourish qua human beings to the extent that they are supported by friendship as a *different* source of commitment. The struggle for equality and justice begun by the disability-rights movement is important; but in order for it to be truly inclusive, that struggle must be nourished by moral resources beyond the realm of politics. This is something that the controlling framework of the disability-rights approach tends to ignore.

To substantiate these claims I must explain one further aspect of why I consider the disability-rights approach insufficient: "insufficient" here does not mean that beyond "access" there is a further goal, "friendship," that we need to reach for, as if it were the icing on a cake. The point is not that we should move beyond equality and justice, because that would presuppose that we already have realized these goals, which is at best only partially true. The goals of equality and justice are not realized within most of our churches, not even at the minimal level of physical accessibility. Therefore, it is not that we add "friendship" to the list of goods people with disabilities need to have. Friendship is not merely complementary to the goals of equality and justice. Especially regarding intellectually disabled persons, the point is much more critical than that: it is that the disability-rights approach leaves unquestioned what causes the exclusion of these humans in the first place, which is that most people in our moral culture do not want them to be part of their lives.

Of course, most people in our society are civilized enough not to want to kill them (though some debates in contemporary bioethics render even this minimal commitment uncertain). It is probably also true that many of us are sufficiently decent to support the provision of care and support for these people and their families. It may even be true that we support their claims to equal rights and social justice. But all of this is still a far cry from wanting to include them in the lives we aspire to live, while none of it prevents us from thinking that it would be better if no disabled lives existed.[4] People with intellectual disabilities, let alone profound intellectual disabilities, do not fit easily within our conceptions of the good life. That's what the focus on friendship is meant to show, not only in a critical sense but also in a constructive sense. I want Christians to consider friendship with a disabled person as a vocation that, once they have entered into it, will change not only their own lives but also the life of the church. This goal is clearly different from theologies that argue for equal access. My primary aim — rather than opening up buildings, jobs, or positions — is to change people's mind.

Therefore, in Parts II and III of this book, I will turn to the Christian tradition in order to think about the human good of friendship in a way that may make a significant difference in how we respond to persons with disabilities. That the church frequently does not answer to this calling is nothing less than shameful, which is one reason why the question of theology's own voice is crucial.[5] It needs to correct its own

---

4. Writing from the experience of a progressive physical disability, Paul Hunt makes some very perceptive but sobering comments on our able-bodied sympathy. The able-bodied person's rejection of superiority implies that he admits equality, at least in theory, Hunt writes, "but when you *act* as though you *are* equal then the crucial test comes. Most people are good-willed liberals towards us up to this point, but not all of them survive close contact with disability without showing some less attractive traits (Hunt, "A Critical Condition," in *The Disability Reader: Social Science Perspectives,* ed. Tom Shakespeare [London: Cassell, 1998], pp. 13f).

5. It appears that many churches in the United States are still struggling with the exemption clause in the Americans with Disabilities Act, which does not allow federally

mistakes. Another reason is that many hold the prime sources of the Christian faith — biblical texts — responsible for the religious stigmatization of disabled people that pervades Western culture.[6] It is not only for these negative reasons, however, that church and theology must correct their failures on their own terms. There is another, decidedly positive, reason for insisting on theology's own voice. As the existing literature abundantly shows, you really don't need theology to justify a disability-rights claim. Other disciplines can do that for you in various ways. But things will turn out to be different when it comes to thinking about friendship. While there are philosophical views about friendship as the essence of the human good (Aristotle is the first who comes to mind), it is not at all clear that they can envision being friends with an intellectually disabled person as part of the good life. If theology is going to make a difference, it must be because of what it can teach us, precisely in this respect, about friendship as foremost among the many graces of God.

I will begin Part II with two chapters that present what in other disciplines is called "the state of the art." This involves a critical assessment of how theologians in recent times have been thinking about the inclusion of people with disabilities. In this chapter and the next one, I will distinguish four different approaches within the literature, particularly the Anglo-Saxon literature: the first is labeled as "a liberation theology of disability"; the second as "a theology of access"; the third as "a theology of community"; and the fourth as "a theology of being human." Each of these approaches represents a different strategy that aims at a different concern. The goal of my presentation of these four approaches is such that the questions they leave unanswered point in the direction of where the next stage of our theological reflection needs to go. This means that the argument for a different theological agenda proceeds hand in hand with the analysis presented in these two chapters.

---

funded organizations to arrange matters of access at their own discretion. No wonder that many disability-rights activists have not found churches to be strong allies in their struggle. See Nancy L. Eiesland, "Barriers and Bridges: Relating the Disability Rights Movement and Religious Organizations," in *Human Disability and the Service of God: Reassessing Religious Practice,* ed. Nancy L. Eiesland and Don E. Saliers (Nashville: Abingdon Press, 1998), pp. 200-229; see also Betenbaugh, *A Theology of Disability.*

6. Eiesland, "Barriers and Bridges," p. 217.

does not represent intell. dis

2. A Theology of Liberation

The first approach to theology and disability that I will discuss is that of a liberation theology of disability. The main protagonist of this approach is without doubt Nancy L. Eiesland, who deserves to be credited for at least two reasons: not only has her book *The Disabled God* inspired many people in the field with new ideas about theology and disability; she has also devoted more attention to methodology than have most other authors in the field.[7] As we shall see, Eiesland's thought follows the paradigm of the disability-rights approach in many respects, particularly her reliance on what I call the anthropology of liberal citizenship. Since the key to this anthropology is the notion of purposive agency aiming at self-representation, it is difficult to see how her theological and moral claims could do anything for those with intellectual disabilities for whom purposive agency and self-representation must remain empty notions.

In contrast to many other authors, however, Eiesland is well aware of this limitation. When she speaks of people with disabilities, she means to speak of persons with physical disabilities only (p. 27). Despite the fact that she calls the lack of theological exploration of those with intellectual, social, or emotional disabilities "scandalous," she does not include them in her work,[8] not only because of the significant differences that exist between the various categories of disabilities but also because of "the prominence of physical disability in the sociological theory and the theological argument employed here" (p. 28). While this exempts the author from responsibility for her lack of representation of intellectual disability, it is nonetheless important to understand why the theoretical framework she uses does not allow her to represent them.

7. Eiesland, *The Disabled God: Toward a Liberatory Theology of Disability* (Nashville: Abingdon Press, 1994) [page number citations given parenthetically in the text refer to this publication]. See also Jane S. Deland, "Images of God Through the Lens of Disability," *Journal of Religion, Disability and Health* 3, no. 2 (1999): 47-79.

8. It is not unusual for authors who identify with the disability-rights movement not to include people with intellectual disabilities in their argument; and usually they do not show awareness of that fact. See, for example, Deborah Creamer, "Finding God in Our Bodies" (n. 2 above). Like Eiesland, Creamer refers exclusively to experiences and examples from the world of physical disability. People with intellectual disabilities are also absent from James I. Charlton, *Nothing about Us without Us: Disability, Oppression and Empowerment* (Berkeley: University of California Press, 1998), p. 6.

Eiesland

SOC.
SC.

A second reason for me to discuss her work is her way of "locating" theology and the church in her argument. As we shall see, Eiesland does not regard the *logia tou theou* as the place to begin theological reflection. Her primary concern is to identify a body of theoretical insight that will enable Christian symbols to be transformed, because that is what she thinks needs to be done. This she finds in a social-scientific theory that she introduces as "the minority group model" (p. 24). It provides her with a sociological appropriation of the experience of stigmatization, as well as with an account of how this experience is defeated by disabled people speaking up for themselves, showing that her method of theological reflection moves "from the outside in." In Eiesland's case, the nontheological frames the theological. Starting from the minority-group model, she argues her way into theology and the church. The reason for this approach is, presumably, that both theology and the church are to be regarded as the objects of change. The meaning of Christian symbols in both theology and the church must be transformed, according to Eiesland, in order to reflect the experience of persons with disabilities in the sense explained by her sociological theory. I will raise a critical point about this procedure below.

Finally, the third reason for my discussion regards the question of the "other" in Eiesland's theology. How does she construe the audience to whom she addresses her claims? A dichotomy seems to be at work in her reflection, one that separates people with disabilities from others whose "ableist" attitudes are the object of her critique. Eiesland will say, of course, that this separation actually exists in the life of the church — that it is not a function of her theoretical framework. This is undoubtedly true, but it does not eliminate the question of how she construes the audience of her claims. The church must change, and thus the people who embody it must change. How are they supposed to receive her criticisms and change their attitudes?

My interest here is an issue of moral motivation. Eiesland's theology has to face the question of why and how people in the church are supposed to change their conceptions of themselves and of disabled people so that they drop their attitudinal fences. Surprisingly, her theology answers this question by appealing to enlightened self-interest, as we shall see. The church and its people are worse off if persons with disabilities are not present in their midst. Because of these three features — the lack of representation of intellectual disability, the primacy of so-

ciology, and the appeal to self-interest as the motivation for change —
the discussion of Eiesland's book will be mainly directed at matters of
strategy and method.

3. Self-Representation

The reason Eiesland's theoretical framework of the minority-group
model does not allow her to represent people with intellectual disabilities is, as I have indicated, that this framework is premised by the crucial importance of *self-representation.* Being herself physically disabled,
Eiesland knows from personal experience that people with disabilities
are not singled out because of their individual characteristics. General-
ized ascriptions of disabling features of her body, or her life, are usually
inadequate and frequently not true. Therefore, Eiesland supports the
social-constructionist claim that disability has very little to do with actual "defects" inherent to people's bodies, but with conceptions that
the "temporarily able-bodied" have of both themselves and others.
What these people believe about persons with disabilities like her is informed by social and cultural prejudices and stigmas. This can be demonstrated in the fact that the lives of people with disabilities are as diverse as those of any other segment of the general population. Since
there are no characteristics or traits that hold for all people with disabilities, what brings them together as a minority group is a "common set
of stigmatizing values and arrangements" that operates against them
(p. 24). In Eiesland's view, the minority-group model provides "a theoretical lens" for understanding how negative stereotypes and prejudice
affect people's lives (p. 66). Without such an understanding, no real
communication is possible because persons with disabilities will not
recognize themselves in how they are approached. This is why the
minority-group model is a necessary tool, she claims, if there is to be
any change in the negative attitudes to disability that currently dominate society and the church.

There is a strong focus in Eiesland's work, then, on what people
think and believe to be true about "disabled people." In her view, it is
the social-symbolic order of the "able-bodied" that produces inequality
and injustice toward people with disabilities. This is why self-
representation is crucial. In order to break through the barriers of nega-

must become subjects
self-representation

tive stereotyping, persons with disabilities must become the subjects of their own lives by naming themselves, by telling their own stories, and by identifying their own needs and ambitions: "The act of naming something grants the namer the power over the named" (p. 25). Consequently, "naming" is not just an exercise in semantics; rather, it is part of the "political work of empowerment" (p. 26).

This account of the primacy of the minority-group model provides the key to how Eiesland understands her own strategy as a theologian. Liberation from marginalization and discrimination will not be possible unless the minority group in question is united in self-identification, which is precisely what the disability movement has been doing.[9] It has created a group solidarity that changes the label that the majority group has used for negative identification into a source of pride (p. 64). Since she is personally involved in that movement, Eiesland intends to use "sociological theories and methods that empower" as the starting point for constructing her "liberatory" theology.

> Recognition of the sociopolitical dimensions of physical disability is vital if we hope to restructure and reconceive contemporary theology about disability and to ground a liberatory theology of disability in the individual and collective bodies of people with disabilities. (p. 50)

Using the minority-group model as a sociological paradigm, Eiesland makes "exclusion" the outcome of "rejection" and "discrimination" by the "non-disabled majority," to which people within the disability-rights movement have responded with a growing sense of self-awareness (p. 64). This again indicates that, in her view, the move toward self-representation is the *conditio sine qua non* of their political struggle. The consequence is that human beings incapable of self-representation have no place in this strategy. They are dependent on being represented by others, but this dependency is part of their problem of marginalization. It excludes them from what Eiesland regards as the source of the liberating experience, namely, to assert the embodied

---

9. This "group building" aspect of empowerment is also vital in Charlton's account of the emergence of the disability rights movement: "Persons with empowered consciousness . . . begin to speak of 'we' instead of 'I' or 'they' (Charlton, *Nothing about Us without Us*, p. 119).

claim "this is who we are."[10] In her view, posing themselves as subjects in their own right is the source of liberation.

4. Moving from the Outside In

Eiesland's declaration that the theological task based on this embodied self-assertion is to "restructure and reconceive contemporary theology of disability" introduces the second theme of my discussion of her book: the question of theology's own voice. Striking in Eiesland's strategy is the fact that the important things to be said have been said already, before she even begins to think theologically. The experience of the disability movement and its theoretical appropriation by sociology is decisive. The motion of the argument is from the outside in: from "liberatory" disability experience and its sociological appropriation to theology and the church as objects of transformation.

This reading is confirmed by the first chapter of her book, which begins with a celebration of the Americans with Disabilities Act (1990) as a "landmark legislation declaring equality for people with disabilities" (p. 19). The law was the result of disabled people coming together in political action and presenting themselves as claimants of equal rights and social justice. It is from this perspective that Eiesland then introduces the church.

> The liberatory impulse evidenced in the disability rights movement has propelled people with disabilities to resist their marginal status in the full range of social institutions, including the Christian church. . . . We have resisted our experience being reformulated to conform to crippling theological categories. We have recovered our

10. The crucial role of a collective subjectivity for persons with disabilities in Eiesland's argument makes the use of first-person pronouns in the plural (e.g., "we," "our," "us") particularly sensitive. As a rule, she uses these pronouns to refer exclusively to people with disabilities, which produces sentences such as this one: "We need symbols that affirm our dignity in relation not only to other people with disabilities, but also to able-bodied persons. We need symbols that call both people with disabilities and the able-bodied to conversion" (p. 92). Restricting the use of first-person pronouns to people with disabilities, Eiesland makes the very few exceptions to this rule in her text all the more interesting.

hidden history and exposed the church's complicity with our marginality. (p. 20)

Given the sociological perspective from which she argues, it is entirely appropriate for Eiesland to regard the church and theology as the objects of change. That is, together they define the field where a transformation needs to take place, but they are not seen as the agents — let alone the sources — of this transformation. However, though her argument clearly leads her down a one-way street from sociology to theology, that is not what she wants. In fact, Eiesland seems to explicitly reject this when, in introducing her method, she talks about "two-way access" and "two agendas that must be recognized" (p. 20). However, from the way she elucidates how this two-way access is supposed to work, it is clear that what she advocates is in fact a one-way street. To see why, we need to know what agendas she has in mind, and then we need to consider what she says about how they are related.

The first agenda is, of course, enabling people with disabilities to participate fully in the life of the church (p. 21). This agenda deals with all the accessibility issues, both material and social; this is basically the agenda of the disability-rights movement. The second agenda then turns to theology and the church: the task of this agenda is to discover "a means by which the church can gain access to the social-symbolic life of persons with disabilities" (p. 23). This somewhat cryptic formulation seems to say that Christians within the disability-rights movement have come to their own explanation of the Christian symbols, and that it is important for the church to recognize this fact.[11] However, though one might expect the "two-way access" to mean some sort of dialectic between two operations moving in opposite directions, this is not in fact what Eiesland has in mind.[12] Instead, she claims:

11. This reading is confirmed by how Eiesland introduces her own "discovery" of the symbol of Christ as the "disabled God" (*The Disabled God,* p. 89).

12. This problem is the key issue in methodological accounts in liberation theology as it has developed since the 1970s. Particularly influential has been Clodovis Boff's *Theology and Praxis: Epistemological Foundations* (Maryknoll, NY: Orbis Books, 1987). For a discussion of this book that aims at the same problem — the relationship between social theory and theology that forms the perspective of liberation theology — see Reinders, *Violence, Victims, and Rights* (Amsterdam: Free University Press, 1988), Ch. 5. (I should warn

Two-way access necessitates that the Christian tradition recognize the lived experience of persons with disabilities and that people with disabilities are able to acknowledge the symbols of the Christian tradition, not as over against us, but as part of our hidden history. (p. 23)

While the first move is clear, the second one is not as clear. The disabled need to be able to appropriate the symbols of the Christian tradition as part of their "hidden history," which is partly the result of the church's complicity. Eiesland apparently means that, when properly understood, the Christian symbols reflect the subversive reality of a marginalized people, which is why she can say that their position is "not over against" these symbols. But this means that the appropriation of these symbols is, in fact, presupposed. Eiesland conceives of her method as "the *interplay* between what is already known to the theologian and active engagement with the particular people who teach them to rework their theories, labels, and depictions of reality" (p. 22; italics added). It is unclear, however, how there can be interplay between two entities when one of these is effectively reduced to the consciousness of the other. Thus it is difficult to see how "what the theologian already knows" has a part in this "interplay," when it does not have some kind of independence and is presented only as the object of reconstruction and reconceptualization. In terms of theological method, there is no second moment in this strategy that asks theology to shed its light on the disability movement and its experience. There is only the repetition of the first moment in different terms.[13] First, the church is summoned to listen to people with disabilities; then the theologian is summoned to do exactly the same. The method of transforming the Christian symbols in this way will allow people with disabilities to affirm their "bro-

---

the reader that this was my doctoral dissertation, and that the chapter on Boff's theological method is one of the few parts of the book that today would survive my own reservations about it.)

13. Eiesland explains her theological method in reference to Rebecca Chopp's critique of David Tracy's "critical correlation method," which she opposes with a "critical praxis correlation," the "moment" of which includes "a de-ideologization of scriptures," "a pragmatic interpretation of experience," "a critical theory of emancipation and enlightenment," and "a social theory to transform praxis" (p. 22). Somehow one wonders whether theology's own voice should not be among the "moments" of this method. The answer, I am afraid, might well be that "theology's own voice" supposedly does not exist.

ken bodies" and enable them to reconsider the church as an inclusive "community of justice" (p. 94). Therefore, the transformation that Eiesland envisions begins with the experience of disabled people as a minority group, it is continued by their struggle for access to the church, and it is completed by the church's recognition of their appropriation of the Christian symbols. There is no "interplay" whatsoever: neither the church nor theology is allowed the position of an independent agent in its own right in the process.

In order to avoid misunderstanding, let me add that, in leveling this objection to Eiesland's work, I do not mean to quarrel with any of her moral claims on a substantive level. That is, virtually everything she says about the exclusion of disabled people, its cause, and the struggle against it is justified, as far as I can see. Nonetheless, her argument is seriously flawed in terms of its formal characteristics. No "two-way access" exists between the sociological minority-group model and symbolic theology in her approach. And that is not inconsequential, as we shall see.

5. Breaking the Barrier

The third reason for reconstructing Eiesland's argument, the reader will recall, poses an issue of moral motivation. Since the strategy of her argument allows the church and its theology only to appear as objects of change, the question is, where does this leave those who embody what needs to be changed? The opposition is one between people with disabilities who have achieved their own liberation within the disability-rights movement, on the one hand, and those who represent and embody the "ableist" church and its theology, on the other. Given this division of roles, the question is, how are the recipients of her criticisms supposed to be changed?

To be in a position to answer this question, we must reconstruct how Eiesland arrives at the notion of the "disabled God," a task that will take us through several stages of her argument. To introduce this notion, she begins with an epiphany.

I saw God in a sip-puff wheelchair, that is, the chair used mostly by quadriplegics enabling them to maneuver by blowing and sucking on a straw-like device. Not an omnipotent, self-sufficient God, but neither a pitiable, suffering servant. In this moment, I beheld God as a survivor, unpitying and forthright. I recognized the incarnate Christ in the image of those judged "not feasible," "unemployable," with "questionable quality of life." Here was God for me. (p. 89)

The image of God in a sip-puff wheelchair bears remarkably little resemblance to the conquering Lord that Eiesland detects in the theological tradition. Since the use of this symbol in church and theology has often been hostile toward disabled people, because it is premised by the notion of strength, this image needs to be replaced (p. 91). This can be done by transforming the image of Christ from a servant who is a model of virtuous suffering to the image of Christ as the disabled God whose body has been broken (p. 94).

In order to arrive at this transformation, Eiesland first reads the incarnate Christ into the image of people with disabilities; then she reads their experience of rejection and resistance into the symbol of Christ crucified and resurrected.[14] The theological voice that Eiesland embodies thus appropriates the gospel as the story of God's participation in the experience of being disabled. However, the distinctive one-sidedness of her method raises the question of whether and when this act of transformation includes people without a disability as subjects. In addition to the church and its theology, the people to whom Eiesland's argument is addressed are the "temporarily able-bodied." What role are they to play?

The next step is recognizing the fact that a liberation theology of disability is embodied theology; it is not abstract theory. Therefore, Eiesland argues for the crucial role of bodily experience in the act of transforming the symbol of Christ. It is "grounded in the bodies and actions of people with disabilities and others who care" (p. 90).[15] Trans-

---

14. "To speak of a liberatory proclamation for people with disabilities is to recognize . . . that a voice is the creature of the body that produces it" (*The Disabled God*, p. 90).

15. The mysterious phrase "others who care" appears several times in the text of *The Disabled God* (e.g., pp. 90, 98, 103). As we shall see, Eiesland uses it to break through her restricted use of the indices of subjectivity for people with disabilities. There are nondisabled others who care. Eiesland does not clarify who these others are and where they come from. In fact, my formal critique of her theology can be summarized in the

173

forming the symbol of Christ, she claims, "is the work of the bodily figuration of knowledge" that reflects the "struggle of resistance and revelation of our long-masked knowledge and images" (90).[16] When this act of transformation succeeds, it has the power of unsettling the social-symbolic order that produces the stigmatization of disabled people. For Eiesland, this "unsettling" is achieved by turning around the signs: the despised and broken bodies of the physically disabled are dignified in the disabled body of the resurrected Christ. Here the reference to the stigmata of the resurrected Christ is crucial, for they are the signs of both his true humanity and divinity.[17]

> In presenting his impaired hands and feet to his startled friends, the resurrected Jesus is revealed as the disabled God. Jesus, the resurrected Savior, calls for his frightened companions to recognize in the marks of impairment their own connection with God, their own salvation. In doing so, the disabled God is also the revealer of a new humanity. The disabled God is not only the One from heaven but the revelation of true personhood, underscoring the reality that full personhood is fully compatible with the experience of disability. (p. 100)

This very powerful language has justifiably earned Eiesland a great deal of admiration. However, while her theology is presumably very inspiring for people with disabilities, the question remains how the objectified "others" of this theology — the "temporarily able-bodied" who are captured by prejudice and fear — are supposed to be inspired by it.

---

claim that it does not enable her to account for these "others," with respect to neither their presence nor their contribution.

16. In her own account of "body theology," Deborah Creamer emphasizes the task of reflecting on *common* experiences of our bodily existence while not overlooking differences ("Finding God in Our Bodies," p. 30). Creamer thus seems to depart from Eiesland's conception of liberation theology in that she thinks in a more inclusive way. Embodiment brings understanding and engagement together, not merely with respect to disabled bodies, but also with respect to "all bodies." Since each of us is truly "differently-abled," we all experience our bodies in a different way, which for Creamer raises the question of how the particularities of our different experiences are overcome.

17. The one text from the New Testament that is crucial to Eiesland's constructive proposal is Luke 24:36-39, where the resurrected Jesus confronts his friends who are frightened by his appearance by showing them the scars on his hands and feet.

They are never participating in the act of transformation; they nowhere appear as subjects of change in Eisland's argument. Since her strategy is entirely based on the premise that liberating experience is the experience of subjects, this must be a serious flaw, specifically from her own point of view.[18]

That it is indeed a serious flaw appears from what she claims the transformation of the Christian symbols must establish. Empowering symbols are vital for any marginalized group, Eiesland says, but this cannot be its only aim. The transformed symbol must also "alter the regular practices, ideas, and images of the able-bodied" (p. 91). We do not need "separatist" symbols, she argues, because the implied "separatism would deny our real interdependence with able-bodied people" (p. 92).[19]

---

18. See Creamer ("Finding God in Our Bodies," p. 39), in whose analysis "objectification" is also a crucial issue. The symbolic exclusion works with two sets of stereotypes: disability as a dreadful tragedy and as a heroic inspiration. Either set "objectify" people with disabilities. "They are objectified for our pity, our inspiration or our curiosity." This theme appears in virtually every American text on theology and disability. Religion has forced people with disabilities into one of two roles: sinner or saint. It reinforces these stereotypes by using disabled people "as examples of heroic faith or the brokenness of the world." My critique is not to deny that people with disabilities are "objectified," but to argue that theology must find its own way of transcending objectifications. It requires a logic of redemption to do so, which is what Eiesland's "liberatory" approach fails to supply.

19. While Eiesland is no doubt sincere — and certainly correct — in her objection to separatism, she writes sentences that make one wonder how they can be read other than as being separatist. For example, she declares her theology to offer a new vision of "a God who is for us and a church that is for God and persons with disabilities as the people of God" (*The Disabled God*, p. 90). Taking into account that "us" in her language refers to persons with a disability, where is the able-bodied "other" in this vision? Against her intentions, this way of describing the new vision invokes the image of a partisan church. A moment later in her text she speaks of "a vision of people with disabilities as theological subjects and historical actors." A few pages later, she says her theological construction intends the creation of symbols and rituals that allow people with physical disabilities to "affirm their bodies in dignity and reconceive the church as community of justice for people with disabilities" (p. 92). Finally, when she considers the source of attitudinal barriers, she mentions "deep-seated unconscious aversion to people with disabilities," and of "inappropriate fascination with their bodies," which she then explains as "ritual enactment of the social power" of able-bodied people (pp. 92-93). The implicit message, here and elsewhere, is that there is no space for the liberated subjectivity of "the other." In addition, one may add, how could that be, since their subjectivity as it stands is apparently wrongly constituted?

Curiously, however, this insight of an interdependent relationship between people with disabilities and "the able-bodied," a "we" that potentially includes all, does not receive a great deal of attention in Eiesland's book.[20] This is quite strange because the strategic question about why and how those in the majority are supposed to identify themselves positively with the cause of disability rights must be an important question. Even though Eiesland does not raise the question explicitly, there are a few observations that suggest what her answer might be.

First, one is struck by the occasional sobering voice that Eiesland raises when it comes to expectations about the positive effects of political action. Able-bodied people do not change their views easily. Political action is necessary to break down material and institutional barriers, but it remains to be seen what it can do with regard to attitudinal barriers.

> While I hope with Pat Wright, once director of the Disability Rights Education and Defense Fund, who writes: "You can't legislate attitudes, but attitudinal barriers will drop the more disabled people are employed, the more they can be seen on the street and when we become not just a silent minority, but fully participating members of society," I am less confident that the presence of our bodies in public will displace the pervasive belief structure that thrives on our subjugation. As the history of the disability rights movement demonstrates and as marginalized people already know, political action does not thoroughly alter the attitudes that underlie discrimination. (pp. 97-98)

I take this comment to signal a very important problem. Attitudinal barriers between different people are by definition mediated by binary conceptions of "self" and "other." Breaking those barriers thus requires both a change in one's conception of oneself and of the other. The one does not work without the other. How do you get able-bodied people to change their conception of themselves based on an experience that is not their own? As we have already seen, the appropriation of the Christian symbol by the minority presupposes unevenly distributed subjec-

---

20. There is a brief digression on the notion of interdependence, but there the notion is attributed to Jesus Christ (*The Disabled God,* p. 103).

What kind of conversion?

tivity, so that the "temporarily able-bodied" have to be satisfied with the role of being dispossessed of their current self-images.

Second, in order to avoid separatism, Eiesland talks about conversion. She aims for symbols that "call both people with disabilities and the able-bodied to conversion" (p. 92). What kind of conversion? Eiesland answers that all human beings have to accept the contingency and vulnerability of their bodily existence. Human bodies fall ill, they become disabled, and they ultimately die. All human beings have to become reconciled to a stage in their lives of being disabled, which is what the revelation of the disabled God does for them. It reveals that the brokenness of all our bodies is the location where God's grace, freedom, and wholeness become real. Accepting the disabled God enables both people with disabilities and those temporarily without a disability to be reconciled to their own bodies (p. 101). This is what conversion is about.

> As the church becomes the site for the difficult work of finding that oneself includes a body, the temporarily able-bodied as well as people with disabilities may come to understand what bodily integrity means as a spiritual and physical practice. Conversion then is, in part, learning to love what is carnal, which is our own already existing body. (p. 111)

Again, I find no reason to quarrel with Eiesland about the material content of these claims. On the contrary, these are insights that we desperately need in a moral culture that is obsessed with bodily perfection. However, when it comes to the question of what may inspire the "able-bodied" to accept these insights, Eiesland makes a rather curious move. Nobody looking at Christ as the disabled God can ignore that all bodies are subject to contingency, she says (p. 104); but it is hard work for able-bodied people to accept that fact about their own existence, and they would rather deny it. Self-delusion allows them to disregard the fact that they are only "temporarily able-bodied." This is a mistake, Eiesland reminds us, because "a 50 percent chance exists that an individual who is currently able-bodied will be physically disabled, either temporarily or permanently" (p. 110).

This reminder is curious because it suggests that the able-bodied better pay attention to people with disabilities for reasons of enlightened self-interest, because at some point in their lives they will most likely find themselves in a similar position. In other words, why and how the temporarily able-bodied may drop their attitudinal fences concerns their own well-being. Indeed, Eiesland says in effect the same thing when she explains the Eucharist as the church's "body practice." As they participate at the Lord's table, the disabled people and their broken bodies will be a reminder to the able-bodied that Christ's body is broken for them to become reconciled to their own vulnerability.

> Eucharist as a body practice of justice and inclusion welcomes us and recognizes the church's impairment when we are not included. The church is impoverished when we are not included. Our narratives and bodies make clear that ordinary lives incorporate contingency and difficulty. We reveal the physical truth of embodiment as a painstaking process of claiming and inhabiting our actually existing bodies. People with disabilities announce the presence of the disabled God for us and call the church to become a communion of struggle. (p. 115)

While it is not unusual for those in the disability-rights movement to remind the able-bodied that supporting inclusion is in their own long-term interest, it is a poor argument in theology.[21] Not because the ap-

---

21. See, for example, Diane Driedger, *The Last Civil Rights Movement: Disabled People's International* (New York: St. Martin's Press, 1989), p. 2; Govig, *Strong at the Broken Places,* pp. 8-9. For another version of Eiesland's argument, see Dennis Schurter: "We dare not exclude ourselves from the family of those who have disabilities, for then we are at risk of excluding ourselves from the kingdom of God, as did the Pharisees of old. We each have our physical, emotional, and spiritual limitations. It is only when we recognize our own needs that we can be open to receive God's healing power in our own lives" (Schurter, "Jesus' Ministry with People with Disabilities: Scriptural Foundations for Churches' Inclusive Ministry," *Journal of Religion in Disability and Rehabilitation* 1, no. 4 [1994]: 33-47). See also Deborah Creamer ("Finding God in Our Bodies," pp. 28-29), who claims that "the church limits its own possibilities for growth and wholeness." Creamer insists that the issue of access is about justice (p. 40), but she argues that the inclusion of people with disabilities is not only important for their own sake: "We do it for ourselves as well. Society loses when we exclude people with disabilities, for their strengths go unacknowledged or underdeveloped, and we are cut off from what these people have to offer." When we create barriers of access, "we lose the additional insight that comes from experience of achievement and fulfillment, of solidarity and community. People with disabilities have as much, if not more, to offer as the rest of the world" (p. 41).

subjectivity is
source of
freedom

Spirit?

peal to enlightened self-interest is wrong in itself, but because in the context of grace it misconstrues the relationship between God and his people. If people with disabilities are welcomed at the table because without their presence the church would be impoverished, then the response should be that without them the Eucharist cannot be celebrated as the communion with Christ at all. This communion is a divine gift before it is an act of the church, and this means that people are welcome for no reason other than that they are invited by God.

6. "The Others Who Care"

Eiesland would probably not deny this, but her theological method does not provide her with other options to overcome the binary opposition inherent in her argument. I must say that this is unsurprising, because the antagonism between the subject and the object of liberation has proved to be a methodological problem for all liberation theologies. And the root of this problem, it seems to me, is the modern assumption that governs Western thought since the days of Kant and Fichte: the assumption that our subjectivity is the source of our freedom as human beings. While different schools in modern social theory are divided about what causes the lack of freedom for so many, they stand firmly united on this one cause: the free expression of the human subject as the author of his or her own story. Eiesland's "liberatory" theology is strongly committed to this assumption.

One approach to this apparent theological deadlock is to ask why she has no recourse to a theology within which God acts toward both persons with and without disabilities.[22] We may well ask why the attempt to think of inclusion of persons with disabilities as the work of the Spirit has no place in her work.[23] At the very best, Eiesland allows

---

22. Here I follow the lead of Peter Ochs, "The Logic of Indignity and the Logic of Redemption," in *God and Human Dignity,* ed. R. Kendall Soulen and Linda Woodhead (Grand Rapids: Eerdmans, 2006), pp. 143-60.

23. There is, as far as I can see, only one passage where she refers to the Holy Spirit. In this passage the pronoun "we" evidently includes all members of the church: "In the resurrection, Jesus Christ's body is not only the transfigured form that yet embodies the reality of impaired hands, feet, and side; it also consists of the body whose life and unity come from the Holy Spirit active in our continuing history. In summoning us to remem-

the able-bodied "other" to be present as "frightened companions."[24] Nonetheless, there is a *tertium datur* in her text: the "others who care."[25] But they are left unaccounted for. How can we account theologically for their presence? What is it that makes their presence intelligible?

The pertinence of these questions becomes particularly clear in the story of "the nuns of North Dakota," about the "body practice" of the laying on of hands, with which Eiesland ends her book (pp. 116-17). I read it as a wonderful example of how the Spirit may work as divine agent in overcoming our antagonisms. Having explained that in the Pentecostal church of her youth this practice was often associated with prayer healing — and thus experienced as stigmatizing — she then tells of a particular church service when the laying on of hands was done by some elderly nuns. She recalls the experience of having her body "redeemed for God as these spiritual women laid hands on me, caressing my pain, lifting my isolation, and revealing my spiritual body" (p. 117). The question of how to account for the redeeming faith of these women in a way that makes their practice intelligible cannot be answered by Eiesland's liberatory theology, I'm afraid. In order to find the answer, she would have to turn to "what theology already knows" and express it in theology's own voice. Eiesland's theology offers an account of "Who God is for her" as a disabled person who has experienced exclusion in the church as well as in theology. She answers in terms of the disabled God, and that answer enables her and her friends to participate in the church as a "community of struggle." In my view, we need a different account, one that explains *who we are before God* in order for us to become a communion of redemption.

---

brance of his body and blood at the table, the disabled God calls us to liberating relationships with God, with our bodies, and with others. We are called to be people who work for justice and access for all" (*The Disabled God*, p. 108).

24. I remind the reader of her explanation of the text in Luke, where she says that Jesus calls for "his frightened companions to recognize in the marks of impairment their own connection with God, their own salvation."

25. See n. 15 above.

7. A Theology of Access

The second approach to theology and disability I propose to discuss is called a "theology of access." Here again the emphasis will be on the formal level of method and strategy. While the liberatory approach primarily appeals to people with disabilities asserting themselves as a minority group, the theologies of access are more about appealing to religious communities as such. This is not to deny that claims to access pose an issue of social justice for them as well, because they also analyze the situation in terms of the marginalization and oppression of people with disabilities; but the binary opposition between the subjects and objects of inclusion is less prominent. Thus Jennie Weiss Block, in her book *Copious Hosting,* prefers a theology of access to a theology of liberation because she wishes to facilitate a "two-sided conversation" and wishes to avoid exclusivism.[26] In her view, access is the first goal of any theology of disability, but she has doubts that a liberation theology serves this goal well: "Could a disability liberation theology ultimately work against inclusion by further segregating the group?"[27]

Theologies of access are distinguished by at least three features. First, they do not express much interest in their own methodology; their emphasis is more pastoral than systematic.[28] Concomitant with this

26. Weiss Block, *Copious Hosting,* p. 21. Like Eiesland, Weiss Block also follows David Tracy's theological method of critical correlation, combining an investigation of Christian texts and of common human experience; unlike Eiesland, however, she does not radicalize this method. For Eiesland, people with disabilities are not evidently "at home" in Christian texts, and their experience is certainly not "common" to all human beings (*The Disabled God,* p. 21). By contrast, Weiss Block has reservations about the radicalization of liberation theology because it might itself become "exclusionary" (p. 99) [page citations given parenthetically in the text hereafter refer to *Copious Hosting*].

27. Weiss Block, *Copious Hosting,* p. 21. Interestingly, the author relates her doubts about liberation theology to the fact that she is not herself disabled. Eiesland's answer to this question would be, presumably, that the development of a disability minority culture suggests that many persons with disabilities participating in that culture apparently do not mind being among themselves with their own art, music, literature, etc. (Eiesland, "Barriers and Bridges," p. 209).

28. Govig, *Strong at the Broken Places,* pp. 134-35, lists these works under the heading of "pastoral care" rather then "theology." I take Helen Betenbaugh's *Theology of Disability* to be an exception: she combines a "hermeneutics of suspicion" in a theological critique of blaming the disabled person for her condition with a practical concern about access on physical and spiritual levels.

characteristic is their particular style, which is much more narrative than analytical and critical.[29] Second, they have a strong concern for biblical exegesis, particularly the stories and passages that deal with disabilities or persons with these disabilities. This concern is apparently related to their pastoral task of educating people in congregations about the sources of religious stigmatization.[30] In contrast, Eiesland's work puts much less weight on biblical texts. The reason may be that many of her friends within the disability movement do not expect the church and its primary texts to be of much help in their struggle.[31] Theologies of access, in contrast, regard it as their task to remove the barriers created by scriptural sources, or, more poignantly, by the ways these sources have been used. Third, because "access" is their main concern, these theologies are strong in offering many practical suggestions and ideas for how to make inclusion a reality in the church. These suggestions and ideas are not only concerned with material barriers — buildings, assembly halls, and so forth — but particularly with symbolic barriers that shape people's attitudes.[32]

Following my discussion of Eiesland's position, I will use Weiss Block's book to explore the difference between a liberatory theology of disability and a theology of access. In my discussion of this book, I will be primarily interested in its method; I will refer only briefly, at the end of the discussion, to the practical implications of the goal of access for which it argues.

With regard to method, there are two parallels to be drawn between Weiss Block's work and Eiesland's liberatory theology of disability. Like Eiesland, Weiss Block underscores the many differences between persons with disabilities, and because of this radical diversity, she calls the

29. To some extent, Weiss Block's book is an exception in this regard. The pastoral emphasis is especially prevalent in much of the earlier work. Examples are Wilke, *Creating the Caring Congregation;* Ohsberg, *The Church and Persons with Handicaps;* and Govig, *Strong at the Broken Places.*

30. Govig's book *Strong at the Broken Places* is forceful in this respect; see also Kathy Black, *A Healing Homiletic: Preaching and Disability* (Nashville: Abingdon Press, 1996).

31. Eiesland, "Barriers and Bridges," 219.

32. Govig, *Strong at the Broken Places,* coins the phrase "stairs and stares" to address these barriers, and he uses various stereotypes ("crippled," "marked," "pitied") to focus on theological and biblical sources. See also Wilke's classic *Creating the Caring Congregation.*

disability movement "the prototype movement of postmodernity." But unlike Eiesland, she nonetheless decides to use a "cross-disability" approach, by which she means an approach that does not distinguish between types of disability (pp. 28-29). The reason for this approach is her belief that focusing on a particular subgroup should be avoided whenever possible because "distinctions often lead the most vulnerable people to further stigmatization" (p. 29). In addition, Weis Block's account of people with disabilities, like Eiesland's, leans heavily toward the philosophy of the disability-rights movement (p. 17). Unlike Eiesland, on the other hand, she does not adopt the antagonistic approach of liberation theology. Not only is she keenly aware of the differences between the philosophical foundations of the disability-rights movement and the Christian community; she also wants to create a conversation that is informed by both sources (p. 18).[33]

> The theological community must learn about the philosophy that drives the disability movement and, then, be willing to critique the Christian tradition in the light of that philosophy. In like fashion, the disability community must be willing to search the Christian tradition for ways that can give meaning to the experience of being disabled. (p. 20)

This statement shows that, for Weiss Block, the space for subjectivity is more evenly distributed than is true in Eiesland's theology. The task for theology is self-criticism; the task for the disability community is to find out which meaning the Christian tradition might shed on their lives. In spite of Weiss Block's appreciation for the liberation-theology approach, she does not want to join it, mainly because she perceives the danger of being antagonistic. Using "oppression" as its primary hermeneutical key, liberation theology is tied to a two-place logic, in which it can assign only two roles: the oppressed and their oppressors. Weiss Block is clearly uncomfortable with this antagonism (pp. 20-21,

---

33. Weiss explains the tension by pointing out that "the disability movement is the product of the democratic liberalism of the Enlightenment based on a political philosophy that values equality, independence, and individual rights." In contrast to this philosophy, "Christianity is a two-thousand-year-old tradition that values the community over the individual, interprets life through ritual and symbol, and believes suffering can be transformative" (*Copious Hosting*, p. 19).

98-99), presumably because it leaves her in doubt about her own position as a white, middle-class woman without a disability.[34] Therefore, in her book she gives much less emphasis to the political nature of the struggle for inclusion. That's not to say that she avoids the language of "oppression," let alone rejects it; but she assigns it to a different location.

Acknowledging oppression in Weiss Block's book follows the reflection on the mystery of God's love rather than precedes it. This is clear from what she says are her guiding principles. First, she commits herself to an anthropology within which persons with disabilities "share fully in human nature"; second, she says that to reflect on disability is "to reflect on the mystery of God's love"; third, she says that "people with disabilities are oppressed"; and fourth, she says that the mandate of access and inclusion "is biblically based" (p. 22). Despite Weiss Block's lack of comment on the lexical order of these principles, it is not accidental that the principle of recognizing oppression comes after the principle of reflecting on the mystery of God's love. Creating access is a "mystical and moral" matter in which Christians attest to their baptismal promise "to welcome with love and stand ready to help" (p. 23). I interpret Weiss Block's logic here to be that Christians who have learned to celebrate God's love for all human beings cannot, without falsehood, ignore the oppression of marginalized people. Moving in the opposite direction — from identifying with the experience of the oppression of a minority group to the celebration of God's love for all — is much more difficult to do.[35]

Weiss Block's constructive program for a theology of access is, as we have seen, to carry out this two-way conversation between people

34. I have already pointed to the apparent inevitability of offering one's credentials as an author in this field (Ch. 1), which Weiss Block does not (want to) escape. She begins by saying that she cannot speak for people with disabilities because she is not disabled herself. Then, by way of offering her own credentials, she tells of her experience as a "secondary consumer" (*Copious Hosting*, p. 12) in her role as primary caretaker for Bobby, the younger brother who was adopted by her parents when he was four and she was twenty. Bobby was intellectually disabled and was diagnosed as seriously abused and mistreated in early childhood. He came into Weiss Block's home at the age of twelve, when their parents died (pp. 12-15).

35. This way of putting it makes one understand why the concept of love is conspicuously absent from Eiesland's book.

with disabilities and the Christian tradition. To articulate the voice of the disability-rights movement, she follows the pattern that we already know. The disability-rights movement in the United States got underway with its struggle for equal rights and social justice in the 1960s, and it won a major victory with the enactment of the ADA in 1990. Since churches are exempt from (some of) its regulations, there is still a lot of work to be done in that realm, which leads Weiss Block to her second task: the "examination of the Christian tradition from a disability perspective" (p. 79).

The theological program she then develops is a complex affair.[36] At its heart is the claim that a communion with others, where inclusion is the rule and not the exception, can only be realized in a Trinitarian context (p. 130). God sent his Son into the vulnerability of human life as a gift to all of humanity; it re-creates the opportunity for a life with God. The Christian community is a community that seeks to live a life "from and for God, and from and for others" guided by the Good News and empowered by the Spirit (p. 132). This is why the church cannot help but be an inclusive community.

> When we live for God, in Christ, through the power of the Holy Spirit, we cannot help but give hope to others, and we cannot help but be inclusive. The gospel of Jesus Christ is a call to a new world where outsiders become insiders. The church as the body of Christ is the quintessential inclusive community, where Jesus Christ, the one who is always identified with the outsider, presides as the copious host. (p. 132)

From this Trinitarian account of the inclusive being of the church, Weiss Block arrives at the moral task for humans of being "co-hosts." Copious hosting, first of all, means "being present" (p. 137): it is to be ready to lay down one's activities, to be still, and to listen before one responds. To clarify the theological meaning of "being present," Weiss Block refers to the Holy Spirit, "the marginalized member of the Trin-

---

36. A broad characterization would be to say that she takes three steps: first, she presents six theological topics from a disability perspective; second, she develops these topics into a full-blown theology of access, in order to arrive, third, at practical suggestions for various aspects of the church and the Christian community (*Copious Hosting*, pp. 129-30).

ity" (p. 139). In its neglect of the Spirit, she says, Western theology has neglected the mystery of God's loving presence in the world. "Being present" is much more than a moral demand; it can only be realized when persons with disabilities are also present, and thus it presupposes true communion. Understood in this way, the inclusion of disabled persons is a sign of the presence of God as the Holy Spirit, mediated by the very presence of people with disabilities. This is not because they represent a particular "holiness," but because their presence proves Christ's promise that the Spirit will be with those who live in Christ.[37]

8. "Beyond Access"

Based on this Trinitarian account of the Christian community as an inclusive community, Weiss Block works out a list of practical things to do: from breaking down attitudinal barriers by being careful in language and behavior — "disability etiquette" — to breaking down material barriers by redesigning buildings (pp. 144-55). But, while the program of inclusive action is itself impressive enough and means a lot of work for every congregation that takes it seriously, Weiss Block is not willing to leave it at that. Instead, she argues that the Christian community must go "beyond access." Unless there is something of a different nature underlying our practices of access and inclusion, she says, they are most likely to fail.

> I am deeply committed to principles of advocacy, social justice, and inclusionary practices. However, my experience has shown me that they are not enough. No laws, bishop's letters, human services paradigms, or parish accessibility committees will ever truly provide access to people with disabilities. Liberation and real access to the community will only be realized through personal relationships that develop into genuine friendships. (p. 158)

37. Weiss Block here depends on Johannine texts on the *paraclete*, "someone called in to help," which is translated by the English term advocate (John 14:26). Since advocacy is a crucial task according to the disability movement, the Holy Spirit is then the special gift to people with disabilities (*Copious Hosting*, pp. 140-41).

The practices and politics of inclusion will not create a lasting change for persons with disabilities unless there will be people willing to invest in friendships with them. Without true friendships, disabled persons will enjoy the new opportunities created by their equal rights most likely as "strangers in a strange land." According to Weiss Block, Christians are called, more than anything else, to friendship (p. 160).

I could not agree more, especially concerning people with intellectual disabilities. Rights open doors, not hearts. Hearts must be opened in order for people to know how to be present with human beings who don't speak, who are restless, who may be imprisoned by destructive impulses, who do not have the ability to fix their attention, or who even don't have a sense of who they are or what they want for themselves. In spite of all these varying characteristics, they nonetheless all share in the human need to be loved. Being loved is being needed, and being needed is more than existing merely as a bunch of problems to be solved.

Despite my agreement with Weiss Block's claim, much remains to be clarified about her concept. Like Eiesland, Weiss Block refers to human interdependence as a basic characteristic of our being; but she does not provide an explanation of what that entails and why. It is quite clear in what sense profoundly disabled human beings like Kelly and Oliver de Vinck need our presence. But in what sense is the reverse also true? Again, like Eiesland, Weiss Block wants to pitch "interdependence" against "independence" in a way that turns it into a primary virtue. In putting "interdependence" in a moral context, however, she opens the door to the kind of misconceptions that she has earlier tried to expel, namely, the idea that we need people with disabilities in our lives so that we may become the kind of people God wants us to be. Friendship is a gift to be received before it is a moral task to be performed. Here Weiss Block leaves the reader behind, puzzled, particularly when she ponders the question of whether there will be such friendships. In many ways, she says, genuine friendship is at cross-purposes with the values of modernity, whose emphases are on autonomy, control, freedom, and rights.

> Although these values appeared to create an attractive vision of society, in reality, they are a movement away from authentic friendship. Language about rights, control, and freedom does not foster situa-

tions of shared commitment to the common good or any willingness to put others before oneself. (p. 161)

This sudden reservation about rights language flatly contradicts much of what Weiss Block has said earlier in her book about the moral necessity to join the disability-rights movement. If ever there was a battle cry uniting all segments of the disability movement, it has been "No charity but rights!"[38] When Weiss Block now reminds us of our calling to friendship, she must surely imply that this is a calling of a different order.

Regarding this conclusion, one story in her book gives us much to think about. It is about Jason, a fourteen-year-old boy with a profound intellectual disability (at least that's the impression the reader gets from Weiss Block's description of him), and about Felicia Santos, a professional caregiver working with him — "truly compassionate, hardworking, dedicated to her work and the children, and so happy" (p. 89). Jason was born with a serious case of spina bifida: he has an enlarged head, his body is underdeveloped for his age, and his arms are twisted. His legs have been broken often because of a bone disease. Jason is also blind; he does not speak or feed himself; and he needs to be bathed and diapered with great care because of his fragile bones (pp. 89-91). Jason is surely profoundly limited in what his body enables him to do, but when he recognizes a voice of someone he is fond of, he claps his hands. Jason and Felicia are devoted to each other, says Weiss Block. She recalls a particular visit when she saw them together, a visit after which she went home from her work, "changed forever" (p. 91).

When I came up to them, Felicia was leaning forward, talking softly to Jason. He was smiling. I stood for a few minutes before speaking and watched their interaction. What I witnessed between them was the purest of love — the kind of love that asks for nothing in return. (p. 90)

---

38. The battle cry appears in titles and subtitles such as Doris Zames Fleisher and Frieda Zames, *The Disability Rights Movement: From Charity to Confrontation* (Philadelphia: Temple University Press, 2001); Richard K. Scotch, *From Good Will to Civil Rights: Transforming Federal Disability Policy* (Philadelphia: Temple University Press, 2001).

Weiss Block recalls this experience as a moment of revelation, because it made her realize that, with human beings like Jason, things are different from what they appear to be.

> I realized that Jason had more to give to me than I had to give him. I knew that in her simplicity and humility, Felicia knew more about life than I did. I understood that within the brokenness, wholeness, and hiddenness of Jason and within the kindness, patience, and generosity of Felicia, God was being revealed. (pp. 90-91)

The reason I bring up this story from Weiss Block's book is that it, like Eiesland's story of the nuns of North Dakota, suggests a fundamental theological insight: being with a person with a disability in a way that overcomes stigmatization requires character. However, even though both these stories record an experience that made a lifelong impression on the authors, both their theologies somehow fail to account for what they signify — though for different reasons. Eiesland's theology does not get beyond the binary opposition between those with and those without disabilities, which leads her to argue for a church that understands itself as a community of struggle. Weiss Block's theology does move beyond this opposition, but in doing so, she has to leave behind the philosophy of the disability-rights movement to which she has committed her approach. Both stories transcend the struggle for political change in the church in that they narrate the flourishing that human beings experience when they receive love that asks nothing in return, as Weiss Block puts it. This experience points to something more fundamental underlying the struggle for change, without which it may very well lose much of its liberating potential. Stories such as these are frequently told, but somehow the theologies fail to make them crucial to their accounts of what it means to include people with disabilities in our communities.

To what extent has Weiss Block's book accomplished its mission? She set out to engage in a two-way conversation between the disability movement and Christian theology. Christian theology must learn about the disability movement's philosophy and be willing to critique its own tradition in light of that philosophy; and the disability movement must be willing to search the Christian tradition for the light it sheds on the experience of people with disabilities. If it is agreed that the philosophy of the disability movement is a philosophy of rights — about which there can hardly be a dispute — then three things follow from the way Weiss Block has pursued her task as a theologian.

First, despite the many virtues of her book, Weiss Block has not interpreted the Christian tradition in terms of the philosophy of rights, because in the end what she suggests is that this philosophy must fail its own objectives. Second, if she is correct at this point, as I believe she may well be, then the Christian tradition *should not* be critiqued from the perspective of the philosophy of rights; instead, it should go the other way around, as Weiss Block shows. Third, if the two previous conclusions hold, then it appears that Weiss Block's task must be obsolete from the perspective of the disability-rights movement. From the perspective of its own philosophy, it has not much to gain by searching the Christian tradition for "meaning" in ways that contradict its own insights. Wherever the reader finds himself with regard to these conclusions, at least it is clear that Weiss Block's contribution to the two-way conversation leaves a few important questions unanswered.

Chapter Six

Theology and Disability II

The Class of "neighbor" has no bounds.

David Pailin[1]

1. Introduction

The two remaining theological approaches to disability are different from the ones I discussed in the previous chapter in that they do not present themselves as "theologies of disability." That is, they are not constructed as a project of theological support for a particular moral cause, as are the theologies of Eiesland and Weiss Block. Eiesland's liberatory theology applies a model that can be used — indeed, has been used quite frequently — in support of any oppressed group seeking to subvert a symbolic order that imposes a negative identity on it. Weiss Block's theology of access shares this concern, but it presents itself as a more moderate version of the same project. Within this model, "disability" is inscribed into the very being of God, thereby enabling a positive identification that subverts the negative identity of disabled people. Social stigma is transformed into Christian symbol. The positive self-identification that supports this theological move, in turn, helps marginalized people find their own identity. I take this to mean that restoring subjective agency is the ultimate aim of these the-

---

1. David A. Pailin, *A Gentle Touch: From a Theology of Handicap to a Theology of Human Being* (London: SPCK, 1992), p. 17.

ologies. In spite of historical and sociological differences, the aim is to restore their subjects to the power of using their human capabilities.

The theological accounts I will discuss in this chapter pursue a different course. First, they focus explicitly on *intellectual* disability; second, their approach does not depend on disability as a social construct that needs to be theologically deconstructed in order to liberate people from a particular negative identity. Instead, their accounts tend to construe intellectual disability as part of the human condition, albeit in different ways.

For reasons that I set forth in Chapter 1, there is much to be said for this approach insofar as the condition of being intellectually disabled construed in this way defies any kind of hierarchy of being human as we have discussed it above. In contrast, emancipatory and deconstructionist methodologies (particularly as we have seen them in Eiesland's work) tend to underscore rather than subvert the limited capabilities implied in intellectual disability. This tendency comes from their aim to restore human agency.

The first approach to intellectual disability outside the emancipatory framework is found in the work of Stanley Hauerwas, who has a track record of writing about intellectually disabled people long before the field of bioethics considered disability to pose an "ethical issue." Hauerwas's work stands out in that he refuses to give any kind of justification for the existence of these people. In fact, in most of his writings on the subject, he uses the existence of the intellectually disabled as a way to detect the presuppositions underlying the culture of modernity. The culture of modernity, according to Hauerwas, seeks to get rid of people whose very existence makes a mockery of its most cherished ideal, namely, that individual freedom defines the moral meaning of being human. By way of contrast, Hauerwas refers to the Christian church as a community within which the existence of such people is not regarded as a calamity or catastrophe that needs to be avoided or repaired, but a community in which they are welcomed and appreciated. This is why his approach is appropriately called a "theology of witness."

The second approach I wish to discuss is found in David Pailin's book *A Gentle Touch,* which was inspired by Pailin's acquaintance with Alexander, a severely disabled newborn child whom he grew very fond of during the brief span of Alexander's life. Pailin understands that, up to the point where he meets Alexander, most of his theological thinking about humanity had no place for his little hero. Coming from a background in process theology, Pailin had just finished a theological essay arguing that the meaning of our lives consists in what we contribute to God's creation when he realized that this view imposed a standard that rendered Alexander's life meaningless. This realization gave him the urgent task of rethinking his earlier claims and replacing them with a more inclusive view, which he presents as a "theology of human being." A particularly strong point in Pailin's reflections is his resistance to any instrumental justification of Alexander's painful life that might turn it into a means in service of a greater good.

My point in discussing the work of Hauerwas and Pailin, as indicated, is that they do not seem to be interested in a theology of disability. Rather, one might say that their respective approaches reverse the order of theological representation. "Disability" represents the human before God rather than the other way around. This is most clearly the case in Hauerwas's work. Whereas Eiesland inscribes "disability" in the body of the resurrected Christ, Hauerwas describes the lives of the disabled as embodying the very meaning of human creatureliness. Whereas Eiesland regards disability as the representation of divine being — as "God for me"[2] — Hauerwas regards it as the representation of being human *coram deo*. Either way, however, the remaining problem is that "disability" is constructed in terms that continue to rely on the distinction between "us" and "them," which is a distinction that both authors are, at the same time, eager to expel. Eiesland's thought attempts to overcome this distinction by affirming that God himself participates in disabled human existence as all human beings inevitably must do at some point in their lives.

Hauerwas seeks to overcome the distinction by affirming that disabled existence represents the core of being human as dependent being vis-à-vis its creator. Pailin moves in a direction similar to Hauerwas's, but his argument does not rely on a theological interpretation of the distinction between disability and ability. However, his an-

2. Nancy L. Eiesland, *The Disabled God: Toward a Liberatory Theology of Disability* (Nashville: Abingdon Press, 1994), p. 89.

thropology continues to rely on the notion of agency as the default marker defining our humanity. Thus, where Hauerwas wants to argue that "disability" represents creatureliness in a most exemplary way, thereby using the notion of disability as a theological trope, Pailin leaves all theological exemplification behind. However, his account unintentionally remains captive to a hierarchy of created being that retains achievement as its implicit standard.

2. Digging Up Presuppositions[3]

The lives of people with intellectual disabilities have for a long time been a recurring theme in the writings of Stanley Hauerwas.[4] In his many collections of essays, there are a number of essays on caring for the "mentally handicapped," as he calls them.[5] However, Hauerwas has

3. The sections on Hauerwas contain material from Hans S. Reinders, "The Virtue of Writing Appropriately. Or: Is Stanley Hauerwas Right in Thinking He Should Not Write Anymore on the Mentally Handicapped?" *God, Truth and Witness: Engaging Stanley Hauerwas,* ed. L. Gregory Jones, Reinhard Hütter, and C. Rosalee Veloso Ewell (Grand Rapids: Brazos Press, 2005), pp. 53-70.

4. His earliest publication on the subject is "Christian Care of the Retarded," *Theology Today* 30, no. 2 (1973): 130-37. Further essays are: "Community and Diversity: The Tyranny of Normality," in *Suffering Presence: Theological Reflections on Medicine, the Mentally Handicapped, and the Church* (Notre Dame, IN: University of Notre Dame Press, 1986), pp. 211-17 (originally published in *National Apostolate with Mentally Retarded Persons Quarterly* [Spring/Summer 1977]); "Having and Learning to Care for Retarded Children," in *Truthfulness and Tragedy: Further Investigations into Christian Ethics* (Notre Dame, IN: University of Notre Dame Press, 1977), pp. 147-56; "The Retarded and the Criteria for the Human," in *Truthfulness and Tragedy,* pp. 156-63; "Suffering, Medical Ethics, and the Retarded Child," in *Truthfulness and Tragedy,* pp. 164-68; "The Gestures of a Truthful Story," *Theology Today* 42, no. 2 (1985): 181-189; "Suffering the Retarded: Should We Prevent Retardation?" in *Suffering Presence,* pp. 159-81; "The Retarded, Society, and the Family: The Dilemma of Care," in *Suffering Presence,* pp. 189-210; "The Church and the Mentally Handicapped: A Continuing Challenge to the Imagination," in *Dispatches from the Front: Theological Engagements with the Secular* (Durham, NC: Duke University Press, 1994); "Timeful Friends: Living with the Handicapped," in *Sanctify Them in the Truth: Holiness Exemplified* (Nashville: Abingdon, 1998), pp. 143-56.

5. Hauerwas has never had much patience for politically correct speech, so he does not bother about the changing terminology in the field and continues to speak of the "mentally handicapped." The term commonly accepted nowadays is, of course, "people with intellectual disabilities," which is the term I use in this book.

never written about the subject to discuss an "ethical issue." The first thing we should consider about his writings is, therefore, what he is actually doing in these texts.

Generally, Hauerwas's aim is to question the belief that the existence of people with disabilities confronts us with a "problem."[6] Suggesting ways of getting away from that notion, he repeatedly turns our attention to those who dedicate their lives to the task of caring for people with intellectual disabilities. In other words, he intends his writings on the subject to report and sustain Christian "witness." And with this intention he seeks to undermine the project of so-called applied ethics, to which he objects because of its presupposition of ethical expertise. Ethical experts are those who consider it their job to address "ethical issues" on our social and political agenda in ways that help establish a moral consensus. Hauerwas is not interested in moral consensus; he is interested in how we learn to live a Christian life.

A clear example of his way of subverting the project of applied ethics is found in his collection of essays *Suffering Presence,* where he takes on the question "Should we prevent retardation?"[7] People involved in applied ethics who have faced this kind of question usually begin by identifying the "dilemma" that this question evokes; then they lay out some procedure of ethical thinking that defines the moral principles that are to be applied to the case in question. And with this procedure, ethicists ideally arrive at the kind of taxonomy that enables them to distinguish between the morally right, the morally wrong, and the morally permissible. Hauerwas is not at all interested in this project. Consider the following quotation, where he discusses the prevention of disability:

6. Hauerwas, "The Church and the Mentally Handicapped," p. 177: "The challenge of being as well as caring for those called 'mentally handicapped' is to prevent those who wish they never existed or would 'just go away' from defining them as 'the problem.' It is almost impossible to resist descriptions that make being mentally handicapped a 'problem,' since those descriptions are set by the power of the 'normal.'"

7. Stanley Hauerwas, "Suffering the Retarded: Should We Prevent Retardation?" pp. 159-81 [page references in parentheses in the text refer to this work]. It is appropriate to acknowledge my indebtedness to Hauerwas's views, particularly as he expresses them in his book *Suffering Presence,* a book that in many ways paves the way for the argument in my book *The Future of the Disabled in Liberal Society: An Ethical Analysis* (Notre Dame, IN: University of Notre Dame Press, 2000). The critical questions that are to be raised in this chapter are an attempt to move beyond the scope of both our arguments.

> Surely, we ought to prevent retardation. Certainly as many couples as
> can ought to be encouraged to maintain good prenatal care. . . . For if
> retardation can be eliminated, then the amount of money needed for
> constant care will be significantly reduced. Better a short-term outlay
> now than a continuing cost.

Within the context of "applied ethics," the first sentence in this quote
reads as if it states a moral principle of action; the second sentence
reads like a straightforward utilitarian justification of the same. Anyone
reading Hauerwas in this way cannot help but be surprised at his incon-
sistencies, for on the next page we encounter a statement that claims
exactly the opposite position.

> Nevertheless, there seems to be something deeply wrong [with] the
> message "prevent retardation." (pp. 159-60)

From the perspective of a carefully argued moral taxonomy, his reasoning appears to be very puzzling. In order to understand what he is doing, we must embark on a quite different kind of inquiry: "To say what is
wrong with such a policy involves some of the most profound questions
of human existence, including our relationship with God" (p. 160). Apparently, Hauerwas is not mapping a moral issue; instead, he is raising
a theological question. What on one level appears to be a straightforward consequentialist justification of the policy of prevention appears
on another level as a deeply questionable practice — but for very different reasons. Hauerwas is not interested whatsoever in whether or not —
and if so, when — we should, or may, engage in the practice of prevention. He is interested in why people think these questions are important moral questions to begin with.

> It has become common in our society to assume that certain chil-
> dren born with severe birth defects who also happen to be retarded
> should not be kept alive in order to spare them a lifetime of suffer-
> ing. But why do we assume that it is the role of medicine to save us
> from suffering? By exploring whether we ought to try to eliminate
> the retarded I hope, therefore, to make explicit a whole set of as-
> sumptions about suffering and medicine's role in its alleviation.
> (p. 160)

Hauerwas has no intention of solving moral dilemmas, or in assisting other people in solving their moral quandaries. Instead, he wants to know what makes us believe we have such problems. In order to find out about these beliefs, his strategy is to bring to the surface what lies beneath our views. Hauerwas's theoretical aim is always to dig up presuppositions.

3. "Suffering Presence"

In the present case, he is digging up presuppositions about suffering. For example, why should it be obvious that we must prevent intellectual disability? The answer appears to be that most people take for granted that people with intellectual disabilities suffer from their condition, despite the fact that their lives may be as full of different kinds of experiences — good and bad — as any other lives. Added to this premise, that "the disabled suffer from their disability," is another one, which is that the prevention of suffering is a necessary end of moral action. Hauerwas takes this to be a "deep" conviction that is widely held in our society.

> No one should will that an animal should suffer gratuitously. No one should will that a child should endure an illness. No one should will that another person should suffer from hunger. No one should will that a child should be born retarded. That suffering should be avoided is a belief as deep as any we have. That someone born retarded suffers is obvious. Therefore, if we believe we ought to prevent suffering, it seems we ought to prevent retardation. (p. 164)

Though Hauerwas does not want to challenge the belief that we ought to prevent suffering, he does want to question that people commonly identify "retardation" with suffering. Do people with retardation suffer from being retarded, or is the problem rather "the suffering we feel the retarded cause us" (p. 165)?[8] To answer this question, Hauerwas attempts

---

8. Against his own habit, in this text Hauerwas is quite unclear about who is included in "we," "our," and "us." Apparently, he has in mind people who do not know from firsthand experience what it is to live a disabled life or to share one's life with someone living such life.

a phenomenological analysis of suffering, within which he places suffering in the context of human fate and action (pp. 165-70).

Sometimes we suffer because of what happens to us — floods, diseases, and so forth — and sometimes we suffer because of who we want to be, or what we have done. Our suffering has both objective and subjective causes.[9] In the present context, I have already noted the example of young parents of disabled children looking back on their first reactions. "Our world fell apart," is a common expression for that devastating experience. That kind of statement indicates a subjective cause of suffering, which is shown in the fact that at later stages these parents often manage to rearrange their world and then are capable of speaking about parenting a disabled child in terms of "enrichment." In other words, suffering is very often the result of our own act, namely, the act of living our lives with particular ideals and expectations.

Of course, not everything stressful or painful results from human action. Some things just happen without any involvement on our part. Many people in our culture think of giving birth to a child with a disability as a tragedy, a misfortune caused by Stepmother Nature. On a larger scale, hurricanes and earthquakes are natural disasters that come to mind. But, as Hauerwas is quick to point out, such examples also show that the distinction between objective and subjective causes of suffering cannot be pushed too far. Nothing is apparently more fateful than the natural catastrophes that sweep entire regions away, until we start to notice that sometimes earthquakes have been predicted, or that warnings about vulnerable coastlines and threats of floods have been ignored.

However, the line between fate and action does not get blurred merely on the level of causation; the same is true on the level of consequence. Hauerwas cites the well-known example of how sick people can overcome suffering from a disease once they receive a diagnosis. What until that moment appeared to be a blow of blind fate has acquired a

9. Much of the argument with the social constructionist approach to disability in Ch. 2 is relevant here. That people in our society usually respond negatively to disability has both subjective and objective causes. The latter we attribute to impairment, the former to culturally mediated ideas and expectations about a "normal" life. See Reinders, *The Future of the Disabled in Liberal Society,* Ch. 3, where I use Hauerwas's analysis of suffering as a lead to disentangle "disability" and "suffering."

name, "cancer," or "autism." With that name usually comes a course of action, such as a therapy, or a program in which one learns to adapt. Fate gets infused, and is thereby transformed, through action. Hauerwas does not wish to suggest, of course, that the entanglements of fate and action show how suffering is *always* a matter of our own responsibility; nor does he wish to say that human beings should always accept suffering as an opportunity for redemptive action. Nonetheless, he does wish to say that the interrelationship of fate and action may lead us to reconsider the kinds of sufferings we are inclined to reject as unbearable.

> It may well be that those forms of suffering we believe we should try to prevent or to eliminate are those that we think impossible to integrate into our projects, socially or individually. It is exactly those forms of suffering which seem to intrude uncontrollably into our lives, which appear to be the most urgent candidates for prevention. Thus our sense that we should try to prevent those kinds of suffering turns out to mean that we should try to prevent those kinds of suffering that we do not feel can serve any human good. (p. 167)

It is no exaggeration to say that many people in our culture believe that the condition of being intellectually disabled is precisely that: a condition of suffering that cannot serve any human good. Since many also believe that the proliferation of genetic testing and screening has brought the prevention of disability into the ambit of human responsibility, people tend to support a general policy to that effect. This explains a growing concern about "responsible reproductive behavior."[10] Hauerwas insists, however, that this presupposition must be questioned. His argument can be spelled out as follows.

First, it is not at all clear that, when people with an intellectual disability suffer, they suffer from their disability (p. 171). If only for the fact of their limited understanding, the source of their suffering may well be our culture's response to their limitations. They may have learned to

10. As a matter of fact, Hauerwas's essay was inspired by his objections to a film promoting the prevention of disability that was sponsored by the American Association of Retarded Citizens ("Suffering the Retarded," p. 159). For a critique of the linking of the proliferation of genetic testing and screening with the concept of responsible reproduction see Reinders, *The Future of the Disabled,* pp. 66-102.

suffer from the ways they have been treated as defective human beings. Even though a person with Down's syndrome needs to learn to deal with the effects of his limited powers of understanding, it does not follow that he suffers from his syndrome for that reason. That people with disabilities always suffer because of their disabling condition is not evidently true; in some cases it is obviously false.

Second, if there are forms of suffering that stem from how we want to live our lives, then the suffering attributed to disabled people and their families may well be a matter of projection. To explain what he has in mind, Hauerwas refers (somewhat surprisingly, one might say) to Adam Smith's *Theory of Moral Sentiments* (p. 174). Usually our empathy for other people's fortune or misfortune is based on a sympathetic imagination that leads us to either rejoice in their happiness or deplore their state of misery. This psychological mechanism does not work well with respect to the intellectually disabled, according to Hauerwas, because frequently we find them quite cheerful and happy with their situation. But, he observes, that doesn't stop us from deploring their lives.[11] The feeling we have about our perception cannot be the reflection of "any sentiment in the sufferer," as Adam Smith puts it. Instead, Hauerwas infers, it must be informed by considering how we would feel in "being retarded," which we necessarily do from our present perspective as people with reason and judgment (p. 174). Therefore, Hauerwas concludes, our view of disabled lives may not be informed primarily by the experience of the people living such lives but rather by feelings about *ourselves* that we generate by imagining ourselves in their situation. The presupposition that the disabled suffer from their disability has its origin in the conception we have of ourselves and our own lives. Our presuppositions about disabled lives, according to Hauerwas, may be self-reflective more than anything else, in which case it is merely presumptuous and inconsequential.[12]

---

11. We should recall that these sentences refer to a hypothetical "we" that does not reflect the views of many "insiders" who have learned to see differently. As indicated, Hauerwas argues here from an "outsider" perspective.

12. This conclusion concurs with my earlier claim that the question concerning the lives of people with intellectual disabilities is not so much what we think about "them," but rather how what we think about them is informed by how we think about ourselves (Ch. 1 and Ch. 3).

Following this analysis, we can see how the self-images dominating our contemporary culture become crucial to Hauerwas's critique. The self-images of our age are prone to the illusion of self-possession, which has the denial of suffering as its flipside. Contrary to popular belief, Hauerwas claims, our identity cannot be grounded in self-possession, because as human beings we are necessarily dependent on our environment — both natural and cultural. We survive in interaction with it, which by definition entails that we do not control it. We deny this, according to Hauerwas, at our own peril. The refusal to accept the fact that suffering from our own world is part of our existence signals for him the denial of our incompleteness. As human beings, "we are inherently creatures of need," which is why we suffer, because suffering indicates the absence of fulfillment (p. 170). This does not imply that we have to accept our sufferings, but it does indicate that there is a risk in losing sight of our humanity when we reject them as contrary to the human good.

Hauerwas believes that the illusion of control leads us to identify intellectual disability with suffering. Consequently, we not only tend to deny that suffering is part of our human existence; we also tend to turn away from those who confront us with it. People who suffer experience loneliness, which is one of the reasons that we fear it. They confront us with nonbeing rather than being.

> The retarded, therefore, are particularly troubling for us. Even if they do not suffer by being retarded, they are certainly people in need. Even worse, they do not try to hide their needs. They are not self-sufficient, they are not self-possessed; they are in need. Even more, they do not evidence the proper shame for being so. They simply assume that they are what they are and they need to provide no justification for being such. It is almost as if they have been given a natural grace to be free from the regret most of us feel for our neediness. (p. 176)

Clearly, "natural grace" is not a term Hauerwas would use accidentally. People with intellectual disabilities are "prophet like" in that their existence reveals what is hidden in "our false sense of self-possession" (p. 169). In revealing their neediness in unencumbered ways — not as deliberate choice, but simply by being who they are — they offer us true

201

insight into our own condition, which liberates us from our own mis-conception of ourselves as "authors" of our own lives (p. 177).

> That is why in the face of the retarded we are offered an opportunity to see God, for like God they offer us an opportunity of recognizing the character of our neediness. In truth, the retarded in this respect are but an instance of the capacity we each have for one another. That the retarded are singled out is only an indication of how they can serve for us all as a prophetic sign of our true nature as creatures des-tined to need God and, thus, one another. (p. 179)

There is a strong sense in which intellectually disabled people exem-plify true human being for Hauerwas. What both these quotations also show, however, is that in his reflections, people with intellectual dis-abilities somehow continue to appear as strange. His rich phenomenol-ogy of human suffering notwithstanding, Hauerwas's default percep-tion of disability remains that of a condition that is *alien* to us. Even though the source of alienation has shifted as a result of his argument, and lies in our false illusions rather than in their "neediness," there continues to be some kind of distance.

> That such fellow feeling is possible does not mean that they are "re-ally just like us." They are not. They do not have the same joys we have nor do they suffer just as we suffer. But in our joys and in our suffer-ings they recognize something of their joy and their suffering, and they offer to share their neediness with us. Such an offer enables us in quite surprising ways to discover that we have needs to share with them. We are thus freed from the false and vicious circle of having to appear strong before others' weakness, and we are then able to join with the retarded in the common project of sharing our needs and satisfactions. As a result, we no longer fear them. (p. 177)

Hauerwas's language continues to use the distinction between "us" and "them," and one cannot help wondering whether this is only a question of language. His claim that in the face of the "retarded" we have an opportunity to see God comes close to substituting "God" for "them," which may explain why Hauerwas may think there is a remain-ing distance. But this explanation does not seem to fit his argument. If it is true, as Hauerwas has argued, that suffering is falsely attributed to the intellectually disabled on grounds of a self-conception in denial of our own vulnerability, why should it be true that they "are not really just like us"? Why should it be true that "they do not have the same joys we have nor do they suffer just as we suffer"? Whence this categorical difference?

Another way of raising the same question emerges when we look at how Hauerwas uses Adam Smith's theory of sympathy. He suggests that the psychological mechanism of sympathetic imagination does not work well with respect to the intellectually disabled because, if it did, we would rejoice in the perception that such people are frequently quite cheerful and happy with their situation. Hauerwas declares that we do not, which claim in my experience is plainly false. His explanation is, as we have seen, that in considering ourselves in the position of "being retarded," we cannot help but proceed from our own condition as persons with reason and judgment. When one actually believes that "they" are not really like "us," however, the appearance of cheerfulness may trigger a different response. On that assumption, what appears as cheerfulness is more appropriately characterized as tragedy.[14] That is not what Hauerwas wishes to say, but what he is saying does not sound like rejoicing in their cheerfulness either. All his argument shows is why we may no longer fear them.

4. Writing about the Disabled

A number of years ago, Hauerwas decided not to write anymore on the subject of intellectual disability.[15] He acknowledged its importance for

13. Hauerwas, "Suffering the Retarded," p. 176. This quote indicates that Hauerwas is far from promoting self-affirmation and self-identification as acts that are critical to human being in the way Eiesland does, together with all other social constructionists.

14. Note Adam Smith's description in the passage quoted by Hauerwas: "The poor wretch, who is in it, laughs and sings perhaps, and is altogether insensible of his misery" ("Suffering the Retarded," p. 174). On the supposition that there is a "real" difference, grounded in the fact of "them" not understanding their own condition of being intellectually disabled as "we" understand it, can their cheerfulness, then, be truly appreciated as cheerfulness?

15. Stanley Hauerwas, "Timeful Friends: Living with the Handicapped," in *Sanctify Them in the Truth: Holiness Exemplified* (Nashville: Abingdon, 1998), pp. 143-56 [following page citations in parentheses in the text refer to this work].

his theological thinking over the years, but he realized that it had primarily served a theoretical purpose in his work. In fact, he was not writing about the "mentally handicapped" at all, as he puts; in a sense, his purpose in using it was as a theological critique of modernity, and particularly of its moral beliefs (p. 145). According to Hauerwas, the moral beliefs of modernity cannot make sense of the lives lived by intellectually disabled people. Modernists would say that our lives are meaningful only to the extent that they are meaningful to ourselves. We are supposed to be the "authors" of our own lives. And what modernists believe, Hauerwas tells us, is in sharp contrast to what Christians believe. "As Christians," he says, "we know we have not been created to be our own authors, to be autonomous. We are creatures. Dependency, not autonomy, is one of the *ontological characteristics* of our lives" (p. 147; italics added).

This claim indicates why and how the existence of persons with intellectual disabilities is pertinent to Hauerwas's theological project. It shows why the modern rejection of dependency is mistaken: disabled lives testify to what it means to be a creature. The fact that people have not chosen these lives, he writes, and that these people are not the authors of their own narrative, "reveals the character of *our* lives" (p. 147; italics added). Consequently, in Hauerwas's conception, the lives of humans with intellectual disabilities are paradigmatic for, rather than exceptional to, human existence. The theoretical status of the subject is acknowledged in the claim that the lives of disabled people provided him with a warrant for his theological realism: "I have used the mentally handicapped as *material markers* to show that Christian speech can and in fact does make claims about the way things are" (p. 147; italics added).

Theological realism for Hauerwas is, of course, couched in the narrative of the cross and the resurrection of Jesus Christ.[16] Only the Christian narrative can make us free to face our incompleteness without despair and share our lives with each other as gifts. Therefore, the presence of intellectually disabled lives does not present Christians with a particular challenge, at least not in the sense that their lives need some kind of moral justification. On the contrary, the Christian com-

16. See Hauerwas, *With the Grain of the Universe: The Church's Witness and Natural Theology* (Grand Rapids: Brazos Press, 2001).

munity is formed by practices that enable us to share our lives with them (p. 147). "Theologically thinking about the mentally handicapped," Hauerwas affirms, "helps us see that claims about the way things are cannot be separated from the way we should live" (p. 148).

Nonetheless, his theological writings about people with intellectual disabilities caused him uneasiness, despite their crucial importance to his project. Writing "about" these people is not what you do when you really care for them, he said. If you care, you write "with" and "for" them. But in order to write "for" them, you need to know such people.

> By "know" I mean you must be with the handicapped in a way they may be able to claim you as a friend. I was once so claimed, but over the last few years, I have not enjoyed such a friendship. So when I now write about the ethics of caring for the mentally handicapped, I fear I am not talking about actual people but more of my memories of the mentally handicapped. (p. 144)

Writing about disability, I take it, cannot be done truthfully without being witness to the love of Christ. Reflecting on where his uneasiness was coming from, Hauerwas suggests that he may have fallen prey to "the Kantian narrative" that teaches us never to use other people merely as a means for our own purposes. This appears as a somewhat curious explanation for a Christian theologian who is inspired by Aristotle and Aquinas. It suggests that, if we dispel the Kantian narrative, the moral objection to using other people loses its force. Even so, the question for an Aristotelian to ask would be a different one: it would not be whether we may use persons with intellectual disabilities for our own agendas, but rather what good we are giving up by depriving ourselves of their friendship. Obviously, Aristotle could never have asked the same question, because friendship with an intellectually disabled person would be inconceivable for him. Nothing could have been more obvious to Aristotle, presumably, than that "they" are not like "us."

Much the same is true of liberals who believe that because intellectually disabled people cannot be the authors of their own lives, their existence is unintelligible; there need to be "reasons" to make sense of their existence (p. 144). Christians do not believe this, according to Hauerwas, and thus they do not need any justification for that existence. Instead, the Christian narrative shapes a community that knows how to appreciate the presence of people with disabilities, intellectual or otherwise, as a gift. This is what being a witness of Christ Jesus means.

Given this assertion, which appears frequently in Hauerwas's writings on the subject, it is curious to see that the role of being this witness in his work is always assigned to particular people.[17] In the final essays of his book *Suffering Presence,* Hauerwas celebrates the witness of families that raise children with intellectual disabilities and accept these children as they are.[18] Similarly, in the last part of his essay "Timeful Friends," he refers to the people of L'Arche, a community founded by the French Canadian priest Jean Vanier. These are people who share their lives with persons with intellectual disabilities as a way of witnessing Christ. Learning from the experience of their communities, I think we need to move beyond the vicariousness of the witness of these people and face the question of what being committed to a person with an intellectual disability would mean for our own witness. Our lives may be changed in ways far exceeding the mere loss of fear of these people. Facing friendship as our vocation would be a first step.

5. "A Theology of Human Being"

David Pailin's book *A Gentle Touch* is a rewarding place to start, because Pailin begins with the confession of having his life changed by Alexander, the newborn son of his friends. Alexander did not make it beyond the age of thirteen months because of his severely disabling condition.[19] Pailin informs us that, at the time of Alexander's birth, he was working on a paper on human salvation in which he was defending the

---

17. See John Swinton, "Introduction: Hauerwas on Disability," in *Critical Reflections on Stanley Hauerwas' Theology of Disability: Disabling Society, Enabling Theology,* ed. J. Swinton (Binghamton, NY: Haworth Press, 2004), pp. 1-9.

18. Hauerwas, "The Retarded, Society, and the Family: The Dilemma of Care," in *Suffering Presence,* pp. 189-210; see also "Community and Diversity: The Tyranny of Normality," pp. 211-17.

19. Pailin, *A Gentle Touch: From a Theology of Handicap to a Theology of Human Being.* [following page citations in parentheses in the text refer to this book].

thesis — inspired by process theology — that with all of our experiences we contribute to the qualities of God's everlasting existence. God responds to us in ways that make us envision a more creative life, full of goodness and beauty. God saves, Pailin's paper concluded, "by preserving what people have achieved and by evoking in them creative responses to their situation" (p. 4). But then he met Alex, and he realized that he had written off this child's life. He was saying that the worth of human beings consists in what they are able to contribute to the divine experience, which made "development" and "achievement" the key notions in his theology of human salvation. The realization turned into a nightmare.

> The nightmare arose from a possible inference from my paper, namely, that a person's worth could be graded according to the richness of his or her contribution to the divine experience. . . . My nightmare was that if the worth of human beings depends on the value of what they contribute, some might argue that those who cannot contribute significantly (and even more those whose demands leave them net debtors of value) should be deemed disposable when resources are limited. (p. 13)

Seeing the possible implications of his paper, Pailin revoked his entire argument and set out to argue for a different view, in which "we are of worth not because of what we contribute to God but because of the value God bestows upon us" (p. 14). This reversed perspective then became the guiding principle of Pailin's account. The book about Alex was his attempt to explain what that principle implies.

In this section, I will describe the central claim of Pailin's book; in the next, I will raise some questions about it. A strong point is his critique of evaluations of the presence of people with disabilities in terms of instrumental value. Pailin confesses that he had initially set out to write a liberation theology about disability after Alex's death, but then changed his mind. Since the reasons he adduces for changing his approach do not conflict with my earlier discussion of Eiesland's work, I will focus here only on the constructive position he develops in terms of "a theology of human being."[20]

20. Since Pailin's book was published two years before Eiesland's, he discusses liberation theology only as a possible approach to his subject. The main difference between

Considering the question of what the theological problem of disability is, Pailin begins by eliminating a few answers that he thinks

---

his criticisms and my own is that, where I follow Eiesland's logic from the perspective of her own project, Pailin develops an external critique from the perspective of profound intellectual disability. He presents four reasons why a theology of disability cannot be a theology of liberation as such. The first reason regards the claim to self-representation as the necessary condition of liberating action, which he argues cannot be applicable to those with profound intellectual disabilities. They can only be represented by others (*A Gentle Touch,* pp. 20-22). Pailin immediately concedes that this implies the danger of allowing judgmental assessments of other people's lives; but he claims that, for persons with intellectual disabilities, this can't be avoided. However, it is interesting that Pailin calls the risk of judging other people's lives "the danger of dehumanization," which he explains by saying that "the feelings, insights and desires of handicapped people themselves must be taken seriously" (p. 23). This is no doubt correct, but it does seem to indicate that, for Pailin, dehumanizing people is coterminous with not treating them as subjects.

The second basis for his argument against a liberation theology of disability is that it tends to promote the development of minority-group culture. Apart from the right to name their own experiences, they must also be encouraged to work out their own patterns of "authentic life" (p. 24). Here Pailin anticipates what Eiesland and others will later identify as "disability culture." His argument against it is that it would reinforce the segregation of persons with intellectual disabilities. At the same time, however, Pailin also seems to favor the continuation of some sort of separatism when he expresses his doubts about so-called community care as "an excuse for abandoning those who need support to situations with which they cannot cope" (p. 25).

His third reason why a liberation theology of disability is inadequate is that persons with intellectual disabilities cannot be liberated from their handicap. Pailin recognizes that something similar holds for other "subjects" of liberation theology as well — women, minorities, etc. — but he thinks there is a difference. Even though in each case the aim is to destroy discriminatory attitudes toward the targeted characteristic (gender, race, etc.), the positive goal of making this characteristic socially irrelevant can be made true for women and people of color, but for intellectually disabled people this is only possible to a limited degree (p. 27). We should keep in mind that Pailin's book was written before the emerging discussion on the politics of identity in constructionist sociology and literary criticism.

Pailin's last objection to a liberation theology of disability is the lack of a definition of the term that is in any way compelling (pp. 29-30). "Handicap," Pailin's terminology, is necessarily defined in reference to an implicit standard of the normal, which for Pailin is a sufficient reason to reject the notion as a fundamental concept in theology (p. 31). Here the constructionist rebuttal would be that his argument focuses on the definition of "impairment," which makes his objection commonplace for students in constructionist sociology (diversity among disabled people is just as wide-ranging as between other people). However, had he focused on "disability" the definition of that term is not obscure at all: a disability is a role of social deprivation that is suffered because of social stigmatization and marginalization.

must fail, most importantly the answer that identifies disability with suffering. Not only is the experience of suffering not specific for disabled persons, underlying the identification is often a notion of inferiority. Given certain assumptions about what people deem important in their lives, the recognition that others are incapable of achieving these goods tends to make their lives appear miserable. According to Pailin, however, the disabled are not suffering from their disability. The limitations imposed by their specific condition do not make people with disabilities "essentially different"; but they do draw our attention to the finitude of all human beings (p. 44). Finitude here does not refer to the fact that all human beings will eventually die, but to the fact that they are finite, created with limitations of finiteness. Createdness in finitude entails diversity. God wants human beings to be, but he does not necessarily want them to be the same: "the divine will does not seek uniformity" (p. 50).[21] While contemporary thought tends toward a celebration of diversity, we should ask whether this includes profound disability as well.

Pailin's answer to this question is to uncover the hidden presumptuousness behind it. If embracing human diversity stops short of embracing profound disability, this must imply that there is a boundary somewhere between what we can and what we cannot — or should not — embrace. Furthermore, in the context of theology, implying a boundary to human diversity and adducing the specifications to draw the line implies an assumption about having identified God's will. If the divine will creates diversity, it is quite presumptuous for the human mind to suggest that not all variations are acceptable. This presumption, according to Pailin, betrays the hubris of placing ourselves in the position of God. To suggest specifications for drawing a line is ungodly business, he says, because "so far as I know, no such specifications are available for inspection at God's patent office" (p. 52).

So, if it is not suffering, what is the theological problem of disability? According to Pailin, it is the question of the "worth of human beings as such" (p. 58). Bringing to bear what he has argued with regard to finitude, Pailin insists that this question is not peculiar to persons with

22. In a sense, Pailin's argument is similar to Hauerwas's argument, but given the latter's continuing use of the binary opposition between "us" and "them," the point in Hauerwas appears to be "difference" rather than "diversity."

disabilities. "Every person is to some extent limited, restricted and finite. This is what it is to be human rather than divine" (p. 59). Therefore, unless we attribute to ourselves the quality of divine knowledge, the answer to the question of worth cannot depend on what differentiates between human beings. The answer cannot be different for profoundly disabled human beings, that is, from what it is for the rest of us (p. 60). Since we do not possess divine knowledge, the importance of the many differences between human beings does not matter all that much: "All are finite: temporary products of chance, whose own products perish, they have no intrinsic significance" (p. 62).

Following this chain of reasoning, it is clear where Pailin is heading: the worth of human beings is not grounded intrinsically; it is not inherent in their being but comes from elsewhere. Before he begins to account for this view, however, Pailin goes on at length to dispel the one view that he finds particularly threatening for human beings such as Alex, namely, that their worth consists in the fact of what they contribute to the lives of others.

6. The Contributory View of Worth

It has not been unusual among Christians to argue that the burdens and limitations we face in our lives are intended by God as a challenge that enables us to develop moral character. Whatever the merits of this view, Pailin comments, it is hardly conceivable how being profoundly disabled as Alex is can be honestly regarded as an opportunity for development. Talk of a "challenge to be overcome" concerning a massively brain-damaged baby who has survived birth is nothing but repulsive (p. 80).

However, Pailin wants to consider an alternative view. This is the view that the condition of profound disability is not an opportunity for disabled persons themselves, but for those who care for them.[22] His discussion of this view aims to show that it rests on a mistake. While it may be true that caring for a disabled person is a challenge to those who care, it does not follow that this fact constitutes the worth of that per-

22. I recall the views of Roman Catholic thinkers such as Robert Spaemann, discussed above (Ch. 2).

not a means

son. Caring for a disabled person is an end in itself, not a means to something else, such as developing moral character. Accordingly, Pailin says:

> The state of handicapped people cannot be justified by holding that it is for the good of others. To suggest that it can be so justified is to ascribe immoral purposes to the divine in a vain attempt to make sense of the senseless. (p. 81)

Leaving aside for the moment the apparent implication of this claim — that the existence of the profoundly disabled is "senseless" — it is clear that Pailin plays out the Kantian imperative that we should not allow some people to be used only as a means to other people's ends.

Pailin elaborates this point extensively because of his view that we live in a culture "where the value of persons is widely judged in terms of what they contribute" (p. 92). Given that the question of what people with profound intellectual disabilities contribute to the good of society may well result in a net deficit (they cost far more than they contribute), this is a dangerous view. Pailin wishes to argue to the contrary that "the fundamental worth of each human being — and indeed of everything that exists — lies neither in what a person achieves nor in what a person makes possible for others to achieve, but in God's love for that person" (p. 95).

Unfortunately, however, many advocates for persons with disabilities think they have to demonstrate that disabled persons do have an important contribution to make (p. 95). Pailin considers this response to be a categorical mistake. His point is not to deny their feelings about the positive contribution of disabled people to the good of society, but to deny that the contribution to the good of society is a justifiable criterion for the worth of human beings. Well-meaning Christians who want to balance the scales of costs and benefits are misled by giving in to the wrong kind of standard. In Pailin's view, the problem with the view they oppose is not that cost-benefit ratio is decided on economic value, but rather that worth is determined by cost-benefit ratio at all.

To establish the argument for this claim, Pailin offers two moral considerations. The first consideration is internal to the cost-benefit ratio. Even though we should not accept the "contributory view" of disability as a criterion for human worth, we do need to take the positive value of care seriously. What needs to be questioned, however, is the claim to a surplus of benefit of caring for a disabled person as compared with the costs. Objectively, he says, it is not true that accepting the burden of care always has a positive outcome. In some cases, the burden of care threatens the quality of life for those taking responsibility for it; in those cases "relief may come only with the death of the ones whom they feel they must love" (p. 98).

Therefore, even though caring for a disabled person people may realize positive value, it is not necessarily true that seizing the opportunity outweighs its costs. Both on an individual and on a social level, the claims to net benefit need important qualifications, according to Pailin. From a Christian perspective, there can be no doubt, he says, that there is a duty, both corporately and individually, to help the disadvantaged enjoy as full an experience of life as is feasible (p. 108). Nonetheless, the costs of putting this principle into practice may result in an unhappy balance that demands consideration of the quality of life of the community as a whole. "Similarly, parents with a severely handicapped child will have to try to find a way of balancing the demands which caring for that child makes upon them with the welfare of the other members of the family" (p. 109). While finding the right balance in these matters is agonizing, Pailin argues, the responsibility for doing so cannot always be avoided.[23] Consequently, if we look at the cost-benefit ratio, it is not always true that positive outcomes outweigh negative ones.

7. No Instrumental Value

The important point about Pailin's rejection of the contributory view is not his internal objection to it, however. Instead, it is that it cannot be established as a valid criterion for "worth" of disabled human beings.

23. With this consideration, Pailin is close to assessing disabled lives in terms of their "social utility," which is sometimes adduced in the bioethics literature in connection with issues of the "killing or letting die" of severely disabled infants such as Alex. Pailin does not mention this similarity, which I presume he would reject out of hand; but he leaves us with the question of how these considerations about the quality of life are related to his argument regarding the worth of human being. In this connection, it is unfortunate he does not follow Kant's conceptual distinction between "worth" and "value" regarding the moral standing of the human being, even though this might have shown how the two kinds of considerations he adduces are to be kept separate.

Attempts to do so must fail for three reasons. The first is that it depersonalizes the disabled person. In holding that the important thing about people with disabilities is what they enable other people to contribute, according to Pailin, overlooks what it is to be a person. "To be valued in these terms, however, is to be depersonalized" (p. 101). It entails treating people "as objects of care," which is "demeaning" and "patronizing" in his eyes (p. 101). This criticism immediately evokes the obvious question of whether Pailin means to identify "person" with "subjectivity." Indeed, this is what he seems to be saying.

> Valued by what they offer to the public good, they are neither given the dignity appropriate to every human being as a person for whom God cares, nor seen as individuals having feelings and desires of their own, with whom the primary mode of relationship must be the "I-thou" encounter of person to person, however hard their handicaps may make it to establish such relationships with them. (p. 102)

Every human being is a person for whom God cares, and persons are characterized by the I-Thou relationship with other persons. Here Pailin seems to overlook the possibility that worth resides in being human because God cares for every human being, person or no person. If he wants to argue that "human being" is coterminous with "person," then the move of defining personhood in terms of an I-Thou relationship implies a moral taxonomy of personhood based on subjectivity. At this point Pailin ignores the question of what this claim means regarding his little friend Alex. Even if the possibility of the I-Thou encounter on the level of interpersonal relationship regarding a particular human being is absent, which may be true in Alex's case, it is still possible that God's caring for that human being is sufficient grounds for its human dignity.[24] As it turns out, however, Pailin relies heavily on the identification of "person" and "subjectivity" when he says:

24. This consideration is critical for the constructive argument I wish to develop in Ch. 7. In my view, grounding personhood in the encounter of an "I-Thou relationship" must be distinguished from grounding it in God's love ("a person for whom God cares"). Whereas the latter maintains the primacy of God's action, the former can be — and usually is — understood in Hegelian terms: the encounter of a person with another person evolves from the subjectivity of the "I" to the subjectivity of "thou," rather than the other way around. Pailin fails to make explicit how human dignity is grounded extrinsically, which, as we will see, is what he wants to assert.

> While all human beings are interdependent, nearly all are able to establish their individuality as persons by free, creative actions. Although their awareness of their environment and their capacity for autonomy may be limited, with extremely rare exceptions the most severely handicapped people, so long as they are conscious, have distinct characters. (p. 102)

If we remind ourselves of Pailin's earlier statements about the theological presumptuousness of drawing boundaries, it is curious to see that here he falls into the trap of doing precisely that. The obvious question concerning the above claim is, of course, what "nearly all" means, and what are we supposed to make of the "extremely rare exceptions"? Are they outside the scope of human beings worthy to be dignified as persons? If so, why isn't it sufficient that they are human beings for whom God cares? What constitutes their inclusion if it is not that fact? One also wonders why Pailin continues to regard the capacity for "free, creative actions" as a marker for what it is to be a human person. Clearly, he is willing to lower the standards — "even those individuals who are incapable of showing personal responses may still have their own feelings" — but he nonetheless implies an intrinsic characteristic of personhood that is the basis for "worth" in being human. Whatever else this means, it means drawing a line. Some human beings, extremely rare exceptions no doubt, are "out."

Pailin's second objection to the contributory view is much more convincing, and, for that matter, much more interesting. The contributory view of worth is degrading to the people who are actually engaged in caring for disabled persons, he says, because it misconstrues their motivation for doing so. If the presence of persons with disabilities in our lives is justified by the fact that it allows us to become better people, then obviously a motive of subjective self-interest is involved. On this assumption, we respond positively to human beings like Kelly and Alex because it makes us feel good about ourselves. Caring for a disabled person offers the experience of enrichment; if that is our motive, it is clearly one of self-interest.

Pailin makes a few important points about why this motivation is misconstrued. No doubt there will be people who engage in caring activities for this reason, he says, but they inevitably must fail in achieving their goal. If I engage in caring for my disabled child because it will contribute to the development of my character as a caring person, and in that sense is enriching my life, I will necessarily fail. If my activity is conditioned by the goal of a reward, I will calculate the probability of reaching the goal. But any calculation of that probability shows that my motivation is not that of a caring person. If obtaining my reward becomes unlikely, I may simply lose interest in the job.[25] In Pailin's words:

> Whatever beneficial results caring may have for some careers, it is a mistake to consider that the possibility of those results justifies the need for care and hence establishes the contributory worth of those who are cared for. The most important of those results occur as accidental by-products of the caring. They are not realized if they are its intentional goal. To decide to love in order to enjoy the benefits of loving is not to love. The benefits of love, whatever they may be, only come to those who love for the sake of loving. (pp. 104-5)

My caring for a disabled person can be a very rewarding kind of activity, but only as a side effect that is not part of my intention.[26] Authentic caring requires being motivated by caring for its own sake. Those who believe that all human activity is motivated by self-interest, according to Pailin, however enlightened that view may be, will fail to understand this point. Such people are ignorant of the nature of what it means to care (p. 106). Authentic caring implies, among other things, that people motivated by it would be *surprised* to be asked why they are concerned about those they care for (p. 103). For such people there is no external reason. The only reason there is lies within the activity itself, without which it becomes unintelligible to them.

> It would seem self-evident to them: those for whom they care need care. That is the only explanation they can give for what they do.

25. This argument pertains to the distinction between internal and external motivation discussed in Ch. 4. It also pertains to the discussion of friendship in the practices of caring for people with disabilities within the communities of L' Arche (see Ch. 10).

26. For a parallel argument about finding meaning in the activity of caring, see Reinders, "The Meaning of Life in Liberal Society," in *Meaningful Care: A Multidisciplinary Approach to the Meaning of Care for People with Mental Retardation*, ed. Joop Stolk, Theo A. Boer, and Rut Seldenrijk (Dordrecht: Kluwer Academic Publishers, 2000), pp. 65-84.

There is no reason for their caring in the sense that their actions are directed by an end that is other than that of caring for the well-being of those for whom they care. They thus see their actions as self-justifying. (p. 103)

Here we find Pailin aiming at the same point made by Hauerwas.[27] Their point is to question the assumption that there must be a reason to justify caring for the profoundly disabled that goes beyond the mere fact of their being human. This assumption implies that, taken in themselves, these lives appear "unintelligible," as Hauerwas prefers to put this. Thus the problem with the contributory view is that adducing the reward of caring for these human beings as external ground reinforces the notion that without it their lives are unintelligible. This conclusion, however, can only be grasped by those who understand what it is to love, as Pailin puts it. In contrast, those who are looking for a reason to justify caring

> have not understood that love is a self-justifying and all-sufficient ground for certain kinds of behavior. Those who remain puzzled by love (and even cynical about references to it) should therefore consider whether the contributory worth notion of value has blinded them to what is good in itself. (p. 103)

The alternative to what is good in itself is what is good as a means to another good. To argue that the worth of a human being is grounded in what it contributes to the lives of others changes it from a "good in itself" to an "instrumental value." This move inevitably gets caught in balancing judgments of cost-benefit tradeoffs, as Pailin's earlier analysis indicates. Pailin rejects this view because it forfeits the central claim of any Christian conception of being human: whatever his or her state or condition, there is no disabled human being who exists outside the love of God.

The third reason why the contributory view is to be rejected focuses on what Pailin calls its "bizarre implications" (p. 107). If the worth of profoundly disabled people is grounded in the fact that they enrich the quality of the lives of their caregivers, there is obviously a need to have people living with adverse conditions: disability and disease then ap-

27. See above, pp. 207-8.

216

pear to be socially desirable because they enable the opportunity for giving care. The bizarre implication would be that, in developing medicine to prevent disability and disease, we are in fact depriving society of an important source of social benefit. According to Pailin, this implication shows how the contributory view leads to a *reductio ad absurdum*. Disability and disease cannot be justified on the grounds that they enable us to become better people. To accept this would be to accept the idea that some people's misery can be changed into something beneficial by the fact that other people find virtue in alleviating it.

Pailin's point here is not to deny that some people do indeed find virtue in alleviating adverse conditions for other people, nor that this is generally something beneficial. But it is to deny that the benefit of enabling caregivers to care is what justifies the activity. Caring relates to "worth," not "reward," in Pailin's terms. "Worth" does not reside in contribution but in participation. This consideration takes us necessarily beyond instrumental goodness, and it requires that we ask what participation in "worth" might mean. As I have suggested, the only way to answer this question that holds universally is to say that the good of being human is primarily a gift rather than an act. "Worth" is received rather than earned.[28]

8. The Goodness of Being

With this extensive discussion of the contributory view of human worth, Pailin is in fact pursuing a theological alternative that succeeds in accounting for the worth of human beings *unconditionally*.[29] Since, as we shall see, this claim is necessarily theological in Pailin's view, his conception of human worth as a gift turns on the notion of who God is and what God does. Thus the doctrine of God turns out to be at the heart of Pailin's constructive argument, to which we will now turn.

Central to Pailin's argument is the conviction that created being itself is the source of worth that we are seeking. Pailin points to Jesus' admonition (Matt. 6:25) to pay attention to the birds and the lilies in the

28. This is the thesis that unites the essays in *God and Human Dignity,* ed. R. Kendall Soulen and Linda Woodhead (Grand Rapids: Eerdmans, 2006).

29. See the epigraph for this chapter (n. 1); see also Pailin, *A Gentle Touch,* p. 140.

field as a call to appreciate being. Without romanticizing the "simplicity" of people with intellectual disabilities, there are those among them who are present, according to Pailin, as "an example of peace in the world and with the world," which is in sharp contrast to the ambitious and stressful lives of many privileged people (pp. 110-11). Therefore, the key to coming to terms with intellectual disability is to consider the ways in which many of those living with this condition "find intense joy in what is given in the present moment" (pp. 111-12). In other words, the key to the problem of disability is the value of being per se.

To explain this, Pailin returns to his claim that persons with intellectual disabilities are persons in the sense discussed earlier: "Each of them has his or her individual capacities and limitations, just as every person has" (p. 112). But now he adds that the worth of being human is not found in these capacities, nor is it in any way affected by a limitation of these capacities. To presuppose that it is would be to presuppose that worth is determined by one's actions, which would imply that the basis of worth is found in the person as agent (p. 113). Pailin rejects this presupposition because it advances "an anthropocentric view of value." Against this view he wishes to argue that "ultimate worth can only be established on a theocentric basis" (p. 113). The reason is, as already indicated, that the differences between human beings regarding their capabilities may not be very significant in God's eyes. "In relation to the scale of the divine reality, the differences between a Michelangelo and an Alex are not important," Pailin declares (p. 113). This is not to deny that God is pleased with the creative freedom that enables people to act and respond to him; but it does not follow that he is less concerned with those who cannot. "The grace of God is not like that," says Pailin. "It is there for all, indiscriminately" (p. 114). A theocentric basis for the fundamental worth of being human requires that we humans speak in the passive voice.

> It is grounded not in what they can do or give, but in what they can be given. Worth is not a quality that belongs to a person in herself or himself; it is a matter of a relationship with another person. . . . Worth is something that is bestowed by being loved, being wanted, being respected, and being cherished. It is not a quality that is inherent in an object or a person: it is a quality that is given to an object or a person by another. (p. 116)

In other words, worth is received. Whatever has worth, has worth for someone, Pailin explains; if it does not, it is worthless. The same is true of value: "No object has any value apart from its value for someone; and whatever value it has for someone is its value — for that person."

With this argument Pailin seems to be defending what is known as a subjectivist theory of value, but this is only appearance. In fact, he is saying that from a theocentric point of view there can be no subjectivist theory of value. A subjectivist theory of value postulates a necessary connection between a value and the positive wish or desire of a valuing agent such that the latter is a condition of the former. Whether that condition actually obtains is, for every value, a contingent question. From a human perspective, then, value is never unconditional because it always depends on someone valuing it.

But according to Pailin, things are different for God. God is the only being whose worth is not contingent on desire.[30] Rather, the relationship works the other way around: God's love is the source of all that is valuable (p. 116). This love is unconditional. But things are different from a nontheistic perspective. Obviously, if worth is received, then it must be given. There are people who do not receive the gift of being loved and who certainly feel worthless. If their worth were to depend on the gift of other human beings, as it necessarily must be in a nontheistic perspective, they would be justified in that feeling.[31] From a Christian point of view, according to Pailin, one would have to say that this judgment is mistaken. On the contrary, no human being can be without worth because every human being is loved and accepted by its Creator. There are no worthless human beings, because — to repeat — no human being exists outside the love of God (p. 119).

Leaving aside whether there are alternatives to subjectivist theories of value other than theism, one would have to say with Pailin —

30. Again, it is somewhat surprising that Pailin uses "worth" and "value" interchangeably, as if there is no philosophical point in distinguishing between the two.

31. Pailin seems to conflate a nontheistic position with a naturalist position, because secular Kantians, for example, would not accept that the worth of a human being depends on being valued by others. However, given its specific context, Pailin's argument will not be affected by this mistake, because Kantians have no way of attributing worth to nonrational beings like the profoundly disabled. At best they are objects of natural kindness.

219

from a Christian perspective — that no human being does exist with-out worth. Therefore, questioning the worth of a human being such as Alex, given the apparent absence of a capacity for purposive agency, does not make sense: "There never is a person for whom no one at all cares if, as theistic faith holds, God, as the one whose relationships are always perfectly loving, knows each person each moment of his or her being" (p. 119).

Thus the worth of any human being is neither instrumentally nor intrinsically but always extrinsically grounded, not in the value they have for others, nor in a quality they have in themselves, but in the love of God.

> It must be insisted, it is not anything that a person experiences or anything that a person produces that is the ground of her or his ulti-mate worth. Each person has ultimate worth just because he or she is, and as such is one whom God cherishes. Worth. . . belongs to each person because it is cherished by the divine and thereby given worth. (p. 121)

Pailin applies the same argument to explain the notion of the human being as *imago dei*. Being created in the divine image does not refer to something that the human being and divine being have in common. "It is not an intrinsic quality of human existence that is referred to when people are held to be 'in the image of God,'" Pailin contends. Instead, the image marks "the status that is given to each person because God is concerned about her or him" (p. 157). Human being as *imago dei* is thus qualified by God's concern. It is unconditional in the sense that no one has to meet any criteria in order to be worthy of God's love. Simply be-ing human is sufficient for this extraordinary gift.[32]

9. "Freely Creative Activity"

The foregoing account of Pailin's project should be sufficient to indi-cate its promise for the question that is central to my inquiry. It is prom-

---

32. Pailin does not address the point explicitly, but the logic of his argument com-mits him to the Aristotelian view that human beings are all those of human descent (see the discussion in Ch. 2 above).

ising in the sense that it purports to offer a theology that, in my own terms, transcends the metaphors of space — metaphors such as "barriers" and "access" — so that even key terms like "exclusion" and "inclusion" lose their force. If only we dare ask how the lives of Alex and Kelly appear in the eyes of God, we will understand that there are no human lives beyond redemption.[33] Following on that insight, the question of ethics as a quest for the human good becomes an entirely different question, a question in which appropriate theological understanding of our being is prior to the discernment of appropriate human achievement.

However, there is a weakness in the way Pailin carries out his project precisely at this point, and we need to spell that out. It originates in the overall theological framework of his argument, which is the framework of process theology. It consists in the fact that, on the one hand, Pailin insists on the unconditional acceptance of persons with disabilities by God, regardless of their state or condition, but, on the other hand, simultaneously retains a conception of the human good in which the importance of what he calls "freely creative" agency looms large.

To trace my source of concern here, I need to focus on Pailin's conception of "the reality of the divine being" (p. 121). On the one hand, the reality of divine being has the character of all-inclusive love, which accounts for the claim that the worth of human beings is grounded in the fact that all are embraced and cherished by the divine (p. 120). On the other hand, however, God is not merely an "outsider" to their existence. "God shares their experiences of being as fully and as intimately as they do. . . . No experience happens which God does not completely share" (p. 120). In technical language, Pailin explains, we can say that God is both "externally" and "internally" related to every experience. This is why we can say that the differences in what human beings experience do not result in a different relationship with God, because God is present in each of their experiences. Nonetheless, according to Pailin, it does not follow that the results of these "functional differences" are insignificant.

---

33. Pailin coins the felicitous phrase: "the class of 'neighbor' has no bounds," referring to Luke 10 and Matthew 25 (see n. 1 above).

Although the divine care for each individual does not vary according to the depth of the experiences of joy, effort, satisfaction and fun that attend each person's existence, it does not follow that the qualities of a person's experiences are of no account. (p. 121)

Wherein lies their significance, then? It appears that here Pailin has in mind primarily the "external" relationship between God and creation. The qualities of the experiences of his creatures "all contribute to the richness of the wholly inclusive reality of the divine being" (p. 121). In other words, the quality of all of our experiences adds up to an ever-expanding divine reality. The reason is that God's creative activity is "expressed through open-ended processes" that are found in the world, in which its potential is explored and actualized (p. 151). Therefore, creation is not a fixed state of natural being that merely follows predetermined patterns, because God delights in the play of free creativity in the processes of reality. As Pailin puts it, "God's creative intention is partly realized through the free creative acts by which human beings give concrete form to their existence," such that "God delights in the good which is thereby actualized" (pp. 151-52). Consequently, the way humans explore and actualize their potential in the world adds to the enrichment of ultimate reality, which is God.[34]

Pailin has repeatedly denied that our capacity for actualizing our potential is a condition of our worth before God. As we have seen, this claim pertains to the "internal" relationship between God and his creatures. From the point of view of the "external" relationship, however, a different picture emerges: this is a picture of the "reality of divine being" that makes one wonder how the lives of human beings with profound disabilities fit in.

> To believe in the Christian gospel is to affirm the reality of God as the gracious ground of being whose presence is found in, whose will desires, and whose spirit promotes life, health, vigor and activity. It is to participate in the fullness of life enjoyed by those whose existence is characterized by the wholeness, sense of worth and creative openness which comes from being grounded in the faith that ultimate reality is perfect love. (p. 129)

34. The word "God," Pailin explains, refers to that which "embodies this ultimacy in being and value" (*A Gentle Touch*, p. 127).

Again, his conclusion is not that the worth of human beings is conditioned by their contributions, but their contributions do make a difference for the richness of the ultimate reality that is God. God is not indifferent to what we produce (p. 152). This view no doubt allows in principle for all of humanity's responses to be favorable to God. As Pailin puts it, "He enjoys the values realized in all that they do, whether it is the grin of a happy infant or the playing of a Chopin" (p. 152). Nonetheless, Pailin cannot help but accept that the identification of human beings as intellectually disabled must imply that their scope for creativity is less than average (p. 153).[35]

It is clear from this view how Pailin succeeds in theologically establishing the "status" of profoundly disabled human beings by grounding it unconditionally in the love of God; but it remains unclear how he evaluates their existence teleologically. That is, it is unclear how the profoundly disabled fit into his conception of "the fullness of life." In fact, it appears that they do not fit very well. The reason, it seems to me, is that he implicitly assumes that humans' contribution to the life of God exists in the variety of goods they can pursue in their lives. But we cannot help accepting, on that assumption, that the contribution of some human beings must be "less than average." Thus, the question Pailin's theology leaves us with is how his account of the unconditional worth of being human relates to his account of the vigor, the vitality, and the creativity that contribute to the fullness of God's being. It certainly seems that that account marginalizes the profoundly disabled to the point of irrelevance.

My suspicion is that the apparent tension in Pailin's argument ultimately inheres in his abstract conception of the divine. The divine is the absolute and ultimate reality. As such, it incorporates the contingent and finite world that it brings forth. But an adequate theological account of profound disability requires something other than a concept of the divine as the ultimate consummation of all being. When Pailin identifies the divine with love itself, unbounded and limitless, we can-

---

35. To be sure, Pailin explicitly denies that this diminished creativity in most people with intellectual disabilities should have any consequence with regard to how we evaluate their being; but all the caveats he imposes here relate to their status. They are all meant to say: the diminished capabilities of these people do not constitute a separate class of beings in the eyes of God. However, the consequence that they contribute less to the richness of the divine being stands unaffected by these caveats.

absence of
the Cross

not help but notice the absence from his account of the Cross in human history. God has given himself for us on the Cross, which renders the measure of our response quite irrelevant for determining what our existence means to him. The Christian gospel announces that in Christ we have been drawn into the communion of the Father, the Son, and the Spirit. It also announces the promise that, through the act of God's self-giving, we will be restored in the fullness of being. Pailin wants to argue that the reality of divine love includes all human beings in a relationship with God. However, the fact that divine love is mediated in the gospel by the self-giving of God points in a different direction of understanding the fullness of being than as mediated by "life, health, vigor, and activity." When God sees humans, he sees woundedness in need of redemption. While unconditional love certainly is the key notion, to account for its possibility requires a Trinitarian understanding of who God is and what God does.

10. Conclusion

The work of both Hauerwas and Pailin on theology and disability gives us pause for reflection in that they raise the extremely important point of unconditional acceptance. This is important particularly with regard to persons with profound disabilities because only the claim to God's unconditional acceptance can avert the logic of subjectivity that sooner or later appears in anthropocentric views.[36] That is the strength of both Hauerwas's and Pailin's theological accounts.

At the same time — though for different reasons — both theologians remain caught in some kind of negativity. Hauerwas cannot rid himself of the sense of profoundly disabled humans as strange creatures; Pailin cannot rid himself of the sense that they do not have much to contribute to the fullness of life, even though he denies that their worth is in any way affected by this. I do not have a quarrel with either of these views, however. Yes, profoundly disabled persons like Kelly *are* strange creatures; and yes, it is a pity that they cannot share the joy of freely creative activity. But those aspects of their existence do not only, not even primarily, signify something to be regretted. It is precisely be-

36. See Ch. 1 above.

cause the profoundly disabled contradict the innermost core of our own being — the "reflective self" — that their presence is crucial to a Trinitarian account of who God is and what God does, and consequently who we are and what we should do. If anything important is to be learned from being with a profoundly disabled person, it is precisely to learn how to be human, theologically speaking, without relying on the reflective self as our inner core. As human beings, our vocation is friendship with God, but usually our reflective self gets in the way of trusting God. Being with an intellectually disabled person teaches us precisely this painful lesson. It paves the way for our friendship both with them and with God by teaching us that we can only give friendship after we have learned to receive it.

To pursue the strategy of the extrinsic grounding of being human in the relationship with God, I will turn to Trinitarian theology in order to arrive at a theological understanding of this relationship. Following Pailin's logic, I will argue that any difference between human beings can be freely accepted and welcomed simply because it has no significance in the eyes of God — except, perhaps, that he cannot help but favor them as his "little ones" whose guardian angels secure his attention (Matt. 18:10-11). In view of this claim, however, we can expect an objection from the skeptical outsider who may wish to push the door that Pailin's (and Hauerwas's) arguments left open: "If it is true that God loves each of us, why should he not regret the fact that some of us are born with such a dim prospect of enjoying the fullness of life? And if so, why should we not seriously regret this fact and try to do something about it? Who, after all, desires a life that means living with such a condition?"

This objection is seductive in that it suggests that God, too, may have preferred these human beings to be different from what they are, that is, more like us. The seductiveness is in the suggestion that we can pry into the divine mind independently from what has been revealed in Christ. Again, we need to be aware of the temptation to find a reason that can make the existence of disabled lives intelligible. I strongly believe, with Hauerwas and Pailin, that this is a temptation that Christians should resist: not only because we do not have knowledge or insight into the divine mind, but also — and more importantly — because of what we do know, which is that the God whom Christians confess to believe in has drawn all his creatures into the promise of his unending

225

love that is revealed in Christ. If correct, this means that it is an eminently cultural responsibility of contemporary Christians to resist the idea that, when a profoundly disabled child is born, something must have gone wrong. Not because this claim is necessarily mistaken but because it is at best *irrelevant* and at worst *obstructive* in terms of how we represent God's love for this child. Given what our contemporary culture suggests is a life worth living, what on earth is one to make of a human life like Kelly's? In my view, Christians should freely admit that they don't know; at the same time, they should claim that their ignorance does not matter at all with regard to knowing how to respond. Therefore, to overcome the need for justifying reasons, we need habits and skills rather than arguments. This is why the task of learning how to be friends with the intellectually disabled is particularly crucial.

Chapter Seven

A Trinitarian Concept of Divine and Human Being

We think of our capacities or potentialities as "inner," awaiting the development which will manifest them or realize them in the public world. . . . But as strong as this partitioning of the world appears to us, as solid as this localization may seem, and anchored in the very nature of the human agent, it is in large part a feature of our world, the world of modern, Western people. The localization is not a universal one, which human beings recognize as a matter of course, as they do for instance that their heads are above their torsos. Rather it is a function of a historically limited mode of self-interpretation, one which has become dominant in the modern West and which may indeed spread thence to other parts of the globe, but which had a beginning in time and space and may have an end.

Charles Taylor

1. Introduction: Intrinsic Qualities

Within the Christian tradition, one cannot address theological anthropology without speaking about the doctrine of *imago dei*. As obvious as this theological intuition may appear, however, as soon as we look into what the tradition has done with it, we are in for a disappointment, as far as the humanity of profoundly disabled human beings is concerned. I will highlight a few episodes of the history of the doctrine in order to suggest that what we mean by human being created in God's image is determined by what we think about God's being. This means that the logically prior task is to argue from our understanding of God to our understanding of being human.

The first thing to notice, particularly in the context of my argument in this book, is that the tradition is to a large extent dominated by the explanation of the divine image in terms of the human faculties, most of all — as by now will be expected — the faculties of human reason and will. Consider the way Thomas Aquinas voices this tradition: reason is what explains how human beings are created in God's image. Aquinas sums up this way of understanding *imago Dei* in this statement:

> Since man is said to be after God's image in virtue of his intelligent nature, it follows that he is most completely after God's image in that point in which such a nature can most completely imitate God.[1]

In our capacity as rational beings, we are capable of imitating God. This claim, according to Aquinas, holds true for every human being. He does not consider the question of what this means for people whose capacity of reason remains underdeveloped, but he does raise another question. He asks whether God's image is only found in human reason, or whether there are other qualities in which the divine image could reside. But he answers that question in the negative: beings without the capacity of reason cannot reflect the image.

> While all creatures bear some resemblance to God, only in a rational creature do you find a resemblance to God in a manner of an image. . . . Now, what puts the rational creature in a higher class than others is precisely intellect or mind.[2]

Reason has thus been elevated time and again as the mark of the divine image, thereby setting it apart from the rest of creation. Aquinas's notion of a "higher class" confirms that the Christian tradition is not alien to a hierarchy of being that marginalizes people in whom the faculties of reason and will remain underdeveloped. The same idea is found in Augustine: he says that human excellence consists in the fact that God

---

1. *Summa Theologica,* Ia, q.93, a.4.
2. *Summa Theologica,* Ia , q.93, a.6.

created the human being in his image "by giving him a rational soul, which raises him above the beasts in the field."[3] Even if one wants to maintain that these Christian thinkers never meant to imply a subdivision of inferior human beings, it is still difficult to deny that their views imply the possible existence of marginal cases in the sense explained in Chapter 2. While all human beings are doubtless human according to their origin, some human beings are only human in a marginal sense from the point of view of their final end.[4]

Augustine and Aquinas represent mainstream Christian thought on this point. As the history of this doctrine shows, the case for theological inclusiveness grounded in *imago Dei* is at best ambiguous. Theological reflection has always been tempted to explain the divine image in terms of human capabilities.[5] Not surprisingly, the moral and intellectual powers of reason and free will have frequently served as the prime candidates for the seat of the divine image.[6] While the explanation of *imago Dei* in terms of human capabilities has been opposed within Protestant theology, this variation among Christian denominations can easily be exaggerated. Even though Protestantism tried to stay away from the question about how human being resembles divine being, it did maintain the dominant view that the powers of the rational soul determine what it means to be created human.

An important question, therefore, is what the driving force behind

---

3. *De Genesis ad Litteram,* VI, 12.

4. Consider Aquinas's claim that the rational soul in which the divine image resides does admit neither of intensity nor remissness because it is a "substance," not an accidental thing; that is, it does not come in degree. According to Aquinas, this is to deny that "a species of substance is shared among different individuals in a greater or lesser degree" (*Summa Theologica,* Ia , q.93, a.3.).

5. Berkhof claims that the tradition has mostly explained the image in terms of a "static-idealistic-individualistic conception" of humans; see H. Berkhof, *Christian Faith: An Introduction to the Study of the Faith* (Grand Rapids: Eerdmans, 1979), p. 180.

6. A recent example is Joseph Fletcher, who understood the divine image to refer to the capacities for "intelligent causal action" (*Morals and Medicine* [Boston: Beacon Press, 1954], p. 218). That Fletcher stood in a long tradition in this respect is shown in D. J. Hall, *Imaging God: Dominion as Stewardship* (Grand Rapids: Eerdmans, 1986), pp. 89-98. Hall says: "A long and influential tradition of Christian thought looks upon the *imago Dei* as referring to something inherent in *Homo Sapiens*. Humankind in God's image, according to this view, means that as it is created by God, the human species possesses certain characteristics or qualities that render it similar to the divine being" (p. 89).

the notion of resemblance was. As Robert Jenson has explained, the Christian tradition was indebted at this point to the metaphysics of late antiquity, in which the concept of a divine image was used as a mediation bridging the gap between pure being of timeless deity and earthly existence that was always threatened by the nonbeing of temporality and change.[7] Given the weight of this problematic, the early Christian fathers reached for the biblical notion of *imago Dei* to explain the church's creed that Jesus Christ was truly the image of God in terms of this metaphysics. But when this explanation was then connected with the creation story in Genesis, the question of how human beings in general are to be regarded as resembling God turned out to be unavoidable.

Two equally compelling answers could be given to this question. On the one hand, some claimed that the image resides in the fact of the human's rational soul, for that is the substance grounding our potential to respond to God. There were those who contested that view, on the other hand, because they regarded reason and will as the source of human sinfulness. Luther famously remarked that, if reason and will were all there were to being created in the image of God, then we should acknowledge that Satan himself reflects that image, for surely he is in the possession of these powers.[8] Protestant theology, thus following Luther, held that being human only reflects the divine image when an actual relationship with God exists. However, whether the faculties of reason and will were regarded from the perspective of fallen rather than created nature, the anthropological content was largely the same. What theology saw as the characteristically human was simultaneously regarded as the cause of both the grandeur and the misery of humankind, depending on from which angle one approached the issue.

We can surmise that, given these two alternatives, the understanding of profoundly disabled human beings might have gone in different ways, had it been a theological issue; but since it was not, the issue is —

7. Robert W. Jenson, *Systematic Theology: The Works of God* (Oxford: Oxford University Press, 1999), II, 53-54.

8. "If these powers are the image of God it follows that Satan was created according to the image of God, since he surely has these natural endowments, such as memory and a very superior intellect and a most determined will, to a far higher degree than we have them" (Luther, *Works*, I, 61).

historically speaking — a matter of speculation. When seen from the exaltation of reason and will as the "seat" of the image of God, the being of the profoundly disabled would have thus been regarded as "defective." On the other hand, when these powers were seen as the root of human sinfulness, then the presence of human creatures with diminished rational capacities could acquire a very different meaning. Contrary to the sinfulness of the rational person guided by the light of reason, disabled persons could be understood to be much closer to God because of their innocence. Understanding profoundly disabled human beings has never been a theological issue, however, so what it *might* have looked like must remain speculative.

It appears that the opposing readings of the doctrine of *imago Dei* outlined above never really reached a state of equilibrium in the development of the tradition. Despite the fact that the biblical sources for this notion are rather scarce,[9] doctrinal theology has placed a heavy burden on this notion. The classical approach has often been to look for an analogy between God and the human being, but the tradition could not settle beyond dispute the question of what the analogy was supposed to inform us about.

2. The Double Portrait of Man[10]

The history of this analogy as a basic theme in theological anthropology started with the struggle against Gnosticism in the early church. In that struggle the reading of *imago Dei* by Irenaeus of Lyon turned out to be pivotal.[11] Playing on the language of Genesis 1:26-27 ("Let us make

---

9. Hans Reinders, "*Imago Dei* as a Basic Concept in Christian Ethics," in *Holy Scriptures in Judaism, Christianity and Islam: Hermeneutics, Values and Society,* ed. Hendrik M. Vroom and Jerald D. Gort (Amsterdam: Rodopi, 1997), pp. 187-204. For a recent update of the biblical scholarship, see also Richard J. Middleton, *The Liberating Image: The Imago Dei in Genesis 1* (Grand Rapids: Brazos Press, 2005).

10. This section contains material from Hans S. Reinders, "*Imago Dei* as a Basic Concept in Christian Ethics," pp. 187-204.

11. For this account of Irenaeus's views, I am indebted mainly to Peter Schwanz, *Imago Dei als christologisch-anthropologisches Problem in der Geschichte der Alten Kirche von Paulus bis Clemens von Alexandrien* (Halle: VEB Max Niemeyer Verlag, 1970); see also David Cairns, *The Image of God in Man* (New York: Philosophical Library, 1953), pp. 73-83.

humankind in our image, according to our likeness"), Irenaeus created what became known as the "double portrait of man." He held that the divine *image* reflects the very nature of human beings, which exists in their faculty of the mind and its capacity for symbolic language and discursive thought. Apart from this general notion of human nature, he took the idea of the divine *likeness* to refer to something specific, namely, the state of human perfection that is attained through the mediation of Christ. So, on the one hand, humankind exists as it is "in itself," that is, as a being constituted by a "substance" of a particular kind. On the other hand, humankind exists as a sinner before God, having lost its original perfection, to which it can only be restored in Christ.[12]

Central to Irenaeus's thought in this connection was the doctrine of the *recapitulatio,* according to which Christ "recapitulated" the generations of descendants of Adam by restoring to humankind what Adam had lost in the Fall. In the Spirit of God claiming him as his beloved Son, Christ became the savior of humankind: those who accept him as their savior will partake in the divine Spirit, and the result will be their restoration to the state of *justitia originalis.*

This doctrine was crucial to Irenaeus's criticism of the Christian Gnostics for their claim that the salvation of humankind was the spirit being saved from imprisonment in the body, ascending to God and thus gaining immortality. Irenaeus strongly opposed this anti-materialism of the Gnostic teachings: he claimed that our "fleshly nature" was the location of the divine image. This he understood in holistic terms of body and soul present in each man and woman and expressed in free will and in the power of reason; thus, contrary to the Gnostic teachings, Irenaeus said that sinfulness was the consequence of human freedom.[13]

One of his reasons was to ascertain that Christ — the divine image

---

12. The question concerning the foundation of Irenaeus's distinction in the Old Testament, and of the way he used it, is easily answered, because — as many scholars have pointed out — the occurrence of the image in the genealogy of Adam (Gen. 5:1-3) and in the story of the God's covenant with Noah (Gen. 9:1-7) indicate that the Old Testament does not teach anything like the partial loss of the *imago Dei* in the Fall.

13. *Adversus Haeresis,* V, 37, 39, 41. Irenaeus criticizes the Gnostic doctrine of the creation of three kinds of humans, of whom those created in the spirit, the gnostics themselves, are beyond good and evil (see V-VI).

par excellence, according to Pauline theology — is the true savior of human beings in this world because of his incarnation as the divine image.[14] As Irenaeus pointed out, there were many among his Gnostic opponents who wanted to exclude Christ's participation in the flesh. This was unacceptable because, if only human beings — not Christ — were created from earthly dust in the artful hands of God, then he could never have restored the image in which humans were created.[15] The following passage makes the point with regard to humans and contains the *locus classicus* for the distinction introduced above.

> If anyone take away the substance of the flesh, that is of the handiwork of God, and understand that as which is purely spiritual, such then would not be a spiritual man, but would be the spirit of man, or the Spirit of God. However, when the spirit here blended with the soul is united to God's handiwork, the man is rendered spiritual and perfect because of the outpouring of the Spirit, and this is he who is made in the image and likeness of God. But if the Spirit be wanting from the soul, he who is such is indeed of an animal nature, and being left carnal, shall be an imperfect being, possessing indeed the image of God in his formation [in his fleshly nature], but not receiving the similitude through the Spirit.[16]

The imperfect being, then, is the human before God in the condition of sinfulness, who, still being the "handiwork of God," retains in body and soul the divine image. There is no identity of the divine Spirit with the human spirit as opposed to its incarceration in the body, because the result would be a distortion rather than the restoration of the image.

Irenaeus's double portrait of humankind set a pattern for Christian anthropology that the tradition never abandoned, though the explanation of it changed throughout the ages.[17] This claim also holds for the

---

14. See Schwanz, *Imago Dei as christologisch-anthropologisches Problem*, pp. 122-30.

15. *Adversus Haeresis*, III, 22, 1.

16. *Adversus Haeresis*, V, 6, 1.

17. Aquinas, for example, further elaborated the dual aspect of the image in a perfect and an imperfect sense. While likeness is essential to the image, it does not necessarily follow that there is equality between Creator and creature: "Yet this [equality] is of the essence of a perfect image; for in a perfect image nothing is wanting that is to be found in that of which it is a copy. Now it is manifest that in man there is some likeness to God,

Protestant tradition, even though many Protestant theologians regarded Irenaeus's legacy as a distortion of biblical faith.[18] In their view, there is only the human being appearing before God as a sinner; there is no aspect of "natural man" that is not tainted by sin. There is no "neutral ground" for theological anthropology to build on.[19] In constructing

---

copied from God as from an exemplar; yet this likeness is not one of equality, for such an exemplar infinitely excels its copy. Therefore there is in man a likeness to God; not, indeed, a perfect likeness, but imperfect" (*Summa Theologica,* Ia, q.93, a.1). Irenaeus's suggestion to use the words *imago* and *similitudo* to explain the distinction between "imperfect" and "perfect" is gone, but the distinction itself has survived. Aquinas adduces a further differentiation by saying that the image is found in human beings in three ways. First, the image consists in "the natural aptitude in man for understanding and loving God," which belongs to the very nature of the mind "common to all man." Second, there are those who "actually or habitually know and love God, though imperfectly," in whom the image consists in "conformity of grace." Third, the image consists in the likeness of glory when God is known and loved perfectly (*Summa Theologica,* Ia, q.93, a.4). According to Aquinas, "the first is found in all men, the second only in the just, the third only in the blessed." In each instance the image is said to consist in knowing and loving God, or at least a tendency to do so, not in a mere potentiality of having the capacity to do so. On the other hand, however, are Aquinas's metaphysical explanations of the image as a likeness in species, implying that God and the human being are of one species, sharing the same substance of a rational soul, even though this likeness in species is "according to a certain analogy or proportion" (*Summa Theologica,* Ia, q.93, a.1).

18. For a Lutheran account of the Protestant tradition, see Helmut Thielicke, *Theological Ethics: Foundations.* Vol. I, trans. W. H. Lazareth (Philadelphia: Fortress Press, 1966). The distinction between "image" and "likeness" was put into service to the Aristotelian scheme of potentiality and actualization, according to Thielicke, culminating in the well-known phrase that divine grace comes to human nature as a *donum superadditum,* which implied that the tendencies in human nature were not destroyed by sin, but made perfect by grace. Thus the distinction between "natural endowment" and "supernatural destiny" becomes decisive, in Thielicke's view, for scholastic anthropology, which he describes as follows: "The sphere of the imago includes nature. In terms of its substance [reason and free will] this nature is static and self-contained; it cannot be augmented or diminished, improved or destroyed. It cannot be destroyed because it consists of an accumulation of ontic parts, each of which is in itself unalterable. If this nature is to point out or lead beyond itself, it cannot do so itself, there must be a new creative act. There must be the impartation of the supernatural gifts, which lead from the natural imago to the supernatural similitude" (pp. 206-7). This shows that Thielicke read the distinction made by Irenaeus into the very structure of Roman Catholic thought (p. 202). This judgment is shared by Emil Brunner, *Man in Revolt: A Christian Anthropology,* trans. O. Wyon (London: Lutterworth, 1939), pp. 504-7; see also James M. Childs, *Christian Anthropology and Ethics* (Philadelphia: Fortress, 1978), pp. 18ff, and Berkhof, n. 5 above.

19. The debate saw a revival in the last century in the well-known dispute between

theological anthropology from this perspective, however, these Protestant theologians faced a serious problem. If the condition of sinfulness affects human nature per se, as they claimed to be true, then it must also be true that the image of God has been lost due to the Fall, and not just "partially," as the Roman Catholic position in line with Irenaeus maintained. If so, how could one avoid the claim that human beings had lost their humanity?

In facing this problem, most Protestant theologians settled for Augustine's doctrine of the *reliquiae,* the "remnants" of the divine image in humankind that remained intact despite the condition of total depravity.[20] They understood these "remnants" to consist of the "natural" capacities of human being. Consequently, the Protestant tradition took a position not all that different from Roman Catholicism's explanation of *imago Dei.*[21] While most of it habitually starts with the rejection of any analogy of being between God and man, this tradition nonetheless returns at some point to thinking about Christian anthropology in terms of the human faculties independent of an actual relationship with God.[22]

Karl Barth and Emil Brunner, in which the former accused the latter of betraying the Protestant legacy by returning to what the Reformation had rejected as the Roman Catholic view of human salvation. According to Thielicke, there is no doubt that the Reformers, and especially Luther, were right in opposing the scholastic view of being human with the claim that Christian anthropology has to start from the distorted relationship with God. Human being is distinguished by being addressed by God, not by its capability of being so addressed. The German original has it even more succinctly: "Das Angeredetwerden durch Gott" as distinct from "die Ansprechbarkeit des Menschen" (*Theological Ethics: Foundations,* I, 164).

20. This notion of "remnants" appears in Augustine, who argues that God's image "has not been so completely erased in the soul of man by the stain of earthly affections, as to have left remaining there not even the merest lineaments of it" (*De Spiritu et Littera,* XXVIII). This argument appears in the context of his explanation of Paul's view that the gentiles, though not in possession of the law, do by nature what is contained in the law. For Augustine the divine image in the human being under the condition of sin apparently was effective in appropriate conduct. See Jenson, *Systematic Theology,* II, pp. 62-63, where he uses the Protestant distinction between "gospel" and "law" to arrive at the same view.

21. See Jenson, *Systematic Theology,* II, 55 (esp. n. 11).

22. Thielicke acknowledges that the image cannot be wiped out completely because that would mean that God would have forsaken the intention that led him to create humankind in the first place. To lend credibility to this claim, he points out that Luther — despite his rigorous rejection of anthropological "dualism" — also prized the ontic as-

It is not only in the Protestant theology that being human as it is *before God* is difficult to reconcile, theologically speaking, with human beings as individual centers of consciousness and agency. Contemporary Roman Catholic theology also reflects this problem, as Robert Jenson has argued in his *Systematic Theology*.[23] Jenson discusses the example of Henri de Lubac's contribution to so-called *nouvelle théologie*. De Lubac constructed his theology, according to Jenson, to overcome the dissociation of the two orders within which human beings were understood to exist: "natural man" and "man before God." De Lubac holds that human nature is open to God's grace — the "vision of God" as the final end of our existence. But that does not mean that God's granting this end is in any way promoted by the exercise of our natural capacities or powers. It is not that the correct use of these natural powers is in any way prejudging being human before God. Receiving God's grace, de Lubac insists, has nothing to do with ability or capacity.[24]

Though Jenson is appreciative of this attempt, he nonetheless

---

pects of the image and maintains that human beings are not so thoroughly inclined toward evil that there is left no "portion" in them that is inclined toward the good. Accordingly, Thielicke says: "There is, of course, a negative mode of the divine likeness. But this negative mode of the imago, being merely a mode, still bears witness to the existence of the imago, and is therefore different in principle from the imago's non-existence or ceasing to be" (*Theological Ethics: Foundations,* I, 167). This claim shows that the opposition to the Roman Catholic position as developed by Aquinas has virtually ceased to exist. That much is clear when Thielicke goes on to say that the loss of the actual relationship with God indirectly points to the greatness of humankind in its previous state of perfection. But more than that, "testimony is also borne to the prior greatness by the fact that man can reflect upon this loss, that he can be addressed on the basis of it. Herein is manifesting his continuing function as a responsible subject, his un-interrupted obligation to reply. Hence his dignity as the image continues vis-à-vis the rest of creation" (I, 167). With this claim Thielicke has come full circle, because it implies that, regardless of the actual relationship with God, there is in any case "addressability." Not only is the resulting position close to what Irenaeus already defended: the powers of reason and free will mark the particular position of mankind in creation; it is also driven by essentially the same concern, which is that, in denying the importance of these powers, one is in fact abrogating God's creation. In Irenaeus's words, quoted above: "Set aside the handiwork of God as it appears in man's body and soul, and you have no longer man but something else."

23. Jenson, *Systematic Theology,* II, 65-68. Jenson discusses these reflections in terms of the Roman Catholic response to Protestant charges of "semi-pelagianism."

24. This kind of argument will be prominent in my discussion of charity in Ch. 8.

thinks that de Lubac's elimination of the dissociation between "nature" and "grace" falters somewhere halfway. The faltering is apparent when de Lubac finds himself compelled to say that the gratuitous gift of grace presupposes "a fundamental and interior aptitude for receiving that gift," which brings back the tension he intended to expel.[25] De Lubac's concession of being caught in a "paradox" especially reveals his argument's similarity to the arguments of Protestants such as Helmut Thielicke, which I have described above. The object of contention — human being "as it is in itself" — is simultaneously accepted and rejected. The theological doctrine of grace affirms — and at the same time questions — a positive appreciation of being human. Having presented his account of the tension as it appears in de Lubac, Jenson then succinctly summarizes where the foregoing discussion has left us:

> The traditional teaching of God's image, whether in Catholic or Protestant modification, is right in seeing the uniqueness of humanity strictly in relation to God; and no other assertion of human uniqueness is likely to be sustainable in the long term. Its difficulties arise from not conceiving humanity's specific relation to God as itself our uniqueness, but instead seeking a complex of qualities, supposedly possessed by us and not by other creatures that are claimed to resemble something in God, and so to establish the relation. In Genesis, the specific relation to God is as such the peculiarity attributed to humanity. If we are to seek in the human creature some feature to be called the image of God, this can only be our location in this relation.[26]

The Christian tradition in general, according to Jenson, is in trouble when it tries to answer the question of how the divine image remains effective in terms of particular features that are supposedly intrinsic to human nature. In his view, any such attempt is wrongheaded. Instead of locating the image in some intrinsic feature, it must be located in the relationship of human beings to the triune God.

---

25. Jenson, *Systematic Theology,* II, 67. Note how de Lubac at this point reflects the analysis of Aquinas's threefold way in which the divine image appears in human beings. The first regards the claim that the image consists in "the natural aptitude in man for understanding and loving God," which belongs to the very nature of the mind "common to all man" (see n. 17 above).

26. Jenson, *Systematic Theology,* II, 58.

3. "Relationality"

If the image is identified with uniqueness, as the first chapter of Genesis maintains, then all attempts to ground uniqueness in some quality to be found only in humans will sooner or later fail. This will be clear when we realize how scientists persistently undercut such attempts by showing that all the proposed qualities are in some form and to some degree found in the animal world as well.[27] Jenson's conclusion reflects a relatively new approach to Christian anthropology that centers on the notion of relationship as the main characteristic of human being. In Protestant quarters the main push in this direction came from Karl Barth.

Having rejected the understanding of the image of God in the Old Testament from what is only its consequence — mankind ruling over the rest of creation — Barth follows the lead of Bonhoeffer, who argued that God created human beings in his own freedom and that they thus resemble God in this freedom. Following Bonhoeffer, Barth wants to say that this is not the negative freedom of nondetermination — as a quality in and of itself — but the freedom of being free for somebody, in the sense of "being committed to." Created freedom, according to Barth, finds expression in a relationship. He continues:

> It is expressed in a confrontation, conjunction and inter-relatedness of man as male and female, which cannot be defined as an existing quality or intrinsic capacity, possibility or structure of his being, but which simply occur. In this relationship, which is absolutely given and posited, there is revealed freedom and therefore divine likeness. As God is free for man, so man is free for man; but only inasmuch as God is for him, so that the *analogia relationis* as the meaning of the divine likeness cannot be equated with the *analogia entis*.[28]

Consequently, according to Barth, the divine image exists in the freedom to be for the other. Thus the "inter-relatedness of man" is to be understood as an expression of "revealed" freedom; it is not to be explained ontologically in terms of being human, because it is given by

---

27. A well-known example is found in Frans de Waal, *Good Natured: The Origins of Right and Wrong in Humans and Other Animals* (Cambridge, MA: Harvard University Press, 1996).

28. Barth, *Church Dogmatics,* III/I, 195.

God "absolutely." Thus the "inter-relatedness of man as male and female" refers to the simple fact that human beings always find themselves related to others, but this fact is not to be taken as an indication of human potentiality.[29]

"Relation" in Barth's usage has a theological warrant: because God is free for his creation, so human beings, who are created in the image of this freedom, are similarly free for one another. Following the Protestant tradition, Barth identifies the divine image as the actuality rather than the potentiality of relation. God is free for his creatures so that these creatures are free for each other. Thus the community in which human being is created is not grounded in a natural capacity preceding this togetherness but in the act of divine freedom.

The theological explanation of this act of divine freedom, however, requires an account of God as triune communion. God's freedom is theologically misrepresented in the Scholastic account of God's indetermination (without beginning, without end, without change, without suffering, etc.). Instead, it requires an account of how God is free in God's self-determining act in trinitarian terms. In Barth's terminology, God's act of freedom exists in the addressing, the being addressed, and the address itself. It is the loving Father who is addressing, it is the beloved Son who is being addressed, and it is the Spirit of love that is the address passing between them. It is also in this act of divine freedom that God creates. Therefore, in terms of the "I-Thou" language that Barth prefers at this point, God's addressing "I" relates to the divine "Thou" that is thus being addressed; similarly, God thus relates to human beings as he creates them, and thus human creatures relate to one another as "I" and "Thou."[30]

With this theological explanation, Barth anticipates the grounding of his theological anthropology in Christology, which he elaborates in

---

29. The language in the original German text is much stronger and directly shows the connection with Barth's overall concept of God's revelation as "Ereignis," which constitutes human potentiality rather than building on it: human freedom in the creational sense expresses itself "in dem als keine vorfindliche Qualität, als keine dem Menschen eigene Fähigkeit, Möglichkeit oder Struktur seines Seins zu bestimmenden, in dem einfach geschehenden, einfach sich ereignenden "Gegenüber-, Miteinderander-, Aufeinander-angewiesensein des Menschen als Mann und Frau" (*Kirchliche Dogmatik* [Zürich: Zollikon, 1947], III/I, 219).

30. Barth, *Church Dogmatics*, III/I, 196.

the second part of his doctrine of creation.[31] True human nature is only visible for us, he says, in its original uncorrupted form in Jesus Christ. Only in him we see that truly being human means being free for others. So it is not that God first created human nature, in which Jesus Christ only then came to participate as its most perfect example; it is the other way around. Because as human beings we are created in Jesus Christ,

31. Barth's attempt was to find his Christological reading of *imago dei* expressed in the text of Genesis as well. Barth wondered why theologians always have been drawn into speculations when the text, "almost definition-wise," tells us that the image consists in the difference and the relationship between man and woman, which he interprets as an analogy of the relationship between the divine persons of the Trinity — his famous *analogia relationis* (Barth, *Church Dogmatics,* trans. G. W. Bromiley (Edinburgh: T&T Clark, 1958), III/1, 192). Barth rejected the reading of the plural in Gen. 1:26: ("Let us make humankind") as referring to the heavenly court; he maintained the ancient church's view that the divine plurality should be understood as in line with the Christian doctrine of the Trinity. The "inner life" of the triune God exists, according to Barth, in an "I-Thou" relationship that is mirrored in the relationship between man and woman (pp. 194-95). However, among biblical scholars, no single author in Old Testament studies has accepted Barth's reading. The obvious exegetical reason for rejecting Barth's proposal has been that the text of Genesis cannot be read as presupposing this doctrine of the Trinity. Barth takes the trinitarian relationship to be constitutive of the biblical view of human beings. Just as there is a "community of disposition and action in the divine essence," so there is also in humans a relationship between "I" and "Thou," a "face-to-face" pattern in human existence that mirrors the pattern of divine existence. Another criticism of Barth's reading of Genesis 1 has been advanced by feminist scholarship. Phyllis Bird, for example, has argued that on Barth's reading, "Adam is characterized by sexual differentiation," which, according to Bird, is like the other creatures, but unlike God" (Bird, "Male and Female He Created Them: Gen. 1:27b in the Context of the Priestly Account of Creation," *Harvard Theological Review* 74 (1981): 129-59). According to Bird, this reading of the text undermines what the text wants to make explicit, namely the special nature of the creation of humankind. Barth is not unaware of this objection, which he meets with the implausible rejoinder that what distinguishes the human being is the fact that, with regard to sexual differentiation, humans are "not radically different from the other creatures with independent life," but are nonetheless honored to be the image of God in the uniqueness of their plurality as male and female (*Church Dogmatics,* III/I, 187). "The animals in their multiplicity are not confronted by different groups and species of human being, but (for all the provisional and subsequent differences in every individual) by one human being, male and female" (*Church Dogmatics,* III/I, 188). In other words, what distinguishes humankind from and constitutes its superiority over the animal world is not sexual differentiation but the fact that there is no further species differentiation in humans (see also *Church Dogmatics,* III/I, 196).

we are able to participate in him: he is the "prototype." What constitutes human nature in him also constitutes it in us.[32] Even the condition of our sinfulness does not alter the fact that human nature as it is constituted in Christ is originally our own. It is neither cancelled nor annihilated by sin, despite the fact that we as human beings have corrupted our own nature. True human nature is saved in Jesus Christ and through him preserved in its "original essence."[33] Through him it has also become knowable to us, where before it was unknowable, because in sinful human beings it cannot express itself. That is why we, as human beings, do not know what we really are.[34]

Barth's Christological grounding of his anthropology leaves much to be explained, however. First, it admits that our sinfulness implies that not everything about being human can be said Christologically. Being human is frequently self-centered and thus not free for others. "Christology is not anthropology," Barth concedes. "We cannot find directly in others the humanity of Jesus."[35] When humanity is constituted in Christ, but as freedom for others it cannot actually be found in the sinful human being, then there must be another way of identifying it. Barth answers this question in terms of "the man Jesus," whose humanity witnesses that "as he is for God, he is also for man, his fellows."[36] He speaks of "the mystery of faith," but then repeats that the humanity of Jesus cannot be a tangible reality in other human beings, given their sinfulness. Second, Barth turns to anthropology in order to explain that Jesus' humanity cannot be entirely different from ours without eliminating the meaning of his being "for other men." There must be something, some sort of continuity. Surprisingly, given his strong claims to the contrary, this is indeed what Barth concedes:

> If the humanity of Jesus consists in the fact that he is for other men, this means that for all the disparity between him and us he affirms these others as beings which are not merely unlike Him in his creaturely existence and therefore in his humanity, but also like Him

32. Barth, *Church Dogmatics,* III/II, 50.
33. Barth, *Church Dogmatics,* III/II, 51.
34. Barth, *Church Dogmatics,* III/II, 52.
35. Barth, *Church Dogmatics,* III/II, 222. The "others" here are human beings other than Jesus (and thus include ourselves).
36. Barth, *Church Dogmatics,* III/II, 221-22.

in some basic form. Where one being is for others, there is necessarily a common sphere or form of existence in which the "for" can be possible and effective. If other men were beings whose humanity stood under an absolutely different and even contradictory determination from that of Jesus, it would be idle and confusing to call both Jesus and these others "men."[37]

Although Barth earlier argued at length against any formal account of the image in terms of an intrinsic capacity, possibility, or structure of human being — the affirmation of which would be tantamount to the affirmation of human potentiality — here we find him apparently reopening the case. If there is to be a shared "form of existence" in which "the 'for' can be possibly an effective," then it seems that we are effectively back to potentiality, namely, the potentiality of being "affirmed by Jesus in our humanity."[38]

Therefore, the conclusion must be that Barth does not escape the double portrait of man that haunts the Christian tradition since Irenaeus's rejection of Gnosticism. The problem in Barth's account originates from his appeal to a shared *form of existence,* which he believes must be posited if we want to continue to speak of our humanity as being free for the other irrespective of whether it is manifest in our actual lives.

There is a further problem with Barth's theological anthropology, however, that needs to be considered. When Christ's humanity is defined as "being free for others," then being human must also be defined in terms of being free for the other person. Furthermore, if this defini-

37. Barth, *Church Dogmatics,* III/II, 222-23.

38. Barth, *Church Dogmatics,* III/II, 224. Barth does not speak of "potentiality," of course, but he uses the language of "mystery" or "secret," which logically seems to be quite similar. Jesus has made visible in his humanity the gift of grace that is also contained in our humanity. The potentiality is not of an Aristotelian kind, because we cannot actualize it on our own account. Barth can even say that the "determination of being for his fellow-man" is not alien to our nature, but "radically belongs" to us. "If there is similarity as well as dissimilarity between him and us, to his being *for* others there must correspond as at least a minimum on our side the fact that our human being is at root a free being *with* others" (p. 274). Alan Torrance reads this passage as indicating that, with his distinction between "being *for*" and "being *with*," Barth anticipates the move Zizioulas will make in arguing that "being for" requires the ecstatic being reborn "from above" (*Being as Communion: Studies in Personhood and the Church* [Crestwood, NY: St. Vladimir Press, 1985], pp. 183-84).

tion is explained as a "form of existence," then we cannot avoid the conclusion that Barth also places human subjectivity at the center of his concept.[39] My humanity exists in and is real to the extent that I am free for another. Even though Barth believed this human freedom to be grounded in the humanity of Christ, in the sense of being constituted by a relationship, this view is not incompatible with the view he intended to leave behind. It is perfectly possible to account for the primordial concept of relationship in terms of the Hegelian principle of reflection that begins with the subject as the "in itself" freely positing the objective "for itself" in order to overcome the separation in the "in and for itself."[40] According to this principle, the "I" reaches out toward the other in order to find itself enriched in the process. In contemporary theological anthropology, "relationality" is in fact often understood as a necessary condition for becoming precisely this kind of enriched being. While such an account may certainly result in a richer and less individualistic concept of being human, it does not abandon but rather presupposes the concept of the human being as individual rational substance.

However, if it is true, as no Christian theologian will deny, that profoundly disabled human beings like Kelly are created in the divine image, then we must leave this inconsistency behind. Barth's reading of the image as relationship will eradicate the primordial distinction be-

---

39. This is mirrored in Barth's account of personhood, where he discusses the attribution of personhood to God. To be a person, he says, is to be a subject, "not merely in the logical sense, but also in the ethical sense: to be a free subject, a subject which is free even in respect of the specific limitations connected with its individuality, able to control its own existence and nature both as particular form and also as living development, and also to select new possibilities of existence and nature" (*Church Dogmatics,* I, 1, 138-39). Given this definition, it is not doubtful whether God is a person, Barth continues, since God is "real person, really free subject," but it certainly is doubtful whether we are: "Can we find among us even one man whom we can call this in the full and proper sense of the term?" Assuming that human personhood is for Barth identical with true human being, such that only Jesus Christ as the divine Word realizes personhood in a full sense, it seems that Barth is not free of individualistic tendencies in the sense that his concept of the human creature presupposes self-conscious agency at his/her center. See Alan Torrance, *Persons in Communion: An Essay in Trinitarian Description and Human Participation* (Edinburgh: T&T Clark, 1996).

40. See Torrance's discussion of Hegelian influence in Barth (*Persons in Communion,* pp. 242-51).

tween ability and disability, but only when it is explained as extrinsically grounded.[41] The fact that profoundly intellectually disabled persons have no awareness of this relationship does nothing to eliminate the image in their case; nor is the fact that one may have an awareness of it constitutive of the divine image in one's own case. These facts lack *theological* significance, unless we want to deny that God created human beings like Kelly in his image in the first place. Therefore, the claim that these human beings are also part of this relationship is warranted by the belief that God loves them and is concerned about them, regardless of whether they have — or can have — any sense of it.[42] Only if this claim is sustained by solid theological argument can Christian anthropology be truly universal.

In developing this argument, we will find it crucial to contend that the shift from "rational substance" to "relation" be only a necessary first step. For as long as "relation" is conceived of as the outreaching initiated by individual subjects as self-conscious centers of human agency, it must be regarded as an enrichment rather than a replacement of the classical concept. Thus the first step needs to be completed by a second one, which is to argue that being human in relationship is grounded extrinsically, that is, "from outside." God's act of love constitutes being human both with regard to its origin and to its final destination, which logically entails that this relationship is inaugurated by divine action, not human action. This is the subject of the next stage of the argument.

As indicated before, however, my interest in developing this argument, which I will attempt in the remainder of this chapter, is not to construct a theology of disability. Rather, it is to contribute to the development of Christian anthropology in a postmodern age. My investigation in this book, the reader may recall, is concerned with our human-

---

41. I use the term "extrinsic" and its derivatives in the sense in which something has an extrinsic cause when it does not have its cause in itself but in another being outside itself. It is then caused "from outside;" see, e.g., W. Norris Clarke, S.J., *The One and the Many: A Contemporary Thomistic Metaphysics* (Notre Dame, IN: University of Notre Dame Press, 2001), p. 179.

42. In making these comments, I am not suggesting that Barth would disagree. On the contrary, the point is rather that his theology enables us to be much more critical with regard to the centrality of human subjectivity in modern thought than he himself actually was.

ity, mine and yours as much as anybody else's, disabled or not. The aim is to develop an account of being human that renders all primordial distinctions between human beings theologically insignificant. To repeat a point I made in Chapter 1, I wish to show that the problem is not how "we" ought to think properly about "them," but rather that anthropology, in focusing on our individual faculties, results in a theological misrepresentation of humanity, theirs as much as our own. This is not to deny, of course, that there is a vested interest in how the argument is constructed. If there is anything that *all* people with disabilities suffer from, it is not what we make of their existence but what we make of our own. Images of imperfection are grounded in images of perfection, which is why I have constructed this inquiry at the crossroads of theological anthropology and ethics — as an argument about the relationship between the genesis and the *telos* of being human.

Therefore, the vested interest of the theological strategy I am using here is to include "difference" in Christian anthropology, even when difference is found at the innermost core of our conception of being human as self-reflective beings. This conception cannot be separated, theologically speaking, from what we are in the eyes of our Creator, namely, creatures who are sharing in his economy of salvation. It includes human creatures whose existence must appear as highly problematic if we take the capacities of reason and will to be definitive of being human. It thus distances itself from attempts to explain our humanity in terms of capabilities intrinsic to our being. Locating itself within the Christian tradition, it proposes to conceive of our origin as well as our final end qua human beings as grounded in God's graceful action toward us.

Up to this point I have given no substantial reason for moving in the direction of Christian theology, other than the fact that I happen to think about these matters in the context of my own faith. Now I can add the systematic reason for doing so. If the logic of the argument I have laid out so far is compelling, as I think it is, then there is no way of answering my initial question about Kelly's humanity securely in strictly secular terms. I believe that I have convincingly established that her humanity cannot be grounded in features that are intrinsic to her being. This means that, in terms of secular reason, there is only one option left, which is to argue that Kelly's humanity is grounded in other people's responses to her being. But in our moral culture, as

well as in many others past and present, this would not result in a secure grounding, which is clear from the fact that many people would
question Kelly's humanity precisely because she lacks the capacity for
self-consciousness. What follows is that if the humanity of human beings like her is to be securely affirmed at all, it must be affirmed *unconditionally.* Given the limitations of our human existence, however,
this is tantamount to saying that it is going to be securely affirmed
only by the One who affirms the humanity of human creatures unconditionally. In other words, if Kelly's humanity is to be securely affirmed at all, it must be affirmed on the grounds of who God is and
what God does.

Of course, this reasoning needs to reckon with a postmodern rejoinder: Is it not precisely because of the contingent nature of our human existence that we cannot reckon with any claim that holds unconditionally, so that in the end there is no secure grounding of anything?
It may be true that the alternative to making the affirmation of the humanity of Kelly dependent on other people's moral beliefs is a weak
one, but it is all that can be hoped for. Trying to move beyond historical
contingency betrays a delusional clinging to a *Grand Recit,* to use
Lyotard's famous phrase.

In the face of this rejoinder, I must plead guilty: I fail to see why
Christian theology should be content with postmodern historicism.
Surely theology must try to speak God's words in its own voice in order
to account for the way things are.[43] That is, it surely must claim to speak

43. With the phrase of theology's own voice I intend to oppose the method of theological reflection that proceeds "from outside in" (see Ch. 5). With this phrase I characterized the strategy of making theological reflection relevant to particular experiences by
means of reading Christian symbols and creeds in the light of these experiences. Against
this procedure I insisted on the importance of "theology's own voice." At least since the
late nineteenth century, theology has been shaped to a significant degree by the
historicist notion that there is no such thing as theology's own voice; there is only contingent theological reflection. That is, when theologians speak of God, they usually project images of themselves and their class, or sex, or race, or culture, as the case may be.
Consequently, the language of theological reflection *as such* is suspect and stands in
need of justification from a critical perspective. In more recent times the emergence of
liberation theology, black theology, and feminist theology presents some of the most
pertinent examples of this history. In the context of our inquiry, Nancy Eiesland's
liberatory theology of disability is an example of the same approach. As a result of this
development, many colleagues in theology have come to regard the notion of theology's

the truth about God, who lets his light shine on true human being, rather than accept that its concept of being human should shed its light

---

own voice as obsolete. In their view, the continuation of this notion merely betrays the lack of critical-historical consciousness. Theology does not have a voice of its own, because the voice with which it speaks is always owned by a particular historical subject. This means that before anything theological can be said, one first has to offer an account of the historical subject that embodies one's own theology. In Eiesland's case, I recall, the sociological theory of the "minority group model" was assigned this task.

In view of this critical method, whatever its particular shape or form, I want to maintain the outrageous suggestion that it rests on a simple mistake. While there is no point in denying the apparent correlation between historically contingent explanations of divine and human existence, it does not follow that theology therefore necessarily proceeds from the deconstruction of the "subject" of its reflections, as most of the critical appropriations in the past century have assumed. What is descriptively true of theological knowledge is not necessarily prescriptively true of its method. That is, to acknowledge its inevitable historicity is by no means sufficient to answer the question of how to proceed in theological reflection.

The argument for this claim is that theological reflection, at least in the Abramaic traditions, is by definition a response, so that it must be self-defeating not to at least suppose the reality of the message to which it purports to be a response, as especially Karl Barth has taught us in recent times. Any critical appropriation of theological speech can only hope to succeed *because* God's Word has been spoken. Otherwise, it could not be a theological appropriation, which means that theological reflection at any stage proceeds *a posteriori* if it is to be theological in a Christian — or Jewish, or Islamic — sense at all (see Torrance, *Persons in Communion,* pp. 22-28).

Theologically speaking, therefore, the particularities of the historical conditions of our insights are as such not very interesting. Of course, human subjectivity necessarily takes shape as a historically contingent reality that is active in all our understanding. And, of course, we need to understand our historical condition if we are to speak to the vicissitudes of our own times. But it does not follow that we therefore have to start with "unmasking" the claims of particular subjects as "impure" in order to replace them with other subjects — or differently constructed subjects — that are supposedly less contaminated by the powers that be. There is a lingering Cartesianism in the suggestion that only on the basis of a critical appropriation by a purified subjectivity, theological reflection can be saved from becoming enmeshed in the vested interests of "received wisdom."

The problem here is not so much that the ascription of any epistemological privilege in theology is necessarily trapped in self-contradiction, even though this is in fact the case. The problem is rather that this privilege already has been established by the notion of a "chosen" people. God chose his own historically conditioned subject to proclaim what he has to say to us. Christian theology has no credibility whatsoever unless it is rooted in the biblical story according to which God called Israel to be his privileged people in order to be their God. Subsequently, the gospel proclaims that the God of Israel has renewed his covenant and graciously sent his Word into the world, for the salvation not

on the truth about God. Theology precedes anthropology, not the other way around. That's why, in this constructive part of my argument, I want to move from anthropology to theology in the strict sense of making the question of how we understand being human dependent on the question of how we understand God's being. In the context of current debates in Christian theology, this means that we need to turn to recent developments in Trinitarian theology. True Christian speech about God will speak of the communion of the Father, the Son, and the Holy Spirit.

4. Trinitarian Theology and "Relational Being"

According to its proponents, the renewal of Trinitarian theology in recent years is an attempt to recover theology's own primordial sources, particularly the understanding of the gospel by the early fathers of the church. With its understanding of the gospel as the gift of participation in the life of the triune communion of Father, Son, and Holy Spirit, Trinitarian theology is seen as a rich source for new orientations on a wide range of theological topics, among them Christian anthropology and ethics. In this respect, Trinitarian thinking is concerned with how human beings are drawn into the divine life, which presupposes the Christian narrative that begins with creation and is followed by the fall, and which is overcome by God's initiative in the incarnation, the decisive event of his death and resurrection, and its completion in the kingdom. In other words, the biblical story underlying a theological account of being human regards both its origin as well as its final end. This characterization indicates that Trinitarian thinking has developed not as a focus of a particular part of the Christian creed but rather as a comprehensive enterprise of rethinking a wide range of questions in the light of who Christians understand God to be.[44] If they understand the triune God to exist as being in communion, then the inevitable question for Christian anthropology and ethics is how this understanding

---

only of the Jews but of people from all nations, that is, for every human being. Consequently, whatever theology wants to say about the experience of marginalized people, it seeks to illuminate that experience from this center — not the other way around.

44. See Christoph Schwöbel's characterization of this development in his introduction to *Trinitarian Theology Today: Essays in Divine Being and Act* (Edinburgh: T&T Clark, 1995), pp. 1-5.

plays out in their understanding of being human.[45] In this chapter I join this enterprise by thinking through the implications of the new Trinitarian theology for the questions central to this book, particularly the question of how to account for human beings affected by profound disability.

The work of the Greek Orthodox theologian John D. Zizioulas is particularly relevant to this point.[46] True human being, in Zizioulas's view, entails that the freedom of the human creature is its most critical component. But, unlike many other accounts of the freedom of the person, his account does not assume "interiority" as its source. Truly being human is not constituted by intrinsic features that mark the domain of the self, nor is it a developmental stage of potentialities entailed in human nature. On the contrary, any humanistic attempt to ground the freedom of the person intrinsically must fail, according to Zizioulas, because human beings cannot negotiate the conditions of their own existence. If there is to be true human freedom, it must be different from the limited moral freedoms that are constituted by human agency. The only possibility of a freedom independent of natural conditions lies in an account of the human person that is constituted by a free act of love by God the Father, Son, and Holy Spirit. In other words, true freedom is grounded in the economy of grace that draws human beings into the communion of the triune God. The argument for these claims is based on Zizioulas's reading of Greek Orthodoxy, particularly the theology of the Cappadocian Fathers on the doctrine of the Trinity in the fourth century C.E.

However, this turn toward the founding fathers of Greek Orthodoxy has spurred extensive debate.[47] On the one hand, many theologians

45. Jürgen Moltmann in his *Trinität und Reich Gottes* (München: Kaiser, 1978) argues that the connection between the doctrine of man and the doctrine of God should be taken in such a way that it explains *imago dei* in terms of humanity in communion, rather than in terms of a single individual human being. This explanation in turn would not refer to God as absolute being but as Trinity of the Father, the Son, and the Spirit (p. 173).

46. For different assessments of Zizioulas's work, see Torrance, *Persons in Communion;* Robert Jenson, *Systematic Theology: The Triune God,* Vol. I (Oxford: Oxford University Press, 1997); Miroslav Volf, *After Our Likeness: The Church as the Image of the Trinity* (Grand Rapids: Eerdmans, 1998); Matthew Levering, *Scripture and Metaphysics: Aquinas and the Renewal of Trinitarian Theology* (Oxford: Blackwell Publishing, 2004); Lewis Ayres, *Nicaea and Its Legacy: An Approach to Fourth-Century Trinitarian Theology* (Oxford: Oxford University Press, 2004).

47. For some of the recent work on the recovery of trinitarian theology other than the

have been following the lead of Zizioulas and his colleagues in arguing in favor of a "relational" concept of the human person. The assumption guiding their thinking is that a reorientation to the tradition of Greek Orthodoxy provides a rich source for a theological critique of modern individualism. On the other hand, however, a growing chorus of theological voices has emerged that is very critical of these claims, particularly regarding their grounding in patristic sources.[48] The contested issues, both systematic and historical, are manifold and quite complex, and I claim no expertise whatsoever in solving them. But I will attempt to portray Zizioulas's thought by striking a fair balance between conciseness and depth in addressing some of these complex issues.

Furthermore, apart from the historical basis of the new Trinitarian theology and its focus on "relationality," there is a systematic concern about the notion of relational personhood per se to which I wish to draw attention. Some writers who are inspired by this notion have assumed that modern individualism is adequately countered by a Trinitarian concept of "relational being."[49] However, there are at least two reasons to doubt whether this is actually true. First is the obvious question about why we need theology for something that philosophy and so-

---

ones by Zizioulas, Moltmann, Torrance, Jenson, Levering, and Ayres mentioned above, see Eberhard Jüngel, *Gott als Geheimnis der Welt: Zur Begründung der Theologie des Gekreuzigten im Streit zwischen Theismus und Atheismus* (Tübingen: J. C. B. Mohr, 1977); W. Kasper, *Der Gott Jesu Christi* (Mainz: Matthias Grünewald, 1982); Bernd Jochen Hilberath, *Der Personsbegriff der Trinitätstheologie in Rückfrage von Karl Rahner zu Tertullians "Adversus Praxean"* (Innsbruck: Tyrolia Verlag, 1986); Ronald J. Feenstra and Cornelius Plantinga, Jr., eds., *Trinity, Incarnation, and Atonement* (Notre Dame, IN: University of Notre Dame Press, 1989); Catherine M. LaCugna, *God for Us: The Trinity and Christian Life* (San Francisco: Harper, 1991); Colin E. Gunton, *The Promise of Trinitarian Theology* (Edinburgh: T&T Clark, 1991); Christoph Schwöbel and Colin E. Gunton, eds., *Persons, Divine and Human* (Edinburgh: T&T Clark, 1991); Colin E. Gunton, *The One, the Three and the Many: God, Creation and the Culture of Modernity* (Cambridge, UK: Cambridge University Press, 1993); Ted Peters, *God as Trinity: Relationality and Temporality in Divine Life* (Louisville: Westminster/John Knox Press, 1993); Stefan Tobler, *Analogia Caritatis: Kirche als Geschöpf und Abbild der Trinität* (Ph. D. diss., Amsterdam: Vrije Universiteit, 1994). For an overview covering much of the literature, see David S. Cunningham, *These Three are One: The Practice of Trinitarian Theology* (Malden, MA: Blackwell Publishers, 1998); see also Gilles Emery, "Chronique de théologie trinitaire," *Revue Thomiste* 101 (2001): 581-82.

48. Among the authors mentioned above, Volf, Levering, and Ayres are particularly critical of Zizioulas's theology of the Trinity, though for quite different reasons.

49. See, for example, Gunton, *The Promise of Trinitarian Theology*, pp. 12-14.

cial theory have established long ago. Apart from German idealism, such as Hegel's philosophy of identity, or Søren Kierkegaard's existentialism, or the developments in Jewish personalism as exemplified by Martin Buber's work, a social theory of being human has been established in the social sciences at least since the social philosophy of George Herbert Mead in the 1920s.

Second, relational being *as such* need not be incompatible at all with modern individualism when its specifically theological subject matter is ignored. It is no doubt true that modern secular thought has underscored the social nature of our being, but its understanding is limited to an explanation of how the individual human self *comes into existence.* For example, Barth's anthropology has been read in support of the claim that theology is in agreement with the findings of the social sciences in insisting that only in our interpersonal relationships are we "homo sapiens in the fullest sense."[50] Such an account raises the question of whether relational being abstracted from its theological meaning carries any significance. I doubt that it does. The important thing, theologically speaking, is not that our subjectivity only exists because of the fact that others have taken on the responsibility of caring for us; the important thing is that God has confirmed the uniqueness of his relationship with us as human beings in giving himself to us in the man Jesus Christ.[51]

Unless it takes this shift of perspective seriously, Christian anthropology still remains focused on self-conscious subjectivity as the center of being human, but now conditioned by sociability. Therefore,

50. Daniel J. Price, *Karl Barth's Anthropology in the Light of Modern Thought* (Grand Rapids: Eerdmans, 2000), pp. 13-14.

51. Arguing for a "theological anthropology of relationality" M. I. Iozzio observes that "not one of us has achieved what appears and is commonly referred to as independence without having first been dependent (and radically so) on others" (Iozzio, "The Writing on the Wall . . . Alzheimer's Disease: A Daughter's Look at Mom's Faithful Care of Dad," *Journal of Religion, Disability & Health* 8, no. 2 (2005): 49-74, n. 21). This indicates the view that "relationality" is important because of what it implies for the genesis of the human individual: "Interdependence and relationality become the necessary preconditions of human flourishing by attention to the needs of the basic physical, intellectual, emotional, social, and spiritual growth and development of every distinct person" (p. 58). What the author implies, in other words, is that relationality is instrumental to the development and growth of the human subject. This is the theological view one commonly finds under the header of "relational anthropology" that I will criticize.

if "relationality" is to make a difference, it must be followed by a much more radical second step. This second step does not limit relational being to the genesis of the human person but aims at its interpretation in terms of our human destiny. Relational being, understood from a Christian perspective, aims at communion and not merely at an enriched subjectivity. Moreover, the communion it aims at is not constituted by our subjectivity but by God's self-giving gift to humankind.

To take this notion a step further, therefore, we must move beyond many current proposals of relational personhood that continue to think from the center of human subjectivity. With this aim in mind, I will turn specifically to Zizioulas's concept of "ecstatic being."[52] Ecstatic being is being that is grounded in communion, as distinguished from being that is grounded in itself as substance. As we will see, however, Zizioulas himself interprets ecstatic being as a "movement *towards* communion," which, from the perspective of my analysis, again raises the question of the initiating subject of this movement. Contrary to his intentions, his account seems to reopen the case for relational personhood in terms of human subjectivity. A theological conception of "ecstatic being" should explain why God is and remains the initiating subject of human interrelatedness in a way that neither depends on nor reinforces the importance of features intrinsic to our being. In other words, the task ahead is to account for the ecstatic nature of being human as *extrinsically* grounded.

5. The Contribution of John D. Zizioulas[53]

In his seminal study entitled *Being as Communion*, Zizioulas argues that the main quest for human beings is to affirm their own identity in free-

52. Pannenberg also speaks of the ecstatic nature of all living beings to the extent that they live for the future, but he considers human beings to be distinguished in their capacity for developing a consciousness that bridges time because it can distinguish past and present — and thus the future (W. Pannenberg, *Anthropologie in theologischer Perspektive* [Göttingen: VandenHoeck & Ruprecht, 1977], pp. 524-25).

53. The sections on Zizioulas contain material from Hans S. Reinders, "Human Dignity in the Absence of Agency," in *God and Human Dignity*, ed. R. Kendall Soulen and Linda Woodhead (Grand Rapids: Eerdmans, 2006), pp. 121-39.

dom. Identity is what makes one human being different from another; it makes me who I am.[54] Affirmation of my identity as an intentional act presupposes freedom, but it must be a much more fundamental freedom than the moral freedom that is well-known from Western philosophy (p. 42).

> The moral sense of freedom. . . is satisfied with the simple power of choice: a man is free who is able to choose one of the possibilities set before him. But this "freedom" is already bound up by the "necessity" of these possibilities, and the ultimate and most binding of these "necessities" for man is his existence itself: how can a man be considered absolutely free when he cannot do other than accept his existence? (p. 42)

The possibility of affirming my existence, not as the recognition of a given fact but as the result of "free choice," says Zizioulas, marks the quest for freedom in modernity. Its philosophy is grounded in the idea of an immediate connection between agency and self-reflexivity. But this immediacy can never completely secure the basis of human freedom, because it cannot escape the determinations of the self as a biologically and culturally mediated datum. If human freedom were to be grounded in self-reflexive agency, Zizioulas contends, the human person should be capable of creating itself *ex nihilo,* which it cannot do.[55]

Zizioulas arrives at this conclusion by observing that the capacity of choice — which is at the core of the Western conception of freedom in his view — cannot possibly escape the condition of necessity because the choosing agent does not only fail to control the range of alternative options, he does not even control the existence of his own being. Human beings cannot attain the fundamental freedom of affirming their own existence; at best, they attain the freedoms (note the plural) that are obtained by accepting obedience to the rules of social institutions. That is, according to Zizioulas, they can manage to create a kind of soci-

---

54. John D. Zizioulas, *Being as Communion: Studies in Personhood and the Church* (Crestwood, NY: St. Vladimir Press, 1985), p. 34 [page number citations in parentheses in the text refer to this work].

55. The problem is discussed by Pannenberg with regard to Fichte's theory of self-positing subjectivity (Pannenberg, *Anthropologie in theologischer Perspektive,* pp. 201-4).

ety allowing them freedoms that are attached to particular roles, for example, the role of being a citizen (pp. 34-35).

It is not freedom per se that is obtained in these social contexts, but only the conditional freedoms that are accidentally attached to them. The human being, in Zizioulas's view, is caught in a web of conditions that do not allow real freedom, because real freedom is unconditional. The human being is not able to free himself absolutely from his "nature" or from his "substance," or "from what biological laws dictate." Human beings aspire to true freedom as their final end *(telos),* but this end cannot be attained by means of their natural faculties. According to Zizioulas, real freedom is only possible because "the being of each human person is *given* to him" (pp. 18-19). Contrary to the tradition of Western philosophy, personhood in Zizioulas's concept is identical with ontological freedom rather than with purposive agency. The freedom of the human person is only possible, according to Zizioulas, when being human is freed from ontological necessity.

To establish the possibility of personhood as ontological freedom, Zizioulas turns to Trinitarian theology as it has been taught and practiced by the church. Personhood as ontological freedom can only be predicated of the triune God: there is nothing in God that binds him to being, not even the necessity of his own existence (p. 41). God's being as the communion of the Father, Son, and Holy Spirit is the result of precisely this freedom. What follows, according to Zizioulas, is not that personhood cannot be attributed to being human, but that it can be attributed to being human only to the extent that it participates in the divine life. Human beings can be really free only because they are drawn into the history of salvation, that is, because of *God's action.*

The theme of participation in the divine life introduces the place of the church in Zizioulas's account of human freedom. The concept of the person as the mark of human freedom could never have entered the realm of human experience without the mystery of the church (p. 18). Zizioulas wants to show how both the experience and the understanding of real freedom became possible within the context of ecclesial communion.[56] It is only because theology revolutionized the concept of the person that Western culture could develop the ideal of personhood

---

56. "*Historically* as well as *existentially* the concept of the person is indissolubly bound up with theology" (*Being as Communion*, p. 27).

as freedom. This revolutionizing discovery of the person as essentially free Zizioulas attributes to a development within Trinitarian theology in the fourth century C.E.

To present his case in support of this claim, Zizioulas shows how the stage for this development was set in the world of Greek theater, where the notion of the person seems to have obtained its original meaning.[57] Greek theater provided the scene where the antagonism between human freedom and natural necessity was enacted as tragedy; it also provided the space where the tragic hero revolts against fate but only in order to learn that there is no escape from it. Tragedy thus expressed the revolt against the never-changing order of being that dominated the Greek worldview. Within this view, everything that exists derives its existence necessarily from *to hen* ("being") as the first ontological principle of the cosmos.[58] Consequently, the concrete particularity of things is not their real being, but is merely accidental. This holds for human beings as well. Zizioulas explains that, in Greek theater, the actor playing the tragic hero disappears behind the mask (*prosopon* in Greek; *persona* in Latin) of his theatrical role. Embodying a role, the person does not participate in "being"; it does not have ontological content.

Against this theatrical background, the notion of the person was developed in the theological disputes in the fourth century. To the Greek mind, things are real to the extent that they participate in ontological necessity; personhood, by contrast, individualizes human beings under the aspect of their illusory freedom. For that very reason, according to Zizioulas, personhood could not touch the very core of being human in the world of Greek antiquity; at best it could signify something accidental to it. Zizioulas summarizes the story up to this point:

> This is as far as the Graeco-Roman world takes the idea of personhood. The glory of this world consists in its having shown man a dimension

57. The notion of *prosopon*, which is the Greek equivalent of the Latin *persona*, was used both for "mask" as well as for the theatrical role in the tragedy (*Being as Communion*, p. 31).

58. "Ancient Greek thought remained tied to the basic principle which it had set itself, the principle that being constitutes in the final analysis a unity in spite of the multiplicity of existing things because concrete existing things finally trace back to their necessary relationship and 'kinship' with the 'one' 'being'" (*Being as Communion*, p. 29).

of existence, which may be called personal. Its weakness lies in the fact that its cosmological framework did not allow this dimension to be justified ontologically. Prosopon and persona remained pointers towards the person. But they consciously. . . constituted a reminder that this personal dimension is not and ought never to be identical with the essence of things, with the true being of man. (p. 35)

Since the idea of personhood originated from the fateful revolt against ontological necessity, it established the thought of essential human freedom under a negative aspect, that is, as a desperate impossibility (pp. 32-33). A major change in worldview was required that could liberate human beings from ontological necessity. According to Zizioulas, two developments in patristic theology prepared the way for this change to become possible.

The first was to deny that the world was ontologically necessary to itself, as the ancient Greeks believed it to be. The fathers of the church responded to this claim to necessity with the doctrine of a creation *ex nihilo*.

The biblical doctrine of creation *ex nihilo* obliged the Fathers to introduce a radical difference into ontology, to trace the world back to an ontology outside the world, that is, to God. They thus broke the circle of the closed ontology of the Greeks, and at the same time did something much more important, which is of direct interest to us here: they made being — the existence of the world, existent things — a product of freedom. (p. 39)

The principle of the world, its *archē,* was transposed from *being* to *freedom.* In other words, the world was extrinsically grounded, and it did not have its being from itself.

The second development concerned divine being as it came to be understood with respect to the Trinity. Here it was argued, mainly by the Cappadocian Fathers, according to Zizioulas, that the *being of God himself* was identified with the three persons of the Trinity. This was how the doctrinal formula of the church (*mia ousia, treis hypostaseis* ["one being, three persons"]) was explained, particularly by Basil the Great.[59] Basil argued that the being of God does not reside in "sub-

---

59. According to Zizioulas, there is a crucial difference at this point between the Cappadocian Fathers and the Western tradition, particularly through the work of Augus-

stance" *(ousia)* but in the *hypostasis,* that is, in the free act of the person of the Father, who generates the Son and brings forth the Spirit in freedom and is thus the "cause" both of the generation of the Son and of the procession of the Spirit.[60] According to Zizioulas, this was a necessary step because, as long as the being of God was identified with "being itself," as it had been in Greek ontology, human beings could never attain authentic personhood. Freedom cannot plausibly be derived from ontological necessity, as Zizioulas explains.

The revolution in Greek philosophy, then, was the explanation of the *hypostasis* of the Father as the first ontological principle (pp. 36-37, 40ff.). Until then, *hypostasis* and *ousia* in Greek ontology had indicated two senses of being: the one was concrete, particular being; the other was general, universal being. In explaining God's being as the communion of the three persons, however, the Cappadocians in fact dissociated *hypostasis* from *ousia* and identified the source of the *kosmos* with an act of freedom by the Father. Therefore, the concrete existence of Father, Son, and Spirit was not traced to being itself but to divine personhood, that is, to the person of the Father.

---

tine. In the West, the Nicean formula was taken to express that the divine being as substance precedes the existence of the persons. Thus the West repeated the pattern of Greek thought by charging "being" (Augustine's notion of God as *ipsum esse*) with ontological priority. This reading mistakenly reiterated classical Greek ontology in locating the "principle" of God in his being rather than his personhood *(Being as Communion,* p. 40). This is one of the strongest points of contention between Zizioulas and the new Trinitarians, on the one hand — Gunton, LaCugna, Schwöbel, and others, all of whom follow Zizioulas at this point — and the patristic scholars who deny any really significant difference between the theological tradition of East and West, on the other hand. There is no primacy of God's being over against the persons of the Father, the Son, and the Spirit in the theology of the Western fathers. See, especially, Lewis Ayres, *Nicea and Its Legacy,* pp. 364-83; see also Michel René Barnes, "Rereading Augustine's Theology of the Trinity," in *The Trinity: An Interdisciplinary Symposium on the Trinity,* ed. Stephen T. Davis, Daniel Kendall, S.J., and Gerald O'Collins, S.J. (Oxford: Oxford University Press, 1999), pp. 145-78.

60. "This thesis of the Cappadocians that introduced the concept of 'cause' into the being of God assumed an incalculable importance. For it meant that the ultimate ontological category that makes something really *be*, is neither impersonal and incommunicable 'substance' nor a structure of communion existing by itself or imposed by necessity, but rather the *person* . . . . The fact that God exists because of the Father shows that His existence, His being is the consequence of a free person; which means, in the last analysis, that not only communion but also *freedom,* the free person, constitutes true being" *(Being as Communion,* p. 40).

It is this argument, says Zizioulas, that breaks away from classical Greek ontology.[61] The decisive step consists in the ontological implication of God's fatherhood as the source of the deity, namely, the implication that the Father is ontologically prior to "being itself."[62] The being of God is no longer seen as ontological necessity — that is, as absolute, "ingenerate" being — but as having the freedom of the loving Father as its "cause."[63] With this step, according to Zizioulas, the divine being came to be understood at once as personal and as relational. "True being," he says, "exists only as the person who loves freely — that is, who freely affirms his being by means of an event of communion with other persons" (p. 18). This was a major shift in the history of Western thought, Zizioulas says, because it meant that the ontology of *hypostasis* was understood in terms of the relational categories of existence: "*To be* and *to be in relation* becomes identical" (p. 88).

61. "Entities no longer trace their being to being itself — that is, being is not an absolute category in itself — but to the person, to precisely that which constitutes being, that is, enables entities to be entities. In other words, from an adjunct to being (a kind of mask) the person becomes the being itself and is simultaneously — a most significant point — *the constitutive element* (the "principle" or "cause" of beings)" (*Being as Communion*, p. 39).

62. As appears from the recent literature, this is frequently seen as the key issue in the renewal of Trinitarian theology; see LaCugna, *God for Us*, pp. 247-48; see also G. Larentzakis, 'Trinitarisches Kirchenverständnis', in *Trinität. Aktuelle Perspektiven der Theologie*, ed. W. Breuning (Freiburg/Basel/Wien: Herder, 1984), pp. 79-80; Cornelius Plantinga, Jr., "Social Trinity and Tritheism," in *Trinity, Incarnation and Atonement: Philosophical and Theological Essays*, ed. Ronald J. Feenstra and Cornelius Plantinga, Jr. (Notre Dame, IN: Notre Dame University Press, 1989), pp. 21-47; Christoph Schwöbel and Colin E. Gunton, eds., *Persons, Divine and Human: King's College Essays in Theological Anthropology* (Edinburgh: T&T Clark, 1991), pp. 11-12.

63. The introduction of causal relation within the Trinity is one of the elements in Zizioulas's theology that worries theologians in the Western tradition. In making the Father the cause of the divine being, Zizioulas implies that the *hypostases* of the Son and the Spirit must be contingent and derivative (see, for example, Alan Torrance, *Persons in Communion*, pp. 290-91). Introducing a hierarchy into the Trinity, Zizioulas is saying that, ontologically, the One Person — of the Father — is prior to God's being as communion, which seems to be inconsistent with his major thesis, because he seems to make intradivine communion a secondary rather than a primordial concept. In any case, it is curious to hear Zizioulas frequently speaking of divine personhood primarily with regard to the Father rather than the Trinity. See also Schmaus, *Die psychologische Trinitätslehre* (pp. 18-19), where he shows that the Cappadocians were following the specifically "Greek" tradition in theology in this respect.

This analysis of the ontology of personhood as found in the Cappadocian Fathers implies, in Zizioulas's view, the primacy of theology over philosophy when it comes to understanding the possibility of human freedom.[64] Philosophy can affirm the reality of the person, but it cannot provide an adequate grounding of its freedom so that this freedom must remain an aspiration rather than a reality.

> Philosophy can arrive at the confirmation of the reality of the person, but only theology can treat of the genuine, the authentic person, as absolute ontological freedom, because the authentic person, as absolute ontological freedom, must be "uncreated," that is, unbounded by any "necessity," including its own existence. If such a person does not exist in reality, the concept of the person is a presumptuous daydream. If God does not exist, the person does not exist. (p. 43)

The only person who can absolutely affirm its own existence, then, is the person who is not bounded by necessity, not even the ontological necessity of its own being. By the same token, however, theology cannot assert the primacy of God's being as *ipsum esse* (Augustine's definition of God's being), because, as Zizioulas has already explained, freedom cannot plausibly be derived from ontological necessity.

> The manner in which God exercises His ontological freedom, that precisely which makes Him ontologically free, is the way in which He transcends and abolishes the ontological necessity of substance as God the Father, that is, as He who "begets" the Son and "brings forth" the Spirit. This ecstatic character of God, the fact that His being is identical with an act of communion, ensures the transcendence of the ontological necessity which His substance would have demanded — if the substance were the primary ontological predicate of God — and replaces this necessity with the free self-affirmation of divine existence. (p. 44)

God's being is "ecstatic" in the sense that it is identical with an act of communion. That is how God exists, which Zizioulas articulates in saying that God's being is "being as communion."

---

64. As indicated, one of the disputed points regarding Zizioulas's interpretation of the Cappadocian Fathers is whether there is actually any interest in an ontology of personhood to be found in their work. I will return to this criticism later in this chapter.

In order to explain what the notion of *ekstasis* is supposed to clarify, Zizioulas indicates how it is distinct from the notion of *hypostasis*.[65] Both *ekstasis* and *hypostasis* characterize being in different ways. Whereas the latter specifies a particular being in its concreteness, the former specifies a particular being in its relationship to other beings. Like *hypostasis, ekstasis* refers to a concrete being; but, unlike the former, it does not refer to the concrete being with regard to its substance. Instead, *ekstasis* refers to the concrete being with regard to the relationship that identifies its concreteness. God's being as *ekstasis* resides in the relationship of love that is the communion of the Father with the Son and the Spirit. The characterization of God as love itself, which appears in the gospel of John and is at the heart of any Christian concept of God, bears testimony to this. Love is not a qualifying property of God; love is the "supreme ontological predicate." Love constitutes God's being in a free act of communion (p. 46).

6. Ecstatic Personhood as Ecclesial Reality

However, when this conception of ontological freedom is applied to human being, a problem emerges. Zizioulas explains that the end of personhood, which is freedom in communion, is thwarted precisely in our concrete existence. The problem is identified in the distinction between "person" and "personality." Whereas the former refers to the ecstatic movement of "relating to," the latter refers to the complex of natural, psychological, and moral qualities that, as Zizioulas puts it, are "possessed" by or "contained" in individual human beings.[66] The limitation of human being is that it cannot be radically separated from its natural subsistence. Therefore, the freedom of the human person is necessarily limited. In view of its biological and historical nature, the human person can only be "real" in a truncated and limited sense. That is why the secular quest for authentic personhood amounts to a tragic

65. See the critical footnote on the attempt by Christos Yannaras to use Heidegger's concept of *ekstasis* for the explanation of patristic theology (*Being as Communion*, pp. 44-45).

66. Zizioulas, "On Human Capacity and Incapacity," pp. 407-8. This distinction implies that the definition of personhood in terms of psychological characteristics is a definition of "personality" rather than "personhood," according to Zizioulas.

illusion.[67] At the same time, however, this contention raises the question of how authentic personhood can be realized in human existence. To answer this question, we must turn to Zizioulas's distinction between what he calls our "natural" being and our "ecclesial" being.

The condition of human nature implies that there is no free movement of human beings "unto another," as in the ecstatic movement from the Father to the Son and the Spirit. Of course, as human beings, we reach out toward each other, but this movement cannot be the first principle of our existence, nor can this movement ever be complete. At this point Zizioulas explains the ambiguity that resides in the natural condition of human being by considering the ambiguity of erotic love. On the one hand, erotic love is a genuine form of ecstatic self-expression through the individual concreteness of the body. At the same time, however, the procreation in the body causes separation and individuality. What follows is that

> [m]an as a biological hypostasis is intrinsically a tragic figure. He is born as a result of an ecstatic fact — erotic love — but this fact is interwoven with natural necessity and therefore lacks ontological freedom. . . . By the same erotic act with which he tries to attain ecstasy he is led to individualism. His body is the tragic instrument which leads to communion with others, stretching out a hand, creating language, speech, conversation, art, kissing. But at the same time it is the "mask" of hypocrisy, the fortress of individualism, the vehicle of the final separation, death. (p. 52)

Zizioulas thus describes the conditions of biological and psychological existence as the two "passions" that govern human being. But even

---

67. These considerations help us understand why Zizioulas says that personhood when applied to God is perhaps the only notion that does not imply the danger of "anthropomorphism." As this danger is usually perceived as attributing features of human being to the divine being, it cannot arise in this case because "ecstatic personhood," as Zizioulas understands it, has no roots in human nature. Thus anthropomorphism is a conceptual impossibility in this case (Zizioulas, "On Human Capacity and Incapacity," p. 420). Incidentally, Zizioulas's comment at this point is exactly parallel to what Barth says about the concept of personhood when applied to the divine *Logos*. Having defined personhood as unrestrained free subjectivity, he adds, "If we consider what this implies, it will not occur to us to see in this personalizing of the concept of God's Word a case of anthropomorphism" (*Church Dogmatics*, I, 1, 138-39).

more decisive in his view is the third "passion," which is death. It finalizes the fact that, from the perspective of our natural being, the hope of survival of the person is illusory. The human person cannot exist without its biological and psychological being, but as such it cannot exist in ontological freedom either.

To explain how we can overcome this impossibility, Zizioulas points to the Christian church. The church proclaims the reality of human freedom from natural necessity as it is attested by the resurrection of Jesus Christ. Because Christ remained faithful to his love of God the Father, he embodied what Zizioulas calls "authentic" personhood. That's why the church insisted on identifying this man, in his biological concreteness and individuality, with the person of the Son in the Trinity. But this does not mean that Christ's mission came out of his development as a human being. As Zizioulas insists, it was not a matter of natural potential. The man Jesus was the Son of God the Father incarnate. An authentic human person is only possible "from above." Zizioulas points to the account of Jesus' baptism in the Gospel of John: the good news to human beings is that in baptism they are born anew, this time not as natural beings but as ecclesial beings.

As an ecclesial being, the individual is introduced by the church "into a kind of relationship with the world that is not determined by the laws of biology" (p. 56). Within the church, being human transcends the exclusivism of its natural bonds (p. 57). The bonds of natural kinship are transcended because, as ecclesial beings, we love differently from how we love as natural beings. This love is not a response to a moral command, Zizioulas explains, but springs from "the fact that the Church has made them part of a network of relationships which transcends every exclusiveness" (p. 58). As ecclesial beings, we find our individuality as the mark of our separation, which is to be transcended. We are drawn into the communion of the Father, Son, and Holy Spirit. Being drawn into this communion justifies our hope of being authentic persons in the final outcome of our existence (pp. 58-59). However, because participation in the life of the church does not take away the concreteness of natural being, the fullness of authentic personhood remains on the plane of eschatological promise. Consequently, participating in the act of communion that is the life of the church is a foretaste of what is to come.

The ecclesial hypostasis reveals man as a person, who, however, has its roots in the future and is perpetually inspired, or rather, maintained and nourished, by the future. The truth and the ontology of the person belong to the future, are images of the future. (p. 62)

According to Zizioulas, this foretaste is realized in the Eucharist: the Eucharist is the center of the life of the church that binds all ecclesial activity to the reality of the living Christ.[68] This means, Zizioulas adds, that the Eucharist is much more than a "sacrament." It is the act that includes us in God's freedom. The Eucharist is both assembly and movement.

As assembly, meaning a network of relationships between human beings related to one another in Christ, it is different from how its members exist as natural being. This is not to say that ecclesial being implies the denial of their natural being; ecclesial personhood does not abandon the concreteness of the human body, nor does it ignore differences between concrete bodies (p. 63). Both aspects, concreteness and difference, are included in the transformation through the Eucharist. Consequently, the Eucharist is not only assembly but also movement. It progresses toward its realization as movement (p. 61). The Eucharist aims to re-create the human person in God's unconditional love. It can only succeed in that it proclaims this re-creation to be realized by God. It is not of this world. Therefore, the paradox of Christian existence between the historical reality and the promise of the world to come is not tragedy but promise. Ecclesial personhood marks an existence from the future as it is expressed in the Eucharist" (p. 63).

7. Zizioulas's Critics

Zizioulas's account of Cappadocian theology has been contested in recent years, particularly his claim that "relation" has been downplayed in the Western tradition of Trinitarian theology due to Augustine's in-

---

68. Zizioulas, *Being as Communion*, p. 60. It is for this reason important for Zizioulas to note that the conceptual shift that was brought about by the Cappadocian Fathers occurred in the context of their ecclesial experience as bishops of the church rather than as doctors of theology (pp. 16-17).

sistence on the primacy of ontology.[69] According to the critics, there is no significant difference between how the fathers of "the East" and those of "the West" have explained Trinitarian personhood.[70] Second, the critics argue that, contrary to what Zizioulas and others have maintained, the Cappadocian Fathers were not at all interested in the ontology of personhood.[71] Allow me to offer a few observations regarding each of these points.

Those who attribute a limited understanding of personhood in the Western tradition to the influence of Augustine's *De Trinitate* describe his concept of the person as a "self-enclosed entity." For example, both LaCugna and Gunton have traced the limitations of this concept back to a lacking differentiation between the persons.[72] In their view, the root of the problem is that Augustine's Trinitarian theology remained subservient to the doctrine of the unity and simplicity of the divine being. This means that, for Augustine, God as person relates to himself under the aspect of his being one God. Following this conception of divine being, Augustine's analysis of the "trinity in man" as it appears in *De Trinitate* shows the same limitation: it is explained likewise in terms of how the human soul relates to itself. Thus the concept is established of the human creature as a self that appears to itself, which, according to Augustine's critics, then becomes the hallmark of the Western concept of the person.[73] Augustine does not deny that the person is relational, of course, but the relationships he describes are exclusively

69. The charge against Augustine is widely dispersed and can be found in authors with otherwise very different theologies such as LaCugna, Gunton, Moltmann, and Jenson, to mention only a few. (See above, n. 45.)

70. See, for example, Ayres, *Nicaea and Its Legacy,* pp. 364-83.

71. Ayres, *Nicaea and Its Legacy,* pp. 312-17.

72. LaCugna, *God for Us,* p. 93; Gunton, *The Promise of Trinitarian Theology,* p. xxiv. (See also Chapter III, of Gunton's book.)

73. See, for example, LaCugna, *God for Us,* pp. 247, 250. I followed the same kind of analysis in my essay "Human Dignity without Agency," which introduces Kelly and then develops an argument that makes the Western tradition as inspired by Augustinian "radical reflexivity" responsible for her disqualification as a subhuman nature. (See Reinders, "Human Dignity in the Absence of Agency," in *God and Human Dignity,* ed. R. Kendall Soulen and Linda Woodhead [Grand Rapids: Eerdmans, 2006], pp. 121-39). After I learned from the emerging criticism of the "new Trinitarians" — particularly in Ayres's work — I reconstructed the argument in this book without relying on this historical claim.

intrapersonal rather than interpersonal.[74] The response to this charge has been to show that the patristic fathers of both East and West were in complete agreement on the importance of the doctrine of divine unity and simplicity. In their account, this unison was grounded in the prime task that the fathers assigned themselves, which was to explain Scripture as the church read it.[75]

Although I do not see why the claim that the fathers of the church were in agreement on the doctrine of divine unity and simplicity should render invalid the critique of Augustine's concept of the person as "self-enclosed entity," I will not pursue that point here. My reason is that a critical distancing from the Augustinian tradition is not central to the argument Zizioulas presents. Central to his claim is how the Cappadocians revolutionized the concept of the person as it had been developed up to that point, which concerns the second objection of the new Trinitarians' critics.

Zizioulas claims to present an accurate account of Christian orthodoxy as it was presented by the great Cappadocians, making his claim to a revolution of ontology in their thought crucial indeed. In his book *Nicaea and Its Legacy*, Lewis Ayres has strongly objected to this notion of a revolution in Greek ontology that Zizioulas attributes primarily to Basil the Great. Ayres says that the fathers of the church in East and West had no interest whatsoever in "relational personhood." They had no interest in a philosophical concept underlying the differentiated relationships between and among Father, Son, and Spirit, Ayres argues, because they all taught the "inseparability of operations."[76] This means that, whenever the Father acts, the Son and the Spirit act simultaneously so that there is no relationship of the Father and the Son that is

---

74. This reading of Augustine's anthropology in the West has become quite influential, as can be seen, e.g., in Charles Taylor's book *Sources of the Self*, where he depicts Augustine's view of humanity in terms of "radical reflexivity," which allows him to characterize the fourth-century bishop as a "proto-Cartesian" (Taylor, *Sources of the Self: The Shaping of Modern Identity* [Cambridge, UK: Cambridge University Press, 1989], pp. 132-33, 140-42).

75. For example, Augustine's emphasis on divine being as *ipsum esse* should be read as his attempt to explain God's name as proclaimed in Exod. 3:14, "I am who I am," as well as the *Shema* in Deut. 6:4: "The Lord is our God, the Lord is one." Brian Daley suggested this to me.

76. Ayres, *Nicaea and Its Legacy*, pp. 280-81.

distinct, for example, from the relationship between the Father and the Spirit.[77] With this doctrine the fathers of the church sought to avoid any implication of polytheism, according to Ayres. Not three Gods but one, united in each of the operations of the three persons. Therefore, Ayres accuses Zizioulas of finding an ontology of relational personhood in patristic theology that is simply not there. There are no textual references, says Ayres, to sustain Zizioulas's claims in this regard.[78]

Leaving aside the historical merits of Ayres's objection, which I am in no position to assess, I nonetheless think that a formal point is justified. It regards the systematics of Zizioulas's claims: Ayres's objection overlooks the fact that Zizioulas never explicitly claims that the Cappadocians had an interest in the ontology of personhood. He also overlooks the fact that the force of Zizioulas's argument does not depend on such a claim. Zizioulas never claims that his patristic sources shared his own interpretation of what they were doing. Presumably, like the other fathers of the church, the Cappadocians intended to defend what they took to be its principal teaching on the scriptural account of the divine economy. But even so, this does not at all exclude the possibility that, in the context of classical Greek thought, against the background of which their own thinking evolved, their views had major ontological implications. It seems to me that when one rereads classical sources, it is certainly legitimate to find implications that the authors themselves did not know were there.[79]

Thus the claim that the Cappadocians had no interest in the ontology of personhood does not invalidate the possibility that their theology in fact implied a major conceptual innovation concerning it. Ayres's objection logically depends on the assumption that the only legitimate way to explain a theological concept is by way of explaining the intention guiding its articulation. As it stands, however, this claim does not

77. This is basically Ayer's defense of Augustine in terms of the first issue: the unity and simplicity of the divine being is taught widely in both East and West.

78. Ayres, *Nicaea and Its Legacy*, p. 313.

79. A nice example of this phenomenon is provided by Wilfried Joest's study *Ontologie der Person bei Luther* (Göttingen: VandenHoeck und Ruprecht, 1967), p. 15, where the author makes a parallel point. Even though Luther clearly had no formal interest in ontological thinking as a prerequisite to theology, this does not rule out a particular ontological conception of "being," though Luther in his theology did attempt nothing but to read Scripture (see also p. 251).

seem to be true, even when one shares Ayres's criticism of Hegelian supersessionism in the history of ideas.[80] In view of the inevitably limited perspective we have on our own thinking, given its historical condition, it is always possible that later generations will arrive at a different understanding of what we ourselves believed we were saying at the time we were saying it, given the context of *their* historical conditions. At any rate, beyond what Zizioulas thinks was the contribution of Greek Orthodox theology to the Christian tradition, his aim is clearly to give an account of the roots of the Christian faith "in the context of the existential quest of modern man" (Zizioulas, p. 19). I do not see why it should be illegitimate to read historical sources with a particular interest that is different from — which is not to say contrary to — the interest with which they were written.

8. Extrinsic Movement

My argument in defense of Zizioulas's project does not imply, however, that the way he carries it out is beyond criticism. This is not the case, not even on its own terms. Despite its powerful theological claims against human subjectivity as the center of personhood, Zizioulas's account does seem to be bound to what he aspires to leave behind. I will make the argument to sustain this objection in two steps.

First, however, let me begin by underscoring the relevance of Zizioulas's theology of personhood to my inquiry in this book. Given his distinction between "person" and "personality," according to which only the latter refers to human capacities, his account of the former creates new possibilities for the development of Christian anthropology that we have been looking for. "Personality," as it refers to our natural being, is not the source for "personhood," according to Zizioulas: this implies that any kind of developmental delay does not eliminate the possibility of being a person. In Zizioulas's terms, "personhood" is not a matter of becoming; it is a gift that enables the participation of every human being in the final end of our humanity — as it is envisioned in the church.

---

80. Ayres, *Nicaea and Its Legacy*, pp. 387-92.

This consideration of the human person from the point of view of a telos must not be interpreted with the help of an Aristotelian entelechy, that is, with the help of a potentiality existing in man's nature which enables him to become something better and more perfect than that which he is now. Through all that I have said in this study, I have excluded every possibility of regarding the person as an expression or emanation of the substance or nature of man. . . . Consequently, there is no question of the ecclesial hypostasis, the authentic person, emerging as a result of an evolution of the human race, whether biological or historical. (p. 59)[81]

Living a human life in which natural capacities remain underdeveloped is a condition on the level of "personality." Such a condition does not eliminate the possibility of participating in authentic personhood, because this is not grounded in human potentiality but in the reality of the triune God. As ecclesial beings, we are drawn into the communion of the Trinity that is given to us in the Eucharist. Ecclesial being, the being of personhood, is relational being.

However, a problem emerges as soon as we look more closely at Zizioulas's account of the Eucharist as movement toward authentic personhood that takes the form of "being toward the other" (p. 63). Zizioulas characterizes this "being toward the other" in terms of *ekstasis*. But when we look at the direction of this movement, we find that "the other" appears as *terminus ad quem,* which raises the question as to the *terminus ab quo* of authentic personhood. We find Zizioulas describing the Eucharist primarily from the perspective of our participation in it. Thus he can say, for example, that it is the assembly of the faithful in movement that "makes the Eucharist liturgy" (p. 61). But the Eucharist as movement of the faithful raises the question of how it relates to the conception of the Eucharist as primarily the gift of God's act. For example, when Zizioulas says that authentic personhood does not deny the biological nature of the body (now identified as "eros"), he explains:

In accordance with what I have said so far, in practice this means basically that eros as *ecstatic* movement of the human person drawing

81. This quotation indicates how Zizioulas's theology of personhood is distinct from the Roman Catholic position precisely at the point of discussion in Ch. 2: the connection between human potentiality and personhood.

its hypostasis from the future, as it is expressed in the Eucharist (or from God through the Eucharist, as it is expressed in the Trinity), is freed from ontological necessity and does not lead any more to the exclusiveness which is dictated by nature. (p. 63)

The human person is drawing his or her ecclesial being from the future as expressed in the Eucharist, or from God through the Eucharist as expressed in the Trinity. What is striking in the above quotation is what Zizioulas has put in parentheses, almost as though it were an afterthought. The problem is that this statement seems indifferent to the relative ordering of giving and receiving; as such it tends to misrepresent the movement of what actually happens in the Eucharist. There is in Zizioulas's description a focus on ecclesial being as a renewed form of human agency, rather than on what it is that we receive to be so renewed. This is also true of his description of ecstatic being; that description remains primarily agent-centered. To be is to be in relationship, we have learned, but he depicts "to be in relation" as a movement initiated by the agent and directed toward the other. Therefore, it is difficult to avoid sensing a lingering residue of reconstructed subjectivity at the center of Zizioulas's concept of personhood.

We are strengthened in this impression when we study his text further. For example, Zizioulas can say, "Thanks to Christ *man* can henceforth. . . *affirm his existence* as personal not on the basis of the immutable laws of nature, but on the basis of a relationship *with* God which is *identified with* what Christ in freedom and love possesses as the Son of God with the Father" (p. 56; italics added).[82] The focus seems to be on the person who affirms his own existence based on a relationship with God that is identical with the relationship of the Son with the Father. I am not suggesting that Zizioulas does not presuppose the primacy of God's act of love; however, I am suggesting that he pays little attention to the most crucial implication of God's act of communion, which is, first of all, that personhood is a transformation that we receive.[83]

---

82. If I understand this correctly, it suggests an analogy between the human person and Christ, both under the aspect of free agency.

83. See Torrance, *Persons in Communion*, pp. 294-95, where he criticizes Zizioulas for linking the "monarchy" of God with the Father instead of with the Trinity. Linking the monarchy with the Trinity would establish "God's free, creative and gracious initiative in bringing humankind to participate in the eternal and ontologically ultimate communion

Theologically speaking, therefore, the *ekstasis* that Zizioulas seeks to delineate needs to be centered in God's action, which is another way of saying that the eucharistic movement toward ecclesial personhood is not only extrinsically grounded but also ecstatically directed. The Eucharist presents the risen Christ, whose body is broken for us, and *in this act of God* we are drawn into the divine life. We can be persons in the ecclesial sense only because our being is unconditionally affirmed by God's self-giving. Our participation in the communion with God is constituted by an act of God; this is what the church celebrates in the Eucharist. When Zizioulas declares, quite rightly in my view, that he has excluded the possibility of personhood as "caused" by human nature, he intends to rule out any view that makes psychological conditions — self-consciousness, reflexivity, the capacity of reason and will, and so on — constitutive of the human person. In view of this declaration, is it really true that as ecclesial beings we affirm our own existence on the basis of a relationship with God? The theological truth of the matter seems to be that our being is transformed in the movement by which God relates to us. The person constituted in an ecstatic movement by an act of communion is extrinsically grounded because the act that constitutes it remains God's act.

In other words, the problem with Zizioulas's account of relational personhood, which it shares with many other accounts, is that it fails to acknowledge the primordial aspect of our receptivity: it is a gift that can only be received. In other words, the movement of ecclesial being is shaped by the passive voice.[84] As human beings we find ourselves at the

---

with the Trinity. And in this way it denotes the being-in-act of God as it 'takes place' in the economy of divine love *toward us*."

84. This aspect is particularly developed in Joest's *Ontologie der Person* as characteristic of Luther's concept of the human person, which Joest describes as "eccentric" (p. 296). As Joest shows, Luther rejected the notion of the human person as a bearer of properties ("Träger von Eigenschaften"). He rejected the Thomistic concept within which the creation of human beings in the image of God was understood as analogous to divine being. Behind the Thomistic conception was the Aristotelian notion of a "substance" that exists of itself and has its active properties of itself rather than from something else. In Thomas's view, this notion applies only to God because only God exists per se, while all other beings have their existence from him, which, with regard to human beings, means that being created in the divine image, they represent relatively the highest stage in the hierarchy of being (pp. 62, 236). More than other creatures, "man" is in the possession of his own being and capable of controlling his own operations by virtue of

receiving end of the act of unconditional divine self-giving. God affirms himself not as being but as giving — ultimately as self-giving. Zizioulas would not deny this, of course, but when he looks in the opposite direction, he ignores how the eucharistic movement continues to be re-enacted by God's act of self-giving. Furthermore, the eschatological dimension of ecclesial personhood implies that its fulfillment must remain a matter of hope, which necessarily implies that God's initiating act of love retains its primacy throughout our existence.[85] Thus the eucharistic movement that draws us into God's being as communion remains dependent on God's *continuing* act of love toward us. And when Zizioulas claims that the human person as ecclesial being proves "that what is valid for God can also be valid for man," he has lost track of the fact that human freedom cannot be conceived in analogy to divine freedom, because it does not originate from an analogous act of self-affirmation.

Therefore, the problem is that Zizioulas consistently understands ecstatic being as a movement *unto* the Other. Given his insistence on

---

his reason and will. Luther rejected this view because of what he saw as its implications in the context of the doctrine of grace, as Joest argues (pp. 113-15, 250-52, passim): his biblical exegesis taught him that, not the operation of being human, but God-given faith was what makes "man" just before God. Consequently, as Joest also shows, Luther's criticism of the Aristotelian-Thomistic concept regarded being human *coram deo*. Outside this particular theological context, Luther did not seem to be troubled by the philosophical ontology of human being and human personhood: he could speak without reservation of reason as "something divine" (*De Homine*, p. 9; Joest, p. 188). While such qualifications pertain to how human beings attend their business *in hac vita*, Luther's concern was the justification of human beings in light of eternity. Despite his praise of reason *coram mundi*, he could even say that, compared to theology, philosophy hardly knew anything about "man" (*De Homine*, p. 11: *Si comperaretur Philosophia seu ratio ipsa ad theologiam, apparebit nos de homine paene nihil scire*, quoted in Joest, p. 189).

85. "The eschatological character of the ecclesial hypostasis contains, of course, a kind of dialectic, the dialectic of 'already but not yet.' This dialectic pervades the Eucharist" (p. 62). How Zizioulas identifies the "not yet" is revealing. He continues: "It makes man as a person always sense that his true home is not in this world, a perception which is expressed by his refusal to locate the confirmation of the hypostasis of the person in this world, in the goods and values of this world." Apparently, the "not yet" has to do with the condition of the world rather than with the condition of being human itself. However, since the Eucharist crowns the liturgy that begins with the confession of sin, the eschatological dimension must also be related to the fact that, even as ecclesial beings, we fail to live up to the reality of authentic personhood that is given to us in Christ. In other words, the Eucharist celebrates the Cross as well as the Resurrection. Christ is present in it as the broken body that is risen.

the monarchy of the Father within the Trinity, it appears that he understands ecclesial being as an analogy to what the Father does toward the Son and the Spirit. The central role of this analogy indicates insufficient attention to the moment of receptivity in the ecstatic movement of divine love toward humankind. A Trinitarian understanding of human being does not result in a formal analogy between divine being and human being, as Augustine attempted, but in the notion that my becoming a person is a gift that exists in being drawn into the communion of the love of the Father, the Son, and the Spirit. The ecstatic movement constituting this gift is "from another," namely, from God as Trinity, rather than "unto another."

In his otherwise positive assessment of Zizioulas's Trinitarian theology, Alan Torrance has raised a similar objection. Sensing the lingering emphasis on subjectivity underlying Zizioulas's account of ecclesial being, Torrance asks what this ontology implies for the presence of human beings whose biological constitution does not allow the kind of subjective transformation that Zizioulas describes.[86] "What is the meaning of the Gospel of grace," Torrance wants to know, "for those of us who may not so easily be described as spiritual or ecclesial 'survivors' for the eternal domain of communion?"[87] When Christ's work is explained in terms of its effect on "the personal transformation and subjective sanctification that is the Church," there is a danger of a limited understanding of human salvation, according to Torrance:

> It is surely imperative that salvation remains a gift of grace, that is, the unconditional acceptance through the New Covenant in Christ of those whose lack of ability, whose weakness and/or alienation may mean that they find no confidence in any new mode of existence conceived subjectively. Is this not the essential message at the very heart of the Eucharist?[88]

I believe that this is indeed the Good News that the gospel proclaims, but I would add that unconditional acceptance is not something that

---

86. Torrance, *Persons in Communion*, p. 301. See also Alan Lewis, "The Burial of God: Rupture and Resumption as the Story of Salvation," *Scottish Journal of Theology* 40, no. 3 (1987).

87. Torrance, *Persons in Communion*, p. 301.

88. Torrance, *Persons in Communion*, p. 302.

only some people need because of their lacking abilities. Surely some people face more limiting conditions than others, but this is hardly relevant in view of the gift of grace embodied in the Eucharist. One may thus conclude that the personalist overtones in Zizioulas's account of ecclesial being result in a picture in which the eucharistic experience remains captive to a focus on subjectivity. Therefore, I would suggest that Zizioulas adhere to his point of departure much more rigorously than he has done, which is that being in the image of God "is not a moral achievement, something that man accomplishes. It is a way of *relationship* with the world, with other people and with God, an event of communion, and that is why it cannot be realized as the achievement of an *individual,* but only as an *ecclesial* fact" (p. 15). Thus it remains true that, in an important sense, my being as *imago Dei* is not to be taken ontologically as a subsistent entity, but as a relationship that is ecstatically grounded in God's loving kindness toward me.

9. Conclusion

In this chapter I have tried to lay out the argument for a Christian understanding of being human that can claim to be properly universal. The argument resulted in a Trinitarian view of human being that manifests an extrinsic relationship between its genesis and its *telos*. With regard to the former, accounted for by the Aristotelian rule "man is born from man," this Trinitarian view precludes the possibility that human beings who fail to develop the capacities of reason and will cannot participate in the latter. Theologically speaking, fulfillment of their being is not the result of developing their potential for intrinsic capacities. The relationship between origin and final end is different. From a theological point of view, the final end of being human is identified by the unique relationship that the triune God maintains with humanity through the economy of salvation. It starts with our being created in his image, which does not refer to our nature as belonging to a particular species — even though our belonging to that species identifies us as humans — but to the relationship God maintains with every human being. As the apostle Paul puts it, God has created each of us in Jesus Christ (Eph. 2:10), which means that his saving grace is "not of your own doing but is God's gift." God regards our humanity in light of the relationship that he has with each of us through Christ. Therefore, the fact that human beings differ with respect to the abilities and capacities characteristic of the human species does nothing to qualify or alter this unique relationship. The reason, I have argued, is that God's love is unconditional and thus cannot be broken because of human limitations.

Surely the argument I have developed in this chapter has taken us far away from where we started. In order to articulate explicitly how the argument can be helpful concerning our initial question, let me return to the human beings with profound intellectual disabilities. Given the nature of their disability, what have we gained? What we have gained is an understanding of their *being* in the light of the gospel. It appears that when seen in that light — that is, seen with the eyes of God — their being is not significantly different from ours, whatever else we must say about them. The notion of truly being human does not spring from an act of self-affirmation: this is as true of my being as it is of yours — or Kelly's. Theologically speaking, we are truly human because we are drawn into the communion with God the Father, the Son, and the Holy Spirit. What this entails in a practical ethical sense will be the subject for Part III of this book. It must have something to do with the relationship that God continues to uphold with each of us, however, whether we are aware of it or not. If the chaotic forces of the human condition had had their way, human beings like Kelly and Oliver de Vinck would have little chance of surviving the impact of their condition. They live among other human beings who regard them as "one of us," not because of their presumed contribution, but because they have accepted them unconditionally. My argument has been that the gospel explains why unconditional acceptance is the gift each human being receives as freely given. It also explains that unconditional acceptance is only possible because it is grounded in God's act of self-giving. What profoundly disabled human beings share with every one of us is that God includes them in his gift.

From the perspective of their natural condition, the acts of others that show they are accepted hardly make sense. This is because we have virtually no sign of a natural potency in profoundly disabled human beings like Kelly. Theologically speaking, however, their existence does not need to make sense in any other way than that in the eyes of God all his children are equal, while none of them are more equal than others. Their being human is as securely affirmed as ours in the act of communion by which God has first created us, and then has re-created us. We have learned that our humanity is a gift from the beginning to the end. We received it before we did anything, and we are promised the fullness of this gift in the end, despite our limitations. All these reflections indicate why divine agency, not human agency, is the primary concept of Christian anthropology. Because of who God is and what God does, we know that profoundly disabled human beings are children of God and are as lovable in his eyes as any other of his children.

Part Three

ETHICS

Chapter Eight

The Fullness of Being:
God's Friendship

Charity is in us neither naturally, nor through acquisition by the natural powers, but by the infusion of the Holy Spirit, who is the love of the Father and the Son, and the participation of whom in us is created charity.

Thomas Aquinas[1]

1. Introduction: Three Responses

The question of how Christian anthropology and ethics are related, I have argued, comes down to the question of how we interpret the origin of human being in the light of its final end and vice versa. As it turns out, there are in principle three responses to this question. The first response, as we have seen, is to argue that human being is defined by the capacities of reason and will and that its final end (or *telos*) lies in a quality of operation of these capacities. In other words, the end of human being is determined by purposive agency aiming at either "happiness" or "freedom." From both these views (Aristotelian and Kantian) follows the claim that, since not all human beings meet the condition of having these capacities, those who do not cannot participate in the end of human being. The point of their lives cannot be what it is for human beings properly so called, which is to develop and excel in using the capacities that distinguish them as human beings. This view would

---

1. Aquinas, *Summa Theologica*, II, II, 24, 2.

dictate that some people's lives cannot be properly regarded as intrinsically good. They lack the kind of features that warrant such an evaluation because they cannot use the capacities that are constitutive of human fulfillment. First among these unfortunate beings are, of course, those with profound intellectual disabilities.

This response is commonly found among defenders of liberal bioethics who distinguish sharply between human existence in a biological and in an ethical sense. But it is not found only among them. Liberal bioethicists are specifically distinguished by the moral claims they infer from this position, for example, when they argue that, in some cases of profoundly disabled human existence, being alive is a fate worse than death.[2]

The second response rejects this solution because it refuses to accept that some human beings are "more human" than others. That is, it denies that the end of being human depends on psychological characteristics, either as capabilities that enable human beings to pursue the good or as qualities in the perfection of which the human good is to be found. This response takes the position that, even when the existence of profoundly disabled beings cannot be valued in terms of a capacity for purposive action, it does not follow that no value can be found in their existence. Their presence elicits a response in other people that is invaluable testimony to our common humanity.[3] In this view, the moral consideration for dependent fellow human beings characterizes our humanity in a most profound way. Taking this position are a number of Roman Catholic writers, including Robert Spaemann, as we have seen in Chapter 3.

The distinctive characteristic of this position is twofold. First, it answers the question about the humanity of the profoundly disabled in terms of their *contribution to* rather than their *participation in* the end of being human. Second, it retains the condition of intrinsic worth but locates it in their state of dependency rather than in their capacity for agency. Accordingly, their contribution to the good is conceived of as

2. See, for example, James Rachels, *The End of Life: The Morality of Euthanasia* (New York: Oxford University Press, 1986).

3. This is the position underlying Christopher de Vinck's book *The Power of the Powerless,* which I have referred to earlier in this inquiry (Ch. 1). As de Vinck's title indicates, and the stories in his book give testimony to, people like his brother Oliver are said to possess an extraordinary power, namely, the power to move other people.

being mediated by other people's moral responses. However, following David Pailin's critique of what he calls the contributory view of human worth, I think we should reject this view, because it evaluates profoundly disabled lives in terms of instrumental value. If it is true that a caring response to their being constitutes part of the common good, this means that their existence is being valued as a means to the good of human society. This is not to deny the experience of many that the very being of those with profound disabilities can teach us important things about our humanity; but the proper way to understand this aspect of their being human would be to say that it is an unintended byproduct of learning to share their lives.[4] It is not what constitutes their "worth," nor is it what includes them in the participation of the ultimate good of being human.

Furthermore, with regard to Kelly's power to move other people, one would have to say that this is not a power intrinsic to her being at all. That is, it is neither properly regarded as a power to act nor as a power of her presence, because it is a power that is inherent in a particular moral *perception* of her being and hence dependent on how her being is represented by the moral framework guiding the response. Again, this is not to say that Kelly's presence cannot cause a response in people, but it is to say that, as a caring response, it is only intelligible because of a particular moral perception.[5] This analysis indicates that the

---

4. This is a recurring theme in the writings of people of the L'Arche communities, to which we will turn in the last two chapters of this book. For example, L'Arche founder Jean Vanier says: "What has struck me is how people with disabilities, as 'different' as they may be, have a secret power to touch and open people's hearts" ("The Need of Strangers," in *Critical Reflections on Stanley Hauerwas' Theology of Disability: Disabling Society, Enabling Theology,* ed. J. Swinton [Binghamton, NY: Haworth Press, 2004], pp. 27-30).

5. The problem with the view under consideration is that it does not refer to just any response that Kelly's body may elicit, but to a particular kind of caring response. One could try to make the argument that Kelly has a power to act, understood as a power to move others in certain ways, and explain this power in analogy to a stimulus-response connection (this kind of argument was suggested to me by Christoph Schwöbel). But such an explanation would be rather weak, because the connection is not one of efficient causality. Kelly could not be the cause of my caring response in the same sense that I can be the cause of my own action. The missing link would be representation. Kelly needs to be perceived in a certain way in order to elicit a certain response. To use one of the examples I investigated in Ch. 1:"You look cheerful today" is a response to her being that depends on a set of convictions and beliefs on the part of the beholder; without these convictions

second response fails because, contrary to what it suggests, it does not ground Kelly's being human in an intrinsic property. Declaring humanity on grounds of a response is grounding it extrinsically rather than intrinsically. However, we should not accept it even as extrinsic grounding, because we should not accept that Kelly's existence as a human being is valuable because of the response it elicits in other people. The reason is that the presence of profoundly disabled human beings often elicits a negative response, and that is true of our society as it is for many others — both past and present. Their existence is regularly perceived as morally doubtful, to put it mildly, which explains the presumption that it requires a moral justification. Therefore, as a solution to our problem, it is doubtful that we can be content by grounding the humanity of profoundly disabled human beings in how other people respond to them.[6] This leads us to the third answer.

The third answer seeks to establish that our humanity — mine, yours, and Kelly's — is extrinsically grounded, both with regard to origin and final end. It distances itself from any attempt to explain our humanity in terms of capacities intrinsic to our being, either conceived of as the capacity to act purposively or as the passive capacity to elicit a particular moral response in other people. Locating itself within the Christian tradition, it proposes to conceive of our origin as well as our

---

and beliefs this response would hardly make sense. In Taiwan I came across a Christian organization named the Creation of Social Welfare Foundation (CSWF), which has established, among other things, twelve houses where people with PVS in impoverished conditions have been taken in. Given the mediating function of moral perspective in recognizing this response as appropriate or inappropriate, one wonders what moral judgment would be applicable to this kind of charitable action from the perspective of liberal bioethics represented by James Rachels. Utmost cruelty? Religious superstition? Or just plain ignorance?

6. Roman Catholic authors committed to the view that the humanity of profoundly disabled human beings is attested by our response of caring for them must reject the possibility that this response can become extinct. Thus a society that accepts the killing or letting die of these human beings loses its distinctive character as a human society and is turned into a perversion of itself. The empirical fact that some societies appear to be moving in that direction does nothing to deny this position, because one can — according to the Vatican — oppose these societies by arguing that they are moving *contra naturam.* This indicates why and how the Vatican considers its current mission in the world to be to call on any secular government to repeal all legislation that it regards as testimony of this perversion.

final end as grounded in God's graceful action toward us in Christ. This is the position I defended in the previous chapter.

In Part III of this book, I will return to the question of ethics in order to think through the ethical implications of this position. At an earlier stage I made a distinction between the many goods and the ultimate good (understood as the "hyper good") of being human, and I suggested that friendship defines the content of the latter. The burden of these last three chapters will be to spell out the meaning that friendship must have in order to sustain the account of Christian anthropology I have presented. The aim of this chapter will be to consider friendship with God as the substantive matter of charity as the Christian tradition preceding modernity understood it. In order to be consistent, my argument must show that, theologically speaking, "friendship with God" must be taken to refer primarily to God's friendship with us. To make such an argument, I will consider the place of charity in the moral theology of Thomas Aquinas.

2. Difference

Before proceeding with that task, let us consider in more detail the point of consistency. The Trinitarian argument of the previous chapter was designed to give an account of the relationship between the genesis and the *telos* of human being that eliminates the significance of the sometimes profound differences we find among human individuals. I did not intend this argument to deny such differences. On the contrary, the argument shows that the widest possible variety within humankind can be acknowledged because the differences do not matter at the most fundamental level. That is, in order to include "difference" in our conception of humanity, even when difference is found at the innermost core of the conception of ourselves as self-reflective beings, we must start with "sameness." From the perspective of Christian theology, "sameness" is grounded in the fact that all human beings are God's creatures who share in his economy of salvation. In view of the recent celebration of "difference" in postmodern thinking, which posits difference to oppose the alleged violence of sameness, arguing for a theological account of sameness can only be grounded in who God is and what God does. This means that sameness is not constituted on the level of individual identity, which is where postmodern thinking locates its attack. Referring to the preceding chapter, sameness does not pertain to the level where Zizioulas's conception of "personality" applies; instead, it pertains to the fundamental level at which the unconditional relationship inaugurated by God's action determines the humanity of every human being. The unconditional nature of this relationship is grounded in God's faithfulness, which implies that when this relationship is distorted on our part, God still does not abandon it.

This is the one condition of our being, then, that holds similarly for each one of us. It is precisely because the meaning of this particular relationship precedes that of all other facts about our existence that the recognition of difference cannot be threatening. Only because of this unconditional relationship can we positively affirm difference; because without it, the postmodern celebration of difference must necessarily be grounded in human acts of self-affirmation. In other words, difference provides the basis of freedom for those among us who are able to assert themselves in body and mind. This is why the postmodern celebration of difference is necessarily exclusivist in its view of human beings to whom the link between agency and freedom cannot apply.[7]

In this respect, Christian theology must disagree. Difference can be celebrated only because it has no theological significance: in the eyes of God, human beings are equally worthy of his loving kindness, no matter what differences the bodies of these human beings may exhibit. This is the sameness that is true of all of us, which is why difference in the widest possible variety can be celebrated. That is, from a theological perspective, what we are as human beings ("essentially," if you will) cannot be deduced from whatever condition we find ourselves in; thus it cannot be deduced from the state of the development of our capabilities.

Put another way, this means that subjectivity is not the primordial aspect of our being that it is usually taken to be. The point of my life can hardly be dependent on what I take that point to be, theologically speaking, because to say that it is thus dependent is to say that it has no point

7. The presupposition here is that all the varieties of postmodern thinking, whether of Nietzschean, Heideggerian, or Foucauldian persuasion, regard the recognition of particularity as essential to freedom. This tendency is most notably seen in accounts centering on the body as the irreducible "location" of particularity. I laid out the argument for this presupposition in Ch. 2.

"outside" my own self-consciousness. Christians who believe that Creation is a part of God's economy of salvation cannot say that. That is why I have argued theologically for the view that the relationship between the genesis and *telos* of being human is extrinsically constituted. As human beings, we find ourselves at the receiving end of a relationship that is initiated by an act of the triune God, which is an act in the economy of salvation of the Father, Son, and Holy Spirit. The act that constitutes this relationship is a divine initiative, and it remains so.

The argument against the primordial meaning of subjectivity directly affects the notion of human being as "relationality." What usually remains unconsidered regarding this notion is that "relationality" involves time: it evolves. Therefore, it also involves sequence, so that we will find it relevant to ask where the movement begins. Most theological accounts of relationality do not raise this question; unconsciously, they assume a Hegelian movement: from the subject to the other, never the other way around, as theology should do. Here the point of narrative display applies. A relational account of being human must be grounded in the story of how God in Christ Jesus renews his relationship with every human being. Without this narrative grounding, theological arguments in support of a relational anthropology must fail.

By way of example, I propose to look at the argument offered by M. J. Iozzio, whose essay on the compromised existence of people with Alzheimer's disease describes and analyzes her experience with her own father, who suffers from this disease.[8] She claims that, without a relational anthropology, there is no way to understand that experience, particularly with respect to the loving care of her mother. The structure of Iozzio's argument is similar to the one I cited in the preceding chapter in the sense that she also argues from the perspective of Trinitarian communion to a relational concept of being human, but it is different precisely in what she takes its anthropological point to be.

Grounding her argument in Aquinas's Trinitarian concept of the divine persons as "subsistent relations," Iozzio argues for human interdependence against what she rejects as the exaltation of individuality

---

8. M. I. Iozzio, "The Writing on the Wall . . . Alzheimer's Disease: A Daughter's Look at Mom's Faithful Care of Dad," *Journal of Religion, Disability & Health* 8, no. 2 (2005): 49-74.

and autonomy in our moral culture. She then sets up her argument starting from the presupposition of human beings as "rational bodies" that are "indispensable to the individuality of the persons they reveal."[9] However, human beings can only become the distinct persons they are meant to be if they engage in relationships with others.

> Only by being a distinct person can any human being enter into a relation with another and only by being related to another can any human being become a distinct person. Further, only by being in relation can these persons flourish individually and together. Thus, just as the Trinity reveals relational interdependence, human beings, as distinct persons sharing a common nature, reveal the relational interdependence required of personal identity and solidarity within the human community.[10]

Apart from the traditional concept that makes the distinctness of human persons a function of their existence as "rational bodies," it is clear that relationships are something we enter "into." It is also clear that entering into relations is conceived of as a precondition of becoming a distinct person, and that only distinct persons can do so. Furthermore, it is also clear that "relation" has the function to further the goal of becoming a distinct person. According to Iozzio, establishing human interdependence is a matter of acknowledging that the "laws of nature and grace" not only recall the inclination to preserve life but also the inclination "to have companions."[11]

This account of her argument shows that Iozzio repeats the popular view that "relationality" is what enables human beings to become distinct persons. The final end of being human is conceived as intrinsically conditioned by the potentiality of the flourishing of human capacities, to which end "relationality" is invoked as indispensable means. Therefore, we might say that, in Iozzio's view, relationality does not subvert individuality but completes it, to paraphrase a famous dictum in the Roman Catholic tradition. However, theologically speaking, there is no condition that can separate human being from its final end, which means that we need a different perspective. I suggest, therefore,

9. Iozzio, "The Writing on the Wall," p. 57.
10. Iozzio, "The Writing on the Wall," p. 57.
11. Iozzio, "The Writing on the Wall," p. 58.

that we follow the reversed pattern of theological analysis that I laid out in the preceding chapter. The fact of God's unconditional love for humans precedes any affirmation of the virtue of human potentiality, rather than the other way around. The crucial importance of this reversal is indicated precisely by the fact that God's love is unconditional.

How human beings respond, of course, is not unconditional. Being inevitably limited in a variety of degrees and ways, our existence cannot but make us realize that the fullness of life in a Christian sense necessarily has an eschatological dimension. This means that its completion must remain a matter of hope and faith. To the extent that the fullness of life can be enjoyed here and now, this is only because of God's initiating act of love. Put in the language of faith, the fullness of life is inaugurated by God as Trinity. God the Father redeems humanity in the light of his relationship with the Son, because "all things came into being through him," as the Gospel of John says (1:3). In Christ we were created and in Christ we are re-created through the gift of the Spirit. The fact that we are very different as humans with respect to the capabilities that characterize our species does nothing to qualify or alter this unique relationship.

3. "Activities That Direct Us to God"

In order to find out what this view entails in a practical ethical sense, we will now turn from the perspective of theological anthropology to ethics, the other path at the crossroads. The questions I want to answer in this chapter are these: What does the extrinsic grounding of being human in the unconditional love of God entail for our understanding of the human good? How is the fullness of being to be understood from a Christian perspective?

This question leads us once again to some views being expressed within Roman Catholicism, because what I am suggesting here is entirely compatible with how the Roman Catholic tradition would account for the "supernatural end" of human being. The supernatural end, as distinct from the natural end, is to be reunited with God. Regarding our supernatural end, the decisive activity is attributed to God's grace. In the face of eternity, human achievement is meaningless in that it does not in any way differentiate human beings before God. Regarding their natural end, however, matters are different. The natural end of human being lies in the actualization of human potential. Human flourishing is a matter of the development of the capacities of reason and will in attaining virtue. For the question I am pursuing in this study, this position must mean that profoundly disabled human beings such as Kelly and Oliver de Vinck will be included in the saving grace of God, but also that they are barred from attaining a good life for human beings inasmuch as they lack the capacity to do so. Consequently, the Roman Catholic tradition would accept what I have been suggesting about the supernatural end of being human, but it would reject what I suggest about its natural end. Or, better, it would criticize my position for conflating the two.

As I have already indicated in Chapter 2, the question is, therefore: How are these two "ends" of being human supposed to be related? As indicated before, there seems to be much room for debate on this matter within the Thomist tradition, depending on how people understand Aquinas's view on the matter. One thing is immediately clear, however: when the position is that both the natural and the supernatural are "interdependent, interrelated, and fully integrated," as Iozzio puts it, then the questions I have raised in this book return with full force.[12] Analogously, if both these ends mark separate accounts of our being as humans, as some philosophical readings of Aquinas have it,[13] then the argument for lending priority to the theological perspective is reinforced once more because of the limited intellectualist conception of human being that the remaining philosophical account of our natural end necessarily entails.

12. Iozzio, "The Writing on the Wall," p. 58. Iozzio argues that (1) the distinction of human beings as rational bodies composed of faculties such as the will, reason, and sensory perceptions "is the beginning of the fullness of the revelation that human beings are created in the image and likeness of the triune God"; that (2) this distinction is also "the beginning of the fullness of the revelation of the *summum bonum* of human flourishing," which is to be "related intimately with the triune God"; and that (3) a significant number of human beings are excluded from attaining this highest good unless it is agreed that their human faculties have no distinctive role to play because of the primordial fact that the triune God relates to us. One would think that (3) is a sufficient reason to reconsider (1) and (2), unless one assumes that the primordial fact that the triune God relates to us has no implications for how we understand either the origin or the final end of human being.

13. Gerald F. Stanley, "Contemplation as Fulfillment of the Human Person," in *Personalist Ethics and Human Subjectivity,* ed. George McLean (Washington, DC: Council for Research in Value and Philosophy, 1991), appendix.

In view of these alternatives, the direction of the overall argument as I have developed it thus far should be clear. From the perspective of a truly universal account of being human, the answer to the ethical question must have something to do with participating in God's love as our final end. It is for this reason that I will focus on a theological reading of Aquinas's ethics. To spell this out, both in terms of principle and of practical implications, I explore the notion of friendship with God in Aquinas's ethics as interpreted by Paul Wadell's *The Primacy of Love*.[14] Here again, our primary task is to understand that this friendship does not spring from a subjective relationship on our part. Instead, it is to be fully understood as gift — moreover a gift that is to be enjoyed precisely when we understand it to be freely and unconditionally given. Once this is fully understood, it is not hard to see how true friendship between God's people follows from this gift. True friendship must resemble God's friendship in being unconditional. However, because of their fallen nature, human beings fail to achieve this, which means that we need the gift to be continuously renewed.

In order to take on the task of exploring these matters, I suggest that we start at the other side of God's unconditional gift, which is how we respond to it. This is where Christian ethics usually begins when it intends to spell out its understanding of the moral life. That is to say, when it comes to understanding the notion of friendship with God, Christian ethics tends to start with the question of what we need to do to become God's friends.

The theme of "friendship with God" is particularly at home in the Thomist tradition. Thomas calls "charity" the promise of a beauty in life, which brings peace and joy to our souls: charity is friendship with God. However, things can also go terribly wrong. We can fail to become God's friends and end up as the kind of humans we would regret to be. That is why we need the virtues. This is Paul Wadell's version of Thomas's view:

> Thomas has always insisted on the most blessed and promising possibility of our lives; however, precisely because he knows there is something marvelous we can achieve, he also knows there is some-

14. Paul Wadell, *The Primacy of Love: An Introduction to the Ethics of Thomas Aquinas* (New York: Paulist Press, 1992) [page number citations in the text refer to this book].

thing wonderful that can be lost. We are balanced between possibilities for greatness and awfulness. . . . Aquinas calls us to the greatness of charity-friendship with God, for he knows it is only in that kinship with love that we shall find peace and joy for our souls. (p. 108)

Forfeiting friendship with God, we can try our luck elsewhere, but this will end in misery. We will only find peace and happiness in practicing the virtues, Aquinas knows, because "they are *activities that direct us to God*" (p. 108; italics added). The virtues instruct us in living our lives in ways "that focus us on the goodness that is the restoration and redemption of our lives."

In consulting Wadell's account of a Thomist ethics of virtue, I am not directly interested in the exposition of Aquinas's view, but only insofar as it is pertinent to the discussion of friendship with God as the fullness of life. It is clear from Wadell's account of Aquinas's view that he understands phrases such as "the fullness of life" and "our final end as humans" in a theological sense. In Wadell's usage, these phrases refer to the end of all of creation, which is a return to eternity in being reunited with God. This is what friendship with God is all about. This means that Wadell takes the fullness of life in Aquinas's view to be equivalent to what the tradition calls our "supernatural end."

As his remarks on virtue have already indicated, Wadell's way of explaining Aquinas's views on friendship with God starts with the question of our moral action. He views friendship with God primarily from the viewpoint of the part we play in it, that is, in the same way that your friendship with me primarily brings into view the part you play in it. In other words, from the way he starts, Wadell suggests that friendship with God, in Aquinas's view, can be appropriately approached from the perspective of our own doing. This starting point triggers the question I am interested in. What is the role of our action in achieving our final end? In many instances, Wadell's account of how the fullness of life may become a reality for us seems to be saying that this possibility is to a surprising extent conditioned by our own agency. As we shall see, however, this impression does not reflect what Wadell ultimately thinks Thomas is saying.

Since the virtues are activities that direct us to God, as Wadell puts it, they realize a potential that humans apparently possess. "Our lives are ours to make," Wadell says, to which he adds, "Thomas knew this

our action
+ God's actio

and it is why he pleads with us to become virtuous instead of wicked. What becomes of us is in our hands" (p. 108). Whether or not we live a virtuous life depends, at least to some extent, on our own action. Even though Wadell qualifies this view later in his book, here it leads him to make strong claims regarding how we attain our final end.

> We return to God not by change of place, but by change of person, and that is what the virtues achieve. They work the transformation in us that enables our reunion with God. (p. 108)

Since the virtues are our own activities, this claim implies that the transformation that brings us back to God is also brought about by our own activities. "They work the transformation in us that enables reunion with God," Wadell says. This is certainly strong language for Christians who are used to thinking about these matters in terms of the primacy of grace. Far from denying the primacy of grace, however, Wadell announces a "stunning paradox" in Aquinas's thought precisely at this point, which is that the virtues "reach their perfection in a gift" (p. 108). While this indicates that there is something about our final end that is *not* of our own doing, the relationship between "virtue" and "gift" remains unclear, at least at this point. That is, so far the recognition of the primacy of grace does not seem to affect the crucial role of the virtues in what we ourselves are capable of contributing to our own transformation.

The theological question is thus once again a question of how we think our own action is related to God's action, or, in traditional Thomist language, how the "natural end" of being human is related to its "supernatural end." Of course, the notion that divine action is necessarily involved is not in dispute. Nevertheless, the question is how both kinds of agency are related.

> We need the virtues. They are the kinds of activities that continue the life God's grace began. They shape us in goodness; they transform us in the loveliness of God. They move us closer to the fullness we are meant to enjoy. Through the virtues, we sculpt ourselves in goodness and life; however, they are indispensable precisely because the fullness of creation is never assured. If our moral predicament is to be poised between chaos and cosmos, then we never fully escape the pull to dissolution. (p. 110)

291

The virtues do not take us all the way to the fullness of life, and besides, without God's grace we could not even get started on that way ("the life that God's grace began"). At the same time, the virtues contribute to a growth that keeps us on the right track. This does not mean that the alternative track of a corrupted life no longer exists; but it does mean that virtuous acts leave their marks on us, they turn into habits, which means they change us for the better (p. 114). While we have the possibility of turning our appetites to various things, good or bad, the virtuous life nonetheless engenders the habits required for "achieving" friendship with God.

> Achieving friendship with God demands giving our lives a single-hearted focus. It demands restriction, and it calls for certain attachments. In order to grow in charity-friendship with God, which Thomas sees as the purpose and goal of our lives, we need to be attached to some things and detached from others, and to foster a special direction for our lives, and that is what the virtues do; it is in this sense that the virtues involve self-definition. (p. 110)

Obviously the claim that self-definition is involved in directing the moral life toward our final end only confirms what the reader may already have anticipated, which is that human beings who are incapable of mastering themselves in terms of self-definition cannot lead a virtuous life. More important, however, is the implication of Wadell's account, which is that with their kind of life they cannot participate in friendship with God either. This implication is caused by his forging a strong connection between attaining friendship with God and developing our natural capacities for the good. If virtue is to set us on the path leading toward this friendship, then a limited capability of developing virtuous behavior must imply that this path is blocked. No friendship with God for human beings like Kelly or Oliver de Vinck.

4. "Poised between Chaos and Cosmos"

There is thus an unfortunate tendency in Wadell's account, because of what it implies for human beings with limited capacity for growth or development. To explore this a bit further, I will draw attention to

Wadell's terminology of "disorderly behavior." As we already have seen, he posits developing the virtues in perspective of the human predicament of being poised between chaos and cosmos. Since we acquire the virtues by developing our natural capacities, lacking development of these capacities leaves us in the ambit of chaos and disorder, according to Wadell. "Our behavior can work a disordering or it can work for wholeness." If the former, he adds, the return to chaos "requires a bit of disordered behavior" (p. 110). This occurs when we succumb to the power of sin, which he also explains as behavior: "Sin is any behavior that works chaos in our lives." Therefore, the alternative to the wholeness that works virtue is the disorderly behavior that works chaos.

In writing these lines, Wadell doubtless never had in mind the *Diagnostic and Statistic Manual of Mental Disorders* (DSM), but his account does allow the question of whether or not there may be a connection. It seems that there is one — at least conceptually. Conditions such as Prader Willi syndrome, for example, do involve both intellectual disability and behavioral disorders that require very strict regulation. The same is true of disabling conditions within the spectrum of autism that may cause obsessive-compulsive behavior. If, as Wadell says, sin is "any behavior that works chaos in our lives," it is difficult to avoid the conclusion that disorderly behavior in these cases is sinful. Without realizing the connection, presumably, Wadell is implying precisely that when he describes people under the sway of sin as people "whose lives can at best be described as chaotic" and "whose mode of life seems utterly destructive" (p. 110). If it is true, as he says, that disorderly behavior is sinful, then it must also be true that this behavior obstructs disorderly human beings in developing virtue, and, for the same reason, it obstructs their friendship with God.

What do these statements entail, then, in view of behavioral problems classified in the *DSM*? Certainly there are people with intellectual disabilities who do indeed live quite chaotic lives because of their behavioral problems. These people need massive support from the professionals whose primary task it is to bring structure into their lives. Although we usually don't blame such people for their behavior, that doesn't change the fact that, left to their own devices, their lives may turn very chaotic and destructive. Wadell would surely agree that they cannot be blamed, but this does not alter the fact that their lives reflect chaos rather than virtue. If it is true, as Wadell says, that the "virtues make us who human beings are meant to be," and that "it is through them that we fulfill our nature" (p. 114), then it must also be true that lives captured by disorderly behavior cannot result in fulfillment.

Furthermore, let me call attention to the use of the first-person plural pronouns in the previous sentence. It turns out that Wadell's use of them is not accidental, but is to be taken quite literally: "The virtues achieve an actualization of our self that corresponds to the purpose of our self" (p. 115). Consequently, we fulfill our own human nature through our own activity. To assure his readers of the fact that following the path of virtue is for human beings the natural thing to do, Wadell quotes Aquinas's reference to Aristotle:

> Speaking of habits of soul and body, Aristotle says that they are activity-directed dispositions whose possessor has reached the term of its development; and he goes on to explain that something is fully developed if it is disposed in accordance with its nature [ST, I-II, 49,2]. (p. 115)

Fulfillment is a function of a natural being whose dispositions have reached the term of its development. This occurs when this being acts from dispositions reflecting its nature. In the case of human nature, these activity-directed dispositions are the virtues. In view of the behavioral disorders that occasionally characterize the lives of people with intellectual disabilities, the conclusion is quite alarming. Since fulfilling our nature qua human beings reunites us with God, according to Wadell's reading of Thomas, the path of virtue leads us to friendship with him, except that people whose natural condition does not allow them to walk this path cannot have a part in it. Thus we are once more confronted with a view in which the "us" that it describes means "some of us" rather than "all of us," this despite the reassuring language in Wadell's account of Aquinas's ethics.[15]

> If a virtue is a quality that changes us, then for Aquinas it must change us not just for the better, but for the best. It is through the virtues that we reach our optimum potential, the fullness of our life in God. Virtues do more than change us, they transform us unto the goodness we need for the fullness of life. (p. 114)

15. I am not implying that this is what Wadell intends to say, but I am saying that his position as he states it leaves him with no defense against one's drawing that conclusion.

To be brought to the fullness of life means nothing less than to have reached "our optimum potential by becoming godly" (p. 114). The virtues take us to the "term of our development" that, according to Wadell, entails a transformation of ourselves into "persons of holiness and love" (p. 115). We are indeed fully developed through the virtues "because it is by developing and practicing those good-making habits that we accomplish the intended fullness of our nature" (p. 115). Therefore, it is in seeking the fulfillment of our human nature that we will turn out to be friends of God.

> As God sees human nature, the most we can possibly be is to be for God the friend God has always been for us. That is the promise intended by the gift of creation, and it is exactly that grace that the virtues seize and nurse to fullness. (p. 115)

The trouble with these reassuring statements is, of course, that they are only reassuring if we leave out of the equation the fact that the promise of human nature — taken as a capacity for development and growth — is apparently lost for a number of human beings. If one assumes an intrinsic connection between developing human nature and its return to eternity, as Wadell clearly does, then we cannot avoid the problem I am analyzing in this book.

Apparently, Wadell's concept of being human leads him to regard chaotic human lives as "unnatural" in that they fail to attest development and growth. Human beings whose behavioral disorders result from disabling conditions have unfortunately escaped his attention, even though they cannot be held responsible for their chaotic behavior. But it is difficult to see how Wadell's position could be revised to account for this omission, because he would have to allow for the possibility of attaining friendship with God regardless of developing our natural capacities for virtuous behavior. Evidently, such a concession would cause his position to fall apart.

More generally, to define the ultimate good of being human in terms of developing the virtues in order to prepare oneself for God's friendship is to make purposive agency the key to our humanity. In Wadell's case, this conception of human being takes him unfortunately close to doubting the humanity of those whose lives do not show the fruits of virtue.

> None of us is yet who we ought to be. . . . No matter what we have achieved, we are in many ways incomplete. Regardless of the good we have displayed, standing before the loveliness of God, we know we are never good enough. To be human is to have a promise to fulfill, but this suggests that simply being alive is not being human at all. (p. 112)

Even though many of his colleagues in Roman Catholic moral theology would clearly not accept this last sentence, the overall structure of his position points to the same problem that I analyzed in Chapter 3.[16] If the fullness of life necessarily depends on the growth in virtuous action because that is how true human beings are meant to live, then it must follow that, if one is incapable of a virtuous life, one is excluded from the end of human being, as Roman Catholicism understands it. I do not for a moment believe Wadell *means* to say that human beings with mental disorders or intellectual disabilities are in fact "not human at all," even though they "have no promise to fulfill"; but evidently his theoretical framework prevents him from seeing the implication.

The reason I am sure that Wadell never thought about the implications of his view for people with profound disabilities is that, had he done so, he would never have written sentences like the following: "Aquinas' ethic of virtue is immensely reassuring because it helps us to understand why there is always hope for improvement in our lives. If the virtues are habits and habits are qualities of ourselves, then a change is always possible for us through developing the life-giving activities of the virtues" (p. 114).[17] Again, this may be true for some of us, but it is defi-

16. Roman Catholic theologians would never accept that "simply being alive is not being human at all" because, within the overall structure of their Thomist position, "being," as opposed to "non-being," is always predicated as good. The reason is that, as we have seen, on the Aristotelian-Thomist view there is no being without the potentiality of its own nature. However, if it can be argued, as I have in Ch. 3, that there is human being within which the principle of potentiality has no empirical referent, then the conclusion "simply being alive is not being human at all" is impossible to avoid for proponents of the Aristotelian-Thomist view. Again, this indicates that, despite their head-on collision in the field of bioethics, there is a curious structural similarity of their position with the position defended by liberal bioethicists. The similarity is that both views presuppose a concept of human good according to which the good consists in the operation of intrinsic natural capacities.

17. Further reason to think that Wadell does not intend his view to be exclusivist in

nitely not true for all of us. The question I am pursuing in this study is whether there is hope where there is no improvement and whether there is fulfillment if the possibility of development is nonexistent, as it sometimes clearly is. Whereas most theologians will defer this question to the domain of eschatology, I am approaching it in the domain of ethics.

5. From First to Last: All Is Grace

There is another tendency in Wadell's account, however, that must be brought out to develop a quite different story about the fullness of being. The key to this alternative is to replace the language of friendship with God by the language of God's friendship. To see what this other possibility entails, we must remind ourselves that God always has been a friend for us, and his friendship precedes any of our actions. Given the various limitations of human existence — some attributable to faults of our own, some not — this reminder must imply that God does not withdraw his friendship, whether or not we manage to change ourselves and become what he hoped we would be. Grace is not a reward. God's love is unconditional. God has always been our friend, not because of how we manage to live our lives but in spite of it. If God's friendship were conditioned by our response, we would have lost his friendship long ago. The

the sense explained is found in his latest book on friendship. There he writes that neighbor love is a risky and radical undertaking, because we need to overcome our fears and prejudices that make us afraid of others. He says, "[e]mbracing some but excluding others is the way to save neighbor love but is totally opposed to the risky and radical love we see living in Christ" (Wadell, *Becoming Friends: Worship, Justice, and the Practice of Christian Friendship* [Grand Rapids: Brazos, 2002], p. 32). Christian friendship, Wadell argues, cannot be that way because "God embraces, God never excludes" (p. 33). Nonetheless, there is remarkably little attention in Wadell's concept of radically asymmetrical friendships, which is strange given his claims about God's all-inclusivenes. One explanation might be, that Wadell, like may other theologians, argues for the centrality of "relation" without thinking about movement (as explained earlier in this chapter). Thus he writes: "To be human is to be possessed by the aching need to give our self to others and to receive the gift of another's self in return. This is indeed the heart of friendship. An undying need of every human being is the need to communicate our self, to share our soul and spirit with others in the hope that we might live in communion with them" (pp. 45-46). Given this view, it does not come as a surprise when Wadell later in his book argues that, though friends are not in all respects like us, there must be sufficient likeness — "shared interests, cares, and activities we have in common" (p. 61).

Christian church lives on the promise that the risen Christ will always be with us (Matt. 25), which is why it continues to celebrate the Eucharist. God's friendship does not depend, and has never depended, on the realization of our capacity for growth. Instead, it has depended on his continuous act of self-giving, by which he draws us into his communion. Nor does God's friendship depend on our potential for it. Instead, the reverse is true: our potential, of whatever kind that turns out to be, depends on his friendship.

Given his earlier language of the virtues achieving "the fullness of our life in God," it may come as a surprise to find Wadell in support of this the reversed order of human and divine action. This occurs when he begins to consider the *limit* of where "virtue" is actually capable of taking us. It is in pondering what this limit is, and what it means, that Wadell's reading of Thomist ethics loses its activist character. Though the virtues work for the sake of friendship with God, now identified as "charity," charity is not enough, according to Wadell, to gain reunion with God for us. As he explains, Aquinas taught that God is the goodness that constitutes our happiness, but this does not mean that we can somehow capture it. As Wadell expresses this, God is "goodness forever beyond us" (p. 125). It is not merely that, because of our limitation, we will always fail no matter how hard we try; the reason is much more radical than that. Not even the life of perfect virtue could gain reunion with God, Wadell says, because even if we were to live that life, we would "still depend on God's love to do for us what our love cannot do" (p. 125). This is why

> Aquinas' schema of the moral life begins in grace and ends in gift. From first to last, God's love enables us. It is the gift of God's love poured out in our hearts that begins the moral life for us and enables us to respond to God at all; but it is also the gift of God's love in the Spirit that completes our virtue and leads us home. . . . From first to last all is grace. (p. 126)

Wadell emphasizes that the aim of Aquinas's moral theology is to explain how we will be reunited with God, whose love has made us (p. 136). He thus asks the question about what has to happen to achieve this reunion. In answer to this question, Wadell points out that Aquinas concludes his study of morality not with the virtues but with the gift of the Spirit.

It is with this turn toward "gift" that the question of how our own activities relate to God's action finally comes to rest. The strong emphasis on the crucial importance of "self-definition" and on the "transformation of the self" with which Wadell started now receives a quintessential caveat: that though the virtues reach for "ultimate enhancement of the person," this end can never be reached effectively (p. 121). The reason is that "we can grow in goodness, but we can never exhaust goodness" (p. 121). Even though we can become better than we are now, we cannot become best, because "the sublime goodness is reserved for God" (p. 121). Whereas his account so far has focused sharply on the task of changing our selves to prepare us for reunion with God, Wadell now reverses the angle in order to argue that it is only God's goodness that heals and restores us. "In the Christian moral life, we are patients and God is the healer" (p. 136). Charity works through the virtues, but it is only because of the primacy of God's love that Christians will be able to do what they are meant to do (p. 138). Charity can only work in us because it recognizes in God the single love enabling it to achieve the goodness we seek. The virtues are thus "passionate cries of dependence" that express our need for a love we can only receive (p. 137).

This way of reversing the relationship between divine and human action indicates that in Wadell's Thomist view the gift of the Spirit not only completes the virtues and makes them perfect, but it also precedes them and makes their achievement possible. The virtues can never achieve the end they seek on their own, "because they intrinsically lack the goodness they need to break into the heart of God" (p. 138). The necessary condition of human fulfillment must remain God's gift, according to Wadell's rendering of Aquinas.

> Ultimately, Thomas knows, we return to God "in virtue" of God more than ourselves. It is God, not our virtue that redeems us, God's goodness, not our own that heals and restores. It is true that we return to God through love, but the return is through God's love more than our own. (p. 136)

Without it, reunion with God would not be possible, because "the only love capable of God is God's love" (p. 138). At a closer look, however, there seem to be two possibilities of "prioritizing" God's action over human action. One is to say that God's friendship is a gift from first to last, that even the life of perfect virtue would not reunite us with God; the other is to say that God's friendship meets the limit of virtue. On the first reading, the relationship is that both kinds of action operate on a different plane: the achievement of virtue presupposes divine grace in every instance as the condition of its possibility. On the second reading, however, the relationship appears to be complementary: they operate on the same level, whereby the one perfects the other.

> The Spirit is not something totally different from charity, but is what happens to charity at the limit of virtue. At some point in the Christian moral life, our love is exhausted by the very desire from which it springs; however, that charity's love gives birth to the Spirit signals that virtue dies not in emptiness but in God. That charity ultimately breaks forth in the Spirit testifies not that we love in vain, but that our love is perfected when it is in the Spirit. At the limit of virtue, charity becomes the Spirit, that is, our friendship with God is met by God's friendship with us. (p. 138)

If charity becomes the Spirit, that must imply a tendency toward identity. Here one is reminded of Wadell's phrasing that virtue aims at the realization of "our optimum potential by becoming godly." There is "a point" in the Christian life where the one is changed into the other. At the same time, however, there is the thought of two distinct levels, which induces Wadell to claim that the gifts of the Spirit do not replace the virtues.

Wadell resolves this apparent tension by saying that "charity transforms the virtues so radically that through love they reach another kind of goodness" (p. 139). The gifts of the Spirit are the virtues' most splendid possibility: "They represent not another kind of virtue, but their ultimate transfiguration" (p. 139). Quoting Aquinas, he explains the relationship between the two this way:

> The Gifts surpass the common perfection of the virtues, not as regards the kinds of work done, but as regards the mode of operation, inasmuch as we are moved in the case of the Gifts by a higher principle. (p. 139)

That higher principle, Wadell adds, is God. Since, as we have seen, the virtues are incapable of achieving what they seek to achieve on their own, which is why they were called "passionate cries of dependence," it appears that the gifts are to be understood as a kind of fuse: "The optimum possibility of every virtue — as well as our lives — is to be fired by the Spirit" (p. 139). The strategy of the virtues is to become gifts, because it is only in that perfect love that they can fulfill their purpose, but at the same time, that only happens when this "perfect love" already operates in them as the Spirit.

It is appropriate at this point to make three comments regarding my concern in this chapter. As I already noted, Wadell's claim to a necessary connection between the virtues and the final end of human nature cannot but imply that some human beings are excluded from that end. We can now add that, to the extent that being reunited with God's love is dependent on the gift of the Spirit, who completes the virtues, it must be true that those same people are also excluded from that reunion.

My second comment is that, in order to avoid this conclusion, we must insist on the primacy of God's love as a gift from beginning to end. Only the primacy of his self-giving love will answer whether or not we will attain the fullness of life independently from the "quality" of our response. Whatever there is to the fullness of life, it must be God's gift from beginning to end, unless one is willing to accept that there are human beings who are excluded from it.

My third comment is that Wadell's account should be much more explicit about the "limits" to virtue from the perspective of God's unconditional love. Absent from his account is the question of whether our will is at all adequately disposed to return that love. As we saw, Wadell equates "sin" with disorderly behavior and fails to notice the problem of the self-seeking will. Even when it is fully developed in terms of the "kinds of work done," virtue can be changed, theologically speaking, into its opposite when it is motivated by the expectation of its reward. Presumably, that is why Aquinas says that the gifts of the Spirit surpass virtue in its "mode of operation": they shape the human will into conformity with God's will. This fully explains why the virtues "cannot achieve what they seek" on their own, and why it is not by means of our own action that we are reunited with God.

Therefore, from the perspective of attaining friendship with God, the limits of virtue are that it is effective only because that friendship is already operating as a gift. In receiving that gift, we receive the possibility to respond. All of these considerations point to the same conclusion:

God's friendship is necessarily prior to the response we are able to produce in any single moment of our lives.

6. Disability as Moral Failure?

As we have seen in the preceding section, the identification of the *telos* of human being with the development and growth of virtue has its dangers, particularly in view of understanding the humanity of people with profound disabilities. We have also seen how these dangers may result in questioning the humanity of those whose achievements do not reach beyond "simply being alive." Furthermore, in placing "virtue" in opposition to "disorderly behavior," Wadell comes close to implying that such behavior is a manifestation of moral failure. In this respect, Wadell's account evokes one of the earlier theological essays by Wolf Wolfensberger, the "godfather of normalization theory." In this essay, Wolfensberger sets out to explain "what mental retardation is" from a Christian perspective.[18] His argument is quite complex and sometimes difficult to follow, but one can adequately summarize its most salient points in the following way.

Wolfensberger begins with a set of anthropological assumptions that he claims reflect widely accepted Christian beliefs, among which the first and the second are decisive. The first is that human beings are created spirits — "souls" — united to material bodies and endowed with the faculties of reason and will. In view of this belief, according to Wolfensberger, there is ample evidence that God has endowed spirits differentially with respect to reason, which is not necessarily problematic. Much more difficult to understand from the viewpoint of creation, he declares, is the fact that created spirits show differences in strength of will, as we also find.[19]

---

18. Wolf Wolfensberger, "An Attempt to Gain Better Understanding from a Christian Perspective of What 'Mental Retardation' Is," in *The Theological Voice of Wolf Wolfensberger*, ed. William C. Gaventa and David L. Coulter (New York: The Haworth Press, 2001), pp. 71-83 [following page number references in the text are to this work].

19. This claim indicates that Wolfensberger tends toward a concept of disability that crucially focuses on "will" rather than "cognition." In this respect, his views are reminiscent of those of Edouard Seguin, one of the nineteenth-century founding fathers of the scientific approach to intellectual disability. In his *Idiocy, and Its Treatment by the Physio-*

The second belief is that human souls in their fallen state are "multiply hindered." They are hindered by their own fallenness, and thus alienated from God; by the fallenness of the body; and by their imperfect union with the fallen body. How these facts are characterized is also subject to the fallen state of human understanding. In their extra-fallen state, however, human souls do not suffer such imperfections, so that the differences between human souls in the state of fallenness is "infinitesimal" compared to the differences between the fallen and the extra-fallen state of being human (pp. 71-72).

Based on these beliefs, Wolfensberger makes a number of inferences. For our purposes, the most important of these inferences pertain to differences between intellect and will. Patterns of impediments to the soul's faculties may be characterized as "mental retardation," Wolfensberger states, as long as they include a recognizable impairment of the intellect to a sufficient degree. However, with respect to the different intellectual capacities of created spirits, it is very unlikely, he says, that these differences would be viewed as "mental retardation." It is much more likely that people will see this condition to be the result of bodily impairments rather than a poor endowment of the soul's intellect. Insofar as the soul is hindered by an impairment of the body, it is to be expected that this not only affects the intellect but also the will. The more deeply the intellect is hindered in its exercise, Wolfensberger says, the more safely we can assume that the body is impaired, even when this is not directly observable, and the more probable it is that the will is also affected. In fact, there is a "negative feedback loop," according to Wolfensberger, "within which intellectual impairment leads to poor physical competence, and thus additional bodily damage is apt to result in greater impairment of both intellect and will" (p. 73).

Wolfensberger then continues to explore the relationship between volitional and intellectual deficit, which he claims has received insufficient attention in modern psychology.[20] He observes that intellectual

---

logical Method, Seguin argued that there is no qualitative difference between "idiots" and normal human beings. The "idiot" suffers from weakness of will; therein lies the possibility of curability, Seguin believed. This view indicates how "intellectual disability" and "moral failure" can become conceptually linked.

20. Wolfensberger explicitly refers to Edouard Seguin's treatment of "volitional impairment" as an essential aspect of intellectual disability, which led him to think about

impairment without a concomitant impairment of the will is much more rare than its opposite, that is, volitional impairment without a concomitant impairment of the intellect. In other words, willing is often more relevant than understanding, according to Wolfensberger. The explanation of this phenomenon must remain speculative, he concedes, but his basic assumptions from Christian belief suggest that, in the state of fallenness, "the human soul is relatively more capable of willing than of knowing" (p. 74).[21] This would explain why human beings are frequently irrational in the sense that their will subverts the proper use of reason, or why they can love or hate things they have little knowledge of. For the same reason, it explains why they come much closer to God through their will than through their intellect. Due to habitual "willing," the intellect may become less and less capable of exercising the potential it retains even under the condition of its fallenness.

Having set the stage for his central point, Wolfensberger proceeds with two surprising observations. The first of these observations is worth quoting because of what it reveals about his perception of intellectually disabled people.

> Volition probably plays a major role in phenomena such as suggestibility, how easily one is led astray, whether one can form deep and lasting love relationships, how strongly one can and will commit oneself to a cause or faith, etc. Indeed, in such things, retarded people are commonly weak. For instance, their love relationships are often superficial, less enduring unless materially and appetitively reinforced, and more easily undermined by selfishness or distractions. . . . Their judgments . . . are very unstable and can easily be swayed — so much that they might be made to swing from one extreme to another, etc. (p. 73)

In other words, many of the characteristics Wolfensberger claims to have observed in human beings with "mental retardation" can be attributed to weakness of will more than anything else.[22] Consequently,

---

treatment in terms of moral education (Wolfensberger, "An Attempt to Gain better Understanding," p. 73).

21. This claim reflects the author's assumption that differences in intellect are compatible with creation in a way that differences in strength of will are not.

22. This observation justifies the assumption that Wolfensberger probably would

he is now in a position to ask whether volitions of a certain kind can be identified as the source of "mental retardation."

The point Wolfensberger is making becomes even more explicit in his second observation. If fallen human souls are relatively more capable of willing than of knowing, he argues, that would suggest two things. Not only can human beings come closer to God via their wills than they can via their intellect; they may also go in the opposite direction and allow the turning of their wills from God to become habitual. Furthermore, this habitual denial of God is of dire consequence because it may also affect the intellect.

> In other words, the soul in its entirety may fall into such a habit of negation, and thus negativism, that the intellect becomes less and less capable of utilizing the potential it has even within the body's limitations. Indeed the body itself may suffer so much from the soul's habitual negation as to develop malaise and/or new impediments to the intellect. (p. 74)

Brought together, these two observations suggest the possibility, in Wolfensberger's view, that the will turned away from God may indeed be the source of "mental retardation." Although he repeatedly insists on some (quite complicated) qualifications to interpret this claim correctly, he nonetheless maintains that he has known people who seem to have willfully blocked the soul from turning to God by, among other things, repressing mental activity.

> They were mildly or moderately retarded by the usual criteria, had so little consciousness as to seem to be almost sleepwalking, yet showed startling flashes of intellectual capacity — but usually only when wreaking wickedness. Obviously, if such "functional" retardation had its onset still during the childhood of the person, and endured for more than a short period, it might so severely interfere with normal mental growth processes as to become largely irreversible. (p. 75)

Misguided by cognitive psychotherapy, says Wolfensberger, many people tend to believe that the impaired activity of the soul is proportional

---

have rejected the term "intellectual disability" because it entirely focuses on the intellect at the expense of ignoring the will.

to the level of intellectual impairment. If this were true, he argues, then we should expect that severe intellectual impairment is accompanied by severe volitional impairment. However, this is not the case, as we can infer from the fact that even severely "retarded" people can have strong wills. Thus it is possible that inflexibility, stubbornness, and rigidity are manifestations of volitional rather than intellectual impairments. It also means that persons showing these characteristics are not barred from having strong attachments and relationships. Nonetheless, when they appear to be limited in forming these attachments and relationships, this is because these require "volitional investments of a higher order that rise above the level of bodily appetites" (p. 76). Of course, this is true also of non-disabled people, but they often have a greater capacity for learning. Consequently, Wolfensberger concludes, the will is an important factor in shaping the disabled person's behaviors and attitudes without the intellect being capable of redirecting it.

With regard to its religious underpinnings, Wolfensberger wants to safeguard his proposition against potential misunderstandings, some of which should be mentioned here. His essay aims at understanding what "mental retardation" *is* rather than what it *means*. For example, being "retarded" does not mean that the person cannot have a mission in life. Even when the will may be involved in a lack of development and growth of natural talent, it does not follow that "retarded" persons are less lovable in the eyes of God, nor does it imply that they have no gifts to offer. God may even act through a "retarded" person's presence, without using her will or intellect.

Furthermore, the fact that the will is capable of turning toward God as well as turning away from him, even in instances of severe intellectual impairment, does not imply that every human being is capable of such a fundamental choice. Sometimes the person never has been able to grasp the possibility of that choice. Yet, despite this caveat, Wolfensberger says that he sometimes found a "deep spirituality" even in severely "retarded" people, but also a "defiance, and even outright evil orientation" in similarly impaired people (p. 77). Thus he can speak of "retardation" as a "willfully self-afflicted" condition caused by "the sinful turning against God" (p. 79). According to Wolfensberger, this shows how the will can also cause damage to the soul in people with intellectual disabilities.

Finally, Wolfensberger wants to make clear that, when a disabled person's soul is capable of making a choice about its relationship with

God, even though that person may be under great compulsion, or deeply wounded, it does not follow that he is responsible for his behavior. The reason is that we do not know; it is usually unclear what the person can be held accountable for. Some people with disabilities can be willfully destructive, but their behavior may not be culpable because they act with insufficient insight into what they are doing. Wolfensberger concludes that this suggests that it is not true that afflictions such as "mental retardation" must be attributed to personal failure ("sin"), but it is also not true that they never are (p. 79).

7. Steadfast Love without Reciprocation

I have presented Wolfensberger's account of "mental retardation" as an illustration of how the condition of intellectual disability can come to be regarded from the perspective of moral failure. What appears in Paul Wadell's account of Aquinas's ethics as merely an unreflected possibility, Wolfenberger's essay explicitly explores. The crucial point is the turning of the soul toward God or away from God, which in some cases is attributable to ill will. Moreover, Wolfensberger even finds in some cases an "evil orientation" in disabled persons. But the curious thing about his essay is that his claims remain inconsequential when it comes to their ethical implications. Nowhere is there the implication that, in cases of self-affliction, people get what they deserve because their misery results from their own wrongdoing. On the contrary, when Wolfensberger considers the issue of responsibility and accountability, he insists on leaving those questions up to God: "Only God can really know what a person is accountable for" (p. 78). Wolfensberger wishes to say that, even when the person has turned against God, that would still not justify turning against that person, or abandoning or failing to protect her. Not surprisingly, the reason Wolfensberger offers for this claim is that, in the eyes of God, loving-kindness toward another human being is never grounded in the fact that it is "deserved." In the Christian view, love is never a response to merit.

In view of his analysis, it is thus very instructive that Wolfensberger arrives at a conclusion regarding its ethical implications that breaks out of the scheme of responsibility that implies culpability. However, that is not a conclusion he has argued for, because in order to argue for it, one would have to rely on the notion of grace. Whether sinful or not, the disabled person is not to be excluded and abandoned, Wolfensberger declares. In practical terms this means, for example, that even when a disabled person's capacity to receive communication is severely hampered, one can still communicate God's love to that person (p. 80). It also means that, even when limited capacities for a loving relationship are caused by impairment of the will, the response should nonetheless be the extending of "steadfast love" to the person — "even if that love is not reciprocated" (p. 81).

The above discussion of Wolfensberger's essay shows why a Christian response to disability is not a response to what the disabled person did or failed to do. In that sense, Wolfensberger's essay inadvertently corroborates my conclusions about Paul Wadell's account of virtue as the path to the fullness of life. Fallen human beings, disabled or not, are apt to frustrate the development of the gifts they have received because of their selfishness and stubbornness. But that does not alter the fact that God's friendship is a gift that is not withdrawn, because it is not a response to merit. Therefore, it doesn't depend on what we do with our talents; by implication, this means that it doesn't depend on what talents we have either. This is because, in Wolfensberger's apt phrase, God loves all his children even if they do not reciprocate that love.

It is interesting that Wolfensberger arrives at his conclusion via the notion that human beings with intellectual disabilities are "creatures of relationship," referring to Jean Vanier (p. 80). Of course, in using this phrase he cannot mean that disabled people are *creators* of relationships: he tends to believe that lacking the capacity to form relationships is part of their impairment. As it turns out, what he means is that the logic of relationship entails that, as "creatures of relationships," persons with intellectual disabilities are extrinsically grounded. Even when you are incapable of receiving communication because of your disability, Wolfensberger insists, I can still communicate God's love to you. And, to be sure, steadfastness is required for that communication.

> The love of a person who, for and with Christ, enters into a long-term committed love for a retarded person can be expected to communicate God's love more powerfully to such a retarded person than would the love of the Christian whose love is fragmented, abstract, and diffused. Of course, the Spirit is not bound or bindable... but the

point is that with the occasional exception provided by God for good purpose, retarded people probably have greater need of enduring relationships from Christians (yes, "from" even more than "with") than they have for large numbers of brief loving encounters with numerous Christians. (pp. 80-81)[23]

The only thing I should add here is that, if we delete the adjective "retarded" from it, Wolfensberger's statement would still be true (and I think he would readily accept that). As Christians will be the first to admit, all human beings, disabled or not, are in need of having God's love communicated to them in more steadfast and concrete, rather than abstract and diffused, ways, because each person carries his or her own wounds — some self-inflicted, some not — that need healing within relationships that communicate God's lasting friendship.

Charity as the fullness of being communicates this friendship inasmuch as it is, as Aquinas puts it, "a participation of the Holy Spirit."[24] With respect to the Trinitarian account in the preceding chapter, we are drawn into the communion of the Father, the Son, and the Spirit by God's self-giving gift, which is his everlasting friendship.

> Charity is a friendship of man for God, founded upon the fellowship of everlasting happiness. Now this fellowship is in respect, not of natural, but of gratuitous gifts, according to Romans 6:23, *the grace of God is life everlasting:* wherefore charity itself surpasses our natural faculties. Now that which surpasses the faculty of nature, cannot be natural or acquired by the natural powers, since a natural effect does not transcend its cause. Therefore charity can be in us neither naturally, nor through acquisition by the natural powers, but by the infusion of the Holy Spirit, who is the love of the Father and the Son.[25]

Because "friendship" is the adequate description of God's being with us, it is also the adequate description of our relationship with others. In fact, there is a close connection between the two. This is why a lack of

---

23. He continues: "The same need may exist in everybody, but it probably exists to a greater degree in persons of impaired intellect; further, their need may be greater because it is less often met."

24. Aquinas, *Summa Theologica,* II, II, 23, 3.

25. Aquinas, *Summa Theologica,* II, II, 24, 2.

How is this not using them instrumentally for what they can do for us?

congruence between them does not work. We cannot sincerely hope to be friends with God and, at the same time, act condescendingly toward our neighbor. If we don't know how to engage in friendships with other people, it is impossible for us to know how to engage in friendship with God. The reverse is also true. We could never have a close and intimate relationship with God and accept the fact that our relationships with other people are at rock bottom.[26] The reason is that the communion with the triune God does not leave us unaffected: as Wadell rightly saw, it transforms us, not by an act of self-affirmation, of course, but by God's act of unconditional affirmation. Since it is the work of the Spirit to draw us closer to the Father and the Son and to transform us accordingly, it is very appropriate to speak of the Holy Spirit as "the transforming Friend,"[27] because the Spirit prepares us for the task of receiving God's friendship.[28] Why this transformation must be extrinsically grounded is brought out clearly in a saying that has been attributed to an ancient voice, Symeon the New Theologian:

> When the three-personed Deity dwells within the saints and is known and felt to be present, it is not the fulfillment of desire, but the cause and the beginning of a much greater and more fervent desire.[29]

Friendship with God is not the fulfillment of a natural desire. That is, it is not a natural desire in the human condition after the Fall, which is why we have to learn how to receive God's friendship. Learning to see the truth about ourselves is the most important thing, as I have argued. The mission of people with disabilities — to use Wolfensberger's language — consists in what being with them can teach us.

In the next chapter we will turn to those Christians who are answering Wolfensberger's call for steadfast relationships with disabled persons. They live together in communities known as L'Arche communities, which were founded by Jean Vanier. We can learn from their

---

26. See James Houston, *The Transforming Friendship* (Oxford: Lion Publishing, 1988), p. 11.

27. Houston, *Transforming Friendship*, p. 118.

28. Aquinas, *Summa Theologica*, II, II.

29. Symeon the New Theologian, *Hymns of Divine Love*, trans. George A. Maloney (New Jersey: Dimension Books), cited in Houston, *Transforming Friendship*, p. 193. See http://www.monachos.net/patristics/symeon_divine_light.shtml.

accounts of their lives why and how friendship with God is mediated by friendship with their disabled fellow humans. Listening to the stories of the people of L'Arche will serve us well as we attempt to answer the remaining question of my inquiry: *How* do human beings with profound disabilities participate in God's friendship as the ultimate good of their lives? In turning to the stories of L'Arche, we will keep this question before us; but the answer will not be found on the path of self-transforming virtue. On the contrary, it is precisely the endeavor to be good to people with disabilities and become their friends that gets in the way of achieving that goal. The fullness of life tends to be blocked and to escape us when it is the deliberate object of our actions.

Chapter Nine

Receiving the Gift of Friendship

*For God's foolishness is wiser than human wisdom, and God's
weakness is stronger than human strength.*

I Corinthians 1:25

1. Introduction

Presumably, the argument developed in this book so far will raise some
questions. Even though it has used the primacy of God's unconditional
love for human beings as leverage against any view that understands
human being primarily in terms of its intellectual and moral capabilities, it does not follow that these capabilities have no proper function
with respect to God's creative purposes. Theological language such as
"the gifts of creation" or "the gifts of the Spirit" from my discussion of
Wadell's account of Aquinas's ethics immediately evokes a question
about what, in terms of these gifts, God has given to profoundly disabled human beings. On every occasion I have insisted on a theological
reversal of the order in which we think about human being. For example, the claim that the reality of divine being precedes the possibility of
human being; that the reality of the communion of the triune God precedes the possibility of human communion; that the reality of God's
compassion precedes the possibility of human compassion, and so
forth. Nonetheless, this constant reversal of our thinking cannot eliminate the question about what these possibilities amount to; yet this is
what I have seemed to be trying to do.

312

how does friendship entail freedom?

To introduce this question at this stage may suggest that so far the argument has not accomplished very much, since my dismissal of talk of human capacities has probably weighed heavily on the reader's mind all along the way. However, we must be aware that the weight of the question depends on the implicit assumption that these capacities are ultimately decisive for our concept of human being. To subvert this assumption has been the aim of my entire argument, which was designed to make that assumption explicit, and to spell out its implications for how we think about profoundly disabled human beings in order to have it replaced by a different perspective. I have tried to accomplish this in the preceding chapters, with the resulting claim that being created in God's image indicates a unique relationship; that this relationship is affirmed extrinsically by the triune God, who saves us from failing to respond appropriately to his call; and that this affirmation is offered to us as the fullness of our being. From a Christian point of view, all of this is to say that the human being exists truthfully in God's friendship, regardless of his or her abilities and disabilities.

Let me return to the distinction, which I introduced in Chapter 3, between the ultimate good of being human and the various goods that are worth pursuing in our lives. If it is acceptable to posit God's friendship as our ultimate good, as the final fulfillment of our being (as I propose with the Christian tradition), then the first thing we must consider is how the gift of this friendship entails the gift of freedom that is proclaimed with this unconditional affirmation. The importance of this gift of freedom for people with profound intellectual disabilities is immense, but with Zizioulas we have to insist that it is not a moral freedom. It is freedom that comes with being chosen to be God's friends. This means that, whatever the vicissitudes of our lives — our limited opportunities, our ailing bodies, the misguided conceptions we have of ourselves and others, our being repressed, or even being threatened in our existence — none of these things will have the last word. Christian freedom is not freedom from things that make our lives difficult. God never promised us that our lives will be free from all sorts of evil; but God has promised us that he will be with us and that the final judgment about our lives is his. Positively speaking, therefore, Christian freedom is the freedom of being drawn into the divine communion: to be God's friends, and thus to be friends with others.

The Christian church believes that this fundamental freedom is se-

313

freedom w/out agency [handwritten annotation in top margin]

cure because, as I have said, the final judgment on our being is God's judgment, and it has been made public in the death and resurrection of his Son, Jesus Christ. This is the Christian gospel, and it is immensely important for human beings like Kelly and Oliver de Vinck, as well as all those other human beings whose existence is not securely affirmed by the powers that be. Regarding the profoundly disabled among us, this freedom entails being liberated from judgments that elevate our capacities and capabilities to the status of threshold value for what it means to be human. It also entails a freedom that includes them in the body of friendship that is the church.

Second, it is also important to point out that the notion of positive freedom does not necessarily imply the notion of agency. Even when we accept that positive freedom is "freedom to," which by its very logic introduces a verb, that does not necessarily imply action: "freedom to" is sufficiently conceived of as freedom to *be*. The gift that profoundly disabled human beings have received is the gift of being, which is derived from the freedom of judgment. No entrance tickets are needed, no exams have to be passed, and no criteria have to be met to determine whether being human in a biological sense also qualifies as being human in a moral sense. That is, whatever more there is to the gift of God's friendship, it does not demand subjectivity or self-consciousness.

Third, the gift of being entails a mission. Being human is never without meaning, because it always means something to God: because there is God, there is purpose. The gift of being is not an abstraction; it is the gift of being what you are. Therefore, the gift of being entails that what we are means something to God, and this holds for human beings with profound disabilities as well. Since this is the most difficult part for us — the "temporarily able-bodied" — to understand, let alone accept, the mission of the profoundly disabled is aptly characterized as a mission to teach us something. Therefore, the gift that follows from God's friendship is that they have to teach us something about God's purpose. However, if they cannot even respond to God's love — at least not consciously and intentionally — because they lack the capacity for purposive agency, how can they teach us something about God's purpose? The answer is that the condition of purposive agency may not be decisive here; for, as Wolfensberger has suggested, their mission in life may be one that does not depend on the powers of reason and will. It is

314

Wolfensberger's view that the presence of human beings like Kelly is a gift *as such*. What Kelly has received from God is her being; and though her being may not mean anything to her, given the absence of subjectivity and self-consciousness, this in no way entails that it does not mean anything to God. Thus, the question to ask is what the existence of a disabled human being means in the eyes of God, which is another way of asking what there is to learn from the fact that they are here.

Obviously, prying into the mind of God often makes theologians look silly. We need only be reminded of the difficulties of reading another human being's mind to understand the impossibility of reading the mind of the Eternal. Fortunately, however, we have a better way at our disposal: reading what Jesus had to say about our question in the biblical story of the man who was born blind (John 9). On one of his journeys in Galilee, Jesus meets this man, and his friends want to know why he was born this way. The answer comes when Jesus shows in this story what the man's mission was. Reading this story and spelling out that answer will be the first focus of this chapter.

The second focus will be to turn to the stories the people of the L'Arche communities tell about their lives with people with intellectual disabilities. I take their stories to exemplify what the Gospel of John teaches us about the mission of such people, irrespective of their disabilities. I hope that many of the remaining points of our discussion so far will fall into place as we read these stories.

2. Receiving

Before we begin, however, I want to again address a point I have already discussed extensively, namely, the contributory view of worth. Following Pailin, I read this view (in Chapters 6 and 7) to say that the presence of profoundly disabled people like Kelly and Oliver de Vinck provide the opportunity for making us better people. In other words, their presence appears as a means to other people's ends. This kind of reasoning is frequently used in Christian literature. Apart from the examples I have given in Chapter 3, consider the following quotation from Father John T. Catoir's sermon at the funeral of Oliver de Vinck, as reported by his brother Christopher:

Oliver was never able to do anything in that sense of the word. He was virtually paralyzed, but still he did so much for each one of us. He evoked the best love that was in us. He helped us to grow in the virtues of devotion, wisdom, perseverance, kindness, patience, and fidelity. Without doing anything, Oliver made all of us better human beings.[1]

Including a person with a profound disability in our lives may contribute to our own good by offering us the opportunity to become better people. What I have suggested above about their "mission" in life seems to be another way of saying just that. Their mission is to teach us something. How is that different from the view I have rejected, following Pailin? Isn't the language that introduces the disabled person as "gift" again moving us into the sphere of contribution?

To answer these questions, I think we should have a closer look at the argument in support of Pailin's objection. As I indicated in Chapter 6, Pailin suggests a Kantian argument against valuing human being for instrumental reasons. The objection against instrumental value stems from Kant's second version of his foundational principle of morality, the "categorical imperative."[2] According to that principle, one should never use other human beings only as a means to one's own good but always as an end in themselves. The notable point in this version of the categorical imperative is that Kant understands morality as a matter of moral constraints concerning how we treat other people in the pursuit of our own good. In this respect, his philosophy clearly reflects the scheme of morals in modernity.

From the vantage point of Christian theology, however, the Kantian framework of ethics looks quite different (which can be inferred from the argument about charity in the previous chapter). The moral life understood from a Christian perspective is a response to the continuing offer of God's friendship that always precedes human action. This means, among other things, that our ways of dealing with other people are always a response to God's ways of dealing with us. Christian moral-

---

1. Christopher de Vinck, *The Power of the Powerless: A Brother's Legacy of Love* (New York: Doubleday, 1990), p. 111.

2. I. Kant, *Foundations of the Metaphysics of Morals,* in I. Kant, *Critique of Practical Reason and Other Writings in Moral Philosophy,* trans. L. W. Beck (Chicago: Chicago University Press, 1949), p. 429.

ity displays a three-way logic, not a two-way logic: it does not prescribe how to treat the other person, but rather how to treat the other person as a way to respond to how one is treated by God.[3] This is why the classical doctrine of charity did not regard the good of the other person as the direct object of virtuous action; instead, it taught that charity seeks friendship with God that includes seeking the good of the neighbor.[4]

However, in view of this particular object, the Kantian view appears to operate on a very different track. In that it understands the moral quality of our actions in terms of an imperative, it is conceived as regulating the act of the will in terms of duty rather than inclination. Thus it is fair to say that the Kantian account of morality is concerned with a universal constraint on our actions. Since the moral quality of our acts is not derived from the good they seek to realize, it follows that, morally speaking, we can pursue any good we want within the universal constraint of the categorical imperative. From the perspective of charity, however, this account of morality appears to be a perversion of the moral life, because, if the proper aim of my action is to respond to God's friendship, then the main ethical question cannot be how to regulate the pursuit of the good so that it does not transgress the categorical imperative. To the extent that our actions involve the use of other people as means to obtain these goods, the main question cannot be how to regulate using them in a morally justifiable way either.

The reason is that the very object of the action — being an act in pursuit of our own good — shows it to be wrong-headed from the outset. That is, from a theological point of view, the question is not how our action should be constrained in pursuing whatever we want to pursue; nor is it how our action should be constrained in using other people as means. Either way, the question indicates that our deliberation has al-

---

3. This explains why, as I have mentioned in the preceding chapter, relationality occurs within time and thus implies sequence, which is but another way of saying that it implies narrative. When the principle of reciprocity is discussed, for example, in terms of the Golden Rule, as it is found in the Gospels of Matthew and Luke, it does not prescribe that we treat others merely as we want to treated by them. What it says is that we ought to treat the widow, the orphan, and the stranger as God treated us in the days he delivered us from captivity in Egypt (see Hans Reinders, "The Golden Rule between Philosophy and Theology," in *Ethics, Reason and Rationality*, ed. A. Bondolfi [Münster: LIT Verlag, 1997], pp. 145-68).

4. Aquinas, *Summa Theologica*, II, II, 25, 1.

ready lost track of the proper aim of human action, at least from a Christian perspective. Therefore, the constrained use of other people as a means to our own good betrays a perverted concept of the moral life. It is perverted in the sense that it has replaced the true object of human action, the happiness that is found in the friendship with God, with an imperative regarding the act of willing per se, regardless of the object that the will is inclined to pursue.[5]

Therefore, any attempt to set moral constraints on the instrumentalizing of other people, while in itself justified *with respect to these people,* remains within the limits of this perversion. Theologically speaking, moral duty — in the strict sense of the action that one is due or bound to do — is duty to God, because, as I have indicated, our moral lives develop within three-term rather than two-term relationships. We give to the other as we have gratuitously received from God: God is "paying it forward," so to speak.[6] The gift is thus a response to the fact that we have received, which makes the act of receiving necessarily prior to the act of giving. For the same reason, it makes knowing how to receive necessarily prior to knowing how to give.[7]

As my observations on the classical doctrine of charity indicate, I believe that the critique of charity in our moral culture is based on a profound misunderstanding of its original intent. The disability rights movement cannot be blamed for this misunderstanding, however, because what it rejects is the demeaning forms of dependence that have often come with the care provided by charity-based organizations. As

5. Aquinas, *Summa Theologica,* II, II, 23, 1.

6. This phrase refers to the title of a movie that tells the story of a little boy who invents a rule to change the world: people pass on to another person an unsolicited gift that they have received gratuitously. In doing so they pay the gift forward instead of backward, without being bound by duty to the receiver of their gift. In this way they learn to give the same way they have received. That is, they learn to give to those from whom they have not received anything. They learn to give without being in debt in any way, which is how God gives.

7. I am aware that disability-rights advocates do not like the language of gift, definitely not in connection with moral duty, because, as my comment seems to underscore, that language tends to make beneficence rather than justice the main feature of moral obligation. The reason for the suspicion of gift language is that in the past this language usually left dependant people in the demeaning role of being the beneficiary of a benefactor, to whom they were then obliged to be grateful. Hence the battle cry of the disability-rights movement: "From beneficence to rights."

many people with disabilities know from firsthand experience, being the beneficiary of other people's goods will change very quickly when it must be paid back in the form of servitude.[8] More often than not, the result has been "cold charity."[9] However, if charity is grounded in the principle that my relationships with other people are opportunities to respond to God's graciousness, then any perception I have of myself as their benefactor must be completely misplaced. To regard myself as a benefactor, to whom gratitude is due, is equally a perversion of Christian morality; it is only a different perversion in that it misconstrues my proper place in the scheme of morals. There is nothing for me to give other than what I have graciously received. In others words, there is nothing else for me to do — properly speaking — than "paying it forward."

I wish to suggest that the explanation for the demise of charity is the shift in viewing moral relationships from three-way to two-way relationships. Charity as serving the neighbor by way of responding to God's friendship has been altered into charity without God. In the nineteenth and twentieth centuries, institutionalized charity was broadly subjected to this change, which has given charity its widespread and often well-deserved reputation for moral hypocrisy. Nonetheless, this should not prevent us from seeing that it is a perversion of the classical doctrine in the sense discussed above. Nothing is wrong with the notion of "receiving" as the key to the moral life, but there is something very wrong with the notion that charity begins with my benevolent action. Based on that notion, I will be tempted to misconstrue my role as "giving," which leaves the other person at the receiving end of my beneficence.

This analysis opens up a different perspective on the claim that one

8. Snyder and Mitchell describe the Puritan version of charity as it developed in America in these terms: "The 'rich and mighty' cultivate qualities such as mercy, gentleness, temperance towards the socially subordinate, and the 'poor and despised' learn to accept such sentiments with faith, patience and obedience." Charity served two functions — one religious, the other economic and political — according to the authors: for the rich a "path to salvation," for the poor to refrain from rebellion (Sharon L. Snyder and David T. Mitchell, *Cultural Locations of Disability* [Chicago: The University of Chicago Press, 2006], pp. 51-60).

9. I borrow this term from John Williams-Searle, "Cold Charity: Manhood, Brotherhood, and the Transformation of Disability, 1870-1900," in *The New Disability History: American Perspectives,* ed. Paul K. Longmore and Lauri Umanski (New York: New York University Press, 2001), pp. 157-86.

of the gifts of God to the disabled is that they may teach us something about his purpose. While this claim inevitably implies that the presence of such people appears as a gift that contributes to our lives, it doesn't follow that lives are dignified because of what they contribute. I believe that Pailin's criticism of the contributory view of worth is correct: the basis of their dignity is in the fact that people receive their being as a gift from God. Yet, despite Pailin's criticism, people with disabilities have important contributions to make. Too often our society lets the contributions these people make as citizens go to waste, not only what they contribute as employees in the workplace, and as students in the schools, but also their contributions to the arts — their painting, theater writing and design, and music. Finally, and importantly, there are the contributions they make as members of their families. As I discussed in Chapter 3, people with disabilities contribute many goods that we think are worth pursuing in our lives.

Yet, apart from contributing these goods, they contribute on a deeper level: the level of their mission of teaching us something about our friendship with God. Here the shifting terminology, from "God's friendship" to "friendship with God," is deliberate. While the former introduces friendship as gift, the latter introduces it as our response to this gift. It is in knowing *how to receive* that the presence of people with intellectual disabilities will appear as a gift. They teach us a few things about ourselves that we, the "temporarily able-bodied," have a hard time understanding on our own, for example, the fact that being accepted by God does not depend on our goodness. Even when people with profound disabilities do not teach by way of explanation, they do teach by way of witness. The gift of disabled persons is the gift of enabling us to learn what our own unshaken belief in our abilities usually prevents us from seeing. Given the problems disabled people face in managing their affairs in life, they cannot help but depend on others for assistance in what they cannot do for themselves. In this sense, they necessarily depend on "receiving." I will argue that in this particular way they are close to God, which follows from what I have argued in the last two chapters. Our being, at every moment of existence, originates from the gift of God's friendship, which makes "receiving" the gift of God a task that is central to both the life of the church and our moral lives as Christians.

Persons with disabilities, even profound intellectual disabilities,

320

have mastered this task far better than most other human beings have. This is particularly true of those among us — the "temporarily able-bodied" — who are impressed by their own abilities. Our moral culture values personal achievement more than anything else, which explains the high premium on abilities that center on purposive agency. We praise ourselves, and are praised by other people, for what we are capable of doing, which, in one way or another, elevates the capacities of reason and will to the core of our being. Thus, we will frequently find that the loss of these capacities is deplored as a fate worse than death. Knowing how to receive is very difficult for people raised in such a culture; in fact, it is much more difficult for such people to receive than to give. In our culture, "giving" is a sign of wealth and power; "receiving" is a sign of dependency and want. The gift of people with disabilities is that they can teach us something different: they can teach us how to receive. That is their mission, or so I will argue in this chapter.[10]

Finally, regarding the pitfalls of thinking about their presence as a gift that contributes to our lives, we need to remind ourselves of the nature of friendship. The argument for friendship as the final end of our lives is not that, in excluding the disabled, we are depriving ourselves of a particular good that only their inclusion can secure — though that may also be true. God's friendship is only properly returned when returned for God's sake. However, charity as the return of this friendship implicates the neighbor, as Aquinas explains.

> The aspect under which our neighbor is to be loved, is God, since what we ought to love in our neighbor is that he may be in God. Hence, it is clear that it is specifically the same act whereby we love

---

10. Of the many suspicions that this claim will evoke, one can be dealt with right away. I am not proposing to revisit the notion of the "holy innocent" with respect to the profoundly disabled. This notion sets the disabled person as an example of the human being who is close to God because she cannot sin. I believe that this notion rests on a mistake: many people whom I know with profound disabilities can be just as mean-spirited as you and I can be. With regard to those who cannot — humans such as Kelly and Oliver de Vinck — the notion of "innocence" fails to apply because it presupposes a capacity for agency. Therefore, "innocence" is not presumed; on the contrary, being with an intellectually disabled person can be a very demanding task, and there is no reason to romanticize that. In fact, the notion of innocence betrays the condescending attitude that it is our task to help. It is quite unlikely that we will succeed in fulfilling this task, however, as long as we continue to assume that "giving" is our part, while "receiving" is theirs.

God, and whereby we love the neighbor. Consequently, the habit of charity extends not only to the love of God, but also to the love of our neighbor.[11]

Thus the claim we should argue for is that only when we seek the presence of persons with intellectual disabilities *for their own sake* will we be able to return God's friendship. But in order to be able to do this, we first have to know what it means to receive it. It is only by seeing them in the light of God's unconditional love that they can reveal his gift. This insight can be gained from reading the story of the man who was born blind.

3. The Story of a Man Born Blind[12]

What is the mission of disabled human beings, according to Jesus? The proper thing is to say that we don't know. What we do know is what he said about the mission of this one particular human being, a man who was born blind, as it is told in the Gospel of John. It will be important to remember this qualification because, as the story unfolds, it will become increasingly clear that John is not giving a general statement about disability. Jesus recognizes something in this man that actually has little to do with his blindness. Therefore, before we start drawing systematic conclusions from the story, we should pay very close attention to the specifics of the narrative as it develops.[13]

11. Aquinas, *Summa Theologica,* II, II, 25, 1.

12. This section contains material from Hans S. Reinders, "Being Thankful: Parenting the Mentally Disabled," in *The Blackwell Companion to Christian Ethics,* ed. Stanley M. Hauerwas and Samuel Wells (London: Blackwell, 2004).

13. For the same reason I think the story must not be read as an attempt to answer the theodicy question. In the way John sets up the story, Jesus is clearly not interested in that question, as we shall see. Nor am I interested in that question, because of the problem it seeks to resolve. A theodicy seeks to explain both why there is evil in a world that is supposedly ruled by a benign God, and why this evil is unfairly distributed by a benign God, who is also supposed to be a righteous God. I doubt that there are lasting responses to this problem, but that is not the point. The point in our context is that the theodicy question can only arise when it is assumed that living a life with a disability qualifies as evil. Even though I am sometimes tempted to agree, seeing the kind of suffering that intellectual disability can afflict on families, at other times so much delight and joy is being

Jesus meets a man who was born blind. His disciples ask him why he was born that way, and Jesus answers that it was so that God's work may be revealed in him.[14] Then the question, of course, is: What is God's work that is revealed in this man? Before continuing in that line, we need a bit of background information about what is going on in the chapters of the John's Gospel that precede this story.

The story appears in the midst of on ongoing hostile confrontation between Jesus and the Pharisees in which Jesus repeatedly insists that they will not understand him unless they believe that he is from the Father. To believe him is to be enlightened by the Spirit; not to believe him is to remain in the dark. Jesus' opponents think they know God, but they fail to recognize the one God has sent for their salvation. Blindness has kept them from seeing it. This is, briefly, Jesus' posture toward his opponents, as John tells it. As he sets it up, there is clearly a dialectic between seeing and blindness, and this dialectic is played out dramatically in the story of the man born blind. Light and darkness are the opposites, and there is no third way. This is Jesus' message: "I am the light of the world; he who follows me will not walk in darkness, but will have the light of life" (John 8:12).

Throughout the Gospel of John, the Pharisees confront Jesus with questions about his credentials. He claims to be "from the Father," but there is no testimony but his own to warrant this claim. Jesus responds that his testimony would be ludicrous unless it is indeed the truth. Even though his testimony is on his own behalf, it is nonetheless valid because the Father sent him to testify.[15] Take away this validation, and all that remains is plain blasphemy. Jesus is fully aware of that. He is also aware of how his words will appear to those who do not believe him. However, he does not point to himself: "If I glorify myself, my glory is

---

shared that the overall picture changes quite radically. But leaving those impressions aside, there is the more general concern that raising the question of theodicy presupposes that God does not necessarily give the gifts we think we should be given and that disability belongs in that category. This presupposition needs to be questioned, because it dwells on the tacit assumption that disability is at odds with what people "normally" are entitled to expect from life, so that when it occurs, they are right in asking for a justification.

14. John 9:1-12; 13-34; 35-41 (quotations are from the RSV).

15. "I bear witness to myself, and the Father who sent me bears witness to me" (John 8:18).

nothing; it is my Father who glorifies me, of whom you say that he is your God" (8:54). Being sent with God's Spirit is what justifies Jesus' mission; without the Spirit, no one will be able to see the truth about him.

The story in John 9 is supposed to illuminate these connections. As Jesus walks by a man who has been blind from birth, his disciples ask him whether it was the result of the man's sin or that of his parents. The logic behind the disciples' question, suggesting that blindness must be somebody's fault, is the logic of retribution: Who committed an offense that was punishable by blindness? Jesus does not answer the question as it stands. In fact, he completely ignores the issue it raises (Can guilt be passed on from one generation to another?); instead, he puts the question in an entirely new light. The man was born blind so that God's work may be revealed in him.

As the story proceeds, it tells about Jesus' healing of the man's blindness — and how this gets both of them in trouble. Nowhere does John reiterate the initial question. Instead, he tells about how Jesus' healing of the man is once again an occasion for a hostile confrontation with the Pharisees. After the man is healed, the Pharisees interrogate him to find fault with Jesus, but without success. They then turn to the man's parents (9:18-23): "Is this your son, who you say has been born blind?"

The parents confirm that he is, but they refuse any further comment because they are also afraid of getting into trouble. The Jews had decided that whoever testified to Jesus as a man of God would be thrown out of the synagogue. Then the Pharisees turn to the healed man once again and ask him to withdraw his earlier testimony, because Jesus is a sinner (9:24-34). The man refuses, but he does not pretend to have insight into God's judgment: "Whether he is a sinner, I do not know. One thing I do know, that though I was blind, now I see" (9:25). The Pharisees want to know how Jesus healed him, but he mocks them: "I have told you already, and you would not listen. Why do you want to hear it again? Do you too want to become his disciples?" The Pharisees get angry: they are the descendants of Moses, and they have received the law and the prophets, so they should know about God. Yet nobody knows where Jesus comes from. The healed man puts them on the spot:

Why, this is a marvel! You do not know where he comes from, and yet he opened my eyes. We know that God does not listen to sinners, but if anyone is a worshiper of God and does his will, God listens to him.

324

Never since the world began has it been heard that anyone opened the eyes of a man born blind. If this man were not from God, he could do nothing. (9:30-33)

The Pharisees retort: "You were born in utter sin, and you would teach us?" (9:34). They are offended and send him away.

It is clear that this story depends heavily on the interplay of metaphor and miracle. When challenged to reject Jesus, the man testifies that he was blind but now he sees. This statement refers as much to the fact that he now recognizes who Jesus is as it does to his healing. Surely the story of how Jesus heals the blind man is intended as a miracle, something unheard of. At the same time, though, the man bears testimony to seeing Jesus for who and what he is, that is, as the one sent by the Father. In contrast, the Pharisees, who claim to know God but reject the one he has sent, are spiritually blinded. Because they do not see that Jesus was the one sent by the Father, they must remain in the dark. Had they claimed no knowledge of God, no harm would be done; but now that they have claimed to know, their rejection of the one he sent is exposed as their sin.[16] In contrast, the man born blind has come to see, not only in the sense of having received his eyesight but also in the sense of seeing the truth about Jesus. After the man has been cast out by the Pharisees, Jesus meets him again and asks whether he believes in the Son of man. The man responds by asking who that might be, whereupon Jesus answers: "It is he who speaks to you." Then the man addresses Jesus: "Lord, I believe." This confession leads Jesus to declare what is clearly the point of the story: "For judgment I came into this world, that those who do not see may see, and those who see may become blind" (9:39).

4. Seeing

The question of how the blind man reveals the work of God, I want to suggest, does not primarily have to do with healing as restoring someone's eyesight, though that clearly plays an important part in the story

---

16. "If you were blind, you would have no guilt; but now that you say, "We see!" your sin remains" (John 9:41).

as John tells it, but rather with healing as bringing to light the truth about Jesus. The crucial notion is that of seeing Jesus as the one sent by the Father. Those who accept Jesus as the one who obeys God will see; those who pretend to know God but who reject Jesus will be left in the dark. In giving his testimony of Jesus, the man reveals God's work. His confession of Jesus as Lord reveals the sin of those who claim to possess knowledge of God but nonetheless reject him. It is with regard to the Son of man that the question of our relationship with the Father is decided.

What is revealed in the blind man, then, is that faith with regard to Jesus' mission changes one's relationship with God. We should note that Jesus says about the blind man that God's work may be revealed *in him*. Jesus has been sent into the world so that those who do not see may see. This is the work that God has revealed in this blind man: he sees Jesus as the Son of man. Jesus has not only given him eyesight, which is a marvel in itself, but he has opened the man's eyes for the Spirit of God. This he could not have done, as he himself is the first to acknowledge, had not the Father sent his Spirit upon him. The healed man shows that he understands this when he says that, if Jesus were not from God, he could do nothing.

Had the Pharisees understood this, they would not have thrown this man out of the synagogue. That's why Jesus confronts them the way he does. It is very clear that the people who reject him fail to see what the man born blind accepts without hesitation, namely, that Jesus' mission does not require other testimony than that he "works the works," in this case healing the blind man. The Pharisees act as the guardians of ecclesiastical establishment; that is, they act as though they are in control of what people may expect from God. In that they don't see the truth of Jesus' mission, however, they show that they do not know God. In contrast, the man born blind does not claim any kind of significant insight into the divine will whatsoever; he simply accepts Jesus' testimony about who he is because of what he did.

We learn that the story, thus interpreted, is not primarily about the man's blindness, nor about his healing, but about his relationship with God. The former two are instrumental to the latter. The work revealed *in him* is about Jesus' role in this relationship. Once we understand this, it throws light on the mission of the blind man. He should not be seen as a sinner, nor should his disability be seen as a sign of sinfulness, either

326

his own or his parents'. Instead, he should be seen as chosen by God to shame those who reject the Son sent by the Father "to work his works." The one thing that distinguishes the blind man from his adversaries is that he raises no questions about who Jesus is, and on whose authority he acts. Nor does he show any pretension of claiming to possess knowledge of God. He never asks for Jesus' credentials; he simply puts his trust in him.

At this point I will venture an analogy between the blind man and disabled people in general, an analogy that pertains to how they are seen by those who confront them. Take Jesus' disciples, for example, who want to know about blindness in connection with sin. It is only when impairment is seen in a negative light that the question they pose before Jesus makes sense. That is, only when one assumes that the man's blindness manifests "sin" can the question arise concerning what his disability testifies to. Only then is there a need for the kind of justification the disciples are looking for. Something similar is true of the Pharisees. They rebuke the man for lecturing them on Jesus while ignoring the fact that he was born "in sin." There is no doubt in their minds that this man — or his family — stands condemned in the eyes of the Almighty.

The disciples' question and the Pharisees' rebuke are not at all alien to our own culture. Being socialized in a frame of mind that marginalizes disability, Christian people in our own culture often see disabled people in that same negative light, whether they are aware of it or not. Disabled people are certainly not supposed to teach us anything, particularly not about our relationship with God. The Gospel of John rejects this view; but it does so indirectly — in retrospect, as it were. It is only when we accept that we are the ones who need healing from blindness that we will be able to see the blind man as God sees him. In bringing out the blind man's response to Jesus, John shows how the Pharisees, in retrospect, might have understood something about their own relationship with God. This should be true for Jesus' disciples as well. What assumptions about God made them raise their question in the first place? Consequently, seeing the blind man in such a way that God's works may be revealed in him implies first knowing how to regard ourselves in that same light. The point of the analogy is that not being able to see the disabled person as God sees him puts us in the same relationship with that person as it did the Pharisees, not to mention Jesus' disciples, regarding the man born blind.

The analogy I suggest, then, is not directly concerned with the healing of people with disabilities but rather, if one wants to use that language, with the need for our own healing. This need concerns the self-images that get in the way of our friendship with God because, in relying on our own judgment about other people and about ourselves, we misunderstand God's friendship. Our own eyes must be opened for this.[17] What I wish to suggest is that the "mission in life" of people with disabilities, even profound disabilities such as Kelly and Oliver de Vinck have, is to help us do just that. That is, the crucial point is about "seeing" not only them but also — and primarily — ourselves.

In order to discern the meaning of this in practical terms, we may find it helpful to be reminded of the ways of "seeing" that have dominated the history of people with disabilities in recent times. First is the habit of stereotyping: people with disabilities tend to be seen in a negative light, usually in images tainted by imperfection and deficit. Scholars in disability studies have targeted the so-called "medical model" as a dominant source of negative stereotyping because the medical profession has a track record of approaching persons with disability as a "problem." The medical profession has regarded disability as a condition in which those afflicted are suffering from a particular pathology: it assumes that their bodies and minds don't function well compared to the functioning of "normal" human beings. Thus the medical model has been a defect model and is now widely criticized for that reason.

Later, the medical model was replaced by the social model, which viewed disability from the perspective of the behavioral sciences. Given the physical and/or mental "malfunctioning" behavior of people with disabilities, the behavioral professionals took them to be failing in adaptive skills: this explains why, particularly in the case of intellectual disabilities, the most commonly perceived problem was that they usually lack the skills to run their own lives. Therefore, scholars in disability studies have considered those trained in the medical or behavioral

---

17. When we read stories such as the one told in John 9, it is always useful to ask ourselves which of the characters in the story marks our own position in the drama. Here I have assumed our place — meaning the place of the "temporarily able-bodied" — to be the role of the Pharisees. Of course, Christians may claim not to have rejected Jesus, but that doesn't seem to be the issue here. Rather, the issue is whether we would know how to recognize the work of God as it is revealed in a disabled person.

seeing
— they are our teachers

sciences to show a propensity for seeing intellectually disabled persons as people with "special needs."

Both the medical and social models of "seeing" have been replaced. Within the last decade, social services have adopted the support model, which is committed to seeing people with disabilities as human beings with their own potential. This model believes that their lives should be given back into their own hands, and that they should receive adequate support to develop the skills enabling them to run their own lives as much as possible. The emphasis has changed from what they "cannot do" to what they "can do." The support model is backed up by a different model, the civil-rights model, which views the disabled person in yet another light, that of equal citizenship. As we have discussed in the opening chapters of this book, this model prevails in political contexts where the issue of equality and justice is pursued. People with disabilities should have every opportunity that other citizens enjoy, which includes housing, paid labor, medical treatment, recreation, and so forth.

Whether it is a medical, social, or political viewpoint, each of these contexts constitutes its own ways of seeing. However, in the last decade the tendency has been to promote a way of seeing based on self-representation. The rest of society will see people with disabilities properly when we see them the way they see themselves.

In contrast to these various models of "seeing," I would like to suggest that "seeing" within the Christian church should spring from the question of what it means to see in the light of the gospel. I would also like to suggest that the story of the man born blind shows how disabled persons may help us see ourselves properly in that light. This is their mission in life.[18] As I have repeatedly argued, the problem of thinking about disability is primarily the problem of understanding how we, the "temporarily able-bodied," regard our own lives in such a way that it throws a negative light on theirs. In order for us to learn to understand this, we need people with disabilities to be our teachers.

18. This does not mean that they have no task in pursuing a variety of other goods in their own lives. To the extent that they can be supported to develop themselves this is what they should be supported to do. What I am saying here relates to the "hyper good," the ultimate good of human being. In this they participate, irrespective of state or condition, which cannot be said of the other — more mundane — goods. They participate in God's friendship, which means, among other things, that their mission is to become "teachers" (see below).

5. Three Caveats

However, I must offer these inferences from the story in John 9 with great caution. Attempts to explain that disabled people have a particular role to play in the divine economy are usually met with suspicion, as far as their families are concerned, because those attempts continue to make them "special," which is not what they want to be. Although the "special" designation no longer casts them in negative imagery, suggestions that they are somehow special in the eyes of God are still excluding them from the rest of humanity. Therefore, before we continue, let me introduce some caveats.

Given the widespread adherence to a "hermeneutics of suspicion," it is impossible nowadays to read biblical stories about disability without raising questions about how the text construes "disability" or how it depicts a particular disability, such as blindness. An extensive literature points out that biblical images are often used to set disabled people apart and reinforce their marginalization. Therefore, my first caveat is that we need to ask how a blind person reads the story in John 9. "Blindness" and "healing" are major themes, both in how John tells the story and how I read it. My own reading translates what Jesus says about the blind man into a question of theological perspective ("seeing as"). How does that make a blind person feel?

John Hull, who is blind himself and an emeritus professor of theology at Birmingham University (UK), answers this question directly.[19] From his own experience as a reader of the Gospel of John, Hull reports that the imagery of light and darkness and of seeing and blindness that informs the scene in John 9 caused him to feel abandoned. He notes several texts in which Jesus is reported to have spoken about blindness as a kind of ignorance; this, says Hull, feeds on existing prejudices about blind people. For example, he takes the story of the encounter between Jesus and John the Baptist from the Gospel of Luke. John asks Jesus whether he is the Savior, and Jesus answers that the blind have received their sight, the deaf can hear, the dead are raised, and blessed is he who takes no offense (Luke 7:22-23). Hull comments:

19. John M. Hull, "How I Discovered My Blind Brother," in *The Bible in Transmission: A Forum for Change in Church and Culture* (London: Bible Society, Spring, 2004), pp. 9-11; see www.johnmhull.biz.

Perhaps there are blind Christians like myself who have become con-
scious of the negative implications of such miracle stories. However,
no matter on which side of the abyss dividing blind and sighted people you may be, the saying retains its force: blessed is the one who
takes no offence. But I wondered, how can I not take offence? You
misunderstand my lifestyle, you use my state as a term of reproach
and you think I have nothing to offer at feasts and parties![20]

Hull is not impressed by the rejoinder that these sayings about blindness are to be read metaphorically, because the metaphor could not
work unless it was based on a shared perception of how blind people
behave. Therefore, Hull claims, "Jesus as a sighted prophet often at-
tacks the vanities of the sighted world but at the same time he shares
many of the prevailing attitudes."[21]

Although I do not mean to belittle the experience of feeling excluded by language that feeds on prejudice, I do not think that in this
particular case Hull's conceptualization of "sightedness" is correct.
The fact that the eyes of a blind person are shut out from light does not
at all imply that this person cannot see. Various expressions support
this point. People are guided by "the light of reason"; we can "illuminate" our reasoning with an analogy; someone can appear to us as an
"enlightened mind." In each case, the person can be blind in a physical
sense and yet actually see in an intellectual and spiritual sense. In fact, I
suspect that there are numerous occasions on which Hull has used the
expression "I see your point." The blindness of which Jesus speaks is
blindness as a mental state. Regarding the Pharisees, this refers to their
understanding as blurred: their "mind's eye," if you will, fails to see
what he is telling them.[22] The claim that the story is about that kind of

20. Hull, "How I Discovered," p. 10.

21. Hull, "How I Discovered," p. 11.

22. There is an aspect of Hull's paper that I find hard to sympathize with, but it does
not have much to do with the theme of blindness. He tells us how he has overcome his
alienation from the biblical texts he discusses, namely, by focusing on the fact that Jesus
himself has shared the experience of being barred from sight at the time of his trial. Not
only was he blindfolded, but he also lost the sight of daylight when the sun eclipsed at
Calvary. Hull comments: "Since I discovered the blind or the blindfolded Christ my attitudes have changed . . . . He leads me, not as a sighted savior but as a blind brother" ("How
I Discovered," p. 11). Like Eiesland, Hull also takes a particular experience as determining legitimate appropriation of theological speech (see Ch. 5). In his case, this is con-

blindness is bolstered by how Jesus defines his own mission: he is there to carry out God's judgment so that those who do not see may see, and those who see may become blind. Clearly, the focal point of the story is about either being enlightened by the Spirit or remaining cast in the darkness of self-righteousness.

This rejoinder to Hull's essay does not answer wider-ranging questions about the uses and abuses of biblical language, of course, but I do think that there is more to what Hull calls "the metaphorical defense" than he wishes to accept. It is true, first of all, that the use of metaphor presupposes a basis of similarity. For example, there is a sense in which "foothills" reminds us of "foot." However, its *metaphorical* use depends on a change of context, and thus depends on difference. This is, in fact, amusingly played out in John's story of the man born blind: after Jesus' verdict on the Pharisees, they ask, in apparent confusion, "We aren't blind, are we?" It is only because of Jesus' metaphorical use of blindness that his response can give yet another twist to its meaning: "If you were blind, you would not have sin. But now that you say, 'We see,' your sin remains" (John 9:41).[23]

Second, however, is it really true, as Hull says, that Jesus' language of blindness only works as a metaphor because of a shared conception of how blind people behave? It does not appear so. Nowhere in these passages do we see Pharisees and Jews "behaving" in ways that remind me of blind people; nor do I see them behaving in ways that do not remind me of blind people. There is simply no connection. In fact, the language of "seeing" referring to mental states is not metaphorical at all: it refers to a different way of seeing. The images I see in my mind are properly seen, only not with my eyes.

But there is yet another reason for caution in putting people with disabilities in a position that ascribes special meaning to their condition, which also relates to the experience of disability — but now in a different key. I have often heard parents of disabled children scorn

---

cerned primarily with the appropriation of biblical language. That is, biblical language referring to blindness is interpreted legitimately to the extent that it reflects the experience of blind people.

23. I take the first clause, "If you were blind," to indicate the perception of their own spiritual blindness, so that Jesus in fact tells them that if they knew their sins, they would no longer be blind but would see the truth about Jesus, and hence their sin would be forgiven.

those who attempt to answer the question of what it means that their child is disabled. "Meaning" is not a subject these parents can spare their energy or time to engage, and they do not think highly of those who do. Obviously, there is good reason for skepticism: things may go very wrong when families are told that their disabled sibling is a blessing, or that she is a special gift of God, or that sharing their lives with her must be an enriching experience. As I observed in Chapter 1, it takes credentials to speak or write about these matters. Very often these things are said by the wrong people at the wrong time. This is the case whenever what such people do does not match what they say. When Jesus tells his disciples that the man has been born blind so that the work of God may be revealed, he immediately adds: "We must work the works of him who sent me while it is day."[24] In other words, true knowledge of God goes with keeping his word. Saying that a disabled life is a blessing can be utterly false and deceitful when one does not underwrite it with an act of friendship.

This is particularly true with regard to suffering. Parents know when their children suffer. The sight of a child with severe epileptic convulsions, for example, is horrible, and parents cannot witness it without feeling the anxiety and panic in their own bodies. Statements about "blessings" or "gifts" become lies when others make them so that the pain does not get under their own skin. That is, statements about disabled lives revealing the works of God, if they are not embedded in acts of compassion, are self-referential contradictions. *Pia fraus sed fraus.*

This does not mean that it is inappropriate to think of the life of a disabled child as a gift. Many wonderful stories about people sharing their lives with a disabled person use words such as "enrichment," "blessing," and "gift." When spoken in truth, such words reflect experience.[25] They are spoken truly by people who have acquired the skills to

24. "You say 'He is our God' though you do not know him. But I know him; if I would say that I do not know him, I would be a liar like you. But I do know him and I keep his word" (John 8:55).

25. There are many examples of such stories, some of whose outstanding titles are: Christopher de Vinck, *The Power of the Powerless* (Grand Rapids: Zondervan, 1988); Donald J. Meyer, ed., *Uncommon Fathers: Reflections on Raising a Child with a Disability* (Bethesda, MD: Woodbine House, 1995); Kenzaburo Oe, *A Healing Family* (Tokyo: Kodansha International, 1996). A wide range of brief stories has recently been published in Stan-

see the disabled person in such a light that her presence does appear as a blessing. Such statements must not be intended as moral claims about how disabled persons *should* be viewed. They should not claim a moral obligation. That is, they are not properly declared as a premise in an argument about how to think morally about the lives of disabled people. It is only appropriate for those who do in fact participate in the task of "working the works" to speak of blessing. Therefore, those who believe that the meaning of disabled lives is that God's works may be revealed in them must be prepared to take up their part in making these works visible.

My third caveat is closely related: it is about repentance. Given who we are as human beings and what our lives are like, many of us are not very good at taking up our share of "working the works." For my part, I find it much easier to write about people with intellectual disabilities than to spend time with them. This is just another way in which speaking Jesus' words from the John 9 story can turn into a lie, which happens whenever we speak those words without confessing our own sin. The Gospel of John epitomizes Jesus' confrontation with the Pharisees in which he says precisely that: the Pharisees will not be able to witness how God's work is revealed in the blind man because they are incapable of recognizing their blindness to the one who works God's work. If they were capable of confessing their sin of this "blindness," their eyes would be opened and they would see — as the blind man does.

The second and third of these caveats, particularly, may point us in the right direction in determining what we may gain from the story of the man born blind. Much, if not all, depends on where we think we are "located" as hearers of John's story. What characters in the story do we identify ourselves with? I suggest that we identify with those who fail to see because of their arrogance and condescension: being well accomplished and successful prevents them from seeing the truth about themselves. The reason to identify with them lies partly in our disposition to see people with intellectual disabilities in a negative light and partly in our disposition to see ourselves in a positive light. "Seeing"

---

ley D. Klein and Kim Schive, eds., *You Will Dream New Dreams: Inspiring Personal Stories by Parents of Children with Disabilities* (New York: Kensington Books, 2001). For a discussion of this literature, see my *The Future of the Disabled in Liberal Society: An Ethical Analysis* (Notre Dame, IN: University of Notre Dame Press, 2000), pp. 175-92.

both ourselves and the disabled person in the light of the gospel does not come easily.

Finally, I suggest that these considerations also answer, to some extent, the problem of biblical language that Hull and others have addressed. This problem would not exist if most Christians contradicted the prejudices about people with disabilities instead of reinforcing them. Unfortunately, we cannot say that they do, and this may very much depend on a misconception of their "location" in God's story. Appropriate seeing — of the kind that the Pharisees are lacking, according to John — would result in Christians' witnessing to the fact that Jesus' "blindness" language is viciously abused when it is used to rebuke physically blind people. The same holds true, of course, for people with other disabilities.

6. Being With

Like most people in our present culture, Christians do not seem particularly comfortable with relating to humans with intellectual disabilities. The presence of such persons in the life of congregations in the church is seldom a matter of course, nor is their participation explicitly welcomed.[26] If they are welcomed, it usually happens by way of ignoring their impairment, as if it did not exist. Similar to life in society in general, it is safe to say that church life is influenced by social stigma. Therefore, seeing disabled people as members of God's church continues to be the exception rather than the rule.[27]

Among the noteworthy exceptions are the communities of L'Arche. The first of these communities was founded in France in 1964 by Jean Vanier. Vanier chose to share his life with two men who came to his home after having stayed for years in a mental hospital. Together they founded the first L'Arche community in the village of Trosly. During the past forty years, similar communities have been founded in all parts of

26. See Brett Webb-Mitchell, *Unexpected Guests at God's Banquet: Welcoming People with Disabilities into the Church* (New York: Crossroad, 1994).

27. The times I have asked ministers and pastors about members of their congregations who are disabled, the most frequent response is, "We don't have them." The question of how pastoral care is administered to people with disabilities is usually answered with a reference to local service-providers.

the world: their aim is to live a life of sharing the friendship of God with one another, and their stories tell us what it means to be part of a community that has chosen to live this kind of life.[28] These stories testify to how persons with intellectual disabilities become "teachers" in bringing people closer to themselves by bringing them closer to God. They show how one needs to see the truth about oneself in order to really understand what it means to be loved by God.

The most important thing to understand about the community houses of L'Arche is that they are shaped by choosing to *be with* the disabled before *doing something for* them.[29] "Being with" is the expression for the act of sharing one's life with somebody because one has chosen to be with that person.

> This is the challenge of L'Arche. It can be professionally interesting and profitable for someone to work with handicapped people as a teacher or a therapist. But who will live with them if they have no family or if they cannot get on with the family? And particularly, who will create a relationship with those who are severely handicapped and what happens if the relationship is not immediately rewarding and gratifying? Who will be prepared to accept anger, violence or depression, hoping that under all the confusion and darkness lies the light of the person? Who will believe and trust in him more than they believe and trust in themselves?[30]

The difference between "doing for" and "being with" marks the crucial distinction between what professionals in social services do for the disabled and what the people of the L'Arche communities intend to do: it is the distinction between professional intervention and personal pres-

---

28. *The Challenge of L'Arche,* intro. and concl. by Jean Vanier (London: Darton, Longman & Todd, 1982); Vanier, *Our Journey Home: Rediscovering a Common Humanity Beyond Our Differences* (Maryknoll, NY: Orbis Books, 1997); Vanier, *Community and Growth,* rev. ed. (New York: Paulist Press, 1989). A well-known source is also the work of Henry Nouwen; see his posthumously published *Adam: God's Beloved* (Maryknoll, NY: Orbis Books, 1997); *Henri Nouwen: Writings Selected,* ed. and intro. Robert A. Jonas (Maryknoll, NY: Orbis Books, 1998); Nouwen, "The Road to Daybreak," in *Spiritual Journals* (New York: Continuum, 1998), pp. 292-448.

29. Jean Vanier, *Community and Growth,* p. 11 [page number references in parentheses in the text are to this work].

30. Vanier, "Conclusion," *The Challenge of L'Arche,* p. 260.

ence. What stands out in this distinction is that "being with" is not inspired by professional goals of improvement. It is the intention of the professional who provides services to improve someone's condition: that person has acquired certain skills for certain specific tasks in order to be qualified for the job. The people of L'Arche do not define themselves by this kind of division of roles: they usually identify the people with disabilities in their community as "members," and they identify the others as "assistants." One's task as an assistant is to be with the members of the community, especially at times when things are not going well.

Vanier, unlike many other voices in theology, is not inclined to romanticize "community" in any way. The L'Arche communities are communities of the Cross: they are places where people learn to accept their own brokenness (p. 37). The more the community pretends to be at peace with one another, the more pent-up anger and fear there is. But community does not survive falsehood; it begins where these angers and fears are admitted and forgiven. "As long as we refuse to accept that we are a mixture of light and darkness," says Vanier, "we will continue to divide the world into enemies and friends" (p. 35). When people can accept their own weaknesses and flawed characters, they can ask for forgiveness and accept the weaknesses and flaws of others (p. 35). Not because of their strength but because of this sharing of the truth about themselves, such communities can become communities of healing; that is, because they realize to be communities of the Cross, they can become communities of the Resurrection.

This raises the question of what distinguishes the role of an assistant in a L'Arche community from that of a professional working for a service-provider. What kinds of skills does one need, or what kinds of qualifications are required for healing a disabled person from the suffering of not being loved? This practical question brings out how the distinction between "intervention" and "presence" does its work.

> The handicapped person needs a warm, friendly, dynamic milieu where he or she can grow and develop. To create this type of atmosphere means essentially to create authentic relationships, which are a source of security. If the handicapped person needs people who can do things for him, if he needs qualified educators, it is also vital for him to have people who are happy just to live and be with them, who

are ready to commit themselves to a lasting relationship, which becomes a deep friendship and a source of hope.[31]

The challenge of L'Arche is to be the kind of community where these things can happen; but it does not come easy for them to actually happen. Community life is difficult, according to Vanier, because it takes more than a sufficient dose of energy, good will, and a noble ideal to commit oneself to a lasting friendship that can be a source of hope. The skills required are of an unusual kind. In general, the required skills can be divided in a way that parallels the earlier distinction between two kinds of "good." Apart from the variety of goods people pursue in their lives, there is the "hyper good," which is the ultimate good that makes for human fulfillment. Similarly, assistants need the skills to help members go through their daily routines — clothing, feeding, toileting, and so on — so that they can pursue their daily activities. Apart from these skills, however, there is a special one of another kind: this skill that turns out to be crucial to "being with" is the "hyper skill," so to speak, and it has to do with self-knowledge.

An account that is instructive is the one presented by Odile Ceyrac, a French woman who joined the first L'Arche community in Trosly and was called to assist Vanier in his leadership. Describing the spiritual journey of living in this L'Arche community, she mentions a discovery that everyone who comes to L'Arche makes. In the language of the beatitudes often used by the people of L'Arche, Ceyrac speaks of persons with intellectual disabilities as "the poor."[32]

> The poor bring us to the discovery of our weakness, limitations, mental blocks, prejudices and handicaps. When we come to live in community with mentally handicapped people, we often feel we have to prove ourselves and show that we are someone. We need to be "successful." In fact, we are hiding our fragility behind the barriers of success. It is difficult to accept the challenge that our encounter with the handicapped person gives us. We have to pass through many trials before we are able to recognize that it is more often an attitude of

31. Odile Ceyrac, "The Poor at the Heart of Our Communities," in *The Challenge of L'Arche*, pp. 25-26.
32. Thomas Philippe, O.P., "Communities of the Beatitudes," in *The Challenge of L'Arche*, pp. 37-50.

domination behind our coming to be with the handicapped people, than a desire to listen. The discovery of this truth about ourselves implies a real stripping. The handicapped person has already lived through this stripping. If we cannot accept this, if we cannot accept our fragilities and handicaps as they are revealed to us, then we will probably not be able to live very long in community with our handicapped brothers and sisters.[33]

The most important and most difficult thing, Ceyrac indicates, is to learn to see *oneself* in truth. Given the reality that persons with intellectual disabilities confront us with, this truth is about limitation, about fear, sometimes even about disgust. Most of all, it is about learning to see one's own brokenness. However, the most striking thing about Ceyrac's account, an example that could be multiplied many times,[34] is the lack of any self-congratulatory confidence in good deeds done. The dominant theme of the spiritual journey that Ceyrac describes has little to do with becoming a "virtuous" person; it is all about getting rid of false pretences.

I take the key sentence in her account to be that persons with intellectual disabilities are far more experienced than any one of us, the "temporarily able-bodied," in standing naked before others, in their case not only spiritually, but all too often physically as well. They are used to standing in front of others as beings whose lives are deemed deplorable and whose accomplishments go unrecognized because they are measured by the standards of "normality." Since most of the assistants have been socialized in cultures that buy into the same standards, it is likely that they embody these standards as well. In any case, Ceyrac suggests that most people coming to L'Arche have to discover that their own virtuous motives often betray a hidden sense of superiority. That is, all too often the assistants also presuppose that human beings with intellectual disabilities are "receivers" by definition, that is, they approach the disabled person as being in the position of receiving what others have to give. According to Ceyrac, this is the attitude that needs to be exposed. The logic underlying her point, we should notice, is

33. Ceyrac, "The Poor at the Heart of Our Communities," pp. 34-35.

34. I will add three other examples from *The Challenge of L'Arche:* Hubert Allier, "A Place for Growth,"p. 54; Claire de Miribel, "Growth towards Covenant," pp. 72-73; Pat and Jo Lenon, "A Place for a Family," pp. 86-88.

based on the reversal of giving and receiving. If sharing one's life with a disabled person is motivated by ideals of communal life, or seeking to be a good person, or making the world a better place, or anything of that nature, then the truth is that one's motives are self-serving. They are inspired by the desire to be good. Ceyrac suggests that, if that is the case, the lesson to be learned is this: one is not offering much to the disabled person, because one is approaching the person with the presumption that having something to offer is what counts. Learning what it takes "to be with," Ceyrac explains, requires abandoning that presumption. The presumption is false because it assumes that giving is prior to receiving.

In a similar vein, Vanier informs us about the many young people who come to L'Arche to find something, to become acquainted with its spirituality, to discover a life that approaches their ideals. All these may be important objectives, but they are not about community. "If we come into community without knowing that the reason we come is to learn to forgive and be forgiven seven times seventy-seven times, we will soon be disappointed" (p. 37). Community does not live on the basis of ideals, nor does it live from what its members think they should be. "The hope of a community is founded on the acceptance and love of ourselves and others *as we really are*" (p. 40; italics added). For a community that aims at "being with," it is essential that its people learn to face the truth about themselves.

7. No Hiding in Strength

In order to learn how to be this kind of community, Vanier explains, L'Arche embodies a particular vision. It is constituted by a group of people, he says, "who have left their own milieu to live with others under the same roof, and work from a new vision of human beings and their relationships with each other and with God" (p. 17). What does this "new vision" entail?

Allow me to try to answer this question with the help of Henri Nouwen, a Dutch pastoral theologian who left his position at Harvard University to become the pastor of Daybreak, a L'Arche community in Toronto. While he was at Daybreak, Nouwen met Adam, a profoundly disabled youngster who, as it turned out, became his closest friend.

When Adam died at the age of thirty-one, Nouwen wrote a book about their friendship.[35] He had been planning to write a commentary on the Apostles' Creed; but, instead of writing a theological treatise, he wrote about his friendship with Adam and explained how their time together changed his relationship with both God and with himself. According to Nouwen, the story was "probably as close as I will ever come to writing about the Apostles' Creed" (p. 17). In many ways, Nouwen's book is an exact illustration of Vanier's and Ceyrac's accounts of what being with disabled people at L'Arche entails.

The relationship between Nouwen and Adam begins when the former is asked to help Adam through his daily morning routine, which means waking him up, bathing him, clothing him, shaving him, brushing his teeth, feeding him, getting him in his wheelchair and into his daily program. Until coming to L'Arche, Nouwen had been a widely published professor of pastoral theology, and he is aghast: "I don't know the man. I'm not a nurse. I have no training in this kind of thing!" In point of fact, he is afraid of Adam. But, without his realizing it, the source of his fear is something else: he is afraid of making mistakes because he does not want to make a fool of himself. "I didn't want to be the source of embarrassment" (p. 42). In hindsight, Nouwen clearly sees what was troubling him in working with Adam.

> In those early days, I saw him as someone who was very different from me. I did not have any expectation that we would communicate because he [Adam] did not talk. The frequent interruptions of his breathing by moments of silence made me wonder if he would be able to take the next breath. He sometimes flailed with his hands, and intertwined his fingers in and out, which made me think something was bothering him, but I had no idea what it might be. When I walked with him, I had to get behind him and support him with my body and my arms. I worried constantly that he would trip on my feet, fall and hurt himself. I was also conscious that he could have a grand mal seizure at any moment: sitting in the bathtub, on the toilet, eating his breakfast, resting, walking, or being shaved. (p. 43)

35. Nouwen, *Adam: God's Beloved* [page number references in parentheses in the text are to this book]. Nouwen did not live to finish this book; he died seven months after Adam was buried. Nouwen's book was edited and posthumously published by Sue Mosteller, a senior member of the Daybreak community who was named literary executrix in Henri's will.

Nouwen could not see Adam as a human being created in the divine image, because he regarded him as "very different." Actually, he resented his assignment to be Adam's assistant, wondering why he had to spend his precious time with "this stranger." The answer he received — "So you can get to know Adam" — was not in the least convincing: he doubted that there was anything to be known (p. 44).[36] "I wondered if he even recognized me. How could I get to know him? What, I asked myself, was he thinking, was he feeling, was he sensing?" Being encouraged to hang in there, Nouwen tried to master the morning routine, but it still did not make much sense to him.

What is interesting in this account of the first stage of their relationship is that Adam remained "hidden" from Nouwen because of how he was perceived. Nouwen considered being Adam's assistant a distraction from what he "really" was meant to do. Each morning after Adam went off to his daycare program, Nouwen felt "a deep relief" in starting with his own work, "doing what I can do well: talking, dictating letters, counseling, making phone calls, leading meetings, giving sermons, presiding over ceremonies. That was the world where I felt at ease and capable" (p. 45). In other words, Nouwen was hiding himself in his strength. He did not want to be exposed in his anxiety of not knowing how to relate to Adam. As a result, he failed to "see" Adam.

The change came when Nouwen finally opened up and was ready to meet Adam, which was when he recognized his own misconceptions. His world had been exclusively about words, books, and papers. Now a person was confronting him, a complete stranger, with the vulnerability of his body. "Being close to Adam's body brought me close to Adam. I was slowly getting to know him" (p. 46). A very important learning experience was Adam's resistance to Nouwen's pushing him through the early morning routine because Nouwen wanted to get back behind his desk.

> Right here I learned that Adam could communicate! He let me know that I wasn't being really present to him and was more concerned about my schedule than about his. A few times when I was so pushy he responded by having a grand mal seizure, and I realized it was his

---

36. Here we are reminded of the ancient hymn in Philippians 2, where it says that God did not consider it a degradation to become human. Nouwen's account testifies that this was indeed the underlying question in his struggle with being Adam's assistant.

way of saying, "Slow down, Henri! Slow down." Well, it certainly slowed me down! A seizure so completely exhausted him that I had to stop everything I was doing and let him rest. Sometimes if it was a bad one, I brought him back to his bed and covered him with many blankets to keep him from shivering violently. Adam was communicating with me, and he was consistent in reminding me that he wanted and needed me to be with him unhurriedly and gently. He was clearly asking me if I was willing to follow his rhythm and adapt my ways to his needs. I found myself beginning to understand a new language, Adam's language. (p. 47)

Nouwen's appreciation of his daily time with Adam gradually changed. What had been a two-hour delay before he could get to what he believed was his prime task changed into a time of contemplation. Nouwen began to converse with Adam, telling him about his thoughts and worries, or just chatting away about the day's events. He began to see Adam's presence differently, not merely as incommunicability but as peacefulness.

> I thought of him as a silent peaceful presence in the center of my life. Sometimes when I was anxious, irritated, or frustrated about something that wasn't happening well enough or fast enough, Adam came to mind and seemed to call me back to the stillness at the eye of the cyclone. The tables were turning. Adam was becoming *my* teacher, taking *me* by the hand, walking with me in my confusion through the wilderness of *my* life. (p. 48)

This change of perspective taught Nouwen things about himself he had never known before. For example, it taught him to pay attention to his own body as the source of his own being, and this enabled him to see the beauty of ordinary life. Adam taught him to see that the truth of words is "in the flesh." So, instead of caring for a human being very different from himself, Nouwen became a friend of Adam, and it made him realize that in Adam's presence he had found what he had been looking for all his life: "love, friendship, community, and a deep sense of belonging" (p. 49).

The moment Nouwen realized what had happened to him came when a former friend visited him at Daybreak. As it turned out, the friend had come only to rebuke him for leaving his academic career at

Harvard. He said: "Leave this work for those who are trained to do it. Don't waste your time here, you have better things to do." It was then that Nouwen understood the importance of "seeing." He quickly realized that his friend was not seeing Adam as he saw him. "What my friend was saying made sense to him because he didn't really 'see' Adam, and he certainly wasn't prepared to get to know him" (p. 53). Nouwen also realized that this friend could only see Adam's incapacities that made him "very different" from the rest of us, just as Nouwen had seen him when he became Adam's assistant. Adam, of course, had remained exactly the same; Nouwen was the one who had changed since that time. His daily hours with Adam had been a transforming experience for him: "My relationship with Adam was giving me new eyes to see and new ears to hear. I was being changed much more than I ever anticipated" (pp. 53-54).[37] He came to understand that, in this bond of friendship between the two of them, God's Spirit was present. It was "God's event among people." Nouwen had asked himself numerous times how Adam could relate to God. Could he pray? Could he know God? Now he understood that these are "questions from below," questions that reflect our anxiety rather than God's love (p. 55).

By contrast, God's questions — the questions "from above" — were quite different: "Can you let Adam lead you into prayer? Can you believe that I am in deep communion with Adam and that his life is a prayer?" (p. 55). Such questions presupposed the complete irrelevance in God's eyes of any comparison between people with and people without disabilities. God has no need of comparisons between people; nor did Adam. He had neither the ability nor the need to rank people according to what they can do. According to Nouwen, Adam "simply lived and by his life invited me to receive his unique gift, wrapped in weakness but given for my transformation." He testifies further: "Adam couldn't produce anything, had no fame to be proud of, and couldn't brag of any award or trophy. But by his very life, he was the most radical witness to the truth of our lives that I have ever encountered" (p. 56).

I read Nouwen's account as a powerful witness to what the "new way of seeing" that Vanier speaks of and that is embodied in L'Arche is all

---

37. On the theme of transformation, see also my *The Future of the Disabled in Liberal Society*, Ch. 11 (see n. 25 above). Of the literature mentioned there, see some of the stories in *Uncommon Fathers: Reflections on Raising a Child with a Disability*.

about. This new way separates those who do see from those who do not see, and the thing that separates them is the capacity of discerning the gift of Adam's presence. Most "normal" people, Nouwen says, "saw Adam as a disabled person who had little to give, and who was mainly a burden to his family, his community, and to society at large. As long as he was seen that way, his truth was hidden. What was not received was not given" (p. 31).[38] For those who have been transformed, the truth of the matter is very different: Adam's presence enlightened them, Nouwen says. It made them comprehend that "we, like him, are also precious, graced, and beloved children of God, whether we see ourselves as rich or poor, intelligent or disabled, good-looking or unattractive" (p. 31). Thus, Adam's presence in their lives enabled them "to recognize something of God's unconditional love." It brought them closer to themselves and led them gently to those inner spaces they preferred not to look at: "In relationship with him we would discover a deeper, truer identity" (p. 31).

8. Moments of Wonder

Nouwen's testimony thus eloquently explains what Vanier has in mind when he talks about seeing the disabled person in a new relationship to ourselves and to God. Seeing truthfully means understanding the reversal of the order of giving and receiving. To presume that one has something to offer to the disabled person, and to presume that this is the point of relating to that person, is to be forgetful of one's own primordial need for being healed.

It is important to note once again that this "new way of seeing" that Vanier talks about is not a prescription for moral virtue. L'Arche is not at all about "ethics" in the traditional sense of defending an account of growing in virtue; that is, it is not about what kind of people Vanier thinks we ought to be. Instead, it is about accepting the truth about the realities that govern our lives. Most striking in his account of what this means is the logic of how the spiritual journey of being with disabled

---

38. With his wonderful phrase, Nouwen completes the reversal of giving and receiving. It is not only that, theologically speaking, receiving is prior to giving, but also — and more profoundly — that if we don't know how to receive, we necessarily lose the capacity to see the gift we have been given.

persons actually works: it is in the mirror of their relationship with these persons that the assistants of L'Arche renew their relationship with God.

Of course, there are those whose persistent determination to do good blocks them from being led in this journey. What usually happens in these cases is that people become disappointed because of their lack of success. And the blame for the "failure" often falls on the disabled person for failing to be cooperative. Having frustrated the assistant's desire for moral perfection, the person with disabilities is said to be "difficult," "demanding," even "aggressive," the kind of language that is used to keep the disabled person at a distance. According to Nouwen's account, however, one may expect this language from people who are unclear about their own motives. Like many others, Nouwen himself could not see the condescension in his denying that he could get Adam through his morning routine. He also saw Adam as being merely at the receiving end of their relationship. But once he made the discovery that that wasn't true, it turned out to be a salutary truth.

At this very point, all the accounts of the L'Arche spiritual journey that I have seen take the same amazing turn. We find it in Nouwen's account, where he speaks of Adam in his capacity as his "teacher," and we also find it in Ceyrac's account of the spiritual journey:

> In the life we share together, we soon discover that they are our "teachers"; they give us more than we can ever give them, in terms of acceptance of our human condition, in the discovery of what is essential in our lives. This is a terribly demanding discovery. Frequently we want to flee from it. We need to be stimulated and encouraged, on a personal as well as on a communal level, in order to live it. The first moments of wonder in our encounter with the handicapped person have to be nourished and deepened.[39]

The "first moments of wonder" are those when the assistant begins to see that the disabled person may lead her with greater openness to what is essential. Those who are supposedly in need of healing become healers themselves. This reversal of roles entails the most important lesson from the L'Arche stories. The most important thing is not knowing how to love those who need our assistance, but knowing how to let God's

39. Ceyrac, "The Poor at the Heart of Our Communities," p. 27.

love unmask the pretension of our self-seeking motives. Seeing oneself in truth is the hard part, but it is nonetheless essential. There is a profound reason why people with intellectual disabilities may become our teachers: living their imperfections is what intellectually disabled people have been doing all their lives.

> They can help and heal us; they can peel away our illusions and masks and thus they can liberate us. Little by little, they can lead us to greater inner freedom. It is important for the handicapped person that we are free in our relationships with him.[40]

Therefore, the wondrous moment is the moment we discover the reality of God's friendship, not in the fullness but in the brokenness of our own lives. The experience that the disabled person is leading in this discovery is the reason why her presence is seen in the light of the beatitudes. Vanier makes this claim in a way that reverently sums up the spiritual journey:

> Each of our L'Arche communities has experienced men and women, who are chaotic, broken and spiritually dead, evolving — after years in a big institution — into men and women of peace and light. These are not mere words. We have all seen the dead rise. It has happened before our eyes and in our homes. This has told us something about the depth, vulnerability and capacities of the human heart.[41]

"We have all seen the dead rise." This is why the communities of L'Arche are in a profound way communities of witness. They do not seek their power in strength, because they know from experience that it will not result in lasting friendships. Nor do they revel in language of weakness, such as appears in the claims that all of us are disabled in some sense. That language easily falls into the trap of sentimentality, because it suggests that we, the "temporarily able-bodied," must not elevate ourselves above the disabled, thereby implicitly assuming the moral task of "lowering" ourselves. Nor are the people of L'Arche tempted by endearing talk of "dependency," as if it were a moral virtue to embrace. Instead, there is a strong sense of realism guiding the sto-

40. Ceyrac, "The Poor at the Heart of Our Communities," p. 35.
41. Vanier, "Conclusion," p. 259.

ries of L'Arche that appears in their insistence on being truthful about themselves.

What does it take to see disabled people in such a way that God's works may be revealed in them? To sum up the answer I have explored in this chapter, I want to conclude with a few lines by Sue Mosteller, who has spent many years in the service of L'Arche's Daybreak community in Toronto. Her account of her experiences in sharing her life with disabled persons says it all.

> For me the quiet moments spent in God's presence at the beginning and at the end of each day are essential. These moments of silence in the presence of Jesus are necessary in order to try to integrate all the beauty and all the pain. And I feel so small. I am learning, however, that it is essentially in knowledge of my inability to look at the other, in my disappointment at my own reactions in a crisis, in my resentments and my harsh judgments that Jesus, the author of love, can touch me, can teach me, can heal me. In these precious moments, I learn to believe more deeply in the essential mystery underlying "blessed are the poor." I believe it, not because I live with handicapped people, the poor, but because I myself am so poor, so close to my limits, and at the same time so blessed in believing that I am a child of God, called to live with brothers and sisters, who journey together towards the Father.[42]

The people of L'Arche are remarkable people, not because of their moral achievement but because of the way they have probed the gospel as it speaks to us in stories such as the one in John 9. They know that there is no refuge in the illusion of strength. Instead, they have learned to see that "being with" persons with intellectual disabilities enables them to enjoy God's friendship. Aquinas puts it this way: "It is specifically the same act whereby we love God, and whereby we love our neighbor."[43]

The gift of friendship is received as a gift for the sake of our own person, as all true friendship is. God does not love us in order to get something from us. Likewise, we do not extend friendship in order to get something from the other, because the result would not be friend-

---

42. Sue Mosteller, "Living With," in *The Challenge of L'Arche*, p. 22.
43. Aquinas, *Summa Theologica*, II, II, 25, 1.

ship but self-love. Therefore, as a sincere response to God, we extend friendship to the other person for her own sake. This is the reason why receiving the other as a gift from God has nothing to do with using the other only as a means. As the discussion above has suggested, the gift cannot be properly received without a transformation of the self, which exposes the self-seeking motive of "giving." In other words, one cannot reap the fruits of friendship if one's friendship is a means to another, external goal. Friendship is its own reward.

Finally, these reflections complete the answer to the question that concluded the preceding chapter: How do human beings with profound disabilities participate in God's friendship as the ultimate good of their lives? First, they participate in the freedom of being who they are and what they are without any need for further justification. Second, they participate in God's friendship in that they reap the fruits of the friendship we learn to extend to them insofar as we know how to have ourselves transformed by their presence in our lives.

Chapter Ten

Learning to Become Friends

I felt utterly trustful that things were under control, though no control of mine. I was willing to bet that between them, Adam and the Being of Love probably had some kind of plan. Whatever it was, I was in for the duration.

Martha Beck

1. Introduction

Having taken the quest for a Christian understanding of profoundly disabled human beings all the way to the inner life of the triune God, I have taken as my task in Part III of this book to think through the ethical implications. Immanuel Kant notoriously rejected the doctrine of the Trinity as being entirely irrelevant for any practical concern, because, as he said, that doctrine — if at all comprehensible — does not provide one with any practical rule by which to conduct one's life, regardless of whether one believes in a deity of three or of ten persons.[1] Well, the truth of the matter has turned out differently. The call to share one's life with a profoundly disabled person will not be properly heard unless one is prepared to receive the presence of that person as a gift from God. Knowing how to receive that gift, however, is the subject matter of a spiritual journey of transformation. This is a practical rule to

---

1. Immanuel Kant, "Der Streit der Fakultäten," in Kant, *Werke, Band IV* (Darmstadt: WBG, 1983), pp. 303-4.

Why friendship rather than sonship?,
God father
John — Power to become children of God
X born of God

conduct one's life, as we have seen, that will offer guidance on this journey and that will increase one's joy in God's friendship. Kant could not have seen this task as "ethical," of course, if only because his moral philosophy defined ethics as pertaining to moral duty, and moral duty as pertaining to our dealings with reasonable human beings.[2]

I introduced the ethical question, the reader will recall, in Chapter 3 as the question of the ultimate good of human being. The answer we have been pursuing was shaped by the notion of friendship, not just friendship in general, but God's friendship as it is extended to human beings in the divine act of unconditional self-giving. Referring to the witness of L'Arche, I have described the journey of learning how to receive this gift as a prerequisite for friendship with human beings who differ from us at what is seen as the innermost core of our being. From a Christian perspective, God's friendship is crucial to the moral life because of our belief that the final end of our existence is to be reunited with God: friendship is the proper name of this reunion. The theological warrant for this claim is that the Christian story of God is about the promise that he will not abandon his creation, even when his creatures, for one reason or another, do not know how to find him. To restore us to the possibility of that reunion, God became one of us and gave himself to save us. This is, in essence, the story of God with human beings as Christians understand it. We learn from this story what living as human beings created in the divine image entails. Those who believe that this story reveals the truth about their existence will live their lives in the promise of a gift that exceeds all other gifts: being one with God. Since they know that this promise is grounded in God's self-giving and does not in any way depend on their own doing, believers will know that living their lives in truth is possible only because of God's unconditional love. Friendship with God is a gift that is only his to give.

2. Kant's much-quoted second version of the categorical imperative, never to use other people only as means but always also as an end in themselves, presupposes the nature of people as beings endowed with the powers of reason and will (Kant, *Foundations of the Metaphysics of Morals,* in Kant, *Critique of Practical Reason and Other Writings in Moral Philosophy,* trans. L. W. Beck (Chicago: University of Chicago, 1949). The best we can get from his philosophy with regard to our subject is a defense of a natural duty not to be cruel to sentient beings such as animals; however, this duty would not qualify as a moral duty proper, but rather as a duty of beneficence, which for Kant lies outside the domain of the moral.

In the preceding chapter we saw in the L'Arche stories that friendship with disabled people, particularly profoundly disabled people, requires a reversal in the order of giving and receiving. What we found is that people who are used to relying on their own capacities will cling to acts of self-affirmation as a way to assert themselves in the face of the other person; and the spiritual journey of L'Arche is precisely the journey to unmask the attitude of superiority hidden in that strategy. "Being there for the other person" is the ethical motive that stands in need of transformation. Learning about the friendship of God may help as a guide on this journey because it teaches us that the possibility of giving does not originate in the act of self-affirmation but in receiving oneself from the other.

What we have not done, however, is think through the concept of friendship that is implied in this reversed order of giving and receiving. The Aristotelian tradition that Thomas Aquinas was trying to incorporate in his Christian views provides the proper starting point. There are a number of questions here. First of all, for Aquinas, friendship with God as the state of fulfillment of human being is not a state at all but an activity of the soul, an activity of the intellectual soul, to be precise. Thus it is not immediately clear how the condition of intellectual disability would be compatible with friendship as the ultimate end of human being, when friendship is supposed to be an activity of a rational soul. Second, friendship with God entails a kind of likeness, for Aquinas as it did for Aristotle, who said that a true friend is the mirror of the soul.[3] Following Aristotle as his main source for ethical reflection, Aquinas draws far-reaching — and quite embarrassing — implications from this intellectualist concept of friendship.

> No irrational creature can be loved out of charity, and this for three reasons. Two of these reasons refer in a general way to friendship, which cannot have an irrational creature for its object. First because friendship is towards one to whom we wish good things, while, properly speaking, we cannot wish good things to a irrational creature, because it is not competent, properly speaking, to possess good, this being proper to the rational creature, which, through its free-will, is the

---

3. Aristotle, *Nicomachean Ethics,* trans. W. D. Ross (Oxford: Oxford University Press, 1925).

Aquinas

---

master of its disposal of the good it possesses. Hence, the philosopher says (*Physics* II, 6) that we do not speak of good or evil befalling such like things, except metaphorically. Secondly, because all friendship is based on some fellowship in life, since *nothing is as proper to friendship as to live together,* as the Philosopher proves (*Ethics,* VIII, 5). Now irrational creatures can have no fellowship in human life, which is regulated by reason. Hence, friendship with irrational creatures is impossible, except metaphorically speaking. The third reason is proper to charity, for charity is based on the fellowship of everlasting happiness, to which the irrational creature cannot attain. Therefore, we cannot have the friendship of charity towards an irrational creature.[4]

Several comments are in order. First, as the wider context of this passage shows, it is evident that, in speaking of "irrational creatures," Aquinas has in mind nonhuman creatures such as animals and plants. However, since his conception of rational creature — "which, through its free-will, is the master of its disposal of the good it possesses" — clearly excludes human beings with impairments affecting the powers of reason and will, it is not at all easy to see how these claims do not apply to people with intellectual disabilities.

Second, there is a gap in Aquinas's argument that, when made explicit, shows that his claims here cannot be sustained theologically. "Charity," he says, "is based on the fellowship of everlasting happiness." Because irrational creatures cannot attain that, we cannot have friendship with them. However, we should note that he leaves out the fact that this particular fellowship is not based on natural gifts such as the powers of reason and will but on the gratuitous gifts of grace.[5] Thus he is effectively saying that "irrational creatures" do not share in the gifts of grace. It may be that, following Aristotle, these things need to be said, "properly speaking"; but it is obvious that they are not properly spoken, theologically speaking. The only way to avoid this conclusion would be to deny that Aquinas is implicating any form of human being here. But despite this explanation, the next question would be: What would he say, then, about human beings who do not even come close to his conception of rational creatures?[6]

4. Aquinas, *Summa Theologica,* II, II, 25, 3.
5. Aquinas, *Summa Theologica,* II, II, 24, 2.
6. My guess is that, in defense of Aquinas, Thomists can only resort to the Aristote-

353

In view of Aquinas's assertions, what positive thing is there to be said here about friendship with persons with profound intellectual disabilities? Is it merely metaphorical use of language? Given the profound inequalities involved, how could Aquinas not be correct that "friendship" in their case is impossible, properly speaking? My aim in this final chapter is to answer these questions. I want to draw out further implications of what I have argued thus far. A Christian account of true friendship, I would say, must accommodate the friendships that exist in L'Arche between people, regardless of their abilities and inabilities. To provide such an account completes my attempt in this book to think about human beings with profound intellectual disabilities at the crossroads of anthropology and ethics. My guiding intuition why Aquinas must be wrong, theologically speaking, is that, if he were right, God's friendship is only promised to some, but not to all, human beings. This is clearly false. Instead of being guided by Aristotelian friendship, then, let us think about Christian friendship as the task of this final chapter.

2. My Friend Ronald[7]

I have a friend named Ronald. Usually when I tell people about Ronald, they are amused by my stories. Most of the stories are funny, not because Ronald is a particularly funny guy but because he does things differently. He might stop a woman on the street to tell her she has beautiful hair and that he would not mind marrying her. Or he might walk into a department store with 70 or 80 cents in his pocket to buy a new watch. Ronald does not worry about what other people may think of him. He knows what they think — in fact, has known it all his life — because people respond differently when you are disabled. Ronald knows people think he is a little crazy, which he does not like, of course, but other-

---

lian conception of natural kind, and will defend the argument that classification proper to natural kind does not exclude marginal cases. I have discussed in Ch. 3 why I think this argument cannot accomplish what it is supposed to.

7. The following three sections contain material taken from Hans S. Reinders, "The Virtue of Writing Appropriately. Or: Is Stanley Hauerwas Right in Thinking He Should Not Write Anymore on the Mentally Handicapped?" in *God, Truth and Witness: Engaging Stanley Hauerwas,* ed. L. Gregory Jones, Reinhard Hütter, and C. Rosalee Veloso Ewell (Grand Rapids: Brazos Press, 2005), pp. 53-70.

wise it doesn't matter. It is just a fact of Ronald's life, and it doesn't stop him from being the outgoing guy that he is. I once had lunch with him in a crowded fast-food restaurant, when suddenly he began identifying the people sitting around us as look-alikes of the actors and actresses in his favorite TV soap. "Hey, you look just like Ethel," he would say. "And you look just like Sam." And so on. Within five minutes, he had the entire crowd examining each another as to who resembled which actor or actress. That's what I mean by "funny."

However, when I tell people that I consider Ronald to be a friend, they are often surprised — even skeptical. "Oh, really?" they say. Their apparently Aristotelian intuition suggests to them that you cannot really be friends with someone so unlike yourself. After all, I am an academic: I am presumed to embody intellect, which is about the opposite of what Ronald is presumed to embody. Regarding friendship, the old metaphysical truth is still alive: sameness attracts sameness, not otherness. This still appears to be the case despite the postmodern celebrations of "otherness." Friends are people who make you feel at ease with yourself, as Aristotle would say, and "otherness" usually does not do that.

Once you start paying attention to these things, as I have for quite a while now, you will soon find out that friendship is a rare thing in the world of those we call "intellectually disabled." In talking with professional caregivers and support workers, I have noticed that they hardly ever think of their "clients" as friends. They may be very fond of them, they may even say they love them, but only reluctantly do they interpret such affection as friendship. One may assume that the explanation for this reluctance has something to do with "choice," the assumption being that professionals do not choose their clients in the same way they choose their friends. But I don't think this explanation works. Apart from the fact that friends are found rather than chosen, it is simply not true that professionals do not become friends with their clients. It surely makes professional relationships more complicated, but it happens quite frequently. Only in the lives of "clients" such as Ronald does it happen infrequently.

If friends are not chosen but found, how did I find Ronald? Well, I didn't. He found me. I was visiting an institution for disabled people with my wife, when she was approached by a bold-looking young fellow. "I know you!" he exclaimed. That fellow turned out to be Ronald. He was not just being bold, however, because what he said was true. They had lived in the same town years before that and had occasionally met. So they had a little chat, during which Ronald and I were introduced to each other. When we were saying our good-byes, he made me promise to come back and visit him. That is how Ronald found me.

3. "We Are Friends, Aren't We?"

The pitfalls of writing on ethics and intellectual disability as an academic are many. In the last chapter I confessed that I find writing about the subject much easier than spending my time with a disabled person. That confession was about Ronald, of course. One of the pitfalls is the temptation to engage in certain practices as a way to obtain legitimacy. After all, we can use people by becoming their friends. I also have learned, similar to the assistants at L'Arche but in a much less demanding way, that there is a lot of hidden superiority in my attitude toward Ronald. Such an attitude does not produce true friendship, especially in the case of people like him. More often than not, such people do not make easy friends. In fact, trying to be their friend is quite a hopeless undertaking if one is lacking in the virtues of patience, sincerity, and constancy, which I would say are true exemplifications of charity.

My friendship with Ronald taught me that lesson. Allow me to tell you a bit more about him. Where Ronald lives, social life is bleak. As soon as you enter the residence, you sense that there is not much of a shared communal life. Rather, the atmosphere is one that I would call a *modus vivendi*. Ronald's life is regulated by a set of explicit and implicit rules to live and let live. Sharing one another's time in the living room is an obligation for Ronald, whereas being allowed to go to his room is his escape. Living in such a place makes fellowship a scarcity, and competition for positive attention a necessity. Ronald would not call either the people he lives with or the people who work with him his friends. He is stuck with them, which he takes as another fact of life. It is an asset to have a friend in this kind of social environment. Having a friend from "outside" is a cause for envy: such a friendship enhances your status; it is something you can show off with.

Therefore, Ronald is thrilled when I visit him. In fact, he phones two or three times a week to ask when I will visit him, even though he already has our next appointment on his calendar. As soon as I arrive on the grounds of the institution, Ronald hops into my car and wants to leave. His preferred destination is a small nearby village, where he likes to go shopping. Buying things is an obsession for him. CDs, videos, watches, and pens are his favorites. He usually does not have enough money to buy what he wants, but he has no problem relying on the fact that I do.

When we started these trips, it frequently happened that he would run into the local music store, throw a fistful of nickels and dimes on the counter, and ask for the latest CD by his favorite band. When the owner would tell him that he could not buy a CD for that kind of money, Ronald would look imploringly at me. The owner would start to grow impatient with the situation: Was I going to come up with the necessary amount, or what? I didn't like that, of course. I felt used. But I have since learned to anticipate these moments and lay out the rules in advance. I announce that I want to visit him but that I don't want to go buy something. I convince myself that, in setting this rule, I am seeking his good, because buying is a compulsion for him. Ronald is "buy sick," as he himself prefers to call it. So we are not going shopping. You don't give sweets to someone who suffers from diabetes, do you?

Ronald accepts this. Of course, what else can he do? I had a hard time realizing this. In fact, my wife had to tell me that, in refusing to go shopping with him, I am depriving him of one of the very few opportunities he has to exercise some form of power over his life, the power of spending money. Nevertheless, I can't stand the way he does it. It drives me crazy. The other day Ronald wanted to buy a new CD box, one that would hold five disks, to replace the one that he had, which was broken. The old box was broken because it had two holes on the side, at least that was what Ronald believed. But when I looked at it, I realized that it wasn't broken at all. The holes had been there all along; in fact, they were there for opening the box. Ronald remained unconvinced: the box was broken. So as not to be the "bad guy," I gave in and we went to the music store. The owner told him the same thing I had told him, but Ronald continued to explain that we had it wrong. Because he was completely obsessed with the idea of buying a new box, he would not let it go. Finally the owner lost patience, and I had to take Ronald out of the shop. He was disappointed, and I was angry — more with myself than with him. Like most people, I am not a very communicative character when I am angry, so I drove Ronald back to his home in silence. He became very anxious: "Please, Hans, we are friends, aren't we?"[8]

4. Aristotle's Friends

When people respond skeptically to the notion of being friends with someone who is intellectually disabled, do they have a point? Can such a relationship be truthfully called a relationship between friends? As the narrative of my friendship with Ronald suggests, the question is a serious one. In the history of ethics, no one has paid more attention to the practice of friendship than Aristotle, as is well known. It is equally well known, however, that his account of true friendship has its limitations. In the context of this book, his notion of true friendship as friendship between "equals" is particularly troublesome.

Whatever there is to be learned from Aristotle's account of friendship, he does not make it easy to include friendship with persons with intellectual disabilities. First of all, there is "true" friendship, as he understands it: this involves persons of good character or virtue, and persons of good character or virtue are distinguished by a particular kind of life, namely, a life of "activity or actions of the soul implying a rational principle."[9] Even on the most favorable interpretation, it is impossible to include in this view people whose actions and activities do not seem to display a rational principle.[10] Since true friendship is possible

8. To be clear, I should say that being friends with Ronald is not just a pain in the neck. Such a limited characterization would do great injustice both to him and to our friendship. We laugh and make jokes; we have dinner, walk on the beach, go camping, and so on. However, in all this I do want to stay focused on how I might make a true difference in his life, which my account here shows is not an easy thing to do, given who I am, who Ronald is, and what his life is like.

9. Aristotle, *Nicomachean Ethics*, 1098a14. Even though Aristotle's account can be saved from his bad reputation with regard to women and slaves, the disabled are in a different category. The discriminating ground is not social status but impairment of intellectual functioning.

10. Recent discussions on the definition of intellectual disabilities have been fueled by concerns that the focus on individual characteristics tends to disregard the social environment from which such characteristics draw their practical and political significance. These discussions notwithstanding, "sub average intellectual functioning" is still regarded as a dominant characteristic. The classical source is R. Luckasson et al., *Mental Re-*

only between persons of good character whose lives imply a rational principle, it must follow that persons with intellectual disabilities cannot be part of such friendships. That much is obvious. But "true" friendship does not exhaust Aristotle's account of friendship. That is, he does not exclude intellectually disabled persons from friendship altogether, inasmuch as he allows for friendship between persons who are "unequal" or "dissimilar."

Exploring this possibility, one finds that Aristotle's account of friendship is fairly liberal with regard to who can count as a friend: it leaves room for such widely different relationships as mother and child, political rulers and their subjects, and children and their peers. All these relationships can amount to friendships. In this broad sense, friendship is concomitant with justice, according to Aristotle, in that it is concerned with the same relationship of mutuality. "Friendship and justice exist between the same persons and have an equal extension."[11] The difference between justice and friendship is that the demands of justice are independent of the actual presence of fellow feeling, which is impossible in the case of friendship. Friendship, according to Aristotle, is defined by the fact of both wishing and doing well for the other *for the other's sake,* and by the fact that these good wishes and good deeds are mutually recognized.[12] As John Cooper has pointed out, this condition applies to all kinds of communal relationships.[13] Just as there can be a relationship of justice with everyone who is capable of participating in law and contract, says Aristotle, so there can be friendship with everyone "in so far as he is a man."[14]

---

tardation: Definition, Classification, and Systems of Support (Washington, DC: American Association for Mental Retardation, 1992).

11. *Nicomachean Ethics,* 1160a8.

12. *Nicomachean Ethics,* 1156a3. See John M. Cooper, "Aristotle on the Forms of Friendship," in *Reason and Emotion: Essays on Ancient Moral Psychology and Moral Theory* (Princeton, NJ: Princeton University Press, 1999), pp. 312-35.

13. See John M. Cooper, "Political Animals and Civic Friendship," in *Reason and Emotion,* pp. 356-77, esp. 371 n. 18.

14. *Nicomachean Ethics,* 1161b8. It is interesting to note the *conditio sine qua non* that Aristotle defines here. One cannot be friends with a slave insofar as he is a slave. The slave resembles the citizen under the rule of a tyrant: he is used as a mere extension ("a tool") of his master. One cannot be friends with what is only an extension of oneself. "*Qua* slave then, one cannot be friends with him. But *qua* man one can" (*Nicomachean Ethics,* 1161b8). Julia Annas points out that the very broad scope of friendship may raise the question of whether Aristotle's conception is at all coherent when friendship can take so

Within the wide variety of possible friendships, there is a subset that involves personal relationships between people who appreciate particular qualities in each other, and the qualities operative in a given friendship determine its nature. Aristotle distinguishes the qualities of utility, pleasure, and virtue.[15] Friendship based on virtue is the one already described: the friendship between "rational souls" who share one another's lives and seek one another's good. This is "perfect" friendship, according to Aristotle.[16] Not all friendships will be "perfect" in this sense, because there is also friendship between people who are unequal and dissimilar.[17]

Friendships of equality are those in which both parties extend the same benevolence to one another, and each receives the same benefits from the friendship. In contrast, unequal friendships involve the superiority of one party to the other. These friendships are viable only to the extent that the benefits rendered to each of the parties are proportionally compensated. "The better [of the two parties] should be more loved than he loves, and so should the more useful, and similarly in each of the other cases; for when the love is in proportion to the merit of the parties, then in a sense arises equality, which is certainly held to be characteristic of friendship."[18]

More or less the same rules hold for friendships marked by dissimilarity. In these friendships the parties do not necessarily get a proportionally unequal share of the same benefits; rather, they receive benefits of different kinds. For example, a wealthy person may be friends with an intelligent person. In such a case, Aristotle explains, all kinds of difficulties may arise in determining what return the parties are due, because there is no fixed standard.[19] To stick with that example for a

---

many different forms (Julia Annas, *The Morality of Happiness* [New York: Oxford University Press, 1993], p. 250). The answer is found in Aristotle's method of examining ethical questions: he asks how his fellow Athenians use words (*Nicomachean Ethics*, 1155a33, 1157a25, 1157b5, 1159b27), and what can be learned from proverbs and popular sayings (*Nicomachean Ethics*, 1155a35, 1156b26, 1157b12, 1158a1, 1159b31). It is from the many opinions that educated people may have on a given subject that Aristotle seeks to find the truth in some of them (*Nicomachean Ethics*, 1145b2).

15. *Nicomachean Ethics*, 1156a4-1156b12.
16. *Nicomachean Ethics*, 1156b6.
17. Cooper, "Aristotle on the Forms of Friendship," p. 320.
18. *Nicomachean Ethics*, 1158b25-28.
19. Hauerwas explains Aristotle's tolerance with regard to the lesser forms of friend-

moment, how many aphorisms or bon mots equal the value of a copious meal? None of these difficulties will arise in a friendship based on good character, however, because in it the mutual benefits are in proportion to intention.[20] In other words, true friendship does not give rise to problems that derive from inequality or dissimilarity, because friends of good character will seek one another's good for the sake of the other and not for some transient quality such as utility or pleasure.

Not only does true friendship not give rise to these problems; it also fosters a growing equality and similarity. Friends not only seek to promote one another's good for the sake of the other, but they also desire to be in one another's company and share one another's delights and sorrows. Each of these things, Aristotle observes, "is true of the good man's relation to himself."[21] Indeed, a person of good character desires for her friend what she also desires for herself. True friends thus grow together in virtue, becoming more and more similar over time. For the good person, Aristotle concludes, "his friend is another self."[22] So there is a kind of identity that exists between true friends in the fact that they recognize themselves in the other person.

None of this is true of a friendship characterized by inequality, of which my friendship with Ronald is a prime example — at least from Aristotle's perspective. Therefore, let me return to my earlier observation of the typically doubtful response to the notion of friendship with a disabled man. Through the lens of such doubt, Aristotle's claim to equality as the mark of true friendship appears right on target. Whatever the fruits of my friendship with Ronald for each of us, it seems unlikely that what I get from it equals what he gets from it. This inequality may well be what people have in mind when they question whether I can "really" be friends with a disabled person. When I confirm Ronald's claim that

---

ship by arguing that friendship does not presuppose virtue but is itself "a process that makes possible our becoming virtuous." Thus, the lesser forms of friendship have "the potential of putting us on the road to virtue." See Hauerwas, "Companions on the Way: The Necessity of Friendship," *Asbury Theological Journal* 45 (1990): 35-48. This appears to me to be a quite favorable interpretation, considering Aristotle's insistence that inequality and dissimilarity between friends must be compensated proportionally. Between unequal or dissimilar friends, the "better" of the two deserves to get more out of the friendship.

20. *Nicomachean Ethics,* 1164b1.
21. *Nicomachean Ethics,* 1166a10.
22. *Nicomachean Ethics,* 1166a31.

we are friends, the responding look is usually one of incredulity. One of us must be joking.

This incredulity is readily displayed by the professionals in Ronald's home, who regard me as a "volunteer." Being a volunteer usually means doing things that do not pay; that's why most people don't do those things when they are under no obligation. It makes "reward" the critical element in being a volunteer. Presumably, volunteering as a "mirror friend" in a home for disabled people does not rank high among rewarding activities. It's my impression that, for the people who work with Ronald, the benefits of our "friendship" are unevenly distributed. Ronald gets to do fun things with me, and the fun for me is the fact that he has a good time. It is clear to them what he gets out of our friendship — trips to the village, free meals, visits to my apartment; presumably, though, it is much less clear to them what I get out of it. Since one never knows when volunteers consider themselves to be sufficiently rewarded, Ronald's caregivers frequently tell him not to be too demanding. It is as if they are saying to him, "Don't push your luck." Their reaction is probably based on how most volunteers respond when they don't get the rewards they expect. They quit.

In sum, Aristotle's account of true friendship suggests that the skepticism with which people view my friendship with Ronald is warranted. Moreover, Aristotle's theory of unequal friendship explains not only their intuitive response but also — whether I like it or not — my own negative reactions to some of Ronald's habits.[23] I am not supposed to be embarrassed by a friend, which is what explains my occasional exasperated "Don't do this to me!" These are the kinds of things one would indeed expect in friendships that are unequal and dissimilar.

It appears, then, that we can argue the question of friendship with an intellectually disabled person in one of two opposing ways. We can reject Aristotle's account because it excludes people like Ronald from being part of true friendships. But we can also invoke Aristotle's account to explain the tensions in these friendships, as is evident in my own example. Apparently, these tensions attest a lack of virtue that prevents friendship from flourishing, at least for the time being. From what we have learned so far, though, the argument can go either way.

---

23. No doubt, many people with intellectual disabilities are blessed with better friends than me, but I am confident that quite a few of these friends face similar challenges.

5. Christian Friendship

Can a Christian account of friendship accommodate the difference between these two responses to the Aristotelian account of friendship vis-à-vis people with intellectual disabilities? In seeking to answer that question, I will once again address Stanley Hauerwas's work, this time his discussion (co-authored with Charles Pinches) on the difference between Aristotelian and Christian friendship.[24]

In their comments on Aristotelian friendship, Hauerwas and Pinches raise the objection that Aristotle's account leaves no space to appreciate the friend as an "other." True friendship is by definition friendship between persons of good character. For the virtuous person there is no distinction between love for self and love for the friend, because they are similar with respect to the good. Perceiving oneself and perceiving one's friend as a person of good character are the same. In view of this claim, Hauerwas and Pinches notice that, even though Aristotle denies true friendship to be instrumental (the friend is not just an extension of the self), his description "fails to reflect otherness in friendship."[25] It is their experience that, "when we love the friend, we love not just what we share with her, but also, and often more importantly, that in her which differs from ourselves."[26]

Regarding this objection, I would argue that, from a Christian point of view, the point about otherness per se does not capture the real problem in Aristotle's theory. For Aristotle, true friendship can stand the test of time because friends participate in virtue, and virtue remains constant. Therefore, true friendship distinguishes itself in that it excels in constancy. But Hauerwas and Pinches conclude: "Aristotle comes close to requiring that the constancy we share protect us from one another's difference."[27] From a Christian perspective, however, the deeper prob-

24. Stanley Hauerwas and Charles Pinches, *Christians among the Virtues: Theological Conversations with Ancient and Modern Ethics* (Notre Dame, IN: University of Notre Dame Press, 1997).

25. Hauerwas and Pinches, *Christians among the Virtues*, p. 40.

26. Hauerwas and Pinches, *Christians among the Virtues*, p. 40.

27. Hauerwas and Pinches, *Christians among the Virtues*, p. 41. Insofar as Hauerwas and Pinches are offering an internal objection to Aristotle at this stage of their argument, I don't think the objection is very strong. As I observed in my introduction, Aristotelian friendship is what makes us feel at home with the other, which is usually not what "other-

lem is introduced by the question of how one could ever *be certain* of being involved in true friendship. The question is, once again, a question
of "seeing as."

Certainty about one's friendship is only possible on grounds of an
act of self-affirmation, that is, the affirmation by me, in view of my companion, that I am a virtuous person. No doubt Aristotle's magnanimous
man has no problem with this act of self-affirmation, but it is not easy
to see how Christians could confidently see themselves in this way. Not
even saints could perform such acts, because it would mean that they
regarded themselves as no longer in need of the Lord's Prayer (the part
that asks God not to lead them into temptation). Surely, the self-
congratulating act of regarding myself as a virtuous person must count
as a temptation, from a Christian point of view. The virtuous "man" in
Aristotle does not have this problem because he has conquered temptation.[28] As a person of good character, he is defined by well-ordered desires according to reason: he is thus in control of himself.

Christians do not have this kind of conception of themselves. Mag-
nanimity, we can learn from several parables in the New Testament, is
equated with hubris — and therefore with sinfulness.[29] This is why Jesus says, according to John's Gospel, that those who consider themselves to be without sin are blind. In other words, what we need for a
Christian account of true friendship is the recognition of how God's
friendship is different in that it entails judgment revealing our blindness in this respect; that is, we need an account of sin.[30]

---

ness" does. If disregard for otherness is a failure, a quite different view of friendship must
already be in place.

28. Here I use "man" and masculine pronouns to indicate that, in truth, Aristotle
does not allow for women as virtuous characters capable of perfect friendship.

29. For example, the parable of the rich man and the poor Lazarus (Luke 16:19-31),
the widow's offering (Luke 20:45-47; 21:1-4; see also Matt. 19:16-30; 18:9-14). In contrast,
we find modesty and humility characterized as exemplary, for example in the story of Jesus' healing of the centurion's servant (Matt. 8:5-13), where the centurion welcomes Jesus
in his house by saying, "Lord, I am not worthy to have you come under my roof" (see also
Matt. 18:1-5; Mark 9:33-37).

30. Conspicuously lacking in the text by Hauerwas and Pinches on Aristotelian friendship is the notion of sin. See also Hauerwas's "Companions on the Way," where he is more
explicit on this point in arguing that in our friendships we want to mirror "a God who bears
a closer resemblance to Aristotle's 'high-minded man'" (p. 44). That is, in our friendships
we like to affirm ourselves in our self-sufficiency rather than in our capacity to receive.

A Christian conception of true friendship, I suggest, should remind us that Christian friendship is not the friendship of great people who are praised for their good character by their peers. True friendship is about committing ourselves to those who are despicable in the eyes of the world, which is why true friendship, from a Christian viewpoint, is friendship under the Cross. Since most of us do not want to be associated with those who are despicable, we need an account of sin in order to confess our failure to be true friends.[31] The reason for this is not difficult to grasp. As Hauerwas and Pinches point out, Christians believe that "the God of the universe, who has extended Himself to us in the Jewish people and in Jesus, invites us to become His friends by sharing in His suffering."[32] Of course, that is precisely what we want to avoid. We certainly want to be friends with God, but not in order to share in his suffering. Most of us do not want to be affiliated with suffering, nor with poverty, nor with abnormality. That explains why people in marginalized positions suffer from our self-images. Having had their self-images shaped by a culture that reproduces a hierarchy of human being, most Christians do not usually distinguish themselves in seeking friendships with those who suffer from poverty, or abnormality.

Therefore, from the point of view of biblical faith, our confessing to the fact that we forsake our friendships is crucial, not necessarily because we are depraved characters, but because it is critical that we be reminded of our own "location" in the scheme of morals.[33] The proper location is not represented in the assumption that our friendship is a gift we have to give. We do not choose our friends for their virtue, that is, in order to extend acts of good will to them — particularly not when these friends are despised in the eyes of the world. We are called to be their friends. Jesus thus says to his disciples in John 15, "I have called you

---

31. This is a claim Hauerwas does make; see Stanley Hauerwas (with Laura Yordy), "Captured in Time," in *A Better Hope: Resources for a Church Confronting Capitalism, Democracy, and Postmodernity* (Grand Rapids: Brazos Press, 2000), p. 181: "Friendship for Christians is both a necessary activity for the discovery that we are less than we were meant to be and the resource to start us on the journey through which we become what we were created to be."

32. Hauerwas and Pinches, *Christians among the Virtues*, p. 44.

33. The best-known example is, of course, Peter's betrayal of friendship in the face of suffering in the courtyard of the high priest on the occasion of Jesus' trial (Matt. 26:69-75).

friends, because I have made known to you everything that I have heard from my Father. You did not choose me but I chose you" (John 15:14-16). Friendship is our vocation because of what we have heard about the love of God, the forgiving Father.

Without this reminder, a Christian account of friendship might incorporate terrible mistakes. This happens when we offer friendship as an act of compassion toward those who suffer, but without the willingness to consider how we extend their suffering. For example, I might be tempted to regard my friendship with Ronald as an act of compassion on my part, an act by which I seek to respond to God's calling. That would be the mistake of placing myself at the wrong end of the invitation. The important thing about our friendship *for me* is not what I am offering to Ronald. That much we have learned from Henri Nouwen's account of his friendship with Adam in the preceding chapter: there is nothing to give without the prior acknowledgment of what has been received. A history of hypocrisy in Christian charity testifies to our sinfulness in forgetting this. The important thing in friendship for me is what the other person does, in Hauerwas's salutary way of putting it, by *claiming me as a friend.*[34] It is a calling and a task that I am invited to perform.[35] In an important sense, friendship is something I receive before I can give.

> Christians must not only see friends as gifts to one another, they
> must see their friendship itself as a gift. They can do this precisely be-
> cause they understand themselves to be actors within a story
> authored not by them but by God. As Christians, our friendship is not
> made constant by an act of our own will, individual or corporate, or

34. Stanley Hauerwas, "Timeful Friends: Living with the Handicapped," in *Sanctify Them in the Truth: Holiness Exemplified* (Nashville: Abingdon, 1998), p. 144.

35. Let me point to a text in the Gospel of Luke that appears right after the Lord's Prayer, which underscores this characterization. Suppose, Jesus says to his disciples, that someone approaches a friend at an untimely hour for some bread because he has an unexpected guest. Suppose further that this friend makes excuses for not being able to help him because the door is locked and the family is already asleep. "I tell you," Jesus then says, "though he will not get up and give him anything because he is his friend, yet because of his importunity he will rise and give him whatever he needs" (Luke 11:5-8). Accordingly, it is not necessarily my concept of what it is to be a friend that provides me with sufficient motive to respond positively, but rather my friend's persistence in calling on me.

even by our own virtue, but rather because we and others find ourselves through participation in a common activity that makes us faithful both to ourselves and the other. That activity is not, as it seems to be in Aristotle, mutual enjoyment as an end in itself, but rather it is the activity of a task we have been given. That task is nothing less than to participate in a new way of life made possible by the life of the man Jesus.[36]

That task, I might add, is not so much an assignment as an invitation. What is new about it is that it is a life of freedom rather than obligation. It is an invitation to be truthful to the story of the triune God, who has drawn us into the communion of Father, Son, and Spirit. In other words, it is an invitation to remain faithful to the gifts of communion we have received through divine action.

6. Eucharistic Practice

The theological warrant for this view is found in the reflection on how the friendship that God offers is present in our lives. It is offered, literally, as self-giving, as when Jesus told his disciples that no one has greater love than when he gives his life for his friends (John 15:11-17). We have already explored how the presence of divine self-giving is shaped by the Eucharist in discussing Zizioulas's conception of ecstatic being (see Ch. 7, sect. 8). Here we need to draw out the implications of this exploration for our understanding of Christian friendship. There are two points I wish to consider: the first is about the nature of Christian friendship as ecstatic; the second is about the nature of Christian friendship as eucharistic practice.

Regarding the ecstatic nature of friendship, I will begin with reminding the reader of the earlier discussion of Zizioulas's view of ecstatic being as a theological concept. I have argued that the ecstatic nature of human personhood as ecclesiastical being must be interpreted consistently as extrinsically grounded. Human personhood is not the actualization of a potentiality of our biological and historical *hypostasis,* but a possibility that exists in the reality of God's graceful action.

---

36. Hauerwas and Pinches, *Christians among the Virtues,* p. 49.

367

This means that we understand the ecstatic nature of human personhood as "being from" rather than "being unto."

It follows, then, that when we think of ecstatic being as movement, as Zizioulas suggests, we in fact conceive of our personhood not as a condition that is received and thus henceforth our own, but as a gift that continues to be given because it stands in constant need of regeneration. When Zizioulas says, quite rightly in my view, that he has excluded the possibility of regarding the person as a being "caused" by human nature, he intends to rule out any view that makes psychological conditions — self-consciousness, reflexivity, the capacity for reason and will, and so forth — constitutive of the human person. The person is constituted in an ecstatic movement by God's act of communion, but this movement is extrinsically grounded because the act that constitutes it *remains* God's act.

Furthermore, it also follows that when Zizioulas claims that the movement toward ecstatic being is shaped by the Eucharist, this means that it is in fact grounded in the Christian practice of learning to be a forgiven people. That is, according to the Gospel of Matthew, what the Eucharist is about.[37] This introduces the second point. If, as Zizioulas claims, participation in the eucharistic movement means to be inspired to a "different kind of love," this means that eucharistic love comes with the Spirit, in whom we receive this love, and that receiving it creates the possibility of returning it. Ecstatic being, understood as extrinsically grounded, exemplifies the reversed order of giving and receiving that I argued for in the preceding chapter. Experiencing eucharistic love means that we no longer fear the limitations of our biological and historical being because we have been accepted as who and what we are. My being has been affirmed (note the passive voice) by the love I have received. Though participation in this eucharistic love transcends our biological and historical being, it does not annihilate it. We can be persons in the ecclesiastical sense only because our being as biological and historical *hypostasis* is unconditionally affirmed by God in the Eucharist. We have a treasure in heaven, but, as Paul puts it, we have it in the vessels of our earthly being because the transcend-

---

37. "Now as they were eating, Jesus took bread, and blessed, and broke it, and gave it to the disciples and said, 'Take, eat; this is my body.' And he took a cup, and when he had given thanks he gave it to them, saying, 'Drink of it, all of you; for this is my blood of the covenant, which is poured out for many for the forgiveness of sins'" (Matt. 26:26-28).

Our own inability does not matter

ing power belongs to God and not to us (2 Cor. 4:7), which is why it needs constant regeneration.[38] The new creation of human personhood inaugurated by God's self-giving is a spiritual journey, not a mental state.

To be a forgiven people is what the eucharistic practice teaches us. Participating in that practice means that we are offered the gifts of God's self-giving, which breaks through the human need of self-affirmation because it tells us what our souls long for: peace with ourselves and with others, freedom from fear and anxiety — all the things given to us when we put our trust in God. This is why, as we participate in this practice, we may learn to see differently, in the sense discussed in Chapter 9. We do not need human self-affirmation once we understand that our being does not need justification. We do not need credits that prove we have earned God's love. Therefore, we do not need to be afraid that our existence does not matter. It matters to God, so much so that he was willing to give himself in order to prove it. Once we understand that this is what is celebrated in the Eucharist, it goes without saying that practicing what it means to be a forgiven people cannot help but include every human being God brings into our lives. It goes also without saying that this practice includes human beings with intellectual disabilities of whatever kind or degree. How could this not be, if we know that, in view of the gift of God's self-giving, our own inability does not matter? Whatever is true about our biological and historical characteristics, they do not determine whether we are offered the friendship of God.

7. The Face of Friendship

At this point that I want to revisit Henri Nouwen's account of his friendship with Adam, the profoundly disabled young man whom he has come to regard as his teacher. Curiously enough, Nouwen begins to describe Adam's being in terms of the categories of the self precisely at the point where one would think there is no need for it at all, namely,

38. This is why Christian friendship necessarily recognizes its eschatological limits. Accordingly, Augustine said that friendship in our earthly lives will not be perfect: "Our earthly relationships always reflect the limitations of our nature, including our sinfulness." See Paul J. Wadell, *Becoming Friends: Worship, Justice, and the Practice of Christian Friendship* (Grand Rapids: Brazos, 2002), pp. 92-93.

in the context of Nouwen's account of his own transformation. As he
has told us, in the beginning of his career as Adam's assistant, he could
only see Adam's profoundly disabled body with eyes "from below," that
is, as a human being very different from himself. Then the transforming experience of helping Adam through his morning routine has
opened his eyes. He then sees a human being very much like him.
Nouwen confesses that everything he has most desired in life — love,
friendship, a sense of community — he has found in Adam. However,
arriving at this point in his story, the language he uses in speaking of
Adam changes.

> I am convinced that somewhere deep down Adam "knew" that he was
> loved. He knew it in his very soul. Adam was not able to reflect on
> love, on the heart as the center of our being, the core of our humanity
> where we give and receive love. He could not talk with me about the
> movements of his heart or my heart or the heart of God. He could ex-
> plain nothing to me in words. But his heart was there, totally alive,
> full of love, which he could both give and receive. Adam's heart made
> him fully alive.[39]

When the core of our humanity is what Nouwen takes it to be, then it is
necessary, of course, to include these statements about Adam's heart.
However, Nouwen goes further than that:

> As I grew closer to Adam, I came to experience his most beautiful
> heart as the gateway to his real self, to his person, his soul, and his
> spirit. His heart, so transparent, reflected for me not only his person
> but also the heart of the universe and, indeed, the heart of God.
> (p. 50)

The transforming experience that Nouwen has gone through has
brought him to a new way of seeing, but what he "sees" is the reflection
of what he believes human beings are in a fundamental way.

> Adam's humanity was not diminished by his disabilities. Adam's hu-
> manity was a full humanity, in which the fullness of love became visi-
> ble for me and for others who grew to know him. (pp. 50-51)

39. Henri J. M. Nouwen, *Adam: God's Beloved* (Maryknoll, NY: Orbis Books, 1997), pp.
49-50 [page numbers in parentheses in text refer to this work].

The love Nouwen finds is a spiritual love, which, as far as Adam was concerned, does not depend on verbal expression or tangible gesture.

> Still I dare to say we loved each other with a love that was enfleshed as any love, and was at the same time purely spiritual. We were friends, brothers, bonded in our hearts. Adam's love was pure and true. (p. 51)

These statements touch on profound theological questions. We have already seen that Nouwen distinguishes between "questions from below," on the one hand, regarding the kinds of things that Adam may or may not be capable of doing, and "questions from above," on the other. The latter, the reader will recall, were questions about prayer: "Can you let Adam lead you into prayer? Can you let Adam be a living prayer at your table? Can you see my face in the face of Adam?"

It occurs to me that, in the statements about Adam's "real self," Nouwen has lost track of this distinction. The interesting thing about his questions "from above" is that none of these questions needs illumination via a statement about Adam's heart, or his "real self." Each of them makes perfect sense, even when we would say that Adam confronts us with a mystery, to recall the statement of Pope John Paul II (see p. 120, above). However, Nouwen pulls in the opposite direction of "mystery," that is, in the direction of "transparency." It enables him to see that, deep down, there is no difference between Adam and himself.

What troubles me about this direction is that Nouwen seems to return to the notion of a reciprocal relationship, which he deemed utterly impossible when seeing Adam "from below." Now that he has been transformed, he has left the "need for comparison" behind. Now he is capable of seeing Adam "from above," which enables him to see his friend's "real self." From the earlier analysis of friendship, it seems clear that Nouwen's account presupposes Aristotle's perfect friendship. Now he sees Adam's humanity for what it really is, "full humanity," not humanity diminished by his disabilities, which then allows him to say that there is a brotherly love between them, and that it is reciprocal. The reader will recall that Aristotelian friendship implies the notion of "mirroring": the friend is the mirror of the soul in which I find my true self reflected. It appears as though Nouwen's initial "need for comparison" is satisfied, rather than abandoned, in the process of his transformation.

Thus, seeing his disabled friend with the eyes of God enables him to glorify Adam, even to the point of identifying the purity of Adam's heart as a reflection of the heart of God. But seeing with the eyes of God, I would say, is seeing with the eyes of Christ, because in him we know God. Therefore, when Nouwen confronts us with the question, "Can you see my face in Adam's face?" the answer should be that in Adam's face we find the face of Christ reflected, and we should remember that Christ's was the face of friendship. Adam was created in Christ, as was the whole of creation: I take this to mean that, in the eyes of God, Adam's humanity is precious as it is. Being transformed by God's love entails embracing Adam's human being for what it is; it does not necessarily entail the discovery of a "real self."

Probably the explanation of Nouwen's need for transparency is found in his understanding of the Incarnation, which plays an important role in the background of his reflections.

> I always believed that the word of God became flesh. I have preached that the divine became manifest in the human so that all things human could become manifestations of the divine. Adam came with others to worship and to hear me preach. He sat in front of me in his chair, and I "saw" the divine significance made visible in him. Adam, I believe, had a heart where the Word of God was dwelling in intimate silence. Adam, during our time together, led me into that intimate indwelling where the deepest significance of his and my humanity was unfolding. (p. 50)

"Indwelling" is the key notion here, because it indicates that for Nouwen the Incarnation means the divinization of the soul. At least that is what is suggested by the characterization of the heart as the location "where the Word of God was dwelling." I would contrast this notion with the ancient hymn that the apostle Paul gives us in his Epistle to the Philippians, which suggests a view of the Incarnation that is quite different from Nouwen's. The hymn sings the praise of Christ, who did not consider himself to be robbed of his divinity but "emptied himself" when he took on his humanity.[40] Paul prays that the Philippians stay in

---

40. Philippians 2:5-7: "Have this mind among yourselves, which is yours in Christ Jesus, who, though he was in the form of God, did not count equality with God a thing to be grasped, but emptied himself, taking the form of a servant, being born in the likeness of men."

the Spirit of Christ and that they not consider their becoming servants as being robbed of their newly acquired state of being God's people. It appears that the relationship between divinity and humanity in Philippians leads us in the opposite direction of Nouwen's reflections: that is, it goes from divinity to humanity, not the other way around.

Second, and closely related, is the fact that Adam's humanity in Nouwen's telling of it is won by looking away from — or beyond — his disabling conditions. "Adam's humanity was a full humanity," says Nouwen, "in which the fullness of love became visible for me and for others who grew to know him." The imagery is that of a hidden humanity, which he did not see at first — being preoccupied with questions "from below," like the friend who tried to get him to leave Daybreak — but which became fully transparent after Nouwen's transformation. Now, however, he understands the question God is asking him: "In being assigned to help this young man through his daily life, what is your response to me?" Taking this question as an example, we immediately see that questions "from above" follow the three-way logic of charity. In assisting Adam, Nouwen finds himself responding to God; but notice that answering God's question in no way depends on seeing Adam as a manifestation of the divine.

We may recall John Zizioulas's claim that the ecstatic nature of the human person as constituted by God's grace does not alter our biological *hypostasis*. I take this to mean that, in participating in God's communion, we renew our way of seeing Adam, not in the sense that his being is now revealed as a "real self," but in the sense that we know God is with him, whatever Adam's body has to endure. The brokenness of his body is what it was before, but it is taken on by Christ, who shared it with him and has been restored in the fullness of being. That is the promise to Adam and to us, and the Eucharist is its liturgical embodiment.

Finally, it appears that Nouwen's claim to the transparency of Adam's heart is simply saying too much. God's unconditional love means that he is with Adam, but how the relationship between them affects Adam's soul is something I don't think we should pretend to know. This is not because of the particularities of Adam's body, because the same question can be asked about God's relationship with me, and the answer *for me* would be just the same. This is something between God and Adam, as it is something between God and me. I recall Robert

373

Jenson's interpretation of the divine image as a unique relationship between God and being human (see p. 237, above). This interpretation indicates the profound wisdom of John Paul II's statement that in the limitations and sufferings in the body and the faculties of the disabled person we are facing the mystery of the human being. Uniqueness signifies mystery in the sense that God's relationship with Adam, despite his limitations and sufferings, is between the two of them, which seems to defy transparency for other human beings. Moreover, since it is *God's* relationship with Adam, it remains between the two of them. That is why reverence is an appropriate response to any human being, disabled or not: Adam's heart is a mystery that only God knows.

My argument has been that, when we partake in the practice of the Eucharist, we learn to be a forgiven people. Learning this will change our hearts: it will do so in the sense that we will no longer perceive our relationship with others primarily from the perspective of what we have to give. To know how to receive the gift of God's friendship is to know how to receive the gift of God's friends. It is through the Holy Spirit that God's friendship is tangible in our lives, because the Spirit sets free the possibility of love, which comes with gratitude for the many graces of God. Therefore, we must learn to be a forgiven people, because the gift requires that we know how to receive. In Nouwen's memorable phrasing, "what is not received has not been given." If we don't know how to receive the gift, we won't recognize it; but then we won't know how to pass on the gift either. God is paying it forward.

7. Friendship with the Profoundly Disabled

In this third part of my inquiry in this book, I have set out to explore the possibility of Kelly's participation in the ultimate good of human being in terms of its ethical implications. The questions and answers I have offered gradually build up to an overall argument that I hope has convinced at least some of my readers. What does it amount to? Let me summarize.

It is commonly accepted that a conception of the good life draws its meaning from a conception of our *telos,* or final end. From a Christian point of view, this final end cannot be the final stage of developing our natural potentialities. This is because our final end is reunion with

God, which is appropriately understood as God's friendship with us, the full extension of which is promised us as the resurrection of the body to eternal life. With regard to our human lives here and now, this means that, from a Christian perspective, the good life necessarily has the structure of a promised life. At the same time, however, there would be no point to a promised life unless it is grounded in historical reality. The conception of reality that serves as a warrant is found in the biblical story of God's covenant with the Jewish people, renewed in the church, according to which the reality that creates and guides our existence — and brings it to its final end — is God's economy of salvation. That covenant entails the promise that God will be with the people of Israel if they want to receive his gifts and be his people. The "new covenant" entails the further promise that this *if* is not a big *if,* because God's gifts are not a reward for an obedient response. The gifts are given in anticipation of our response: God's graceful gifts always precede our actions.

This claim, we will recall, is the theological basis for arguing that the inability to respond cannot imply exclusion from these gifts. This is not to say, of course, that our response does not matter. It matters very much to God that we respond positively to his invitation, but only if we respond for the right reason. That is, only if we respond out of free love. God wants this loving response to be free, free from fear and from the anxiety that we need to love him in order to avoid his punishment. God is certainly a God of retribution, but he is only so for those who do not trust him. Because they do not trust God, they will misread what happens in their lives and respond mistakenly. God's gifts are paid forward, but this does not mean that God knows no time of payback. God pays back those who seek their salvation by leaving them to their own schemes of protecting themselves.

Human beings must learn to trust in God's forgiveness for each time they fail to return his love freely. No love will be returned when there is no love received. Therefore, knowing how to receive is the primordial task of the Christian moral life. The reality that grounds the promised life of God's friendship with us exists in the offer of God's friendship here and now. God will deliver us from our sufferings, but he will deliver us in the act of *being with* us when we suffer. He never turns away from us when — not if — we truly seek him. Again, seeking is not a condition for God's friendship, because the offer precedes our seeking.

Coming before him with our pain and brokenness and fears demands trust, and what we must learn is to trust that we are accepted.

The stories of the people of L'Arche in these chapters bear witness to the fact of how human beings with intellectual disabilities, even profound intellectual disabilities, can become our teachers when it comes to trust. That is their gift to us. Given the condition that characterizes their lives, they have learned, in one way or another, to trust in order to survive. The reverse is also true: where trust is absent, they barely survive. Given our many capacities and abilities, we, the "temporarily ablebodied," may presume ourselves to be much stronger and may decide to hide our own brokenness in a show of strength. The spiritual journeys of the people of L'Arche show the blessings of giving up this illusion of strength, even though it is a painful process. Facing ourselves in truth is the hardest thing to do. It requires giving up illusions about our own character, which means that we need to unmask both self-seeking motives and the attitudes of superiority from which they spring. This can be done only if we learn to listen and truly see the person with the disability and act for the sake of that person.

Christians who participate in the practice of the Eucharist try to learn to live as a forgiven people. This enables them to find the courage to trust the other and see the presence of the other as gift. The transformation this process entails will teach them how to receive from those who have nothing to give — at least in the eyes of the world. The friendship that results from this transformation is a form of "being with" that reveals itself as the work of God's friendship here and now. God is being with us when we give up the pretensions of invulnerability and strength. I believe that this answers the question of how people with profound disabilities, such as Henri Nouwen's friend Adam, may contribute to the good life.

What about participation? In large part, the answer follows from the same logic. Human beings like Adam or Kelly or Oliver de Vinck certainly participate in the good life, understood from a Christian viewpoint, because receiving God's friendship is not the prerogative of the "temporarily able-bodied." It is not true that you must be capable of doing or understanding certain kinds of things, such as responding to God, in order to partake in the fullness of being. But, as we have seen, the friendship of God takes on two distinct forms. On the one hand, it is the fullness of being that is promised us in the kingdom of heaven, in which we will enjoy reunion with God; on the other hand, God's friendship is offered here and now in the form of God's movement toward us in the Eucharist, in which we find peace and consolation. Being drawn into this movement, we are given the gift of the Spirit to reflect God's presence.

The people of the L'Arche communities are witness to this presence: it is found when "being with" acquires a new meaning of tuning in to the disabled persons and letting them take the lead in forming community. "Assisting" in the truest sense of the word means emptying oneself without considering that as a denial of oneself (note the Philippians 2 hymn), because the primary task is to follow rather than to lead or instruct. In this way, assisting becomes a transforming experience of being the recipient of "the poor." God's friendship can be reflected only when the assistant (e.g., at L'Arche) does not act from self-seeking motives but seeks to work for the sake of the other person. In this respect, there is no difference between assisting persons with mild intellectual disabilities and assisting persons like Adam or Kelly or Oliver de Vinck. Being with a person in the certainty that this is a child of God who is dear to God's heart will bring the peace and quiet that Henri Nouwen has described. As is true of any human being, receiving the gifts of friendship means being loved in an unselfish way, which is clearly to the benefit of a flourishing life. All human lives can flourish to the extent of their abilities. Once assistants have learned how to do that, miracles may happen. "We all have seen the dead rise," as Vanier said, indicating the possibility of people opening up after years of having closed themselves in because they feared being rejected once again. Even when we know that such miracles will not happen, because the nature of the underlying impairment will not allow it, the logic of charity remains the same. God does not withdraw his friendship at the moment we fail to respond as he had hoped. So why should we?

There is one remaining question that I cannot answer. Nobody can — except by rejecting the entire argument of this book. A profoundly disabled person such as Kelly has no relationship with God in the sense of a human act on her part, I have argued, but this does not exclude the possibility that God has a relationship with her. But I don't know exactly what this means with respect to Kelly. Henri Nouwen suggested that his transformation made him see the beauty of Adam's soul. Unless we speak metaphorically, Kelly cannot return gifts of friendship in the sense of a human act. Thus, what we have received is the gift of her presence, not the gift of her response. There is no reason to deny that, in many ways, this is a sad fact about her life. However, there is great consolation in the certainty that God is with her, even if explaining how this affects Kelly's soul is beyond our comprehension. Faith in God's unconditional love for Kelly is a gift of the Spirit, if anything is. Where this gift is received, a transforming love is set free that enables us to welcome her presence in our lives. That is how Kelly reveals the work of God, as Jesus said (in the Gospel of John). As this chapter's epigraph by Martha Beck suggests, there may be some sort of a "plan" between them, but we can't possibly know it. This is why the mystery of her as a profoundly disabled human being must be the last word.

Postscript

In this book I have tried to give an account of Christian anthropology that understands being human in an all-inclusive way. Given its point of departure in the lives of people with profound intellectual disabilities, the only possible way to make the argument work has been to engage in a continuing process of reversing the order of our thinking. Now that I have finished the argument, let me underscore once again that the theological reflections I have presented here are only secondary to the witness of people whose lives testify to the reality of what I have been trying to describe here, particularly in the last chapters. I have not attempted to offer a theological "model"; I have only tried to give an account of what I think these lives are about, understood from a Christian perspective.

I know of no better way to end this book than to recite a text that came to me through my friend Bill Gaventa, who is at the Elizabeth Boggs Center in New Brunswick, New Jersey. It is written by Nate Hajdu, who is a direct support professional at the Jubilee Association, a Mennonite-based organization in Maryland. Hajdu spoke these words at the Interfaith Disability Presummit on September 22, 2005, at St. Margaret's Episcopal Church in Washington, D.C. Hajdu's text reflects how his faith has been impacted by supporting and working with Charlie Swenson, who is a profoundly disabled young man. It exemplifies what I have said about reversing the order of our thinking as a way to understand Christian friendship.

379

My Friend Charlie

He is my friend: I am his friend
I help him out: He helps me to learn
I help him to learn: He helps me to grow
I help him to grow: He teaches me to accept

His struggle: Is my struggle
His vulnerability: Leads to my respect
My respect: Leads him to trust
His trust: Leads to my devotion

His availability: Feeds my desire to be needed
I keep his secrets: He keeps mine
    We have an arrangement
His lack of self-consciousness: Leads to my tolerance
His constant need for stimulation: Leads to my patience
His discomfort: Sharpens my sensitivity
His unhappiness: Is my challenge
His presence: Eases my isolation
His loyalty: Leads to my loyalty
    Which leads to mutual appreciation

His brokenness: Makes me accept my own brokenness
    Which leads to healing
His humanity: Leads to personal connection
His steadfastness: Centers me

His smile: Is my reward
His joy: Lifts my spirits
His happiness: Gives me a sense of purpose
His struggles: Expose my anxieties
    Which tests me
    Then strengthens me
    And in turn bolsters my faith

In guiding: I am guided
In helping: I am helped
In teaching: I am taught

In his laughter: There is joy
In that joy: There is energy
In that energy: There is spirit
In that spirit: there is grace

In his eyes: There is a glow
In that glow: Is his soul
In his soul: There is God
And in God: There is peace

NATE HAJDU
Jubilee Association of Maryland

Literature

Abberley, P. "The concept of oppression and the development of a social theory of disability." *Disability, Handicap and Society* 2 (1987): 5-19.

———. "Work, Utopia, and Impairment." In *Disability and Society: Emerging Issues and Insights,* edited by Len Barton, 61-79. London and New York: Longman, 1996.

Allen, Barry. "Foucault's Nominalism." In *Foucault and the Government of Disability,* edited by Shelley Tremain, 93-107. Ann Arbor: The University of Michigan Press, 2005.

Allier, "A Place for Growth." In *The Challenge of L'Arche,* intro. and concl. by Jean Vanier. London: Darton, Longman, & Todd, 1982.

Annas, Julia. *The Morality of Happiness.* New York: Oxford University Press, 1993.

Aquinas, Thomas. *Summa Theologica.* Complete English Edition in Five Volumes. Translated by Fathers of the English Dominican Province. New York: Benziger, 1948.

Aristotle. "Metaphysics." Translated by W. D. Ross. *The Works of Aristotle.* Translated into English under the editorship of W. D. Ross. Volume VIII. Oxford: Clarendon Press, 1908.

———. "Politics." Translated by W. D. Ross. *The Works of Aristotle.* Translated into English under the editorship of W. D. Ross. Volume X. Oxford: Clarendon Press, 1921.

———. *Nicomachean Ethics.* Translated by W. D. Ross. Oxford: Oxford University Press, 1925.

———. "Physics." Translated by W. D. Ross. *The Works of Aristotle.* Translated into English under the editorship of W. D. Ross. Volume III. Oxford: Clarendon Press, 1930.

Arras, John D. "The Severely Demented, Minimally Functioning Patient: An Ethical Analysis." *Journal of American Geriatrics Society* 36 (1988): 938.

Augustine. *The Literal Meaning of Genesis.* Translated by John Hammond Taylor, S.J. Mahwah, NJ: Paulist Press, 1982.

———. *City of God.* Edited by Philip Schaff. Nicene and Post-Nicene Fathers, Volume II. Grand Rapids: Eerdmans, 1983.

Axelsson, Majgull. *April Witch.* Translated by Linda Schenck. New York: Villard, 2002.

Ayres, Lewis. *Nicaea and Its Legacy: An Approach to Fourth-century Trinitarian Theology.* Oxford: Oxford University Press, 2004.

Barnes, Michel René. "Rereading Augustine's Theology of the Trinity." In *The Trinity: An Interdisciplinary Symposium on the Trinity,* edited by Stephen T. Davis, Daniel Kendall, S.J., and Gerald O'Collins, S.J. Oxford: Oxford University Press, 1999.

Barth, Karl. *Kirchliche Dogmatik.* Vol. III/I. Zürich: Zollikon, 1947.

———. *Church Dogmatics.* Vol. III/I. Translated by G. W. Bromiley. Edinburgh: T&T Clark, 1958.

Barton, Len. "Sociology and Disability: Some Emerging Issues." In *Disability and Society: Emerging Issues and Insights,* edited by Len Barton, 3-17. London and New York: Longman, 1996.

Bashford, Alison, and Carolyn Strange. "Isolation and Exclusion in the Modern World." In *Isolation: Places and Practices of Exclusion,* edited by A. Bashford and C. Strange, 1-19. London: Routledge, 2003.

Beauchamp, Tom L. "The Failure of Theories of Personhood." *Kennedy Institute of Ethics Journal* 9 (1999): 309-24.

Beck, Martha. *Expecting Adam: A True Story of Birth, Rebirth, and Everyday Magic.* New York: Berkley Books, 1999.

Beck, U., A. Giddens, and S. Lash, eds. *Reflexive Modernization.* Cambridge, MA: Polity Press, 1991.

Berkhof, Hendrikus. *Christian Faith: An Introduction to the Study of the Faith.* Grand Rapids: Eerdmans, 1979.

Berube, Michael. *Life As We Know It: A Father, a Family, and an Exceptional Child.* New York: Vintage Books, 1996.

Betenbaugh, Helen. *A Theology of Disability.* Dallas: Perkins School of Theology, 1992.

Bird, Phyllis A. "Male and Female He Created Them: Gen. 1:27b in the Context of the Priestly Account of Creation." *Harvard Theological Review* 74 (1981): 129-59.

Black, Kathy. *A Healing Homiletic: Preaching and Disability.* Nashville: Abingdon Press, 1996.

Boff, Clodovis. *Theology and Praxis: Epistemological Foundations.* Maryknoll, NY: Orbis Books, 1987.

Boyle, M. *Schizophrenia: A Scientific Delusion.* London: Routledge, 1993.

Brown, Steven E. *A Celebration of Diversity: An Annotated Bibliography about Disability Culture.* 2nd edition. Las Cruces, NM: Institute on Disability Culture, 2002.

Brunner, Emil. *Man in Revolt: A Christian Anthropology.* Translated by O. Wyon. London: Lutterworth Press, 1939.

Buchanan, Allen, E., and Dan W. Brock. *Deciding for Others: The Ethics of Surrogate Decision Making.* Cambridge, UK: Cambridge University Press, 1989.

Cairns, David. *The Image of God in Man.* New York: Philosophical Library, 1953.

Cantor, Norman L. *Making Medical Decisions for the Profoundly Mentally Disabled.* Cambridge, MA: MIT Press, 2005.

Carlson, Licia. "Docile Bodies, Docile Minds." In *Foucault and the Government of Disability,* edited by Shelley Tremain, 133-52. Ann Arbor: The University of Michigan Press, 2005.

Cavalieri, Paola, and Peter Singer, eds. *The Great Ape Project: Equality Beyond Humanity.* New York: St. Martin's Press, 1994.

Cessario, Romanus. *Introduction to Moral Theology.* Washington, DC: The Catholic University of America Press, 2001.

Ceyrac, Odile. "The Poor at the Heart of Our Communities." In *The Challenge of L'Arche,* intro. and concl. by Jean Vanier. London: Darton, Longman, & Todd, 1982.

Charlton, James L. *Nothing about Us without Us: Disability, Oppression, and Empowerment.* Berkeley: University of California Press, 1998.

Childs, James M. *Christian Anthropology and Ethics.* Philadelphia: Fortress Press, 1978.

Connery, John. *Abortion: The Development of the Roman Catholic Perspective.* Chicago: Loyola University Press, 1977.

Cooper, John M. "Aristotle on the Forms of Friendship." In *Reason and Emotion: Essays on Ancient Moral Psychology and Moral Theory,* edited by John M. Cooper, 312-35. Princeton, NJ: Princeton University Press, 1999.

Cozzoli, M. "The Human Embryo: Ethical and Normative Aspects." In *The Identity and Status of the Human Embryo — Proceedings of the Third Assembly of the Pontifical Academy for Life,* edited by J. de Dios, Vial Correa, and E. Sgreccia, 260-300. Città del Vaticano: Librera Editrice Vaticana, 1997.

Creamer, Deborah. "Finding God in Our Bodies: Theology from the Perspective of People with Disabilities." *Journal of Religion in Disability & Rehabilitation* 2, no. 1 (1995): 27-42 (Part 1); 2, no. 2 (1995): 67-87 (Part 2).

Cunningham, David S. *These Three Are One: The Practice of Trinitarian Theology.* Malden, UK: Blackwell, 1998.

Deland, Jane S. "Breaking Down Barriers So All May Worship." *Journal of Religion in Disability & Rehabilitation* 2, no. 1 (1995): 5-20.

———. "Images of God Through the Lens of Disability." *Journal of Religion, Disability and Health* 3, no. 2 (1999): 47-79.

De Vinck, Christopher. *The Power of the Powerless: A Brother's Legacy of Love.* New York: Doubleday, 1990.

De Waal, Frans. *Good Natured: The Origins of Right and Wrong in Humans and Other Animals.* Cambridge, MA: Harvard University Press, 1996.

Donceel, Joseph F. "A Liberal Catholic's View." In *Abortion and Catholicism: The American Debate,* edited by Patricia B. Jung and Thomas A. Shannon, 48-53. New York: Crossroad, 1988.

Donum Vitae: Instruction on Respect for Human Life in its Origin and on the Dignity of Procreation. London: Publications of the Holy See, 1987.

Dorris, Michael. *The Broken Chord.* New York: Harper, 1989.

Drake, Robert F. "A Critique of the Role of the Traditional Charities." In *Disability and Society: Emerging Issues and Insights,* edited by Len Barton, 145-66. London and New York: Longman, 1996.

Driedger, Diane. *The Last Civil Rights Movement: Disabled People's International.* New York: St. Martin's Press, 1989.

Dunstan, G. R. "The Moral Status of the Human Embryo: A Tradition Recalled." *Journal of Medical Ethics* 1 (1984): 38-44.

Eiesland, Nancy L. *The Disabled God: Toward a Liberatory Theology of Disability.* Nashville: Abingdon Press, 1994.

———. "Liberation, Inclusion, and Justice: A Faith Response to Persons with Disabilities." *Impact: Feature Issue on Faith Communities and Persons with Developmental Disabilities,* edited by V. Gaylord, B. Gaventa, S. R. Simon, R. Norman-McNaney, A. N. Amado. 14 (2002): 2-3.

———. "Barriers and Bridges: Relating the Disability Rights Movement and Religious Organizations." Nancy L. Eiesland and Don E. Saliers, eds. *Human Disability and the Service of God: Reassessing Religious Practice,* 200-229. Nashville: Abingdon Press, 1998.

Elders, Leo J. *The Metaphysics of Being of St. Thomas Aquinas in Historical Perspective.* Leiden: Brill, 1993.

Emery, Gilles. "Chronique de théologie trinitaire." *Revue Thomiste,* 101 (2001): 581-82.

Erevelles, Nirmala. "Signs of Reason." In *Foucault and the Government of*

Disability, edited by Shelley Tremain, 145-64. Ann Arbor: The University of Michigan Press, 2005.

Evangelium Vitae. Encyclical Letter. Washington, DC: United States Catholic Conference, 1995.

Faggioni, M. "Life and Forms of Life: The Relationship between Biology and Anthropology." In *The Culture of Life: Foundations and Dimensions — Proceedings of the Seventh Assembly of the Pontifical Academy for Life,* edited by J. de Dios Vial Correa and E. Sgreccia, 67-103. Città del Vaticano: Librera Editrice Vaticana, 2002.

Feenstra, Ronald J., and Cornelius Plantinga, Jr., eds. *Trinity, Incarnation, and Atonement.* Notre Dame: The University of Notre Dame Press, 1989.

Fletcher, Joseph. *Morals and Medicine.* Boston: Beacon Press, 1954.

Foucault, Michel. "On the Genealogy of Ethics: An Overview of Work in Progress." *The Essential Works of Michel Foucault, 1954-1984,* vol. I, *Ethics: Subjectivity and Truth,* edited by Paul Rabinow. London: Allen Lame, 1997.

Gallie, W. B. "Essentially Contested Concepts." In *Philosophy and the Historical Understanding,* edited by W. B. Gallie, 157-91. New York: Schocken, 1968.

Gergen, Kenneth J. *Realities and Relationships: Soundings in Social Construction.* Cambridge, MA: Harvard University Press, 1994.

Gordon, Phyllis A., Jennifer Chiriboga Tantillo, David Feldman, and Kristin Perrone. "Attitudes Regarding Interpersonal Relationships with Persons with Mental Illness and Mental Retardation." *Journal of Rehabilitation* 70 (2004).

Govig, Stewart D. *Strong at the Broken Places: Persons with Disabilities and the Church.* Louisville: Westminster/John Knox Press, 1989.

Gray, John. "Political Power, Social Theory, and Essential Contestability." In *The Nature of Political Theory,* edited by David Miller and Larry Siedentop, 75-101. Oxford: Clarendon Press, 1983.

Grisez, Germaine G. *Abortion: The Myths, the Realities, and the Arguments.* New York: Corpus Books, 1970.

Groce, Nora Ellen. *Everyone Here Spoke Sign Language: Hereditary Deafness on Martha's Vineyard.* Cambridge, UK: Cambridge University Press, 1985.

Groce, Nora Ellen, and Jonathan Marks. "The Great Ape Project and Disability Rights: Ominous Undercurrents of Eugenics in Action." *American Anthropologist* 102, no. 4 (2000): 818-22.

Gunton, Colin E. *The Promise of Trinitarian Theology.* Edinburgh: T&T Clark, 1991.

————. *The One, the Three and the Many: God, Creation and the Culture of Modernity.* Cambridge, UK: Cambridge University Press, 1993.

Hacking, Ian. *The Social Construction of What?* Cambridge, MA: Harvard University Press, 1999.

Hall, Douglas J. *Imaging God: Dominion as Stewardship.* Grand Rapids: Eerdmans, 1986.

Hatton, Chris. "Whose Quality of Life Is It Anyway? Some Problems with the Emerging Quality of Life Consensus." *Mental Retardation* 36, no. 2 (1998): 104-15.

Hauerwas, Stanley M. "Christian Care of the Retarded." *Theology Today* 30, no. 2 (1973): 130-37.

————. "The Church and the Mentally Handicapped: A Continuing Challenge to the Imagination." In *Dispatches from the Front: Theological Engagements with the Secular.* Durham: Duke University Press, 1994.

————. "Community and Diversity: The Tyranny of Normality." In S. Hauerwas, *Suffering Presence: Theological Reflections on Medicine, the Mentally Handicapped, and the Church*, 211-17. Notre Dame, IN: University of Notre Dame Press, 1986.

————. "Companions on the Way: The Necessity of Friendship." *Asbury Theological Journal* 45 (1990): 35-48.

————. "The Gestures of a Truthful Story." *Theology Today* 42, no. 2 (1985): 181-89.

————. *Suffering Presence: Theological Reflections on Medicine, the Mentally Handicapped, and the Church.* Notre Dame, IN: University of Notre Dame Press, 1986.

————. "Timeful Friends: Living with the Handicapped." In *Sanctify Them in the Truth: Holiness Exemplified.* Nashville: Abingdon, 1998.

————. *Truthfulness and Tragedy: Further Investigations into Christian Ethics.* Notre Dame, IN: The University of Notre Dame Press, 1977.

————. *With the Grain of the Universe: The Church's Witness and Natural Theology.* Grand Rapids: Brazos Press, 2001.

Hauerwas, Stanley M., and Charles Pinches. *Christians among the Virtues: Theological Conversations with Ancient and Modern Ethics.* Notre Dame, IN: The University of Notre Dame Press, 1997.

Hauerwas, Stanley M., and Laura Yordy. "Captured in Time." In S. Hauerwas, *A Better Hope: Resources for a Church Confronting Capitalism, Democracy, and Postmodernity.* Grand Rapids: Brazos Press, 2000.

Heschel, Abraham J. *Who Is Man?* Stanford, CA: Stanford University Press, 1965.

Hibberd, Fiona J. *Unfolding Social Constructionism.* New York: Springer, 2005.

Hilberath, Bernd Jochen. *Der Personsbegriff der Trinitätstheologie in Rückfrage von Karl Rahner zu Tertullians "Adversus Praxean"*. Innsbruck: Tyrolia Verlag, 1986.

Hughes, Bill. "What Can a Foucauldian Analysis Contribute to Disability Theory?" In *Foucault and the Government of Disability*, edited by Shelley Tremain, 78-92. Ann Arbor: The University of Michigan Press, 2005.

Huitt, W. *Maslow's Hierarchy of Needs. Educational Psychology Interactive*, 2004. Valdosta State University: http://chiron.valdosta.edu/whuitt/col/regsys/maslow.html.

Hunt, Paul. "A Critical Condition." In *The Disability Reader: Social Science Perspectives*, edited by Tom Shakespeare, 7-19. London: Cassell, 1998.

Iozzio, M. I. "The Writing on the Wall . . . Alzheimer's Disease: A Daughter's Look at Mom's Faithful Care of Dad," *Journal of Religion, Disability & Health* 8, no. 2 (2005): 49-74.

Irenaeus, *Against Heresies*. Edited by A. Roberts and J. Donaldson. Ante-Nicene Fathers, Volume I. Grand Rapids: Eerdmans, 1981.

Jenson, Robert W. *Systematic Theology: The Triune God*. Vol. I. Oxford: Oxford University Press, 1997.

———. *Systematic Theology: The Works of God*. Vol. II. Oxford: Oxford University Press, 1999.

Joest, Wilfried. *Ontologie der Person bei Luther*. Göttingen: VandenHoeck und Ruprecht, 1967.

John Paul II. "The International Year of Disabled Persons." In *Ministry With Persons With Disabilities*, Vol. II: Resource File, section III A. Church Documents. Edited by Janice Lalonde Benton. Washington, DC: National Catholic Office for Persons with Disabilities, 1987.

Johnstone, Brian V. "From Physicalism to Personalism," *Studia Moralia* 30 (1992): 71-96.

Kant, Immanuel. *Foundations of the Metaphysics of Morals*. In Kant, *Critique of Practical Reason and Other Writings in Moral Philosophy*. Translated by L. W. Beck. Chicago: University of Chicago Press, 1949.

———. "Der Streit der Fakultäten." In Kant, *Werke*. Band IV. Darmstadt: Wisschenschaftliche Buchgesellschaft, 1983.

Kasper, W. *Der Gott Jesu Christi*. Mainz: Matthias Grünewald, 1982.

Klein, Stanley D., and Kim Schive, eds. *You Will Dream New Dreams: Inspiring Personal Stories by Parents of Children with Disabilities*. New York: Kensington, 2001.

Kuhse, Helga, and Peter Singer. *Should the Baby Live? The Problem of Handicapped Infants*. Oxford: Oxford University Press, 1985.

Kuhse, Helga, and Peter Singer, eds. *Bioethics: An Anthology.* Oxford: Blackwell, 1999.

LaCugna, Catherine M. *God for Us: The Trinity and Christian Life.* San Francisco: Harper, 1991.

Larentzakis, G. "Trinitarisches Kirchenverständnis." In *Trinität. Aktuelle Perspektiven der Theologie,* edited by W. Breuning (Hrsg.). Freiburg/Basel/Wien: Herder, 1984.

Lenon, Pat and Jo. "A Place for Family." In *The Challenge of L'Arche,* intro. and concl. by Jean Vanier. London: Darton, Longman, & Todd, 1982.

Levering, Matthew. *Scripture and Metaphysics: Aquinas and the Renewal of Trinitarian Theology.* Oxford: Blackwell Publishing, 2004.

Longmore, Paul K. "The Second Phase: From Disability Rights to Disability Culture." *Disability Rag and Resource* 7 (1995): 6-7.

———. *Why I Burned My Book and Other Essays on Disability.* Philadelphia: Temple University Press, 2003.

Lorizio, G. "I Believe in the Resurrection of the Flesh." In *The Culture of Life: Foundations and Dimensions — Proceedings of the Seventh Assembly of the Pontifical Academy for Life,* edited by Juan de Dios Vial Correa and Elio Sgreccia, 35-51. Città del Vaticano: Librera Editrice Vaticana, 2002.

Lubac, Henri de. *The Mystery of the Supernatural.* Translated by Rosemary Sheed. London: Chapman, 1967.

Lucas, John R. *On Justice.* Cambridge: Blackwell, 1980.

Lucas, R. Lucas. "The Anthropological Status of the Human Embryo." In *The Identity and Status of the Human Embryo — Proceedings of the Third Assembly of the Pontifical Academy for Life,* edited by J. de Dios Vial Correa and E. Sgreccia, 178-205. Città del Vaticano: Librera Editrice Vaticana, 1997.

Luckasson, R. *Mental Retardation: Definition, Classification, and Systems of Support.* Washington, DC: American Association for Mental Retardation, 1992.

Mahowald, M. B. "Person." In *Encyclopedia of Bioethics.* Revised edition. Edited by Warren T. Reich. New York: Macmillan, 1995.

Mairs, Nancy. *Plaintext.* Tucson: University of Arizona Press, 1986.

Marks, Deborah. *Disability: Controversial Debates and Psychological Perspectives.* London: Routledge, 1999.

Maslow, A. *Motivation and Personality.* New York: Harper, 1954.

May, Tim. "Reflections and Reflexivity." In *Knowing the Social World,* edited by Tim May and Malcolm Williams, 157-77. Buckingham: Open University Press, 1998.

Meyer, Donald J., ed. *Uncommon Fathers: Reflections on Raising a Child with a Disability.* Bethesda, PA: Woodbine House, 1995.

Middleton, Richard J. *The Liberating Image: The Imago Dei in Genesis 1.* Grand Rapids: Brazos Press, 2005.

Miribel, Claire de. "Growth towards Covenant." In *The Challenge of L'Arche,* intro. and concl. by Jean Vanier. London: Darton, Longman, & Todd, 1982.

Mitchell, David T., and Sharon L. Snyder. "Disability Studies and the Double Bind of Representation." In *The Body and Physical Difference: Discourses of Disability,* edited by David T. Mitchell and Sharon L. Snyder, 1-31. Ann Arbor: The University of Michigan Press, 1997.

Mohanty, Satya P. *Literary Theory and the Claims of History: Postmodernism, Objectivity, Multicultural Politics.* Ithaca, NY: Cornell University Press, 1988.

Moltmann, Jürgen. *Trinität und Reich Gottes.* München: Kaiser, 1978.

Moraczewski, Albert S. "The Human Embryo and Fetus: Ontological, Ethical and Legal Aspects." In *Humanae Vitae: 20 Anni Dopo, Atti del II Congresso Internazionale di Teologia Morale,* edited by Aurelio Ansaldo, 339-62. Milano: Edizione Ares, 1989.

Mosteller, Sue. "Living With." In *The Challenge of L'Arche,* intro. and concl. by Jean Vanier. London: Darton, Longman, & Todd, 1982.

Moya, Paula. *Learning from Experience: Minority Identities, Multicultural Struggles.* Berkeley: University of California Press, 2002.

Norris Clarke, W., S.J. *The One and the Many: A Contemporary Thomistic Metaphysics.* Notre Dame, IN: University of Notre Dame Press, 2001.

Norwood, G. *Maslow's Hierarchy of Needs,* 2006. http://www.deepermind.com-/20maslow.htm.

Nouwen, Henri J. M. *Adam: God's Beloved.* Maryknoll, NY: Orbis Books, 1997.

———. "The Road to Daybreak." In *Spiritual Journals.* New York: Continuum, 1990.

———. *Selected Writings.* Maryknoll, NY: Orbis, 1997.

Novak Amado, A., ed. *Friendships and Community Connections Between People With and Without Developmental Disabilities.* Baltimore: Paul H. Brookes, 1993.

Nozick, Robert. *Philosophical Explanations.* Cambridge, MA: Harvard University Press, 1981.

Odozor, Paulinus I. *Moral Theology in an Age of Renewal: A Study of the Catholic Tradition since Vatican II.* Notre Dame, IN: University of Notre Dame Press, 2003.

Oe, Kenzaburo. *A Healing Family.* Tokyo: Kodansha International, 1995.

Ohsberg, H. Oliver. *The Church and Persons with Handicaps.* Scottsdale, AZ: Herald Press, 1982.

Oliver, M. "Social Policy and Disability: Some Theoretical Issues." *Disability, Handicap and Society* 1 (1986): 5-18.

———. "Changing the Social Relations of Research Production." *Disability, Handicap and Society* 7 (1992): 101-14.

———. *The Politics of Disablement.* London: Macmillan, 1990.

———. "A Sociology of Disability or a Disablist Sociology?" In *Disability and Society: Emerging Issues and Insights,* edited by Len Barton, 18-42. London and New York: Longman, 1996.

Outhwaite, William. "Naturalisms and Anti-naturalisms." In *Knowing the Social World,* edited by Tim May and Malcolm Williams, 22-36. Buckingham: Open University Press, 1998.

Owens, Joseph. *The Doctrine of Being in the Aristotelian Metaphysics: A Study in the Greek Background of Medieval Thought.* Toronto: Pontifical Institute of Mediaeval Studies, 1951.

Pailin, David A. *A Gentle Touch: A Theology of Human Being.* London: SPCK, 1992.

Palazzani, L. "The Meanings of the Philosophical Concept of Person and their Implications in the Current Debate on the Status of the Human Embryo." In *The Identity and Status of the Human Embryo: Proceedings of the Third Assembly of the Pontifical Academy for Life,* edited by J. de Dios Vial Correa and E. Sgreccia, 74-95. Città del Vaticano: Librera Editrice Vaticana, 1997.

Pannenberg, Wofhart. *Anthropologie in theologischer Perspektive.* Göttingen: VandenHoeck & Ruprecht, 1977.

Pasnau, Robert. *Thomas Aquinas on Human Nature: A Philosophical Study of Summa Theologiae Ia, 75-89.* Cambridge, UK: Cambridge University Press, 2002.

Pegis, Anton C. *At the Origins of the Thomistic Notion of Man.* New York: MacMillan, 1963.

Perske, Robert. *Circles of Friends: People with Disabilities and Their Friends Enrich the Lives of One Another.* Nashville: Abingdon Press, 1988.

Peters, Susan. "The Politics of Disability Identity." In *Disability and Society: Emerging Issues and Insights,* edited by Len Barton, 215-34. London and New York: Longman, 1996.

Peters, Ted. *God as Trinity: Relationality and Temporality in Divine Life.* Louisville: Westminster/John Knox Press, 1993.

Philippe, Thomas, O.P. "Communities of the Beatitudes." In *The Challenge of L'Arche,* intro. and concl. by Jean Vanier. London: Darton, Longman, & Todd, 1982.

Plantinga, Cornelius, Jr. "Social Trinity and Tritheism." In *Trinity, Incarna-*

tion and Atonement: Philosophical and Theological Essays, edited by Ronald J. Feenstra and Cornelius Plantinga, Jr., 21-47. Notre Dame, IN: University of Notre Dame Press, 1989.

Price, Daniel J. *Karl Barth's Anthropology in the Light of Modern Thought.* Grand Rapids: Eerdmans, 2000.

Rachels, James. *The End of Life: The Morality of Euthanasia.* New York: Oxford University Press, 1986.

Rafalovich, Adam. *Framing ADHD Children: A Critical Examination of the History, Discourse, and Everyday Experience of Attention Deficit/Hyperactivity Disorder.* Lanham, MD: Lexington Books, 2004.

Rautenberg, Joseph F. "Abortion: Questions of Value and Procedure." In *Moral Theology: Challenges for the Future,* edited by Charles C. Curran, 241-63. New York: Paulist Press, 1990.

Reinders, Hans S. *Violence, Victims, and Rights.* Amsterdam: Free University Press, 1988.

———. "*Imago Dei* as a Basic Concept in Christian Ethics." In *Holy Scriptures in Judaism, Christianity and Islam: Hermeneutics, Values and Society,* edited by Hendrik M. Vroom and Jerald D. Gort, 187-204. Amsterdam: Rodopi, 1997.

———. "'The Meaning of Life' in Liberal Society." In *Meaningful Care: A Multidisciplinary Approach to the Meaning of Care for People with Mental Retardation,* edited by Joop Stolk, Theo A. Boer, and Rut Seldenrijk, 65-84. Dordrecht: Kluwer, 2000.

———. *The Future of the Disabled in Liberal Society: An Ethical Analysis.* Notre Dame, IN: University of Notre Dame Press, 2000.

———. "The Good Life for Citizens with Intellectual Disabilities." *Journal of Intellectual Disability Research* 46 (2002): 1-5.

———. "Being Thankful: Parenting the Mentally Disabled." In *The Blackwell Companion to Christian Ethics,* edited by Stanley M. Hauerwas and Samuel Wells. London: Blackwell, 2004.

———. "The Virtue of Writing Appropriately. Or: Is Stanley Hauerwas Right in Thinking He Should Not Write Anymore on the Mentally Handicapped?" In *God, Truth and Witness: Engaging Stanley Hauerwas,* edited by L. Gregory Jones, Reinhard Hütter, and C. Rosalee Veloso Ewell, 53-70. Grand Rapids: Brazos Press, 2005.

———. "Human Dignity in the Absence of Agency." In *God and Human Dignity,* edited by R. Kendall Soulen and Linda Woodhead. Grand Rapids: Eerdmans, 2006, pp. 121-39.

Riddell, Sheila. "Theorising Special Education Needs in a Changing Political Climate." In *Disability and Society: Emerging Issues and Insights*, edited by Len Barton, 83-106. London and New York: Longman, 1996.

Ross, Lainie Friedman. *Children, Families, and Health Care Decision Making.* New York: Clarendon Press, 1998.

Ryan, J., and F. Thomas. *The Politics of Mental Handicap.* Hammondsworth, UK: Penguin Books, 1980.

Saliers, Don S. "Toward a Spirituality of Inclusiveness." In *Human Disability and the Service of God: Reassessing Religious Practice*, edited by Nancy L. Eiesland and Don S. Saliers, 19-31. Nashville: Abingdon Press, 1998.

Schalock, R. L. *Quality of Life: Perspectives and Issues.* Washington, DC: American Association on Mental Retardation, 1990.

Schalock, R. L., and K. D. Keith. *Quality of Life Questionnaire Manual.* Worthington, OH: IDS Publishing Company, 1993.

Schalock, Robert S., and Miguel Angel Verdugo Alonso. *Handbook on Quality of Life for Human Services Practitioners.* Washington, DC: American Association on Mental Retardation, 2002.

Scheerenberger, R. C. *A History of Mental Retardation.* Baltimore: Paul H. Brookes, 1983.

Schockenhoff, Eberhard. *Natural Law and Human Dignity: Universal Ethics in a Historical World.* Translated by B. McNeil. Washington, DC: The Catholic University of America Press, 2003.

Schurter, Dennis. "Jesus' Ministry with People with Disabilities: Scriptural Foundations for Churches' Inclusive Ministry." *Journal of Religion in Disability & Rehabilitation* 1, no. 4 (1994): 33-47.

Schwanz, Peter. *Imago Dei als christologisch-anthropologisches Problem in der Geschichte der Alten Kirche von Paulus bis Clemens von Alexandrien.* Halle: Max Niemeyer Verlag, 1970.

Schwöbel, Christoph, ed. *Trinitarian Theology Today: Essays in Divine Being and Act.* Edinburgh: T&T Clark, 1995.

Schwöbel, Christoph, and Colin E. Gunton, eds. *Persons, Divine and Human.* Edinburgh: T&T Clark, 1991.

Scorgie, Kathryn I. "From Devastation to Transformation: Managing Life when a Child is Disabled." Ph.D. dissertation, University of Alberta, 1996.

Scotch, Richard K. *From Good Will to Civil Rights: Transforming Federal Disability Policy.* Philadelphia: Temple University Press, 2001.

Shakespeare, T. "Cultural representations of disabled people: Dustbins of Disavowal." *Disability and Society* 3 (1994): 283-301.

Shakespeare, Tom. "Social Constructionism as a Political Strategy." In *The*

Politics of Constructionism, edited by Irving Velody and Robin Williams, 168-81. London: Sage, 1998.

―――. "Introduction." In *The Disability Reader: Social Science Perspectives,* edited by Tom Shakespeare, 1-3. London: Cassell, 1998.

Shapiro, Joseph P. *No Pity: People with Disabilities Forging a New Civil Rights Movement.* New York: Times Books, 1993.

―――. "What the ADA Teaches Us about the Value of Civil Rights." *Journal of Religion in Disability & Rehabilitation* 2 (1996): 43-47.

Siebers, Tobin. "Disability Studies and the Future of Identity Politics." In *Identity Politics Reconsidered,* edited by Linda Martin Alcoff, Michael Hames-Garcia, Satya P. Mohanty, and Paula M. L. Moya, 10-30. New York: Palgrave, Macmillan, 2006.

Singer, Peter. *Rethinking Life and Death: The Collapse of Our Traditional Ethics.* New York: St. Martin's Press, 1995.

Snyder, Sharon L., and David T. Mitchell. *Cultural Locations of Disability.* Chicago: The University of Chicago Press, 2006.

Solomon, Andrew. "Deaf Is Beautiful." *New York Times Magazine,* 28 Aug. 1994, 67.

Spaemann, R. "On the anthropology of the Encyclical *Evangelium Vitae.*" In *Evangelium Vitae: Five Years of Confrontation with the Society — Proceedings of the Sixth Assembly of the Pontifical Academy for Life, 11-14 Feb. 2000,* edited by Juan de Dios Vial Correa and Elio Sgreccia, 437-51. Città del Vaticano: Librera Editrice Vaticana, 2001.

Spaemann, Robert. *Personen: Versuche über den Unterschied zwischen "etwas" und "jemand."* Stuttgart: Klett-Cotta, 1996.

Stanley, Gerald F. "Contemplation as Fulfillment of the Human Person." In *Personalist Ethics and Human Subjectivity,* edited by George McLean, appendix. Washington, DC: Council for Research in Value and Philosophy, 1991.

Stroman, Duane F. *The Disabilities Rights Movement: From Deinstitutionalization to Self-Determination.* Lanham, MD: University of America Press, 2003.

Swinton, J., ed. *Critical Reflections on Stanley Hauerwas' Theology of Disability: Disabling Society, Enabling Theology.* Binghamton, NY: Haworth Press, 2004.

Switzer, Jacqueline V. *Disabled Rights: American Disability Policy and the Fight for Equality.* Washington, DC: Georgetown University Press, 2003.

Tauer, Carol A. "The Tradition of Probabilism and the Moral Status of the Early Embryo." In *Abortion and Catholicism: The American Debate,* edited by Patricia B. Jung and Thomas A. Shannon, 54-84. New York: Crossroad, 1988.

Taylor, Charles. *Sources of the Self: The Shaping of Modern Identity*. Cambridge, UK: Cambridge University Press, 1989.

Thielicke, Helmut. *Theological Ethics: Foundations*. Vol. I. Translated by W. H. Lazareth. Philadelphia: Fortress Press, 1966.

Tobler, Stefan. *Analogia Caritatis: Kirche als Geschöpf und Abbild der Trinität*. Doctoral dissertation, Vrije Universiteit, Amsterdam, 1994.

Torrance, Alan. *Persons in Communion: An Essay in Trinitarian Description and Human Participation*. Edinburgh: T&T Clark, 1996.

Tremain, Shelley. "Foucault, Governmentality, and Critical Disability Theory." In *Foucault and the Government of Disability*, edited by Shelley Tremain, 1-24. Ann Arbor: The University of Michigan Press, 2005.

Vanier, Jean. *Becoming Human*. London: Darton, Longman & Todd, 1989.

———. *The Challenge of L'Arche*. London: Darton, Longman & Todd, 1982.

———. *Community and Growth*. New York: Paulist Press, 1989.

———. *Our Journey Home: Rediscovering a Common Humanity beyond Our Differences*. Maryknoll, NY: Orbis, 1997.

———. "The Need of Strangers." In *Critical Reflections on Stanley Hauerwas' Theology of Disability: Disabling Society, Enabling Theology*, edited by J. Swinton, 27-30. Binghamton, NY: Haworth Press, 2004.

Veritatis Splendor: Encyclical Letter. Washinton, DC: United States Catholic Conference, 1993.

Volf, Miroslav. *After Our Likeness: The Church as the Image of the Trinity*. Grand Rapids: Eerdmans, 1998.

Wadell, Paul. *The Primacy of Love: An Introduction to the Ethics of Thomas Aquinas*. New York: Paulist Press, 1992.

———. *Becoming Friends: Worship, Justice, and the Practice of Christian Friendship*. Grand Rapids: Brazos, 2002.

Weiss Block, Jennie. *Copious Hosting: A Theology of Access for People with Disabilities*. New York: Continuum, 2002.

Wendell, Susan. "Towards a Feminist Theory of Disability." *Hypathia* 4, no. 2 (1989): 104-23.

———. *The Rejected Body: Feminist Philosophical Reflections on Disability*. London: Routledge, 1996.

Wilke, Harold H. *Creating the Caring Congregation: Guidelines for Ministering with the Handicapped*. Nashville: Abingdon Press, 1980.

Williams-Searle, John. "Cold Charity: Manhood, Brotherhood, and the Transformation of Disability, 1870-1900." In *The New Disability His-*

tory: American Perspectives, edited by Paul K. Longmore and Lauri Umanski, 157-86. New York: New York University Press, 2001.

Wolfensberger, Wolf. "An Attempt to Gain Better Understanding from a Christian Perspective of What 'Mental Retardation' Is." In *The Theological Voice of Wolf Wolfensberger,* edited by William C. Gaventa and David L. Coulter, 71-83. Binghamton, NY: The Haworth Press, 2001.

———. "The Good Life for Mentally Retarded Persons." In *The Theological Voice of Wolf Wolfensberger,* edited by William C. Gaventa and David L. Coulter, 103-9. Binghamton, NY: Haworth Press, 2001.

Yates, Scott. "Truth, Power, and Ethics in Care Services for People with Learning Difficulties." In *Foucault and the Government of Disability,* edited by Shelley Tremain, 65-77. Ann Arbor: The University of Michigan Press, 2005.

Zames Fleischer, Doris, and Frieda Zames. *The Disability Rights Movement: From Charity to Confrontation.* Philadelphia: Temple University Press, 2001.

Zizioulas, John D. *Being as Communion: Studies in Personhood and the Church.* Crestwood, NY: St. Vladimir, 1985.

Index